CITISTATES

How Urban America
Can Prosper in a
Competitive World

by Neal R. Peirce

with Curtis W. Johnson
and John Stuart Hall

SEVEN LOCKS PRESS   WASHINGTON, D.C.

Library of Congress Cataloging-in-Publication Data

Peirce, Neal R.
    Citistates : how urban America can prosper in a competitive world
    /   by Neal R. Peirce with Curtis W. Johnson and John Stuart Hall.
      p. cm.
    Includes bibliographical references and index.
    ISBN 0–929765–16–8 — ISBN 0–929765–34–6 (pbk.)
    1. Metropolitan areas—United States—Case studies.
    2. Urbanization—United States—Case studies. 3. Urban policy-
    United States—Case studies. I. Johnson, Curtis W., 1942–   .
    II. Hall, John Stuart, 1942–   . III. Title.
    HT334.U5P45 1993

    307.76'0973—dc20
                          93–18709
                            CIP

Manufactured in the United States of America

Seven Locks Press
Washington, D.C.
(800) 354–5348

Table of Contents

Preface

This book began modestly, as a vehicle to reprint the studies—so-called Peirce Reports—we wrote for the leading newspapers of six cities, analyzing the critical challenges each faces now and as it plans for the next century. In each case the newspaper publisher asked us to come to town and make a thorough and independent analysis of the city. Neal Peirce, a journalist, and Curtis Johnson, then head of the Minneapolis–St. Paul Citizens League, were involved with each project. Often a third outside urban expert joined our team. In each city, the team also included a locally based person with university credentials—a well-informed (but not partisan) "insider."

The entire team would conduct several dozen interviews—always "off-the-record" to assure frankness—with local movers and shakers, sages, rebels, and citizens. Governors and mayors and county officials, corporate executives and business analysts, neighborhood and environmental group leaders, nonprofit operators, labor union spokespersons, religious and foundation and media leaders, journalists, academics, school officials, social service agency heads and community volunteers—they and many others were among those interviewed. Those face-to-face discussions (typically lasting an hour each) were supplemented with observations from helicopter, automobile, and walking tours. We examined press reports, academic research, official budgets and plans and census reports, as well as the interview notes we had made on visits to these cities as far back as the 1960s.

Our first goal was to identify the most salient regional problems, then to identify (against the background of our knowledge of other metropolitan areas) a realistic "next generation" of potential solutions that seemed to make sense in the particular region's distinctive civic and political culture. Our findings were then presented either in a special section of the newspaper's Sunday edition or in a day-by-day series over the course of a week.

The Phoenix report, first in the chain, appeared in *The Arizona*

Republic and *The Phoenix Gazette* in February 1987, followed by a series on the Puget Sound region for *The Seattle Times* in 1989. Then, all in 1991, came reports for *The* (Baltimore) *Sun,* the *Owensboro* (Kentucky) *Messenger-Inquirer, The Dallas Morning News,* and the *St. Paul Pioneer Press.*

As part of the process, each newspaper guaranteed publication of the Peirce Report without substantial editorial interference. But because the reports appeared in regular daily newspapers, they were unlike more standard policy research reports. They landed simultaneously on doorsteps across entire regions, meaning that large segments of the region's population read and discussed the report at virtually the same time. By definition, the Peirce Reports were action research, affecting the local policy dialogue.

In each case, we insisted on examining not just the center city, but the entire metropolitan region—the "real city" made up of center city, inner and outer suburbs, and rural hinterland so clearly and intimately interconnected in geography, environment, work force, and surely a shared economic and social future.

Inexorably, a metropolitan focus drives one to visualize our great cities, their suburbs, exurbs, and geographic realms of influence as *citistates*—entities that perform as critical actors, more on their own in the world economy than anyone would have dreamed since the birth of the nation-state in the 16th and 17th centuries. Thus, for this book, we have chosen a new word, *citistate,* to emphasize these entities' transglobal connectedness, their growing domination by a world population. These modern citistates have strong conceptual roots in the city-states of antiquity and the Renaissance; but we believe their late–20th century manifestation represents a new form and justifies a new word.

The first chapter of this book explores the citistate concept and the radical reconceptualization of social and economic thinking it demands of us. Then follow the individual city chapters. Each is introduced by a "Citistate in Brief" section, which provides demographic information, and a "Peirce Report Glossary" to orient the reader to place names and other references in the city chapter that might be unfamiliar to a nonresident of the citistate. Each city chapter ends with a brief update that provides information about policy initiatives and other actions taken—or not taken—to follow through on our recommendations.

We can now see that although we approached each city region as a separate entity, multiple common themes emerged in our reports. Furthermore, the challenges we were prompted to lay down for each city region—a search for civic cohesion; a call for regional planning, genuine citizen involvement, and smart governance; the case for environmentally sensitive land use, drastic education reform, and concerted efforts to bring the poor and alienated into the mainstream of the regional society—were not simply good causes. They represent, as we note in the concluding chapter, the indispensable building blocks of a successful citistate in the new world economy.

Acknowledgments

There is no way we can possibly give due credit to the hundreds of people—professional colleagues, interviewees, publishers and editors, research associates—who made this book possible.

Among those who contributed the most, either by reading manuscript, researching, editing, or giving us a vital hand with arrangements, were Nancy Connors, John Parr, Bill Stafford, Bruce Chapman, Royce Hanson, Henry Cisneros, George Duff, Sam Campana, Richard Bradley, Allan Wallis, Scott Fosler, John DiIulio, Mark Alan Hughes, Richard Hartman, Dwight Vick, Dale Swaboda, Cherylene Schick, Richard Hadley, David Lanegran, Bernard Weinstein, Geri Bachman, and this book's publisher and staff—Norman Sherman, Kathleen Florio, Lisa Rubarth, and Sarah Seage.

Our fellow team members for the interviews in the various cities provided many of the ideas that appear in these pages. We are indebted to all for their keen interest in these reports and for their friendship.

In Phoenix, the report group included, in addition to the three authors of this book, Christopher Gates, vice president of the National Civic League.

For Seattle, our teammate was Betty Jane Narver, president of the Municipal League of King County and director of the Institute for Public Policy and Management at the University of Washington.

In Baltimore, we were assisted by Lenneal Henderson, professor of government and public administration and senior fellow in the William Donald Schaefer Center for Public Policy at the University of Baltimore, as well as Carol Steinbach, free-lance writer and contributing editor of *National Journal*.

Our associates for the Dallas project were Mary Evans Sias, executive director of the YWCA of Metropolitan Dallas and a former college professor; and Ricardo Romo, associate professor of history at the University of Texas in Austin and vice president of the Tomas Rivera Center, a Hispanic public policy institute in San Antonio.

In Owensboro, our additional team members were C. B. (Bob) Darrell, professor of English at Kentucky Wesleyan College, and Robert Guskind, contributing editor of *National Journal* and a free-lance writer.

For the St. Paul report, our chief associate was Ralph R. Widner, chief executive officer of Fairfax House International in Alexandria, Virginia, and head of an informal network of community and regional development leaders who provide help to leaders around the world. Widner served previously as president of the Greater Philadelphia First Corporation and as first chief executive of the Appalachian Development Program. Our other St. Paul associate was Ellen T. Brown, a consultant and former executive of Control Data.

Foundations made these reports possible in Baltimore and St. Paul. We extend our appreciation to Robert Embry and Lauri Gillen (the Abell Foundation), Paul Verrett (the St. Paul Foundation), Michael O'Keefe (the McKnight Foundation), Terry Saario (the Northwest Areas Foundation), and Creed Black (the Knight Foundation). Although they helped to finance the reports, none of the foundations associated themselves directly with the findings.

Without the newspapers, the Peirce Reports would not have been born. Pat Murphy, then publisher of *The Arizona Republic* and *The Phoenix Gazette,* made the first proposal to us for a city report in 1986. We remain indebted to Murphy for his vision in sparking a new form in American urban journalism, not to mention his courage in printing our jarring civic wake-up call for Phoenix and its sister cities of the Valley of the Sun.

Publishers, editors, and many staffers of the individual papers made the city reports possible. Our special thanks go to Michael Fancher, Frank Blethen, Mindy Cameron, Rick Zahler, and Eric Pryne of *The Seattle Times;* Lois Boyles of *The Phoenix Gazette;* Reg Murphy, James Houck, Michael Davies, and Joseph Sterne of *The* (Baltimore) *Sun;* Ronald Clark, Mary Junck, and David Peters of the *St. Paul Pioneer Press;* Burl Osborne, Ralph Langer, Rena Pederson, and John Ostdick of *The Dallas Morning News;* and John Hager, Tim Harmon, and David Berry of the *Owensboro Messenger-Inquirer.*

Neal R. Peirce

Curtis W. Johnson

John Stuart Hall

The New Citistate Age

Across America and across the globe, citistates are emerging as a critical focus of economic activity, of governance, of social organization for the 1990s and the century to come.

Why, after four centuries in the shadows of mighty nation-states, does it seem plausible to revive the historic city-state concept to describe geographic areas that we typically saddle with such ungainly titles as "metropolitan area," "metroplex," or—in the even more dreary European usage—"conurbation"?

The answer lies in a remarkable confluence of events. Telecommunications has become global and instant. With access to an international airport, goods can be moved between any two continents in a single day. Trade barriers are crumbling, opening distant markets, forcing inefficient manufacturers out of business. Nation-states' macroeconomic policies are constantly being thwarted, even as ethnic and provincial sentiment forces them into ceding power to their constituent parts—or even, as in the case of the Soviet Union, forces them to break up into smaller countries. The cold war has thawed, sending ethnic waters racing in every direction.

World population seems to be blowing with hurricane velocity out of the globe's rural areas into citistate metropolises. The focus of global competition is shifting from military power to economics. Nation-states excel at war; they are proving increasingly limited and sometimes shockingly incompetent in the arena of economics. As economic analyst Joel Kotkin observes:

> Just as the decades of East-West tension fostered the creation of a high-tech permanent warfare state, concentrating economic and technological power in a small, domestic elite, the current diminution of the

military erodes what Polish sociologist Stanislav Andreski described as the state's primary power: "the regulation of the use of violence."[1]

John Gardner, planning director for Metropolitan Toronto, suggests that the forces abroad in the world today are simultaneously pushing power *up*, to the international level, and *down*, to the local level. The "Earth Summit" in Rio de Janeiro in 1992 underscored, for example, the imperative for coordinated international attention to such vital issues as the earth's intricately interdependent environment. Yet at the same time, Gardner suggests, we are seeing a "withering away" of national institutions and power—especially in nations like Canada, where ethnic and linguistic divisions threaten to rend the nation-state apart.

Increasingly, it has become clear that preoccupation with macroeconomics at the nation-state level may not be particularly productive, that national economies are, in fact, constellations of regional economies, each with a major city at its core, each requiring specific and customized strategies.

Benjamin Barber, Walt Whitman Professor of Political Science at Rutgers University, has developed an analogous theme—that "the planet is falling precipitously apart *and* coming reluctantly together at the very same moment." He labels the divergent trends "Jihad vs. McWorld." On the one hand there's "a retribalization of large swaths of humankind by war and bloodshed: a threatened Lebanonization of national states in which culture is pitted against culture, . . . a Jihad in the name of a hundred narrowly conceived faiths against every kind of interdependence, every kind of artificial social cooperation and civic mutuality." Yet there's also the McWorld phenomenon, "borne in on us by the onrush of economic and ecological forces that demand integration and uniformity," forces propelling nations into one commercially homogenous global network "tied together by technology, ecology, communications and commerce."[2]

What is certain is that wherever one looks, trends accentuate the rise of the citistate and the eclipse of the nation-state. Telecommunications —"the highway of the future" in the words of Dallas-based, city-corporate consultant James Crupi—enables people to vault national boundaries in nanoseconds.[3] Fiber optics, satellites, and "smart buildings" constantly increase the speed and efficiency of telecommunications.

Citistates rush to be included in the communications revolution. San Antonio is aggressively marketing itself as "TeleCity." Amsterdam hopes to become a critical air and telecommunications port, linking Europe with the world and thus gaining the upper hand in its bid for the European head-quarters of firms from other continents. New York City has a "teleport"—an antenna farm on Staten Island linked to a regional fiber-optic network—that gives the Big Apple's banks, brokerage houses, and travel industries instant access to satellites and other global telecommunications media. Hong Kong (the prototype citistate, some say) is reportedly ahead of practically all the world in laying down fiber-optic cables across its entire territory.

The international flow of capital, constrained until the collapse of the Bretton Woods monetary system in 1971, has become extraordinarily fluid in the last two decades. With the new technology it's possible for millions of dollars to move in seconds from Miami to Milan, Dallas to Dhahran. From New York to Tokyo, the world's major stock markets now respond to one another's movements in moments. Investment capital, the mother's milk of citistates' economic development, becomes increasingly mobile, with immense capacity to aggregate and disaggregate itself, nationally and internationally.

But citistates will have difficulty attracting and retaining that mobile capital unless they show a stable, dependable face to the world. When south-central Los Angeles went up in flames in the spring of 1992, the impact wasn't simply $1 billion or more in canceled Japanese tourist bookings for Southern California. Local business leaders also had to ago-nize about European and Asian capital bolting. When a flood in April 1992 closed down Chicago's Board of Trade, trading in the London futures exchange surged as Chicago tried desperately to get back on line and avert a permanent loss of market share.

Crumbling trade barriers are a leitmotif of our times. Immense liberal-ization has resulted from the years of GATT (General Agreement for Tariffs and Trade) negotiations. By the end of 1992, the 12 nations of the European Community (EC) had completed a process to allow completely free move-ment of goods, services, capital, and people among the member countries, creating an integrated market of 320 million consumers. The process was not likely to be reversed, notwithstanding the currency crises and deep divisions over trade and unity that seemed to grip the continent just before the January 1, 1993, deadline.

North America is rushing toward its own common market. Virtually all trade restrictions between Canada and the United States fell with imple-mentation of the two nations' comprehensive trade agreement in 1989. As these pages are written, a total North American trade agreement, Mexico included, has been written and awaits ratification.

Peter Karl Kresl, an economist at Bucknell University, notes that by destroying trade walls, nation-states are voluntarily relinquishing a significant part of their power to subsidize favored industries or regions.[4] By ceding broad authority to the European Community, the nation-states of the continent are losing formidable powers to bargain with individual corporations or regions. Yet the unified EC appears to have little awareness of regional disparities and how to deal with them.[5]

A similar withdrawal has been under way on a national level in the United States. Over the course of the 1980s, the federal government was so fiscally and intellectually exhausted that ailing cities and regions increasingly felt there was no higher government to look to for assistance. Even with a more politically activist government in Washington, a cavernous national deficit eclipses the prospect of much more than a trickle of regionally targeted federal assistance for years to come.

Unilateral economic moves by nation-states are becoming increasingly perilous. When nation-states "lose control of fiscal and economic and monetary policy," notes James Crupi, "they lose sovereignty."

One might say the same is true when they lose control of immigration. The United States is currently receiving 600,000 immigrants annually—nearly as many as in the peak years of 1900 to 1910. And that figure does not even count the vast, unnumbered flow of illegal immigrants each year. The nation seems unwilling to take the draconian measures necessary to seal its border with Mexico. Virtually all the immigrants head for the cities, adding fresh entrepreneurial energy but also vast social service burdens for which the nation-state accepts very little responsibility.

Whether their immigrants come from abroad or from the countryside of their own nations, citistates are becoming the focal point of world population growth. The spread-out population patterns of the early nation-state period have virtually disappeared. Today, 80 percent of the world's population occupies just 2 percent of the land surface of the globe. It's estimated that by 2000 roughly 50 percent of the world's population will live in and around cities; by 2020, that proportion could rise to as high as two-thirds. With the 1990 census, the United States became a truly metropolitan nation for the first time in its history: 125 million people, or 50.2 percent of the national total, were found to live in the 39 U.S. metropolitan areas with populations of 1 million people or more. The speed of change is reflected by the fact that in 1950, there were only 14 U.S. metropolitan areas of more than 1 million people, and they were home to only 30 percent of the country's population.

Individual citistates are already demonstrating that boundaries often have more to do with sentiment than logic. Seventy percent of the investment in Guangzhou Province in the Peoples' Republic of China comes from the adjacent Hong Kong citistate. The entire state of Georgia, James Crupi suggests, can be seen as the hinterland of the Atlanta citistate, with Savannah as its port. Tijuana, Mexico, clearly falls under the orbit of the San Diego citistate, divided only by one of the world's busiest international crossing points.

Several major league baseball franchises are truly regional, drawing fans, media coverage, and allegiances—to say nothing of millions of dollars—across state lines and into a citistate. Cincinnati, St. Louis, and Boston are obvious examples, as is Baltimore, with its new and abundantly successful Camden Yards baseball park. After 60 consecutive sellout crowds in 1992—a new major league attendance record—sports columnist Thomas Boswell of *The Washington Post* concluded: "This is the year when Washington fans invaded Baltimore and became full partners supporting what has become a true regional franchise. . . . Like it or not—and neither city is totally happy with the arrangement—the team that plays here is the Baltimore-Washington Orioles."[6]

One is tempted to ask: In American terms, does the rise of the citistate mean that state governments are consigned to the shadows of insignificance? The answer, we believe, is emphatically no. American state governments have immense powers—over taxation, over regulation, in determining the basic powers of the local governments.[7] States have original, constitutional power. Many are highly active in attracting foreign investment and have trade offices in Europe and Asia. And in the context of the 1990s, their strategic sense is reflected in the timing and location of their investments, their policies on issues ranging from education to health to renewal of infrastructure, and the relationships they build not just domestically, but internationally.

All too often, the state governments and their major metropolitan areas seem locked in adversarial relationships. A great deal of suburban legislators' energy goes into keeping the big city at bay. Yet a stunning portion of states' economies are bound up in the fate of their citistates—big cities and suburbs alike.

The same truth is evident internationally. The Italian parliament recognized it in 1990, for example, when it gave all its major metropolises— Turin, Milan, Venice, Genoa, Bologna, Florence, Rome, and Naples—a kind of citistate status. Each was vested with powers formerly retained by Italian provinces: planning for land use and transportation, supervision of environmental and cultural resources, and planning of energy and water systems. The territory of each was defined as the existing center city plus nearby towns and communities that formed a coherent urban whole. In the cases where the metropolitan territory failed to correspond exactly with the territory of an existing province, the communities left over were either made into a new province or transferred to adjacent provinces.[8]

No one is suggesting that American state governments give way to citistates, constitutionally or in any other way. But the essential interdependence of the states and citistates has emerged as an indispensable feature of governance in the latter years of the 20th century.

National governments also depend heavily on citistates for their aggregate economic strength. The U.S. federal government, during Ronald Reagan's presidency in the 1980s, abandoned the few national inducements to metropolitan coherence it had in place (such as the so-called A-95 regional review process for federal grants, generally carried out by regional councils of governments). One of the consequences of national disinterest, however, was mounting environmental degradation—especially air pollution worsened by massive, federally subsidized highway building and the absence of metropolitan land use controls.

In the Clean Air Act Amendments of 1990, Congress laid down much stricter requirements that states meet a schedule of stiffening air quality standards. And in the Intermodal Surface Transportation Efficiency Act of 1991 (nicknamed "ISTEA"), Washington went dramatically further by requiring a rational, inclusive transportation planning process at the metropolitan level. A major responsibility was laid on metropolitan planning organizations (usually councils of governments) to make clear, hard choices between highway and mass transit initiatives. The MPOs were also required to involve the public far more in the decision-making process and to give real weight (for a change) to such factors as energy conservation, congestion relief, and even such alternatives as pedestrian walkways and bikeways. The Clean Air Act and ISTEA, with their increasingly rigorous attainment and performance goals, represent the first wave of federal legislation that recognizes the needs and realities of the citistate era.

The Nation-State and City-State in History

One can argue that the city-state was always a more natural political and economic entity than the nation-state. The nation-state began to emerge in the 16th century in the wake of the fall of Constantinople, which closed the land bridge to Asia, frustrating Europeans' lust for easy trade, land, and plunder. The age of colonial exploration and exploitation, the rise of capitalism, and the breakdown of medieval society with its hierarchical rankings all contributed to the rise of nation-states. Then came the decline of monarchies and the rise of broadly based nationalism, fired up in peoples' minds as the Napoleonic wars convulsed Europe. Nationalism in turn stimulated the development of national unity in the United States, as Henry Clay and the "War Hawks" called upon the country to avenge the "insults" to its flag and ravages on its trade, and the nation plunged into the War of 1812.[9]

Over the course of the 19th century, nationalism swept away all competing ideas, and the nation-state came to be accepted as the only "natural" form of organization for government, culture, trade, and all economic activity. The European nations competed heatedly for colonial possessions from Africa to the Pacific, and Russia colonized and exploited great land areas and populations from Bessarabia to Turkestan.[10] As H. G. Wells later wrote:

> All men are by nature partisans and patriots, but the natural tribalism of men in the nineteenth century was unnaturally exaggerated, it was fretted and overstimulated and inflamed and forced into the national-ist mode. Nationalism was taught in schools, emphasized by newspa-pers, preached and mocked and sung into men. It became a monstrous cant which darkened all human affairs. Men were brought to feel that they were so improper without a nationality as without their clothes in a crowded assembly.[11]

By the late 19th century the most extreme form of nationalism in the world was German—an autocratic, unbending, militaristic philosophy that intimidated intellectuals and people of moderation, paving the way for two cataclysmic world wars and the rise of bestial Naziism. And socialism, which had seemed for a while an alternative to blind nationalism and fealty to nation-states, became twisted in the Soviet experience into the horrors of the Stalin regime. Nor did nationalism spend itself in Europe, America, and Eurasia; in the years after World War II it fulfilled the same revolutionary function in remaking the map of Asia and Africa.

The long history of city-states, in contrast, seemed to begin rather naturally around 3000 B.C. They emerged as a way to enhance the security of peasants who periodically were called upon by a king (a leader of a clan) to wage war with other villages and regions. Protective walls were built to provide defense and define city boundaries; the security they provided gave people some release from the drudgery of guard duty and soldiering, more time for assembly, bargaining, the arts, and other creatively productive functions.[12]

Religious identity, linked to cultural homogeneity, was significant in the early city-states. The center of every Greek city-state was an *acropolis,* the home of the city's gods. Yet eventually it was the *agora,* the marketplace, that assumed the central place in the city-states' lives. From 700 to 450 B.C. Greek city-states ran the gamut of violent, constitutional, and practical political change. Yet one can argue that the highest form of effective democratic governance the world has known was achieved, after many stages and changes, by such Greek city-states as Athens around 450 B.C., during the Age of Pericles, when Greek art and literature made their most significant contributions to world culture.

It is true that the democracy of the time was hardly universal. According to Oxford scholar H. A. Davies, the city-state of Athens was made up of 280,000 people, including 100,000 slaves.[13] When women and children are subtracted, this left about 50,000 *freemen*—men for whom *both* parents were Athenians—who directly governed the city-state.

Yet the city-states of ancient Greece not only established political order during their time; they also broke down monarchic, and in turn aristocratic, rule. And they gave birth, in the words of Sir William Halliday, professor of ancient history at the University of Liverpool, to "the conception of the community as a living whole, of which its individual members are living parts."[14]

Of antiquity in general, one can say city-states—whether Athens, Sparta, Miletus, Syracuse, Carthage, or Rome—were the organizing principle. It is helpful to remember that the word *civilization* is derived from the word *city,* and the word *politics* is derived from the ancient Greek word for the city-state, the *polis.*[15]

It is worth noting that the so-called Dark Ages that followed the collapse of the Roman Empire were devoid of both city-state focus and urban culture. Yet despite the several centuries of turmoil and feudal and ecclesiastic rule that characterized that period, in time city-states and a rejuvenated European urban culture returned. Beginning around 1100 A.D., new city-states began to form out of the fragments of small fiefdoms that characterized the early Middle Ages. Economics drove the change. Residents of most medieval towns were either actual or economic slaves to feudal kings or barons. But the advent of interregion trade, together with the avarice and combativeness of many rulers, resulted in kings' needing more cash. Opportunities soon arose for the people of some towns to buy their freedom. Strong economic guilds formed, many of them taking on roles in governance.[16]

Such former city-states of the Mediterranean region as Venice and Genoa gained new life as centers of trade and commerce, dealing with exotic and profitable goods from the Far East. New city-states emerged in Germany, France, and England, among them Cologne, Mainz, Troyes, Reims, London, Bristol, and Norwich. The common theme shared by all of these new centers, according to urban anthropologist Richard G. Fox, was resistance to "the suffocating powers of their feudal overlords."[17]

The city-states of the late Middle Ages were the centers of cultural and democratic development in their time. It was in them that the great works of Greek and Roman civilization were once again esteemed and the Gothic form of architecture was proclaimed most dramatically in cathedrals and town halls.

At the same time, such mercantile city-states as Florence and Amsterdam laid the groundwork for democratic governance by reinstating the rule of law over dictatorial, hereditary power. Obviously universal suffrage as we know it today did not exist; yet in each of the European city-states of the late Middle Ages, "a steady percolation of political weight drew power downward from a small patrician elite to a large urban mass."[18]

The city-states of these times also demonstrated the advantages of opportunism, collaboration, and confederation. The most famous confederation was the Hanseatic League, which at one time (between 1340 and 1450) was made up of more than 80 cities, including Lubeck, Cologne, Brunswick, Wisby, and Danzig. At its peak, the Hanseatic League covered all the important cities of Germany and had factories in Denmark, England, Russia, and Sweden. The league's influence stretched from the eastern boundary of Novgorod, Russia, to the western boundary of London. It monopolized the trade of the Baltic and North seas, fought pirates, and had great fleets reminiscent of those of ancient Venice. Richard Fox has described the confederations of that time as "a coming together of equals, a combination of many small, sharply bound, and aggressively independent urban communities wherein none lost their identity"—though none, Fox noted, "retained membership [in the League] once their individual advantage had been served."[19]

Why have city-states spanned time and continents? The short answer is that they served as vessels for real change. City-states arose as natural responses to real and perceived oppression, weak and ineffective governance by the state, and people's drive to economic expansion and growth. Born as defensive reactions, they thrived as politically and legally autonomous entities, economically free and robust. Over time, they have proven themselves as centers of the world's commerce, government, tribes, and religions. Small wonder that we see them reemerging in our time.

What, in today's world, are the special advantages and driving forces of these entities we are calling *citistates?* In some cases one can argue it is ethnicity. Montreal stands forth, for example, as the epitome of French America, Miami as the principal Hispanic beachhead in the United States. As the Soviet Union has crumbled, the lead cities of the reemergent republics have become their citistate centers. Ask Catalans what city is their natural capital and they will name Barcelona rather than Madrid. Scots will name Edinburgh rather than London. Strands of separatism are even found in Japan's Hokkaido or Kyushu prefectures. In one sense citistates seem the natural entities to fully express the cultural and linguistic ethnicity now bubbling up at the local level across the world—even though one of citistates' greatest challenges is to accommodate diverse nationalities. (Where interethnic tolerance has failed—the Sarejevo, Beirut, Belfast, and Jerusalem–Tel Aviv citistates, for example—a bitter price is paid.)

American citistates, we might note, have begun to develop various programs, forums, and councils to smooth over the ethnic divides. Examples include the Portland, Oregon, program to "unlearn racism"; the race relations forum of the Greater Cleveland Round Table; minority leadership training efforts of Challenge Greensboro in North Carolina; and the cultural awareness training and education sessions of many local governments.[20] The transcendent task for this generation of Americans is to achieve "wholeness incorporating diversity" in our communities and as a nation, argues John W. Gardner, founder of Common Cause and advisor to six presidents. Rather than some kind of homogeneity, says Gardner, the objective should be "a workable level of unity" that is tolerant of diversity, dispersed power, and healthy conflict.[21]

The citistate, given its myriad of interpersonal and practical ties, may be the best arena to respond to challenges such as John Gardner's, to experiment with building a sense of the common good out of diversity.

There seems little doubt, though, that it is economics that has been the cornerstone of city-states' growth and influence through the sweep of history. Jane Jacobs, in her 1969 book *The Economy of Cities,* brilliantly laid out the case that it was cities, not rural areas, that, since the dawn of history have instigated most of the world's economic invention and growth. To that she added the modern corollary: it is cities, not nations, that are the chief generators of wealth on earth. Cities' power stems from the creative power of humans challenging each other in the close, shared society of urban settings. And for centuries, it has been cities that have inaugurated the great trade routes of the world. Jacobs quotes Jerome Carcopino's *Daily Life of Ancient Rome* to underscore how *trade* has for millennia been the hallmark of the city-state:

> Into the three ports of Ostia, Portus and the emporium beneath the Aventine, [wrote Carcopino] poured the tiles and bricks, the wines and fruits of Italy; the corn of Egypt and Africa; the oil of Spain; the venison, the timbers and the wood of Gaul; the cured meats of Baetica; the dates of the oases; the marbles of Tuscany, of Greece, and of Numidia; the porphyries of the Arabian Desert; the lead, silver and copper of the Iberian Peninsula; the ivory of the Syrtes and the Mauretanias, the gold of Dalmatia and of Dacia; the tin of the Cassiterides, now the Scilly Isles, and the amber of the Baltic; the papyri of the valley of the Nile; the glass of Phoenicia and of Syria; the stuffs of the Orient; the incense of Arabia; the spices, the corals, and the gems of India; the silks of the Far East.[22]

In critical aspects, however, the city-state trade of antiquity, even of the recent past, differed dramatically from what we see today. Individual areas traditionally specialized in their exports, either due to a monopoly of raw material supply or preeminence in crafting and manufacturing raw materials. Today monopolies in raw materials and agricultural specialties are rarer. It's become an economic truism that significant and lasting wealth comes not simply from extraction or crop growth, but through ever-advanced levels of processing and manufacturing.

The Reborn City-State

We would be the first to concede that citistates, especially in the United States, are not yet recognized as a major component of the political and economic reality of the late 20th century. Like other new forms of human organization over the course of history, they are evolving because existing forms of organization and governance are less and less successful in meeting the real needs of the times. And, as before, it will likely be economic change that focuses and gives birth to the reality of the new form and then to its broader public recognition.

Consider the harsh character of present-day economic competition. Virtually every manufacturing monopoly in today's international economy is crumbling. With instant communications and rapid transportation, citistate enterprises find themselves threatened by competitors that may suddenly spring up on any continent. Markets mature, peak, and wither with amazing speed; nothing is truly proprietary. An IBM PC becomes just another commodity, like so much rice or grain. In the past, Theodore Hershberg of the University of Pennsylvania suggests, an industry might be able to get along with internal inefficiencies, a mediocre work force, weak local transportation links. No longer. Today's industries don't enjoy a protective envelope of time and distance. Their exposure is immediate, almost total. Only entrepreneurial, adaptive, "thinking" enterprises are likely to remain competitive.

What that means is that skilled human resources are becoming as critical as cheap labor or great belching steel plants were in times past. Economic development specialist Gene DePrez, formerly an executive of PHH Fantus, says the search for low-cost labor that characterized the era of low-tech manufacturing has just about disappeared. Today virtually all processes are using more automated production methods. Firms are decentralizing authority, trying "Total Quality Management" schemes that put a premium on employee intelligence and ingenuity. "Just-in-time" manufacturing—the kind that brings a new product to market precisely when it is needed—similarly requires higher skill levels. Firms considering locations, notes DePrez, weigh quality of labor just as seriously as its cost.[23]

Knowledge, learning, research, information, and skill are the raw materials of commerce in a global society. "Brainpower will be the dominant resource of the 21st century," James Crupi observes. "Cities that do the best job of attracting and educating talented people will flourish. People are the new products."

But if national governments are losing their power to innovate, to reposture a society, who will? To us, the inescapable conclusion is that the citistates have the potential to tackle these challenges. The skill and foresight individual citistates bring to laying the groundwork for their future will determine how well they fare in the harsh, exposed, new global economy. They must have strong physical infrastructures; they must develop capable work forces; they must avoid social dissension and the expense of large impoverished populations. Their internal leadership capacity—to scan the international environment, to make vital changes at home—becomes preeminently important.

States and provinces can play an important part in mobilizing for the new world economy; in the United States, for example, states have taxing and regulatory authority far beyond that of any local government or coalition of local governments, and their assistance is critical. But the citistate, as a focus for planning and mobilization and action, is likely to grow steadily in the public consciousness. It is large enough to take on the cross-jurisdictional challenges of work force preparedness, education, physical infrastructure, environmental quality, and economic positioning. Yet a citistate is generally small enough to allow a measure of personal interaction between citizens and institutions. "All the people" of an Illinois, a Texas, a California, can never hope to become sufficiently and personally sensitive to one another to form a cohesive community. (California, indeed, claims to be a nation-state, and in its fiscal agony of the early 1990s began to act suspiciously like one.) Yet a citistate is sufficiently contained geographically so that there's a chance for people to coalesce within it, forming some direct ties, and then understandings, across a "Chicagoland," a Dallas–Fort Worth "Metroplex," a Los Angeles or San Francisco citistate. For citistates with smaller populations—the Baltimores and Seattles, Phoenixes and St. Pauls covered in this book, for example—the task ought to be even easier.

The question does arise: How large is a citistate? Does it encompass just the original core city and its immediate surrounding areas? Or, in U.S. terms, all of a census-defined metropolitan statistical area? Or the viewing area of the city's television stations? Or the radius of the longest commute, which some would define as that citistate's "commute-shed"? Or virtually all the exurban, rural territory up to the orbit of another citistate? Indeed, given the infinite variety of geographic configurations, the very ambiguity of the definition of citistate may tell us a lot. The citistate *is* the most dynamic form of human settlement today. We are just beginning to sense its full, latent power. But it may be years before we grasp its limits, geographic or political.

What we *can* sense is when the business and political leadership of a citistate begins to coalesce to further the region's common interests. Within the cities covered in this book, a standout for its time was the Goals for Dallas process, born in the painful years after the Kennedy assassination. It led to the creation of the Dallas/Fort Worth Airport and a multiyear series of sensational industrial catches.

The Greater Baltimore Committee (GBC) has been particularly far-sighted, focusing on city, but in some cases metropolitanwide, issues for more than a generation now. At the start of the 1990s, the GBC formulated a plan to make the city and region a center of life sciences—medical, biotechnical, environmental—based on the proven research strengths at Johns Hopkins University and the University of Maryland. Most of the new biotech company sites were expected to be in Columbia, Baltimore County, and other suburban areas; but the city itself would benefit through its new marine biotechnology laboratory, the Christopher Columbus Center in downtown, and through creation of a life sciences training institute at the Community College of Baltimore.

The Greater Seattle Chamber of Commerce has been a national leader in gathering a cross section of business, political, and even scrappy neighborhood leaders to travel to other cities for intensive briefings on how another community grapples with major problems. The Seattleites came back from their Toronto visit fired with a vision for doing things regionally; from that came a growth strategies commission and increased attention to the capital infrastructure needs of the entire region.

The suburban and inner-city political forces of the Philadelphia citistate, all too often at each others' throats over the past generation, coalesced in 1991 to persuade the Pennsylvania legislature to create a long-term tax base for mass transit agencies in the state. Without that decision, the Southeast Pennsylvania Transit Authority, a subway-rail-trolley-bus system that covers a five-county area the size of Delaware and carries 1.2 million riders a day, might have ground to a halt with disastrous consequences for the regional economy.

For concerted regionwide economic planning, few communities have matched the so-called Metro Denver Network, launched with strong support from the Greater Denver Chamber of Commerce. Virtually every chamber and economic development agency in the Denver metropolitan region—53 at last count—signed on to the network, even though many of the counties and municipalities had a history of abrasive relations. The effort amounts to the United States' first regionwide, computerized information system to track every new business lead and all available sites, and to provide unified national advertising and coordinated screening of industrial prospects. Begun in 1987 in the pits of a regional recession, the network by 1992 was claiming some credit for a strong economic turnaround in the region and creation of some 100,000 new jobs. In the meantime, the region's business and political leaders worked full-bore to sell over $3 billion in bonds to build a massive new Denver International Airport. By 1992 they were deep into negotiations with such international carriers as KLM, Lufthansa, Air Canada, and British Airways on future direct connections and were working with hundreds of local firms on potential opportunities in international trade.

Austin, Texas, and its environs may be the 1990s star in high-technology development. In some ways, it all looks like luck or federal largesse. IBM started the chips rolling 25 years ago when it opened an Austin plant. In time, IBM was joined by Texas Instruments, 3M, Motorola, Apple Computer, Advanced Micro Devices, and a couple of the biggest high-tech prizes of our time—the congressionally approved consortium of Fortune 500 companies that formed the Microelectronics and Computer Technology Corporation (MCC) to work on advanced computer technologies, plus the federally supported Sematech consortium to reclaim computer chip domination from the Japanese. Both the MCC and Sematech location decisions came after stiff competition against dozens of competing U.S. cities. In 1992, Silicon Valley's Advanced Micro Devices announced it had chosen Austin for a state-of-the-art semiconductor plant worth more than $700 million.

Big-time support from Texas politicos, not to mention an attractive state capital town and the University of Texas, with its rich supply of ideas and consultants, was said to account for a lot of Austin's success. But a competitor—Steve Vedesco, president of the San Jose Chamber of Commerce—put his finger on what's probably the most critical reason of all. Austin's secret, he told a *Washington Post* reporter, is "community spirit"— government, business, and university leaders working closely together to attract the high-tech firms, talented engineers, and consortia.[24]

The Louisville region presents an interesting case of a kind of economic restructuring. In the early 1980s, the region was suffering an almost cataclysmic loss of manufacturing jobs. Negative national publicity spread when Louisville was dubbed "Strike City" for its contentious labor relations. In fairly standard fashion, regional leaders in 1988 launched a $10-million, five-year campaign to boost the economy by 13,000 additional jobs and $1.5 billion in added economic activity. But they did more. They defined their economic region as all of neighboring Kentucky and several counties across the river in Indiana. They placed major emphasis on helping companies in the region break into international business. They launched a "Buy Louisville Campaign" to match large local manufacturers with smaller local vendors. Major attention went to improving labor-management relations and the local schools. In a community that had gone through two rather bitter city-county merger fights, the mayor of Louisville, Jerry Abramson, was able to cut a deal with the county judge/executive to share the city and county wage taxes.

So when the Louisville area's Ford plant was threatened with extinction, a broad civic alliance sprang to its defense. A worker retraining program was put together with state and local government aid. Then the governor, the mayor, the county judge, senior managers of the Ford plant, and local leaders of the United Auto Workers all got on a plane to Detroit to make an unusual pitch at Ford headquarters: "We're working together, and here's the evidence. We believe we can make the Louisville plant the most competitive in the Ford system." It worked. Ford management was convinced not just to keep its Louisville plant open, but to plow $260 million of fresh investment into it. The plant started making Ford Explorers and pickup trucks and—in an amazing switch from the usual pattern—the Japanese Mazda firm puts its "Navajo" name on the American product, not the reverse. Virtually the entire work force got training in sophisticated new manufacturing techniques. Continuous programs of retraining—from a basic GED to the beginnings of a master's degree—were made available at the plant. The workers recognized that training had become their ticket to a decent living in the fiercely competitive international economy, and they began to participate heavily.

The turnaround in the Louisville area was dramatic, with job totals *and* real income rising by the turn of the decade. In the words of University of Louisville economist Paul Coomes: "The city is now known more for artificial heart surgery than for smokestacks, a world air hub for United Parcel Service than for barge and rail traffic."[25]

Sadly, few American citistates have mobilized more than a fraction of their communities' full skills to address the steadily mounting challenges of the new world economy. There are, of course, sparks of creative planning. Atlanta determined in the 1970s to become an international city and by the 1990s had achieved part of that mission with some 1,200 foreign operations as well as direct overseas air links. Indianapolis's leadership circle determined single-mindedly in the 1980s to make Indianapolis a city of distinction, fell accidently upon an amateur sports strategy, and in a few years was hosting the Pan-American games. Numerous cities have tried to make themselves centers of specialized new technologies, from biotechnology to polymers to computer-age software, and some have made forward strides.

But take the measure of what makes a truly great international citistate on the world stage—economic cohesiveness, cultural distinction, environmental safety, social equity, livability, physical safety—and most American citistates lag well behind their European and Asian counterparts. Up to now, that lag has not had dire consequences. The holdover momentum of what economist Lester Thurow calls the United States' era of "effortless superiority," the time when North America's rich natural resources and manufacturing prowess assured our international hegemony, has kept our economic machine rolling. (In 1945 the United States GNP was a scarcely credible three-quarters of the world GNP). But from today's $4-trillion U.S. debt to the nation's staggering trade deficits, the evidence is long since overwhelming that the future may be extraordinarily perilous for the United States—and its citistates.

What are the chief barriers, or disabilities, that American citistates must vault in the race to make it in today's international economy? We suggest there are three especially dangerous barriers most apparent in the United States. The first is the deep socioeconomic gulf between poor cities and affluent suburbs. The second is physical sprawl—the alarming environmental and social consequences of Americans' inability or unwillingness to contain urban growth within reasonably compact geographic areas. The third is Americans' hesitation, one might say their paralysis, in creating effective systems of coordinated governance for citistates.

A Torn Social Fabric

The social disability of America's citistates is rooted in historic antiurbanism, overlain in our time by ethnic and racial prejudices. It is exacerbated by journalists and scholars who dwell almost exclusively on the deep negatives of inner-city life—failing, in the process, to recognize the rich tapestry of self-help efforts in urban neighborhoods. The initial victims of these attitudes are the disadvantaged people of our societies. But the entire citistate suffers, too, as the so-called downtown, the urban heart, the site of the civilization's great buildings and commerce and communications and arts, also experiences disinvestment, gains a negative image in the eyes of its own citizens and the international community.

No one will deny the immense problems that beset American cities in the late 20th century. The manufacturing-based economy of our urban centers has undergone wrenching change. In cities and working-class suburbs that used to be ladders of opportunity for our poorest migrants, the bottom rungs of the ladder have been sawed off. In the transition to a more information- and service-driven economy, hundreds of thousands of low-skilled jobs have vanished; real wages for a worker with a high school or elementary school education have plummeted, often well below the poverty line. Welfare dependency has ballooned—recently to over one million people in New York City alone. City after city has large neighborhoods of the abject poor, often minorities, frustrated, angry, with little stake in the present system, let alone hope for the future. The housing in these tracts is dilapidated, some of it abandoned public housing. Waves of homelessness, AIDS, the carnage of street-level gunfights for drug turf, sweep over these neighborhoods. Americans cavalierly throw away their old cities, notes urbanologist Mark Hughes: "There are levels of depopulation in urban America that on other continents would require war, famine, or pestilence."[26]

Inevitably the images of violence-plagued streets, of graffiti-stained slums close to the downtowns, darken people's entire vision of the city. Many of the Detroit region's 2.8 million suburbanites have written off the center city as a menacing place infested with crack and boarded-up buildings, *The New York Times* reported. "We can slice off Detroit and let it fall into the Detroit River," said Democratic State Sen. Gilbert DiNello, whose suburban district encompasses East Detroit, a town that recently renamed itself Eastepointe to erase its symbolic connection with the ailing city. In Detroit, there are many suburbanites who have not visited the city in years.[27] We even heard of that phenomenon in Baltimore, a city with a wonderfully rebuilt and entertaining center.

Connecticut's capital city of Hartford, tightly surrounded by affluent suburbs, symbolizes the agonies of urban America today. As the *Hartford Courant* itself reported in a series on the city's future:

> The city has 60 to 70 percent of the region's poor and must carry the baggage of poverty: crime, drugs, welfare dependency, teenage pregnancy, hunger and broken families. Hartford has the highest number of welfare recipients of any city or town in the state. . . . Teen pregnancy shackles city youngsters to the welfare system. . . . The city has so many halfway houses, group homes and social service agencies that some streets threaten to become social service malls. . . . Crime continues to suck the life out of the city. . . . Neighborhoods that drew middle-class homesteaders in the 1970s are losing them now because of crime, taxes and schools. . . . The public schools, more racially segregated than some in South Africa, are a disaster. . . . The four-year

dropout rate in the high schools is more than 50 percent. . . . City government is beset by bureaucratic inefficiency and expensive union contracts. City workers are often accused of being rude or unhelpful.[28]

Hartford does not, of course, live apart from its region. The problem is that crazy-quilt, Colonial-era boundaries cordon off the core city from its suburban territory. Each morning thousands of suburbanites drive to the insurance company towers of downtown Hartford, befouling the city's air and using city streets and resources. Each evening they retreat, taking with them the income to support their safe and prosperous towns.

Evidence is now mounting that American citistates are paying a heavy economic price for cramming the poor into constricted center cities while suburbia maintains its walls of segregation. The National League of Cities released statistics in 1992 showing that the metropolitan regions with the most massive income differential between center city and suburbs had been suffering the most in the recession. Using employment growth as its measure, the study (by Larry Ledebur of Wayne State University and William Barnes of the league staff) showed the averages marching right up the scale—the better center-city incomes compared with the suburbs, the better the regional performance; the worse the economic condition of center-city people, the worse the regional job picture.

There's a rather close tie between center city and suburban performance on three critical growth measures—population, income, and employment, according to economist Richard Voith of the Federal Reserve Bank of Philadelphia. Studying economic performance in 28 major metropolitan areas across the Northeast and Midwest, Voith found that with few exceptions, the better the center city does, the better the suburbs do. Conversely, dismal city economic performance is generally reflected in suburban economic activity well below that of suburbs that surround less impacted center cities. The suburbs around a miserably performing center city, like Detroit, may *think* they're winning some sort of competitive race with the inner city. But in fact they're doing substantially worse than suburbs around more successful inner cities. "Even if the most acute problems associated with decline do not arise in the suburbs," Voith concludes, "central city decline is likely to be a long-run, slow drain on the economic and social vitality of the region."[29]

The most comprehensive study of the relationship between center cities and their suburbs in the 1980s, conducted by H. V. Savitch and his colleagues at the University of Louisville School of Urban Policy, reached the same conclusion. Looking at 59 metropolitan areas (27 with center cities experiencing population loss, 32 with population gain), they found that per capita incomes of center city and suburbs (despite the big differentials) tend to move in tandem. Self-sufficiency of suburbs, they concluded, "is an impoverished idea." They go on to say:

> Suburbs which surround healthy cities stand a better chance of vitality than those which surround sick cities. Suburbanites may feel they can shield themselves from urban decline, but like a hole wearing at the center of a rubber raft, everybody is likely to ride a little lower in the water. Those at the center may be at the lowest incline, but hanging onto the periphery may not be the wisest alternative. Self-sufficiency at the periphery is not a sufficient defense. The challenge of repair is as much for those outside the center as for those in it.[30]

David Rusk, former mayor of Albuquerque, New Mexico, has produced a related study. He identifies nine "cities without suburbs." They include Rusk's own Albuquerque plus such places as Jacksonville, Florida; Colorado Springs, Colorado; Lincoln, Nebraska; and Lexington, Kentucky. These cities, says Rusk, have systematically annexed new growth areas or merged with their surrounding counties, so that little's left outside their boundaries. In fact, their per capita income is actually 16 percent higher than the average in their outlying areas. They keep their wealth, so the center city doesn't get stuck (as is so often the case) with dramatically higher taxes. Subsidized housing gets spread around a whole expanded city. School opportunities are equalized. Middle-class families haven't fled.

Rusk says that "the more an area is organized on a metropolitanwide basis, the smaller the socioeconomic gaps between black, Hispanic and Anglo-Americans. In other words, integration works!" There's no "instant panacea," Rusk acknowledges, in city-county consolidation, areawide housing strategies, or shared areawide education and training strategies. Politically, all are exceedingly tough to effect. But tolerating vast disparities between cities and suburbs, he argues, can be deadly: "Our society deludes itself in thinking that turning America's central cities into the sociological equivalent of giant public housing projects is the path to anything but a garrison state."[31]

Indeed, the heavy toll poverty exacts on any state and its large metropolitan regions ought to be obvious. Poor people not only earn less, they pay less in taxes. Their welfare and criminal justice costs drag down state and local economies. Usually less educated, they're less employable. That makes the region (and the nation) all the less attractive for industrial firms that need skilled job candidates.

Nor is the scourge reserved to inner cities alone. Many working-class suburbs are in severe decline. Analyzing 1992 census data from six representative metropolitan regions, Paul Glastris of *U.S. News and World Report* found that 35 percent suffered real declines in median household incomes in the 1980s. "Many suburbs that have served for decades as stepping stones for the working class found themselves in the same downward spiral as urban areas," Glastris reported. He quotes real estate consultant Charles Lockwood: "The nation that invented the throwaway city is now creating the throwaway suburb."[32]

One would have expected scholars to focus on antidotes to urban distress and a polarized society in which the more fortunate retreat behind their social fire walls. Most academic research, though, has limited itself to describing the dire state of things. From Edward Banfield to Richard Lawton to Douglas Yates to Paul Peterson to Eugene Meehan, the common theme is one of hopelessness—that nothing, indeed, can be done, because urban areas are victims of forces far beyond their control.[33]

The reasons stated run far and wide: cities' narrow geographic limits; racism and white flight; new technology making it easier for businesses to operate in remote locations; shriveling tax bases; inefficient, politically manipulated city workers. The research regularly refers to state and federal governments' indifference to urban social renewal. Some of it has focused on the flight of black and Hispanic families to the suburbs as they reach middle-class status, thus depriving the city's youth of positive role models.

Indeed, Douglas Yates has gone so far as to argue that cities are "fundamentally ungovernable . . . incapable of producing coherent decisions, developing effective policies, or implementing state or federal programs."[34] A few urban scholars, like Terry Nichols Clark, Dennis Judd and Randy Ready, and Deil Wright have taken exception to this perspective and offered more optimistic appraisals of the capacity of local government to cope with pressing urban issues and to deal directly with questions of distribution associated with economic growth and investment.[35]

But these are the exceptions. A recent and comprehensive review of scholarly works on cities and urban governance by Robert Warren, Mark Rosentraub, and Louis Weschler finds mainly malaise:

> The vision of a breakdown in urban governance has been reflected and reinforced in the work of many scholars since the 1960s. They have

put emphasis upon the limitations of cities and their citizens in handling local affairs. Depending on the analyst, urban government has been characterized as fragmented, inefficient, inherently unstable economically because of capital mobility, too large to allow neighborhood democracy, too small to solve metropolitan problems, or possessed of leaders who are elites, subordinate to capital, or incapable of resolving or even addressing basic issues facing citizens.[36]

An old friend, David H. Davis of the University of Toledo, sends us a paper describing a "zone of transition," a band of urban decay first detected by Homer Hoyt in Chicago in the 1920s.[37] The zone starts a little distance from a city's downtown and then "crawls out from the center of a widening circle like a slow tidal wave or the shock from an atomic explosion." At each step, once viable neighborhoods are transformed into blocks of slums, vacant stores, abandoned factories. Although a municipality may find itself the victim, "the external causes are almost entirely beyond a city's control." Examples: national laws for taxation, highways, and environmental protection continue to favor the suburbs. The federal clean air and clean water acts, and federal regulations on the environmental Superfund and other toxic site controls provide powerful disincentives for industrial activities on older urban sites.

"The consequence," writes Davis, "is to create urban deserts in the old industrial land and to force new industrial users onto virgin land." He sees a likelihood of "permanent depression" in older industrial cities, with large city land tracts abandoned without any future reclamation.

A problem with such analyses is that they tend to ignore or discard data or findings that are not "objectively measurable." It is far easier to measure crime rates or poverty problems or rates of population and industrial decline than it is to assess the indigenous, regenerative power of cities. So the analyses miss the qualities of community cooperation, constant experimentation, and optimism that Alexis de Tocqueville detected in the communities of America as early as the 1830s—qualities we have found confirmed a thousand times over in our reporting missions to the cities over the last quarter century. Perhaps it is precisely because they're inherently unquantifiable that the intangible factors are glossed over. The result, in any event, is a systemic antiurban bias in the academic literature.

The unfavorable image of cities that academics throw out is matched by creators of movies and television programs who provide today's strongest images, sometimes the only picture millions of Americans have, of city life in the Age of Suburbia. Today's up-and-coming genre includes *New Jack City* and *Boyz N the Hood,* which, according to their young black directors, carry an antigang message, but which critics hit for glamorizing the rawest violence and hatreds in black ghettoes. Spike Lee, today's most celebrated black filmmaker, depicts seething cauldrons of racial and ethnic tension in urban neighborhoods in such movies as *Do the Right Thing* and *Jungle Fever.* We have apocalypse films such as *Blade Runner,* with its view of a future Los Angeles as a bleak and violent place of warring ethnic groups and high-tech, high-fire-power cops. Miami gets portrayed by *Scarface* on the big screen and blood-stained "Miami Vice" on television.

Considering that the predominant images here are guns, drugs, crooks, poverty, hate, and general rot, you have to wonder why virtually every major American city has a publicly funded film office trying to lure movies and television to do on-location shooting—cinematic, that is.

The academics and popular entertainers alike appear to be associating cities with the seamiest side of our society, as if there were almost a cause-and-effect relationship. Academics use the cities because they're quantifiable. Entertainers use them because the urban backdrop is especially vivid and colorful. Yet in each case, the cities get closely associated with negative social behaviors that are, in fact, growing, serious problems in rural and suburban America as well.

If the popularly conveyed pictures of the inner cities are correct, if the deterministic view of urban life is to be accepted, then American citistates are doomed to failure, because they lack economic viability and because underclass and slum conditions turn much of their territory into an American Beirut.

Without denying the urban horror stories of our time, we insist that the picture is far more complex—and hopeful. The Denver and Louisville stories told earlier in this chapter reflect imaginative efforts by whole citistates to prepare for a future with economic opportunity for poor and rich people alike. The Atlanta Project, launched by former President Jimmy Carter in 1992 to mobilize vast corporate, volunteer, and governmental forces to reverse the poverty and desperation in the poorest neighborhoods of the Atlanta region—not just some demonstration neighborhood—represents a systemic effort on a scale simply unknown in the United States in times past. Focusing especially on bringing major industries into south-central Los Angeles, the "Rebuild L.A." or "R.L.A." effort headed by ex-baseball commissioner Peter Ueberroth represents a rare effort to pull distressed communities into the American mainstream. (The strategy of

locating major corporate outposts in slum areas, we might add, was originally spelled out in the Peirce Report for Dallas, included in this book, a
year before the Los Angeles disturbances and the birth of R.L.A.)

The most convincing evidence for the inherent strength and viability of
the American community, even in the face of what might be paralyzing
impediments, is at the grassroots. Each time someone tells us cities are
hopeless, we recall a blustery winter day in 1977 touring the South Bronx.
The scene was like Berlin in 1945—so many gutted buildings, smoldering
fires, or the fresh ashes of those fires. That day, in a tiny hole-in-the-wall
luncheonette in the South Bronx, we met Megan Charlop. Megan was a
young slip of a woman who'd thought of becoming a lawyer, worked in the
city courts, and decided the only hope was in the neighborhoods. That
winter she had saved 17 South Bronx tenement buildings. Whenever she
heard a landlord had abandoned an apartment building, she went in, called
the tenants together, and told them: "You have two options. You can stick
together, pool your rents, and work with the city and repair people we'll
make available to get this building into shape; or you can all sit here and
freeze one by one."

Megan Charlop was working—often seven days a week, for meager
pay—for the now-defunct People's Development Corporation, one of scores
of neighborhood housing groups that had sprung up in seemingly hopeless
New York neighborhoods. They worked in the midst of devastation: abandoned, gutted, burned-out buildings; garbage-strewn alleys; scenes of drugs
and crime. It was a time when building abandonment was running rampant
in the South Bronx, when Roger Starr, on the editorial board of *The New
York Times,* was urging euthanasia for such neighborhoods—cutting off the
umbilical cord of city services and letting those areas die as part of a strategy
of "planned shrinkage" for the city. But the Megan Charlops were throwing
their lives and bodies into the battle on the other side. And the results were
amazing. When residents of endangered buildings or neighborhoods realized they could make decisions for themselves, attitudes and habits changed
abruptly. Crime, vandalism, and drug use plummeted. Buildings that
police once feared to enter suddenly became self-policing.

Megan Charlop talked to us simply but eloquently of the costs of
abandonment, fires, people freezing. Neighborhoods, she said, don't need
distant urbanologists to tell them "the plan" for their future—or nonfuture.
"We'll tell them the plan," she said. "They're not the city. We're the city."

Visit the South Bronx today and you find quite a different community.
Grass grows over the fields of rubble. Vast amounts of housing have been

built, much of it by nonprofit groups—blocks of tastefully renovated low-rise apartments, senior-citizen and low-income family town houses, several square blocks of pastel-colored bungalows with neat lawns and gardens on Charlotte Street, where Presidents Carter and Reagan came to view the devastation of Dresden in America. A major industrial park has been constructed. Law enforcement is working better. Real estate values have shot upward. The South Bronx still has its problems: poor schools, a huge proportion of the population on welfare, open-air drug sales. Yet on the streets, there's a sense of a very poor but vibrant community.

Much of the credit for the South Bronx revival has to go to scrappy and imaginative community development corporations (CDCs) with such colorful names as Banana Kelly and the Mid-Bronx Desperadoes. And the story is not an isolated one. From Washington's Anacostia to Newark's Central Ward to Chicago's South Side to Miami's Liberty City, CDCs have been the fulcrum of amazing recovery stories. According to a rigorous study by our colleague Renee Berger for the National Congress for Community Economic Development, more than 2,000 CDCs are operating today across the country. In the last several years, they have built or refurbished 320,000 homes and apartments for low- and moderate-income households and have developed 17.4 million square feet of commercial and industrial space. Through an array of programs for business development and entrepreneurship, they also claim credit for the creation of some 90,000 permanent jobs.

The support of progressive local business communities, of forward-looking local governments, of foundations, has been critical to these grassroots efforts. In the 1980s, the community-based groups acquired a new set of supporters—so-called intermediaries, who provide new networks of contacts, assistance in raising funds for housing and commercial projects, and technical assistance. The New York–based Local Initiatives Support Corporation (LISC), founded by the Ford Foundation in 1979, has leveraged over $1 billion in direct investment in the projects of more than 500 community groups. It has helped finance more than 17,000 housing units and five million square feet of commercial development. Through the federal Low Income Housing Tax Credit, LISC's National Equity Fund has brought the financial resources of Fortune 500 companies to community development groups.

A related organization, the Local Initiatives Managed Assets Corporation, offers traditional investors a low-risk opportunity to purchase quality community development corporation loans. The harvest has been housing, shopping centers, supermarkets, industrial parks, and business incubators in hard-off city neighborhoods and rural backwaters where conventional wisdom and the private market said "it couldn't be done."

The Enterprise Foundation, founded by developer James Rouse, also provides grants, loans, and assistance to community-based groups, concentrating on the very poor. The Neighborhood Reinvestment Corporation, chartered by Congress in the 1970s, has generated over $6.5 billion of reinvestment nationwide through its Neighborhood Housing Services (NHS) network. Local NHS partnerships of residents, government, and businesses are active in 241 neighborhoods in 138 cities, towns, and counties. Some 71 neighborhoods, restored to stability, have been able to move out from under the NHS umbrella.

Thus, despite so many American cities' grim slum conditions, the building blocks of systemic recovery have been identified and in many communities put into place. A substantially greater scale may be required, but the tools are no secret.

On a related front, the number of community health centers, prevention-oriented and responsive to neighborhood needs, is now pegged at some 600 locations. (The Dallas effort, organized by the Parkland Memorial Hospital and described later in this book, is a stellar example.) A new generation of community-responsive policing is arising, with the potential to transform law enforcement officers from an occupying force to champions of low-income neighborhoods. Some cities have formed highly responsive social service networks. (St. Paul's may be a model among all cities.) The ferment over school reform has begun to embrace the idea of schools as multipurpose community centers, along with enlarged parental and community responsibility to make school a place of spirited, quality learning.

Advocates in our inner cities paint a bleak picture of how the American economy and political system have bypassed the poor in the last two decades. From Newark to Cincinnati to Oakland, one can find blocks of the most fearful destruction and social chaos present anywhere in the industrialized world.

Yet studies by Isabel Sawhill and others at the Urban Institute suggest there are probably only some 2.5 million people nationwide actually living in underclass conditions in such neighborhoods. And if one looks carefully around major cities, one can easily spot rather hopeful neighborhoods, according to Richard Nathan of the State University of New York at Albany. Nathan calls these areas "zones of emergence," in which blacks, Hispanics, new or old ethnic groups, have bought into the traditional American dream, owning their own homes, anxious to protect their territory, willing to organize crime patrols and fight hard to keep out drugs. The heavily Puerto Rican Sunset Park neighborhood of Brooklyn is one of these; another is Cleveland's Buckeye-Woodland neighborhood, once predominantly Hungarian, now heavily black. Nathan has identified zones of emergence in such widely diverse cities as Indianapolis, Dallas, St. Louis, Columbus, New Orleans, Pittsburgh, Rochester, Milwaukee, and Denver. Many are to be found around New York City: central Queens, which is soon expected to top New York's Chinatown in Asian population; downtown Flushing, which some call a Hong Kong West; and areas of southeast Queens that some local observers believe may be "the largest contiguous well-off black area in the world."[38]

The negative and deterministic view of urban America also ignores the startling and often quite attractive physical transformation of many cities in the last two decades. It is true that citistates' downtowns face such perils as the constant erosion of retail shopping outlets to the suburbs—a trend that only a few cities (Minneapolis, Seattle, New Orleans, New York, and Portland, Oregon, among them) have even partially offset. Many corporate offices have been lost to suburban office parks, following the big factories that fled a few years earlier. The struggle to keep redefining a city's economic role is a tough one.

Yet it is also true that from the 1970s to the 1980s the center cities experienced the greatest downtown building boom of their history. Some great old buildings have been lost and delightful old streetscapes butchered. But many have been rehabilitated, safeguarded through historic preservation guidelines and given a new life with new public open spaces. Hundreds of American cities have rediscovered the long-neglected rivers passing through them; some (like Baltimore) have made waterfront revival the key to a broad city revival. Pockets of gentrified urban neighborhoods can be found coast to coast. Downtown management districts are adding significant new stability. Richard Bradley, executive director of the International Downtown Association, suggests that while downtowns have a massive backlog of office space, they continue to build new public facilities (arenas, theaters, and the like) and are becoming the true *centers of community* within their regions.

After the Sprawl

There is a second peril for American citistates: the historic and natural American tendency to look the other way as the private sector pushes physical growth farther and farther from the original urban center. The result is diffusion across extraordinarily broad land masses. Population growth in metropolitan New York over the past 25 years has been only 5 percent, but the developed land has increased by 61 percent—devouring nearly 25 percent of the region's open space, forests, and farmland.[39] While the Los Angeles region's population has increased by more than four times over the last 50 years, its geographic size has ballooned by a factor of 20. The 1970s and '80s saw metropolitan Chicago's population increase a bare 4 percent, but its size increase 46 percent.[40]

This trend proceeded in rapid-fire fashion during the 1980s. Not only did development proceed farther and farther from urban centers, but corporations—from industrial giants to the smallest upstart enterprises—flocked to the suburbs. The suburban bedroom communities, the gas stations and waffle shops of the 1950s, became passé; the new order was signature office towers, luxury hotels, upscale housing, high-tech firms in clusters that some choose to describe in one of the great oxymorons of our times: "urban villages."

What we were witnessing, of course, was suburbia fast becoming America's prime workplace. In 1970, only 25 percent of the nation's offices were located in suburbs. Today's figure is close to 60 percent.

There are environmental costs to all this. Among them are horrendous traffic, commutes that take hours instead of minutes, serious air pollution, loss of greenbelts and open space, and obliteration of community life. If suburban office centers were supposed to put people closer to jobs, they haven't succeeded well. In the 1980s the number of Americans driving to work alone soared by 22 million, or *35 percent,* several million more than the raw numbers (18.5 million) of workers added to the work force. The actual count of people carpooling went down 19 percent during the decade. Use of public transit actually declined slightly. The length of the average trip to work grew to over 10 miles.[41] In Southern California, global symbol of freeway "freedom," average travel speed has dipped to 33 miles per hour and is likely to drop to as little as 15 miles per hour as population and car ownership keep expanding in the next decade. Without massive new freeways, the Federal Highway Administration suggests, congestion will increase 400 percent on freeways over the next 20 years—even while the mere idea of plowing new roads through existing neighborhoods becomes increasingly unthinkable.

A related problem is that as the growth juggernaut proceeds, the greenbelts of productive open space around our citistates—farms, parks, watersheds, forests—have been whittled back, paved over, many lost forever. One town merges into the next. Community identity is lost.

Then there's the fact that low-density growth is devilishly expensive. It requires many more miles of roadway, more firehouses and schools and sewer lines (mostly billed to the public through taxes). Working on our Baltimore report, we learned that the state of Maryland's excess road bill if it chooses low- instead of high-density development will likely exceed $3.6 billion by 2020.

Finally, but not least seriously, sprawling development separates people by class and race, moving the new jobs farther and farther from center-city people who are in the deepest need of productive employment. In California there's the example of the San Francisco Bay region, where development has spread up and over the hills to the east, in fact spilling far out into the Central Valley, while comparatively little is done to revive and make use of grand old downtown Oakland or offer accessible jobs to Oakland's troubled populations. One can see the same pattern around Atlanta, as vast office and commercial projects, with their thousands of jobs, flow to Buckhead and other developments on the affluent and overwhelmingly white northern periphery, leaving under- and unemployed blacks in south Atlanta trailing figuratively in the dust. The same phenomenon is also apparent around Philadelphia, with the Route 202 boom corridor plowing through verdant Chester County, essentially inaccessible to Philadelphia's poor minorities.

The most desirable new jobs in metropolitan regions—those associated with the export of goods and services, plus region-serving finance, real estate, and professional work—are the very jobs migrating most rapidly to the suburban peripheries, metropolitan analyst Christopher Leinberger notes.[42] In the meantime, traditional downtowns and inner suburbs are stuck with lower-paying "local-service" jobs such as schoolteachers, store clerks, police, and "storefront" lawyers. (Robert Reich makes much the same point when he talks of American society dividing between "the people in glass towers"—and everyone else.)

We saw stunning physical evidence of this trend in our Dallas helicopter tour—obvious disinvestment in downtown and South Dallas, while 25 miles to the north, on open fields, J. C. Penney (which left New York in 1988) was building a large campuslike office park. Leinberger warns an even larger proportion of high-paying jobs may go to the extreme fringe of metropolitan areas in the 1990s.

Some say industries are picking locations on the far periphery because the real estate is cheap, or because big office complexes are hard to site in older suburbs or cities. Sometimes executives just want shorter commutes for themselves. Sometimes they are obviously escaping the cities' minorities and crime. Consider the example of Sears Roebuck, moving its merchandising division to Hoffman Estates, inaccessible by public transit, 12 miles beyond suburban Schaumburg and 37 miles from its traditional location in the downtown Chicago Sears Tower.

We call this pervasive national phenomenon our own American apartheid. We fear the American citistates may be stuck with it long after South Africa's is extinct.

It's true that all citistates of the modern world face, to some degree, the problem of unwanted geographic dispersion. The examples include Toronto, London, and Frankfurt, all of which have attempted to protect themselves with a greenbelt on their urban periphery, only to see development, in time, leap over the greenbelt. Yet the citistate that tries to deal intelligently with this problem—allowing growth, trying to keep it reasonably compact, allowing for generous green spaces—is likely to fare much better than competitors wed to a cavalier laissez-faire approach.

Environmental, fiscal, and social costs mount rapidly in uncontrolled regions. "A decentralized metropolis cannot be sustained for very long," the San Francisco Greenbelt Alliance notes. Degraded air chokes and impairs health. There's no more land to exploit, except at totally unmanageable distances. Social tensions mount. Infrastructure costs soar beyond the public's willingness to pay.

There are some who argue the new, spread-out form of citistate growth is inevitable. In 1991 a prophet-defender of the new order, *Washington Post* writer Joel Garreau, emerged to call the pattern of mushrooming developments circling America's cities *Edge City*. In a book of that name, Garreau even listed all the edge cities coast to coast, among them such places as King of Prussia outside Philadelphia, Bloomington/Edina in the Minneapolis–St. Paul orbit, Houston's Galleria, Las Colinas on Dallas's western flank, and Los Angeles's Marina Del Ray–Culver City office constellation.

"Edge City," Garreau noted, "is a creation of the marketplace, and commercial real estate agents are its most devoted acolytes." It features scads of parking, climate enclosure, and a safe atmosphere to lure female shoppers. If readers doubted Americans are making this choice, Garreau reminded them: "We have not built a single old-style downtown from raw dirt in 75 years."[43]

There are multiple drawbacks to edge cities. Their commercial emporia are full of retailing opportunity but offer zero in the way of truly urban and urbane amenities: symbolically splendid boulevards and public spaces, proud city halls, grand parks, concert halls, museums—all the features of a shared public life and a culture deeper than commerce. Indeed, because the edge cities are privately owned, their owners claim a right to keep the homeless, the poor, beggars, anyone inconvenient, even newspapers they may not like, out of their new American "Main Streets." Edge cities are omnipotent, extraconstitutional within their spheres. If you don't like the terms, the only option is to leave.

Yet edge cities will not float away. They are a geographic fact of life in every citistate of any size. "Downtown" becomes just one of several concentrations of what the technocrats refer to as "a multi-nodal form of metropolitan development."

One would like to think that center cities, with their public places and parks, museums and zoos and seats of government for a region, are still a special place. And there is probably great, untapped potential to make them prosper. Former U.S. Census Bureau director Bruce Chapman, now head of Seattle's Discovery Institute, notes:

> Unused and underused land conveniently close to city hubs is becoming an increasingly valuable resource as the inconvenience and anomie of "edge cities" become more obvious. Depending on the city and the site, large scale, publicly enabled private development of housing and shops close to existing services and infrastructure can make urban living desirable again for members of the middle class. The greatest obstacles are political and bureaucratic shortsightedness. Bureaucrats often make urban development more burdensome. Environmental controls are mindlessly applied. Poverty groups oppose "gentrification." Change these attitudes and center cities will thrive.[44]

Many people today claim that cities are losing their historic advantages, that with instant telephone, fax, modem, and teleconferencing capacity, much of the center cities' inherent advantage has disappeared. Certainly many research laboratories, many cutting-edge corporations, are out on the urban fringe—close enough to the city, one quickly notes, to reach its airport and centralized facilities, but far enough out to escape the tax reach of the center city and older suburbs bearing the brunt of the region's social problems.

We submit that in the final analysis, a citistate's center city, its heart, remains vitally important. It is the meeting place of all the components of a region likely to be ever more ethnically and socially diverse. It does provide a lively, compact area where leaders in business, communications, the arts, and government can interact. It sets the image of the entire citistate for all potential business partners, tourists, visitors, and opinion setters in the new world economy. As we said in a talk to the Central Dallas Association: "Think of telling that businessperson or tourist from Osaka or Rome or Caracas or Johannesburg that downtown Dallas has been discontinued; please take a cab to the LBJ Corridor and then pick some exit."

There are two scintillas of recent good news on the growth-policy front. One is the modest increase in growth-management planning processes implemented in individual states, including Oregon and Hawaii in the 1970s and such states as Florida, Georgia, Vermont, Maine, and Washington from 1980 to 1991. Another is the renewed concept of rational planning across a metropolitan area that was embodied in the federal government's 1990 Clean Air Act Amendments and the 1991 ISTEA regional transportation planning requirements (both discussed earlier in this chapter).

The Governance Gap

The third great disability of American citistates is their common lack of coherent governance—either formal or informal. The result is that fundamentally *public* decisions, on every question from air quality to transportation to solid waste disposal to assuring a competent work force for the future, are reached in piecemeal, often haphazard fashion—or worse still, are never made at all.

The conventional wisdom is that the time for metropolitan government in America has come—and gone. People recall that metropolitan government issues rose up in the 1960s, propelled by federal mandates for regionwide planning. Councils of governments were formed across the nation, often to facilitate capturing federal grants. But they rarely gained substantive power. Americans' inherent desire for localized home rule, their fear of metropolitanism, torpedoed most efforts to create common governance for the dozens, sometimes hundreds, of independent governmental units in any single region. A few cities and counties merged—Nashville–Davidson County(1962), Jacksonville–Duval County (1968), Indianapolis–Marion County (1969). A few thoughtful shared-power arrangements surfaced, such as the Minnesota Twin Cities' Metropolitan Council and the Metropolitan Service District of Portland, Oregon; but they rarely were emulated. Put to local voters, the vast majority of city-county consolidation proposals went down to defeat. America was drifting toward center cities packed with poor minorities. Not surprisingly, the more affluent and whiter suburbs feared that with consolidation they'd be obliged to subsidize the poor, or perhaps even worse, get thrown into school districts with them. Simultaneously, the minorities decided that once they'd seized center-city power, they didn't want to dilute it.

The result was recurrent talk of consolidation, but little action. Take Virginia's Hampton Roads area (Norfolk, Portsmouth, Newport News, Virginia Beach). Hampton Roads is the nation's 27th largest metropolitan area, yet it has only one all-encompassing "regional" agency—sewage disposal—and at least 75 units of government. Government officials have conferred on regional cooperation since 1953. But the area still has two regional economic development departments, several competing tourism and convention offices, three regional planning agencies, and four phone books. There isn't even bus service between the neighboring communities. "Getting cooperation here is like getting that little marble on the Mouse Trap game to make a perfect run," according to Gordon Borrell of the *Virginian-Pilot*.[45]

In contrast, across the Atlantic, the old Hanseatic citistate of Hamburg, exercising clear powers over its geographic area, aspires to become "the Metropole of the North," the connecting city between the European Community on the one hand and the non-EC areas of Scandinavia and the Baltic states on the other. Hamburg's systems of education, environmental protection, and social services are all closely coordinated. The city is confidently working, Peter Karl Kresl reports, to reassert itself as a transportation link between Berlin and the sea, successfully arguing that the first test of Germany's magnetic-levitation, high-speed rail system should be Hamburg-Berlin.[46]

Barcelona, site of the 1992 Summer Olympics, saw its metropolitanwide governance system destroyed by a conservatively minded provincial government in Catalonia. Still, Barcelona and the other communities within the citistate worked hard to maintain their unity and came up with the Barcelona 2000 Strategic Plan. The plan is aimed at inserting Barcelona into the Eurocities network and positioning the city as the center of one of Europe's major regional economies.

One is left wondering how the American citistates can hope to compete with European or Asian counterparts that seem to have their act together in such superior fashion. Often Americans muddle through with rather impressive, albeit totally informal, consultative arrangements. Pittsburgh has quietly allowed a great many governmental powers to float upward, to the Allegheny County level, providing a measure of de facto coordination in a region bedeviled with 4 cities, 82 boroughs, 26 "first-class" towns and 16 "second-class" towns, 42 school districts, and 8 councils of governments, not to mention 17 special districts for parking, 37 for sewers, 24 for water, 7 for recreation, 13 for health, and 16 with miscellaneous powers.

Cleveland, despite the serious poverty of its inner city, tries to be a model of informal consultation to work on shared goals. There are frequent meetings, for example, among representatives of the city Department of Economic Development, Cleveland Tomorrow (an exemplary business-led organization involved in strategic economic research and planning for the region), the Greater Cleveland Round Table, Cuyahoga County, local universities, and two foundations important to Cleveland's revitalization—the George Gund Foundation and the Cleveland Foundation. Effective work on regional agendas is also done by the Citizens League of Greater Cleveland. Inner-city neighborhoods get expert assistance from Neighborhood Progress Inc., which benefits from the active involvement of top business figures, along with foundation, government, and other civic leaders.

But moving from informal consultations to such tangible regional steps as tax-base sharing, cross-border school enrollment, or formation of a work force preparedness plan for the Cleveland region in the 21st century, is very difficult. The "U.S. model" of public-private partnerships and open community participation does maximize creativity, Peter Karl Kresl notes. "But in the absence of a clear and effective structure, the best of plans will have difficulty in the implementation phase."[47]

The problem, of course, is that virtually no problem of the modern citistate—be it strategic economic planning, environmental protection, education and work force preparedness, transportation, parks, recreation, urban growth management—can be handled entirely on a municipality-by-municipality basis.

It is worth noting that when a region does learn to act cohesively, it's rarely tempted to break into pieces again. John W. Walls, president of the Indiana Chamber of Commerce, runs through some of the obvious advantages of Indianapolis's "Unigov" system—combining most Indianapolis and Marion County government functions, eliminating a disruptive county commissioner system, creating a local legislative body responsible for policy and budgeting for *all* city-county units, improving the ability of the mayor to administer governmental functions through a strong "cabinet" relationship. Then he adds:

Psychologically, Unigov has created the perception and reality of a strong, united community, led by a mayor who can literally speak for that community in all competitive relationships.

Does it cost less? No, and we never said it would. Is it more efficient? Probably. Is it more effective? Immeasurably.[48]

Problems and Potentials

In the six Peirce Report cities, we witnessed virtually all the problems of today's American citistates. Dallas's downtown had sprouted a virtual forest of flashy high-rise buildings, for example, yet still seemed, in 1991, in danger of corporate abandonment involving not only potential loss of vast amounts of invested capital but calamitous job losses for residents of heavily black, Hispanic, and poor areas in adjacent South and West Dallas. Baltimore, its exciting Inner Harbor and related revival efforts of the 1980s notwithstanding, was exhibiting a mounting, deep income division—an inner city with only *half* as much average per family income as the surrounding suburban counties. Without the physical renewal, Baltimore might have little chance for human renewal; by the same token, unless it works hard on human renewal, it could one day become a forbidding, not a welcoming, place.

We found Phoenix to be one of America's most extreme cases of a hollowed-out downtown with development sprawling out to distant horizons, an arrangement we discovered was tailor-made for (and politically manipulated by) land speculators and developers. The Seattle (or Puget Sound) citistate, despite a far richer civic culture, was imperiled by haphazard residential and commercial development rolling up and over the broad swath of forested and mountained land stretching from Lake Washington to the Cascades. The movement of such industries as Microsoft to a rural site on the East Side was also undermining the future of the Puget Sounds's "new" suburban city, Bellevue, not to mention Seattle itself and the gritty, historic cities of Tacoma and Everett anchoring the region's southern and northern flanks.

In St. Paul, junior partner in Minnesota's citistate, we found a town that's retained such a strong middle-class population base that it enjoys options effectively foreclosed to many cities. There is no reason, our report suggested, that the growing Southeast Asian, Hispanic, African-American, and Native American populations of St. Paul couldn't be gracefully integrated into the schools, the economy, and local politics. (A rich local infrastructure of sensitive social service organizations helps to make the idea feasible.) St. Paul's downtown, despite widespread movement of corporate offices to Minneapolis in recent years, retains immense charm and good design and is positioned to make arts and culture the organizing principle of an ingenious "Cultural Capital" strategy that could produce a substantial economic payoff.

The government fragmentation problem is well-nigh universal in American communities large and small. Our list included one city so small—Owensboro, Kentucky, a community of only 53,549 people in a county of 87,189—that it would seem a stretch to call it a full-fledged citistate. Yet Owensboro, long distances from any metropolis, has its own regional economy and acts like a larger citistate in many respects. The city had just gone through the agony of a city-county merger fight. (The merger lost). Our report focused on how consensus, a sense of regional citizenship, can be forged in and around Owensboro so that solid cooperation and progress can take place without formalized unitary government.

All the 18 cities of the Phoenix citistate had to do to achieve some common governance, we noted, would be to press for a state constitutional amendment granting full home-rule powers to Maricopa County, which already encompasses 58 percent of Arizona's population. The time was ripe, it appeared, for a unifying Puget Sound Council, starting with King County (the big county that encompasses Seattle) and then expanding over time to take in the neighboring counties.

Indeed, what struck us most was the *potential* of virtually every citistate to alter its environment, to position itself for the new economy. The right civic forces have the potential to coalesce to achieve some form of shared governance. Business has the potential to enlist academic and government allies and start defining the citistate's potential niche or niches in goods and services with national and international appeal. Business-civic alliances can work closely with schools and community colleges and universities to assure preparation of a work force with the needed new skills. Urban universities have the potential to reach out from their ivory towers, engage themselves deeply in every arena from economic planning to environmental monitoring to working intimately with troubled schools and their teachers, to create a spirit of excitement in learning. From the arts to environmental planning, from parks and recreation to making local governments slim and efficient, the possibilities for intelligent, participatory, ahead-of-the-game strategic planning are simply immense.

For the potentials to be unleashed, a community's leaders—established leaders as well as developing leadership cadres—must, of course, be clear-eyed, acknowledging that external factors will surely play a heavy role. Nation-state macroeconomic policies, world trade, migration, climate, corporate location decisions, state taxation and spending policies—each of those forces affects both the limits, and the possibilities, of what any citistate can do.

Yet even with all those "givens," citistate leaders must recognize they need *not* be victims, that the deterministic view of their future is a sure recipe for defeat. Free will lives. The men and women leading our regions must recognize that while no benevolent state or federal or international authority is about to step in to wave a wand and solve their problems, they are free agents, in free communities, able to plan strategically for their future, *able to shape fundamentally what their destiny will be.*

The reports in this book illustrate the rich variety of experiments already under way in citistates across America; the reports then look to even greater possibilities for the future. We did not fly into cities with preconceived notions of solutions to their ills; instead we listened carefully to a broad variety of leaders and citizens in each citistate, hearing how they assessed their own community, its assets, its problems, its possibilities. We then tried, in our reports, to build on what we heard and to suggest next logical steps.

Only history will tell whether American citistates can overcome their disabilities, whether they can make it in the new world order. What we can report is that when one delves below the surface and checks out the civic forces pushing for regeneration, it is possible to discern the outlines of a more coherent, mutually supportive social and economic order, struggling to be born.

The Citistate in Brief

Over half of all Arizonans live in the Phoenix citistate (essentially Maricopa County), which had 2,122,101 people according to the 1990 census—up 40 percent from 1980. The citistate covers 9,204 square miles. Phoenix, with a population of 983,403, is the largest city and Arizona's capital. Chandler, Glendale, Mesa, Scottsdale, and Tempe are major satellite cities, each with populations of over 100,000 as a result of heavy growth in recent decades. The region has 138 governments, 21 cities and towns, 56 school districts, and 60 special districts.

The Peirce Report Glossary

Sky Harbor is the Phoenix regional airport. Businesses and resorts line *Camelback,* the main east-west thoroughfare that runs through Phoenix and Scottsdale. (It's named after Camelback Mountain, a formation that vaguely resembles a camel's back and that lies directly north and parallel to the thoroughfare). *Central Avenue* is Phoenix's main north-south street and major commercial corridor. *North Central* refers to the newer and more affluent section of Central Avenue and adjacent neighborhoods.

The *Phoenix 40,* an elite group of business leaders interested in civic affairs, was founded in 1975 and had an early 1990s membership of about 60. The *East Valley Partnership* was founded by civic and business leaders from Mesa, Chandler, Gilbert, and Tempe to represent East Valley interests and respond to the perceived exclusivity of the Phoenix 40. The *Maricopa Association of Governments* is the regional "COG" (council of governments), consisting of officials from the county's cities and towns, bearing principal responsibility for regional planning in transportation, air and water quality, and solid waste management. *Valley Leadership,* formed in 1947, provides training and networking for community leaders on issues of concern to the greater Phoenix area. The *Phoenix City Club,* dating from 1984, is a nonprofit civic group that has focused on such issues as downtown development and the freeway system.

Finding a Way to Stand Together

(Originally published in The Arizona Republic *and* The Phoenix Gazette *on February 6, 1987.)*

It's not possible to visit the Valley of the Sun—the region of Phoenix and its 17 sister cities—without being struck by its vastness, its dynamism, and its zest for life.

The vastness struck us our very first afternoon in town. Channel 12 helicopter pilot Jerry Foster gave us a grand aerial tour of the Valley. Even from on high, one's vision has to stretch to encompass the 40 miles from Sun City to Apache Junction or the 43 miles from Chandler's southern flank to Scottsdale's northern extremity.

Phoenix proper expanded from 9.6 square miles in 1940 to 343 today, we learned. An incredible 936 square miles lie within the Valley's settled communities. Some people are born, live, and die in the Valley of the Sun without ever traveling its full breadth.

Yet amazingly, this civilization arising among the hauntingly beautiful desert peaks represents no completed metropolis. One is amazed to see the vast spaces still empty and awaiting development, close to the center and out to the farthest horizons.

Across the desert floor march the new developments, sweeping cactuses, alfalfa fields, or orchards before them. Few places on this continent, or anywhere in the world, can compare in rate of growth.

We had been given a mission by *The Phoenix Gazette* and *The Arizona Republic* to visit the Valley, take its civic pulse, assess attributes both solid and weak. And then we were to suggest, against the backdrop of our knowledge of metropolitan areas across the country, how this region could strengthen its collective decision-making capacity; and how it could better prepare itself to assure high quality of life, of jobs, and of community support for citizens of all ages and income groups—not just in good times, but also for a dawning era of turbulent change in national and international economies.

For although the Valley today boasts nearly incredible growth figures, its apparent good fortune is no guarantee of what the future might bring. As the Phoenix Economic Growth Corporation noted in the strategic plan published in spring 1987, many cities that once expanded with population leaps of 50 percent or more in a decade—such as Detroit, Newark, and St. Louis—are struggling for survival today.

Houston, a star of the Sun Belt growth of the 1970s, has seen a collapse of its employment base; Denver, another star, has seen its economy run out of steam. History is replete with stories of great civilizations that failed to make timely provisions for the future and suffered grievously as a result. The critical time for action is before the advent of reversals that rob a metropolis of wealth and forward momentum.

The Phoenix newspapers gave us total freedom in our task. Although the papers' editors did propose names for our consideration, we determined the final list of about 60 Valley leaders to be interviewed. No representative of the papers took part in the off-the-record interviews we conducted.

We were struck by the remarkable unanimity, whether from men or women, old or young, whites or minorities, about the positive sides of life in the Valley. They all view the civilization here as an opening book, full of promise and opportunity.

Here, they told us, is a place to make your start in life or get a new start. Here are cities still developing with freshness, potential, the American dream alive and well, a touch of the old Wild West lingering on. In this Valley, we heard, a newcomer's energy and creativity won't be stymied by entrenched institutions. "The glorious desert sunsets, the expansive sky, the exhilaration, all work positively on your psyche," a relative newcomer said. Many Valley residents stressed lifestyle—the proximity of an outdoors filled with the wonders of the Southwest's geography, "openness and a sense of space."

We checked the figures and discovered that 267,000 residents—one-fifth of the Valley's adult population—own recreational vehicles. More than 140,000 own boats. Hundreds of thousands are into such activities as bicycling, backpacking, golfing, horseback riding, hunting, fishing, tubing, and snow skiing.

Even before they get there, many people conjure up a sparkling vision of what life in Arizona might be like. For young adults, it might include lounging by the pool, a beer or daiquiri in hand, as some smiling swain or lass saunters toward you. Or if you're in life's golden years, a chance to escape the cold, enjoy a reasonable cost of living, socialize with people of your own generation.

The Valley lifestyle stresses low-density living, starting with the single-family home, preferably with its own pool. (Outsiders always gasp when they see how many pools the desert has spawned!) But now, increasing numbers of planned communities offer lakes, golf courses, and open space—a more attractive form of growth than typical Sun Belt sprawl. Visitors can detect some smugness in Valley attitudes—a touch of "we have it good and the heck with the rest of America."

Some people seem to value most what the Valley *doesn't* have. They talk of the absence of crowded cities like those in the East or Midwest, escape from the endless sprawl of modern California, their successful flight from air pollution, snowy or icy weather. Thinking about the pluses of the area, one of our guests looked out the window at a sunny, warm, December day and said, "This is not Buffalo."

The problem, of course, is that "absences" can boomerang. The newcomer might talk about the chance to shuck off a misfired career start, a divorce, ill health, some other misfortune in favor of life in a resort community where the sun almost always shines. But what about the strong and supportive United Way, the cultural institutions, the familiar doctor, the supportive network of friends left behind in some stodgy old eastern city? What happens when one's old personal hobgoblins reappear, even under Arizona skies?

Blizzards are not about to afflict the Valley, but its air pollution has reached alarming levels. Our helicopter ride disclosed an ugly yellow pall hanging over the Valley. Foster told us he'd seen the problem become visibly worse over the past decade.

As for traffic, it's still far below Los Angeles or Orange County levels—but on its way. We heard from several people the familiar Valley joke about how you'll get to a traffic jam in Phoenix more rapidly than almost anywhere else in the world—only to encounter "exquisite gridlock."

We could not help being impressed by the Valley's thriving economy, its high-tech base combined with the resort business and growing service economy. And above all, the phenomenon of rapid, virtually nonstop growth—from a civilization of 633,510 people in 1960 to 1.5 million in 1980 to 1.8 million today to a projected 2.1 million in 1990. The area, we were told, is now reaching a critical level of urbanization in which new local businesses furnish services and goods that were previously supplied from other regions.

Some believe Phoenix is destined to become one of the four major metropolitan areas west of the Mississippi, along with Los Angeles, San Francisco, and Denver. That might or might not come to pass. What is certain is that today, the very process of growth remains the critical factor driving the Valley's economy.

The equation is relatively simple: Add together the forces of developers and land speculators and then consider their "extended family"—from contractors to bankers, lawyers to title companies, sand and gravel operators to builders of schools, roadways, and water mains. Mix in the variables of a warm climate, a low cost of living, and industrial expansion. Result: Phoenix, the premier growth region of western America.

The equation provides an economic ebullience, not to mention economic opportunity, that would make most regions green with envy. But it also spawns severe problems—deteriorating air quality, rapid consumption of open space, traffic sprawls, strained schools, rootlessness and social dislocation. How are these problems, the inevitable byproducts of rapid urbanization, to be addressed? Through the thousands of disjointed private decisions of developers, land dealers, and their associates? Hardly.

This Valley of the Sun, Headquarters West of the American free enterprise ethic, is indeed achieving the breadth and velocity of growth it believes can only be reached in an unfettered private economy. But in the process, an ironic, jarring note has been introduced. To deal with the problems the growth has created, the region will need more collective decision making, more cohesion among its competing businesses, and stronger and more effective government than it ever tolerated before.

It might be true the fight over growth in the Phoenix orbit was waged and lost in the 1970s—that the no-growth group lost and moved to Tucson. But public opinion polls reveal a public shaken by growth's negative consequences.

Sixty-five percent of Maricopa County residents believe Arizona is "growing too fast," the Rocky Mountain Poll of the Behavior Research Center of Arizona reported in October 1986. The survey revealed a "dramatic increase" since 1976 in the public's demand that business and government pay more attention to growth planning and protection of Arizona's natural environment. The percentage of both Maricopa County and Pima County residents who judge Arizona's air pollution laws "too weak" soared from 34 percent in 1980 to 54 percent in 1986.

It would be natural for Valley residents, given their long-standing preference for minimalist government, to look to coalitions of private business to set new agendas and tackle the problems that growth has wrought. But we found the private business community of the Valley much less cohesive, much less prepared for concerted action than its counterparts elsewhere.

In days past, the old lions of the Phoenix business establishment— Walter Bimson from Valley National Bank, Bill Reilly at Arizona Public Service Company, Eugene C. Pulliam at *The Gazette* and *The Republic*, Frank Snell of Snell & Wilmer, and Tom Chauncey, former owner of KOOL television and radio—constituted a small club that could call the shots—or at least appeared to.

But those times are long past. Once a small desert city, Phoenix has become a booming metropolis with hundreds of competing business voices, but scarcely a dominant one in the group. The Phoenix 40, and in more recent years the East Valley Partnership, have played some role, but the former is widely resented as too elitist and the other focuses on just one section of the Valley.

Most seriously, many of the major industries in the Valley are subsidiaries of companies headquartered elsewhere or must report to a distant home office. Phoenix and its sister cities suffer from the branch-town syndrome perhaps more than any other metropolitan area of America. Greyhound has headquarters in the city—though what that means with its bus operations sold is unclear. But the other "biggies"—Motorola, Honeywell, Digital, Intel, even Goldwater's department store—are owned by corporate empires with their offices hundreds of miles away. Of the major Phoenix banks, only Valley National has resisted national conglomerates.

What all this means is that the potentially powerful decision makers are simply not present. The result is painfully clear. Phoenix musters only episodic and ad hoc bursts of decision making.

Virtually each community leader we met expressed pleasure in the common effort mobilized behind the 1985 referendum to increase the sales tax by a half cent and thus raise the megabucks necessary to build the Valley's long-delayed freeways. But one added: "We should never have gotten to that point. Waiting for an overt crisis is no kind of a model for public policy."

As we've looked about the nation, we've noted some of the sinister negatives that can paralyze communities. Among them are apathy, parochialism, ignorance about areawide issues, sometimes destructive media coverage. The Valley is not altogether free of these encumbrances, though on some fronts—race relations, for example—its problems don't appear as severe as in other metropolitan areas.

But we also found the Valley lacking in some of the critical capacities that enable cities or regions to "get their act together" and move in timely, assertive fashion. These capacities include the following:

> Broad and cooperative engagement of citizens, business, and government
> An expectation that interests will differ and a willingness to negotiate to find common ground
> An openness to experimentation and risk taking, with local corporations and foundations providing some of the seed money
> Continuous communication among the interested parties
> Local media as committed to covering constructive partnership building as they are committed to exposing wrongdoing

Leadership that operates from shared knowledge develops the capacity to initiate projects rather than simply block others' ideas. With the development of the capacities noted above, a shared civic culture results.

Without these kinds of capacities, the Twin Cities (Minneapolis–St. Paul) would not have been able to attack escalating medical costs, San Diego would not have its dazzling Horton Plaza, the first multidepartment store inner-city shopping mall. Boston would not have been able to develop its famed "compact" to assure high school graduates jobs in return for the school system guaranteeing graduates would be better qualified. Nor would any of these areas, lacking many of the advantages of the Phoenix region, have been able to improve and "sell" their business climate.

In today's metropolitan politics, civic activism does not conflict with economic growth; they become natural allies. The strategies, across class, race, city lines, become "win-win," not "win-lose."

There is no single, facile formula for civic improvement, because each metropolitan area has its own history, politics, and culture. But there is a requirement: that the leadership of the metropolitan area—business, governmental, neighborhood, academic—sees the need and guarantees whole-hearted assistance.

Perhaps because the Phoenix area has been so phenomenally success-ful in free enterprise growth, in developing a lifestyle envied far and wide, it hasn't felt obliged to move on these fronts. One could say the region has learned to grow incredibly by dividing and multiplying, but it hasn't devised a formula to add up the sum of its parts, to untap its incredible potential for collective action.

We can only hope the region will soon tackle that task. On every front from air quality to land-use protection to the homeless, the need for strategic action appears to be mounting rapidly.* What encouraged us was the number of Valley leaders we met—politicians, business people, civic activists—who exhibit vision and skill to match their counterparts any-where in America.

Economy and Education: Easing the Pains of Transition

Rarely in American history has an area's economy jumped forward with the monstrous leaps and bounds of Arizona and the Valley. The Arizona job total, driven chiefly by the Phoenix region, has soared 75.2 percent since 1975, up from 729,100 to 1,277,500. Personal income has ballooned in 10 years from $11.9 billion to $39.4 billion, a phenomenal 230 percent increase. Not a single other state boasts comparable growth rates.

Inc. magazine recently surveyed the performance of all states in stimu-lating entrepreneurial activity and economic expansion. It devised an index based on raw numbers on job generation, new businesses formed, and the growth rate of young companies. Arizona ranked number one in the country.

Why this incredible record? The economists offered no crisp explana-tion. Top factors seem to include the Valley's favorable image as a winter resort and recreation center, its warm climate and relaxed Southwest lifestyle. Compared to California, the area offers substantially lower labor

---

* Our original report should have noted that Phoenix has protected, through its South Mountain Park Preserve and North Phoenix Mountains Preserve, more than 37.5 square miles of view-rich mountainous land that developers would love dearly to get their hands on. Phoenix voters have repeatedly endorsed the preserve program through bond elections and initiative votes.

costs—a heavy draw for branch operations in high-tech industries, in clerical and data processing jobs. The presence of the Motorolas, Honeywells, and others has sparked a one-way flow of technical and managerial personnel from California and the Frost Belt states. Finally, there are the Valley's traditional drawing cards: low construction costs, a welcome mat for land speculators and developers, and minimal government regulation.

Looking to the future, there's a great temptation to say: Don't tinker with the Marvelous Growth Machine. If it ain't broke, don't fix it.

Few of the dozens of Valley leaders we talked with were so relaxed or laid back, however. They expressed genuine concerns about the economic future. They warned that the advantages of cheap land and inexpensive labor and big federal grants, the catalysts of so much past Valley development, are starting to dissipate.

They worry that the area's high-tech employment is high on quantity but low on quality—that it is overwhelmingly in the type of low-wage, run-of-the-mill assembly jobs that corporations are shifting to Mexico, Taiwan, Korea, or other third world locations. A major business leader agonized that Phoenix is a classic branch town, with few if any major corporate headquarters. "We are all the more vulnerable to restructuring, plant relocations, adverse developments from mergers and acquisitions," he said.

The city of Phoenix's own strategic economic development plan, issued in spring 1986, noted the region is so weak in high-tech research and development capacity that Phoenix wasn't even seriously considered for the highly prized Microelectronics and Computer Consortium facility that eventually was landed by Austin, Texas.

With a little imagination one can list other events that would cost the Valley jobs—for example, a major arms accord with the Soviets closing down defense facilities such as McDonnell Douglas's attack-helicopter plant, or a collapse of the Mexican economy followed by mass illegal migration northward. Far more likely, of course, is a deep national recession deflating the resort and tourism industry and, in turn, the whole development game.

"The business of the Valley is development," said one economic analyst, warning that if the commercial and new-home construction business slumped, there would be a dominolike effect of companies thrown onto the ropes.

"With cutbacks in growth we'd have many businesses in trouble," a leading banker told us. "We haven't learned well to manage under static or declining conditions. The whole mind-set here, so upbeat, seeing land values and population increase nonstop, has covered a lot of mistakes in investing."

Some Valley boosters reply all the fears are manufactured, that the area has recovered relatively quickly from recessions, so it need not worry now. They claim the area is reaching broad economic diversification it previously never enjoyed—that Motorola, for example, accounted for 25 percent of the Valley's manufacturing activity a few years ago but is now down to only 13 percent.

But we found it difficult to dismiss warnings from top business people that search firms representing new industries complain that neither the Valley's schools nor the technical programs in its universities are good enough. And, some said, a community teetering on the edge of closing its major symphony orchestra telegraphs a highly negative message in the modern-day competition for executive talent. To be fair, symphonies in some other major cities—San Diego, Houston, and Pittsburgh, in particular—ran deficits last year.

Adding to the economic worry list, a prominent Hispanic said he feared the Valley's "soft" economic development thrust, based on supposedly nonpolluting, high-tech assembly operations, was suppressing the potential for "hard" industrial facilities that could provide solid jobs, at higher wages, for low-income residents. "How about a Buckeye Rubber?" he said, referring to an imaginary company that would diversify the Valley economy with traditional factory jobs.

On a different track, a leader of the Phoenix 40 told us he feared Phoenix's hope to become a major regional center would remain just that— a hope—for years to come. The reason he cited: Los Angeles's rise as the command and control center for the southwestern United States, a rise based on its supremacy in those areas in which Phoenix trails—banking, corporate headquarters, foreign trade, cultural facilities, and media of national prominence.

What single thing could the Valley do to strengthen its economic prospects, to ensure against a severe letdown? From the leaders we interviewed came a virtually unanimous answer: education. Specifically, what's needed is a multiyear effort to upgrade the learning systems in the Valley, from preschool to postgraduate to adult education. Why? Because, as one college administrator told us, "The K-to-12 (kindergarten to 12th grade) sector here is generally bad and beleaguered." Sadly, he reported, "the problem is not widely recognized by the Valley public."

The educational deficit is no mystery, however, to those engaged in economic development. One business person reported, "We know the educational quality, the disparities in educational resources here, are a terrible problem."

Some told us the problem is most severe in the Phoenix schools, some of which are said to have deteriorated at an alarming rate over the past decade. We heard claims that schools in some of the surrounding cities are in substantially better shape.

But one must consider it a dangerous omen that Arizona has shared only marginally in the massive wave of school reforms initiated by state governments in the 1980s. Tougher grade-by-grade promotion and graduation standards, competency tests and incentive plans for teachers, beefed-up curricula—the specifics have differed from one state to another; but the cumulative progress has been stunning. Most states are moving to a second generation of education reform—from mandates to incentives, from attacking the schools to rebuilding them, even while Arizona awaits its first significant reform.

We heard that Valley teachers and education groups tend to be defensive, claiming the schools are in good shape already. That would be nice, but false. The report card is already in: U.S. schools have fallen disastrously behind those of Japan and other advanced nations. The Valley must compete with Seoul, Taipei, or Rio de Janeiro as much as Dallas, Albuquerque, or Denver.

And when do the schools get a critical spurt of change? Only when education is called too important to leave to the educators.

Experience across the nation shows the major breakthroughs in education reform occur when an area's business community becomes actively involved. Is Arizona business up to that challenge? One veteran political leader expressed doubt. "Arizona's business community barely has a toe in the water on school reform," he told us. "Our business leaders have been conditioned for quick, showy victories," he said. "They don't quicken to the idea of settling into a long, slow, indeterminate kind of thing, which school reform is."

Some business figures might try for a simpler fix by forcing unification of school districts, especially the incredible total of 21 elementary districts within or partly within Phoenix. But as messy, and possibly extravagant, as the proliferation of school districts might be, it's a bit peripheral to the central problem: the *quality* of education, not its administration.

A strategic vision says: Look to the big picture, to the future of the children in school today, who truly represent Arizona's tomorrow. There is no assurance the state will continue to be able to import quantities of young adults trained in the school and university systems (and by the taxpayers) of California, Michigan, or New York. The nationwide dropoff in the numbers of baby-boom kids reaching maturity means the pool of potential young immigrants is destined to shrink anyway.

The Phoenix area has had the image of being a heavily white community. But the picture is changing, especially in the schools, with their increasingly Hispanic, black, and other minority enrollments. A growing number of affluent white parents are opting for private schools for their children. On top of that, only 38 percent of Valley households have children in school at all. We were shocked to hear Sun City and some other retirement communities are not in any school district, so that their residents pay only the basic countywide school tax. Where, then, is the constituency for schools of excellence?

Partly, of course, the constituency will be found in dedicated citizen groups that will fight for better education regardless of their members' personal gain. And partly it will be found among politicians willing to take on a vital cause, even if its constituency is ill organized.

We were impressed by one of Arizona's senior Republican politicians pleading for "more individual attention to vulnerable kids." The politician noted that "a poor single parent just can't match the resources of a wealthier, intact family," and then insisted, "We need to put more money into those schools with more minorities—smaller classes, higher pay for teachers."

But politicians generally do not initiate, they react.

The business community will be ready to act on the school issue when it sees its fate can't be separated from an increasingly Hispanic work force, a veteran legislator said. He added that Valley capitalists will recognize their vision of the Valley's economic future faces "collapse" if the emerging work force is hobbled by having the equivalent of only an eighth-grade education.

A businessman told us Arizona's much-heralded school equalization law of the early 1980s was backfiring because—ironically—it seeks to equalize spending. The practical effect, he said, is to "guarantee inequities." It simply costs more money than the average to bring a minority or poor child up to an acceptable achievement level. And it's a hollow answer, he argued, to suggest that communities in need of special educational programs can "go to the override," asking voters to spend more money on their schools. The reason: those are precisely the communities too poor to afford the extra programs.

51

The same businessman said there is a pressing need for more social support services in schools with a high proportion of disadvantaged children. He said there must be efforts to bring parents—many of whom are themselves only partially literate, oftentimes intimidated—into the youngster's schooling. Allied needs could be addressed, ranging from a renewed emphasis on basic skills to advanced math and science, lower class size, and all-day kindergarten and latchkey programs.

Would many Valley business people see the school needs that broadly? Not likely, we concluded.

But we considered the consequences of drift and deterioration. How would the Valley fare if word spread through America's corporate boardrooms that the region is paralyzed in dealing with subquality schools, or with air that imperils one's health, or with high crime?

These issues simply do not lend themselves to private solution. They require highly effective public-private partnerships, strong business communities dealing, as equals, with strong local governments.

Education might be the toughest challenge of all. The education establishment is so entrenched, the psyches of the practitioners so set, that only something close to a frontal assault by business and government leaders alike will get the mule's attention.

The Arizona business community lags seriously in areas of broad public policy that will determine the future. Until it makes the transition, we suspect that the economy of the Valley, however buoyant it appears today, will be in unnecessary jeopardy.

Governing the Valley

The Valley of the Sun believes it lives with minimal, pared-down government, just the right mix for Barry Goldwater–Free Enterprise country. We found that to be a myth. Phoenix-area government employees, as a share of the work force, actually number quite high.

And let no one be deceived. Power *is* being exercised. It is wielded rather freely by real estate developers who have learned to bend the system to their convenience, by a state legislature deeply distrustful of lower governments and rarely willing to cede power, and by rather skilled city managers and professional bureaucrats who run Phoenix and its 17 sister cities of the Valley.

There's nothing wrong with a vigorous business community making its opinions known and its concerns heard by government. The problem arises when one sector of business lobbies and pressures so effectively, so consistently, that other voices and concerns—including those of the general public—are drowned out.

The development community appears to wield such inordinate power in the Phoenix region. For years, it tilted Phoenix city policy to favor developments farther and farther from downtown and the Central Avenue spine. Zoning for Phoenix's "urban villages" was turned to permit much higher buildings than neighborhoods previously had been asked to accept. Outlying tract development probably gets easier approval in the Valley than anywhere else in America. One need only fly over the checkerboard development to guess how many unnecessary millions of dollars the public is being charged—for roads, utility lines, schools, fire stations, police stations—so that developers can benefit from cheaper land. Efforts to get developers to pay for the new public facilities, beyond basic roadways and the like, have been stymied.

Developer money flows freely into election contests in all the cities of the Valley. Neighborhood concerns about density, good design, trees or parks or amenities, typically are overridden by developers' insistence on commercial strips or whatever projects will turn a quick buck.

There are, of course, exceptions to the story. The adoption of a district system for electing the Phoenix City Council, replacing the at-large system that had been manipulated so easily by development interests, was a giant stride toward more popular democracy. Scottsdale has set standards in land-use control, design, and control of signs and billboards that deserve to be a model for cities across the region.

The region's elected officials, more than their counterparts in most American urban areas, cede substantive authority to city managers and their staffs. That could be called a plus. The Valley is getting generally professional government; the city of Phoenix is known in the literature as one of the nation's strongest city manager towns.

Some interesting cooperative arrangements between the Valley's cities—exchange of fire department services near the boundaries, for example—were only revealed to the councils after the arrangements were operating smoothly and were politically safe to embrace.

But there are immense long-term dangers in a system where innovation and new approaches come from the professionals, while the mayors and councils—the people's representatives—fail to lead public policy. However capable, appointed officers generally will look to protecting their bureaucratic positions, not to the big innovations and policy shifts the community sometimes needs. And if influence of the development community needs to be curbed, it eventually will be elected representatives, not appointees, who will have to do the job.

We were startled by the degree to which Valley governments and the media depend for population predictions and economic growth forecasts on private companies and individuals who work for, or with, the development community, which has a vested interest in high figures. The list of needed reforms might include insisting that public employees carry out population estimates and economic projections.

The realization that more, not less, popular democracy is what the Valley needs came as something of a surprise to us. We had come to the Valley believing the biggest governmental problem would be Balkanization— all those independent cities fighting for status, recognition, to capture tax bases or prestigious facilities from each other.

How many cities of the Valley need symphonies? If major-league football or baseball teams come, who will get the stadiums? What's the answer to an unseemly scramble for new commercial facilities or for a branch plant? How about the splintered lower court system, said to lack "uniformity, efficiency, leadership, and competence?"

Each of the questions needs attention. Peace, concord, and efficiency would be great to achieve. But the fact is that every metropolitan region in America suffers from some fragmentation. Consider the Pittsburgh region, with its 130 cities and towns. It would appear to be a lot worse off than metropolitan Phoenix.

We found there is a broad degree of cooperation among Valley cities on such day-to-day matters as a unified police academy, criminal investigations, firefighting, planning for sewage treatment. The city managers are said to have an excellent working relationship. The mayors claim, for the most part, that they do, too.

The biggest governmental problem of the Valley is not incapacity or quarreling among its cities, we concluded. It is rather that there is no way the region today can *speak with a single, clear voice* and take decisive action on issues that transcend any and all city boundaries.

Chief among those problems is air quality—possibly the most serious short- and long-term threat to the Valley. But there are others, too: land use, growth controls, and transportation among them.

Left unattended, some of the regionwide problems could cast a long shadow over the Valley's future. The existing organizations obviously are not up to the task. The Maricopa Association of Governments (MAG) prepares some good research papers. But it is devoid of power to make anyone listen to its recommendations. We heard the legislature purposely made MAG weak out of fear that anything akin to areawide government might evolve.

One thing that can be said for MAG is that it functions like a little United Nations, inducing leaders of the various cities to talk when they might not otherwise. But MAG uses the same preposterous one-nation, one-vote system used by the UN General Assembly. The city of Phoenix, with 983,403 residents, has the same voting power as the newly incorporated town of Carefree, with 3,330.

Then there's the Maricopa County government. The Valley is lucky to have a single county, not the competing counties with which many metro areas must cope. But as it is constituted today, Maricopa County government lacks home rule powers. It can only carry out duties the legislature assigns to it.

Should one of the great air pollution crises of all time hit the Valley next week, the county government would be powerless to do anything about it. Nor could it act on transit or any other important regional policy issue without specific legislative approval.

Just as bad, the county is encumbered with countless mandates by the state. Some are important, such as provision for medical care for the poor. Others seem arcane or downright ridiculous, such as a requirement that the county treasurer's records be kept on 100-percent-rag-content paper.

The county also is paralyzed by its archaic structure. There are five supervisors, with the chairmanship rotating annually among members of the party in power, so no perceived leader emerges. And "row officers"— the directly elected recorder, assessor, county attorney, treasurer, sheriff, and superintendent of schools—rule over their fiefdoms with little if any accountability to the supervisors.

The supervisors and row officers from the rural counties represent a potent force with the legislature, fighting any effort to abolish their sinecures or make them appointive. In legislative horse trading, one lobbyist told us, they have actually swapped getting home rule powers in return for pay raises!

What is the solution? Some would argue that a new supergovernment is necessary. We think that approach is neither politically feasible nor necessary in the Valley. Is a strengthened MAG the best way to get a unified voice for the Valley? We think not. Councils of governments are rather weak sisters. Most areas initially created them in response to requirements in federal laws for some form of regional coordination. They virtually never gain true governmental status.

We believe there is a reasonable alternative, one that speaks both to the needs and concerns of the people of the Valley: full county home rule under a totally reorganized and reconstituted county government. The slate should be wiped clean. There should be a directly elected county council and a directly elected county executive. For simplicity's sake, the existing state senate districts within Maricopa County might be used as council districts. The new county executive would become the chief spokesperson for issues of true Valleywide significance.

Would strong county home rule undercut the existing cities of the Valley? In no way. With few exceptions, the cities would continue to exercise all the powers they do today. In fact, we propose that while the new county council be elected on a "one-man, one-vote" basis, a special effort be made to deal the mayors into the new arrangement. This might be accomplished by inviting all of them to sit on the county council as nonvoting, ex officio members.

If a strong regional authority is not established, then the almost inevitable result will be the creation of more special regional authorities—bodies that are unelected and essentially accountable to no one. That's already happened on transit issues, and the model is capable of being repeated again and again. Allowing that to occur is tantamount to the people of the Valley saying: "We don't dare govern ourselves. We're so scared of anything even superficially resembling metropolitan government that we're willing to hand off major, substantive power over our lives to unelected, bureaucratic government."

But if the public fails to take charge, special interests will.

Consider Maricopa County's recent green light for a bond issue for what some critics call "a $70-million road to nowhere." It would be a major arterial road running out beyond the White Tank Mountains on the region's westernmost boundary.

The "west is hot" for development because of the new freeway connection into Phoenix, we heard. Land speculators, highway builders, developers, real estate interests, lenders, and others would stand to make multimillions off the public's investment in the road. Then the public likely would pay a second time through utility bills, because Arizona law requires utilities to either extend lines to new communities or to buy lines that developers install.

So powerful are the forces pushing development outward that one wonders whether there is any rational public decision making at all. For at the same time, vast tracts of closer-in land stand fallow and older neighborhoods deteriorate. "We constantly subsidize development at the fringe," one observer complained. "We keep going farther and farther out, while the center is dying, slain by prevailing public policy."

The legislature is not the sole culprit in this scenario, but it is a major one. Consider the issue of using scarce, fresh, drinkable water in the large lakes that developers now are building into their projects. A 1986 bill to ban the practice, forcing the use of "gray," or recycled, water instead, was beaten down by the development community in what a prominent Arizona official described as "a naked exercise of power."

The legislature has more recently been asked to let Westinghouse Communities—and now its successor, SunCor Development—set up a corporate city with the type of tax-free financing normally reserved for governments. It would be difficult to think of a more blatant effort to substitute private government for public decision making, to let private developers charge the public for most of their risk.

How can the people of the Valley effect public control of decisions vital to their lives and future? Only, we concluded, by bidding for and getting full home rule.

Some told us that was impossible—that the legislature would approve home rule about as readily as it would let the Navajo Nation annex the Valley. A quarter century after the Supreme Court's historic one-man, one-vote apportionment rulings, rural interests are alleged to maintain extraordinary influence in the Arizona legislature. We heard that Valley legislators, especially those from the city of Phoenix, are chronically divided and ineffective in speaking up for the region's interests.

Is the situation correctable? Certainly! All it takes is for the people of Maricopa County, 57 percent of Arizona's population and thus over half the legislature, to use the weapon of the ballot to elect a legislative delegation that promises to stand together, man and woman, Republican and Democrat, for the public interest over private interests, for home rule in lieu of exploitation.

A logical approach would be for Valley leaders, including newspaper editors, to rally behind a campaign to elect a "Unified, Home Rule Legislative Delegation" to represent the communities of the Valley.

Would this be a tough campaign to win? Yes. One can imagine the flood of developer cash and pressure that would be mounted in opposition. But the bottom-line issue is quite simple: Do the citizens of this region want to be masters of their own destiny? If they do, we would advise them simply: Go for it.

Tapping the Potential of Neighborhoods and People

The Valley needs strong and explicit public policies to undergird and champion neighborhood life. Valleywide political cohesion is critically important. It's the reason that we endorse county home rule, the idea that the citizens of Maricopa County must insist on control of their own destiny. But without a strong grassroots base, without capable and empowered neighborhoods, progress on a citywide or Valleywide basis might be tenuous at best.

A top aide to former Gov. Bruce Babbitt told us: "Civic culture is the most compelling need in Phoenix and the region. Everything else would flow from that." We believe he was right. But we are convinced that healthy civic culture always flows upward from personal association, not downward from higher governments or any other authority.

Civic culture is a tough question for the Phoenix area. In our interviews with leaders of the region we heard again and again deep concerns about how Valley residents relate to each other, of how a civilization of newcomers becomes acquainted, settled, and finally capable of collective action. The Valley's greatest strength—its newness, its lack of encrusted old institutions, its freedom to let people be who they want to be—is also its greatest weakness.

There is danger in painting any picture with too wide a brush. We recognize there are many sound and mature neighborhoods, many excellent interpersonal support systems in place in the Valley. But we also heard repeated accounts of people seemingly anxious to isolate themselves from others: installing a private pool, erecting a fence, rarely getting to know neighbors; alternatively, moving into homogenous planned communities, surrounded by fences and protected by private security guards; happy to spend a good chunk of time in private autos, closed off from others; refusing to take part in neighborhood activities, politics, or civic life in general.

We were taken aback when one of Arizona's most prominent politicians told us, "The average person here doesn't give a —— about the general interest. They're not willing to participate. Somehow they've opted out. As long as their little piece is protected, they don't care."

Another prominent Arizona officeholder told us how stunned he was to meet a former Arizona university professor in an airport in Iowa. "I have taken a job in a community college in Iowa," the man said. "I would love to live in Arizona. I had a great job as a tenured faculty member. But I am raising children. And the ambiance, the set of relationships, the Arizona neighborhood where I was raising my kids, was not acceptable. It had a quality of transience; it lacked stable relationships. So I felt my teenagers were at risk—that there were no supporting structures for them. So I am in Iowa until my kids are on their own."

Will the bad effects of newness and transience clear away in time? Perhaps. It might take a decade or more for a newcomer to an area to feel comfortable about participating in public life.

A college administrator said he thought many of the young people coming now will remain and develop a stake in the community as the years roll on. But if pell-mell migration into the Valley continues, one must wonder if stability will ever arrive. There is surely little sign of it yet. An astounding 28 percent of the adults in the Phoenix metropolitan region have been here for less than five years. A substantial proportion of the young people who move to the region are birds of passage, picking up and moving on before too long.

A low 43 percent of Valley homeowners have been in the same residence as long as five years. Half of the people who rent apartments or houses in the Valley move every year.

No one has established cause and effect between high transience and social disorders, but there are some disturbing indications. Assuming the federal government's statistics are to be trusted, the divorce rate in the Phoenix area is almost half again as high as the already worrisome national level. Alcoholism is more prevalent in the Valley than nationally. Suicide rates are among the nation's highest. Drug abuse appears to be worse, too.

If you're not making it in a resort culture, you may feel really alone. There may be a thin line between dream and nightmare. And what troubles individuals spills out in problems for the broader society, too.

The rate of serious crimes in the Phoenix area is dramatically above the U.S. average; in fact, it has been 32 percent to 57 percent worse in recent years, according to U.S. Justice Department reports. In one recent year Maricopa County reported no less than 11,503 violent crimes and 130,198 property crimes. The overall crime rate in Arizona is the fourth highest in the nation.

The popular solution to this problem seems to be piling on more police, more prisons. Phoenix spends more on police per capita than such comparable cities of the Sun Belt as San Antonio, San Diego, and San Jose, and nearly as much as crime-plagued Houston. Arizona ranks 10th highest among the states in its per capita prison population. Arizona spends almost as much on prisons as it does on a major academic institution such as Arizona State University.

And while you'll find Valleyites flocking in vast numbers to backpack, play golf, swim, or boat, don't look for many at the polls. The interest in local Valley elections lags badly. And there's no indication turnouts are improving.

It is hard for us to explain the low participation levels. A prominent Arizona public opinion analyst suggested to us that many voters believe powerful interests, especially developers and their allies, are making all the decisions anyway—so why bother?

There is no absolute proof for the proposition, but we strongly suspect that if Valleyites placed more emphasis on neighborhood association, then every problem from social disorder to low voter turnout would be positively affected.

Strengthening the weak identity of Valley neighborhoods might be a first step. People rarely know where one neighborhood stops or another begins. Often a neighborhood's popular name is nothing more distinctive than the intersection of two roads.

The cities of the Valley should make clear identification of neighborhoods a priority—even in the newest subdivisions. And they should bring neighborhood people into the process, inviting them to make the identification. The name game itself could be fun; perhaps residents could do research to identify a natural feature of the surrounding area's terrain, such as a desert peak or waterway, and adopt it. We'd guess that some healthy neighborhood organization could be prompted by this single exercise.

A "civic welcome wagon" should be considered—an organized program of calls on newcomers to tell them where the local schools and libraries and fire and police stations are located. But much more than that should be provided—for example, a rundown on all local civic organizations, where they meet, what kind of activities they're into. Newcomers might also be provided with some history of the neighborhood and an invitation to become active themselves. Schedules and contacts could be listed on how one joins neighbors in jogging, cycling, bridge, stamp swapping—any kind of activity one can think of. It would be ideal if the local neighborhood organization could sponsor the civic welcome wagon, inviting newcomers to a local meeting, perhaps a block party, at the very moment of contact.

The city governments should take an interest in getting such an effort mounted. The only proviso should be *no commercial pitches*. This is too important a civic opportunity to be muddied or even compromised by advertising.

Crime watches, with active police support, should be supported in all neighborhoods. Evidence from around the country is that block watch anticrime efforts are not only the most effective ways anyone has discovered to curb burglaries, but that they also function as a seedbed for other types of civic activity.

Finally, neighborhood vitality can be enhanced many times over if city governments build neighborhoods into the decision-making process of the city, if there is a formal way that neighborhood opinions are heard on city plans, on zoning, on the city budget.

The explicit neighborhood policy being developed by Mayor Terry Goddard and the Phoenix City Council appears to be a significant step in this direction. Under the policy, all commercial projects, for example, will have to go through site planning review that includes a voice for surrounding residents.

Valley political or business leaders also should consider a campaign to encourage more personal and neighborhood ties. Such an effort has virtually no precedent around the country. But surely if leaders made some strong personal expressions of interest in neighborhood-scale activities and then sought personally to help with them, a positive message would be telegraphed. And it would be reaffirmed if the city councils backed that up with a "neighborhoods first" policy.

Is there a danger all this might simply feed the fires of parochialism? Yes. But our observation across America is that organizations of citizens at the most local level, sometimes for very narrow purposes, quite often blossom later into constructive civic outreach. In addition, many of the nation's brightest city council members and mayors got their start in neighborhood organizations.

Special attention also should be paid to the region's lower-income peoples, especially Hispanics, blacks, and Native Americans. Some of these groups have more conscious neighborhood life, more support systems, than the supposedly fortunate and privileged Anglo middle class.

Yet the consequences of isolation are painfully apparent in neighborhoods in these areas. South Phoenix, with the region's highest concentration of minorities, has high ratios of poverty, unemployment, and low educational attainment. Such social problems as alcoholism, drug abuse, and high crime stalk the poor neighborhoods. Services—public and private—are notoriously low.

Across America, government support for neighborhood organizations, especially inventive social service groups and community development corporations, is proving quite effective. Arizona should be no exception.

The Valley might try to encourage development of more community ties in a way few metropolitan areas have considered—at the workplace. One Arizona leader noted that, when visiting industrial facilities in the Valley, he was struck by how many people, particularly single women, relate to the workplace as a source of shared relationships. Society, he suggested, had not fully explored how to create community out of the workplace.

Another promising avenue of exploration would be how young professionals can be drawn more into civic activity. Are special gimmicks—staged entertainment, for example—necessary to snare their attention? Would parties help to get the ball rolling for cooperative projects to deal with some of the Valley's social pathologies, from drug abuse to the plight of the homeless?

Whatever works, it seems to us, ought to be tried. The cumulative intelligence, wealth, skill of the young professional class is immense. If ways could be found to divert just a small share of its energies away from private gain and to public purpose, the dividends could be startling. Organized programs for young executives, such as Valley Leadership, centered in Phoenix, plus parallel efforts in other Valley cities, are a step in the right direction.

The same principle applies to retirees. The Valley's national image notwithstanding, the Phoenix region has no greater share of senior citizens than the nation at large. But whether they live in Sun City, in single homes or condo developments spread from one end of the Valley to the other, a substantial number of retirees do tend to live isolated lives, separated from the support of extended families.

In candor, we must report that the retirees' image among Valley leaders is abysmal. A leader in the philanthropic area told us: "There are lots of retirees who could care less what happens with the schools, or any other public problem. They don't seem to care as long as they can get from their condo to the golf course."

A government official said: "Sun City people do a lot to take care of themselves, with their own police, meals on wheels, cultural events. But they do little beyond their own community." And this is what we heard from some journalists we spoke with: "The retirement communities exercise strong political power in the Valley—but generally for their own narrow interests."

There are major exceptions to that rule. Older people do play a very important part in the civic life of the Valley. But not, we would guess, in the numbers or with the constructive full effect one might hope for. Many more senior citizens could contribute materially to life in the Valley—in classrooms, social service agencies, environmental groups.

Another example of what might be done would be a "Brass Hats" organization. Retired CEOs and other former business leaders could provide some of the civic leadership the region needs so badly. They might, for example, assist in recruiting some corporate headquarters and reducing the region's overdependence on branch plants.

The Valley, in short, has the human resources it needs to make its civic culture excel. The challenge—and we recognize it is an enormous one—is to tap those resources.

Giving and Leading

"First generation wealth is selfish wealth. That's what we have in Phoenix."

"This is a developers' paradise. But few of them have any social vision."

"We have these free riders. They asked my firm to give still more, and I discovered none of my five chief competitors had contributed a cent."

"We have so many wealthy snowbirds—folks here nine months a year, but their allegiance is still to a Chicago or an Indianapolis."

"If leaders don't give, don't care, don't expect the masses to."

The quotes have been synthesized for emphasis. But they reflect what we heard from dozens of prominent Phoenix-area citizens about the problems of leadership and civic giving.

A hallmark of the American way is keeping government strictly limited—a highly prized credo across the United States, and especially in Arizona. But there's an indispensable corollary: high levels of personal and corporate giving.

The "Third Sector"—the entire nonprofit, educational, social service, cultural, philanthropic world—is vital to how American communities work. Without it, we would need dramatically higher taxes, more like those exacted of corporations and individuals in Europe.

The Valley's problem is that it is as low on the philanthropic-civic totem pole as it is on taxes. This could become critical in the future, as heavy population growth continues and the Valley's cultural, environmental, and social needs mount.

We found Valley leaders constantly referring to the crisis over funding of the Phoenix Symphony and how it is obliged to subsist on a budget most other full-time orchestras would find intolerable.

Few would dispute the severity of the cultural-giving problem. A report from Arizona State University's School of Public Affairs shows that Arizona ranks 43rd among the 50 states in its per capita spending for the arts. "So what?" some ask. Maybe that just means Arizonans like the outdoor, barbecue life more than indoorsy, artsy activity—or that they prefer a different brand of music.

"We all get a spastic colon when some guy with a beard gets on the television and tells us we have to save the symphony," a local official said. "Why? When Johnny Paycheck comes to town the line goes all the way around the building. Who's to say what's right?"

As cute as that sounds, the problem goes much deeper. The arts represent a vital part of the "quality of life" factors that major corporations consider when they decide where to locate. The Valley may decide to scorn the high arts. But by doing so it would reject what Western civilization for centuries has found to be one of the great frontiers of the human spirit. And Phoenix also would be turning its back on its chance to be known as a world-class city.

Nor are arts the only problem. Giving for social needs also is perilously low. In 1985, per capita funding for the Valley of the Sun United Way was $7.78, lowest of the 52 U.S. cities considered to have major funding programs. The median of all the cities was $16.55, with a high of $29.37 in Cleveland.

As for the poor, Phoenix might be one of the worst places in the nation to live. According to a 1985 report by the Urban Institute and Arizona State University's John Hall, government funding for human services—social, health, and income maintenance—in the Phoenix area was $563 per capita. Jackson, Mississippi—capital of America's poorest state—spent $911. The figure in Pittsburgh was $1,018, in New York $1,670. Overall, Phoenix ranked 14th of 16 metropolitan areas surveyed, just marginally ahead of Vicksburg, Mississippi, and Dallas.

The region also is close to notorious for its dependence on federal dollars and a refusal to spend its own money for social services. The Urban

Institute study showed 77 percent of all the public human service funds spent locally came from the national government, with just 12 percent from the state government and 11 percent from city and county governments. Given such figures of rock-bottom public spending, the Valley should be a national leader in private philanthropy, not a distant straggler.

Some of the explanations for low giving make sense. Because the communities of the Valley are relatively new, it is scarcely surprising that the second and succeeding generations in families of wealth have yet to form and take a leading role. Cultural and social institutions from Boston to San Francisco might shrivel in the face of a similar disability. "New wealth" gives little anywhere.

We were disappointed but not surprised to hear the leader of a Valley financial institution say that, for his outfit, a big corporate gift would be in the $5,000–$25,000 range. In another city, however, the same institution might give hundreds of thousands, if not a million, dollars.

For some of the same reasons, the Valley has yet to develop private foundations that can underwrite major civic undertakings as well as smaller, experimental efforts on every front from mental health to economic development in poorer neighborhoods. The Valley has, for example, no replica of Indianapolis's Lilly Endowment, dispersing millions each year to build up the downtown, aid neighborhoods, and support social service agencies. The Phoenix-based Flinn Foundation has a corpus of more than $70 million but focuses its gifts almost exclusively in health care services.

We found the nucleus of what could be major philanthropic giving. But can the Valley wait for years for philanthropies, like century plants, to mature? Or will it have to hurry the process along?

We believe that some intense "hurrying along" is appropriate and suggest this small sampling of techniques to be considered:

Media exposure of the philanthropic cop-outs. The newspapers could perform a great public service through periodic investigative pieces providing specifies on which firms are giving and which are not.

Philanthropic SWAT teams. To get at the numerous commercial "free loaders," those businesses that "leave it to George" to do the giving, we propose some friendly visits from the CEOs of companies that *do* give to suggest that giving is part of doing business in the Valley.

Mobilizing the snow birds. Wealthy or not, the people who spend a good chunk of each year in the Valley should be disabused of the idea they have no responsibilities to its public life.

Giving is not some isolated or incidental event, but central to the texture of a succesful civic culture. And there is an intimate tie between philanthropy and leadership. Both reflect what people are willing to give back to their community. Some people can give back financially, others can volunteer time. A community needs both—the things money can buy and those it can't.

We listened with interest to the discussions of "who leads the Valley." We talked several times with members of the Phoenix 40. Its supporters say it is the closest thing the Valley has to a responsible "establishment," while its critics attack it as an elitist, self-anointed group that "couldn't elect a dogcatcher today."

We also talked with leaders of the East Valley Partnership, which is trying to cope with an array of planning, transportation, and cultural issues in its explosively growing part of the region. East Valley's avowed goal is to establish a much broader base than the 40. The best idea for the future of the 40 came from an Arizona political old-timer who suggested the group stop being a debating society, get scrappier, democratize itself into "the Phoenix 400," and become a permanent force.

The Phoenix 40 recently has adopted an aggressive new stance—that it will only declare itself on issues that it is ready to fight hard to win. In a community in which lassitude and indifference often are the worst enemies, that could be a real plus. Another sign of maturity and progress is the appearance of the Phoenix City Club, some 1,000 strong—"a yuppies club," we heard some say. It has about 200 people mobilized into committees on such topics as energy, transportation, taxes, and the future of South Phoenix. But by being 100 percent volunteer, with no staff, the City Club might find its long-term effectiveness limited.

We were surprised to hear that in this Valley where the commercial ethic so predominates, there is no single business figure of regionwide prominence who is looked to by others for leadership. And we noted another curious phenomenon: the most prominent citizens, the so-called movers and shakers of the Valley, quickly tell visitors how difficult it is to make decisions and get things done. In most communities, the comparable movers and shakers would be boasting of how effective they are.

But we suspect it would be a great error for the Valley to search for or to anoint some strong leader. He or she likely would be rejected in this heavily individualistic culture anyway. The era of the big heroes, political or industrial, has subsided across the nation. Effective leadership in American communities today is by consensus, not from a white horse.

What then replaces the old power structure? It is a civic culture that says no one person or clique is singly responsible for the community, but that hundreds—thousands—of citizens need to assume that role, individually and collectively.

The Valley, with its big contingents of yuppies and retirees, might have to work hard to make the idea of mutual responsibility fashionable again. It needs to foster the idea that people get important personal rewards from what they give to the community and that they will be respected for taking risks and shouldering those tasks. When that happens, then the Valley's crisis of anemic philanthropy likely will solve itself.

As an important step in that direction, a very broadly based goals process—akin to the "Goals for Dallas" program and its counterparts in many other cities—should be considered. In this process, people from all sectors—governments, businesses, philanthropies, schools and universities, neighborhoods rich and poor—come to the table to identify some long-range objectives. Winter visitors also should be brought into the picture. We were surprised to hear how regularly the snowbirds get snubbed and disdained—and not just in newspaper cartoons.

The object of a goals process is to forge "win-win" strategies that will benefit multiple income groups, classes, and geographic sections. Economic development, education, arts and culture, social services, and regional facilities all can be part of the goals mix. The seeds for such a movement might be planted in the largely successful Phoenix bond election committees. But that movement needs broadening.

Goals efforts have been suggested before but never taken seriously by the Phoenix 40 or other Valley establishments. Perhaps it is time for a fresh look at participatory processes that would pull together the scores of varying interests.

One outgrowth could be formation of a permanent Valleywide citizens group to monitor implementation of the goals. It should stay around for the long haul, providing a critical, independent look at the series of challenges likely to confront this dynamic region over the years ahead.

The Rio Salado Project

New York's Central Park is 840 sylvan acres filled with sunken roads, miles of paths, bridges, lakes, woods, and lawns. It's the pride of New Yorkers and burnishes the city's image around the globe.

But consider what the great landscape architect Frederick Law Olmsted reported finding when he trekked through the future site of the park in the

1850s—"black and unctuous slime, the low grounds steeped in the over-flow and mush of pigsties, slaughterhouses and bone boiling works."

Flying over the Valley today, one has to be appalled by the sight of the drained Salt River. It is nothing other than a jagged, ugly, dried-out scar cutting across a beautiful Valley. Robbed of its waters, used as a dumping ground, exploited for sand and gravel, today's Salt River is the desert equivalent of central Manhattan before Central Park.

Imagine the magnificent but lost opportunity for greenery, peace, fun, and culture, the enrichment of New Yorkers' lives generation by genera-tion, if Central Park had not become reality. The Salt River represents just as significant a challenge for Valleyites—now.

This is why we find the Rio Salado proposal so exciting—to transform 17 miles of the riverbed into a continuous regional park, straight through the heart of the Valley, a place of water and greenery and sports and beauty, a magnet for development and, most important, a place of meeting and common pride for all the people of the region.

We found ourselves well briefed on the salient problems swirling about Rio Salado:

> The danger of floods and apparent need for more dam building upstream
> The potential of serious toxic substances deposited by decades of careless dumping
> Possible political opposition from sand and gravel operators
> The need to raise some $1 billion to build the project, an endeavor likely to take 25 years

Beyond all that, we found how seriously bogged down the entire Rio Salado effort is. After a burst of public attention and interest in the early 1980s, the project got snagged in funding dilemmas, challenged by South Phoenix interests, picked apart a bit by the media, and politicized by businessman Bill Schulz.

The Rio Salado Development District, created by the legislature, pre-pared a technically excellent master plan for the project and released it in 1985. But a leading friend of the project suggested to us that instead of leadership by a Robert Moses type who could have fired up people's imaginations, the entire Rio Salado concept got "bureaucratized" by the development district.

Maricopa County voters will soon be asked to give the district authority to levy a property tax of up to 25 cents per $100 assessed valuation. "It's risky, but we were dying a slow death anyway," a principal supporter of the proposal told us.

As visitors, it would be presumptuous for us to say whether the property tax or another form of taxation ought to be adopted for Rio Salado. Clearly there is a major political obstacle in getting Valleywide approval, when the parochial view in some cities will be: "Why us? The river doesn't flow through our town."

We were impressed to hear some leaders of other cities, especially Scottsdale Mayor Herb Drinkwater, endorse the project anyway. The Indian Bend Wash in Scottsdale already provides a splendid example of how the bed of an abandoned desert stream can be made into an inviting oasis.

The worst thing that could happen to Rio Salado now would be inaction and paralysis. But that is precisely what might happen unless some form of tax—ideal or not—isn't soon enacted to get land acquisition and the thousands of other pieces of requisite planning under way.

In the long run, we think the interests that benefit most from the project should pay a big share of the Rio Salado costs. First because that's only right and appropriate. The history of America too often has been one of private interests reaping a bonanza from investments made by taxpayers. Just consider the billions earned by people lucky enough to hold land close to the places where interstate highway exits were built, or how so many western agricultural interests have received irrigation water from government projects at a fraction of its true market cost.

In a time of tight public budgets, any thought of massive new giveaways should be shelved. Even more to the point, there appears to be deep suspicion among Valleyites that development interests have been ripping them off regularly and will not hesitate to do the same again. If Rio Salado gets labeled as developer relief, if the public believes its tax dollars simply will prepare a windfall for big money interests, then the project almost certainly will founder, to the immense loss of everyone in the Valley— private citizens and developers alike.

Let no one doubt: the potential business-sector benefits from Rio Salado would be huge. Some 2,300 acres of prime land would be made available for private development between the north and south parkways proposed to be built near the river banks. There would be more private development generated outside the parkways—perhaps another 2,000 acres over 25 years. More than 74,000 jobs would be generated, the development district estimates. The supply of new housing units would increase by

16,055. Land values might be expected to rise eightfold to tenfold over current values.

That's why there needs to be a tax formula that is easy to understand and shows reasonable developer contribution. It probably is not too important whether that is done through tax increment financing—a property-tax shift that would provide funds to retire bonds used in developing Rio Salado—or through some other method such as a special tax assessment district for properties along and near the river.

Perhaps a combination of methods might be worked out over time. The vital principle should be this: those who gain must pay their fair share. We suggest that development interests themselves should want that kind of arrangement, because it would make public approval of the project much more likely.

To bolster public confidence further, a permanent Rio Salado Citizens Committee should be considered. Because Rio Salado would be a truly regional facility, the committee should have ample representation from the communities of the Valley, not just the cities of Tempe, Mesa, and Phoenix, which directly abut the project.

Such a committee would act first as John Q. Citizen's surrogate, lacking legal powers but capable of blowing the whistle, focusing public attention, and presumably forcing corrective action if developers or other interests seemed to be getting a free ride at the public's expense.

It is true that a citizens' advisory group reviewed the Rio Salado Master Plan before its unveiling two years ago, that there were a number of hearings, community meetings, and workshops. But we believe the citizen input into a project of such immense regional import should start earlier, last longer, and go deeper—in fact be a critical component.

The project would be well served if the Rio Salado Citizens Committee were to participate in each stage of planning and implementation. Experience in major public projects around the nation shows that design counsel from a large citizens committee can prompt the professionals to come up with a much superior end product, one that not only looks pretty but truly matches the needs, the interests, the spirit of the community.

We were impressed by the Rio Salado Master Plan as presented. But we suggest the project might better be served by putting that plan to the side, pulling in a strong citizens committee, and providing that committee with competent and permanent staff.

The newspapers and broadcasters of the Valley also owe it to readers and listeners to provide constant coverage on Rio Salado alternatives, to sponsor and report reader surveys and polls. Another secret of success might lie in approaching Rio Salado incrementally—one phase at a time. "Rio Salado is a spectrum of possibilities that can be done on many scales," a prominent Arizona officeholder suggested to us. Another official proposed a pilot project, so that citizens could see a section of the riverbed actually completed.

What of the many obstacles that seem to stand in Rio Salado's way, from toxic substance cleanup to flood control to the interests of the sand and gravel industry? The only answer can and must be: find a way to overcome each.

We heard some fairly scary stories about dangerous substances dumped along the river over the years, of how some of the landfills are like "tea bags," changing the color of water that flows through them. Some day the governments of the Valley must address the problems of toxic substances close by a very floodable riverbed. Rio Salado simply presents an opportunity and challenge to take care of the obligation sooner.

Last but not least has to be finding ways to help the poor in South Phoenix improve their residences, get relocation aid where necessary, and not be "gentrified" out of their neighborhood.

None of these problems should be permitted to cloud the future, paralyze the present, and kill Rio Salado. We cannot imagine a greater tragedy for the people of the Valley, for this project, carried forward with integrity and skill, could have incredible benefits.

Count, if you will, the $10 billion in taxes and associated public benefits that supporters say the project could produce for the Valley over 60 years. Or the total economic gain that some have estimated could reach a staggering $50 billion over the same period. Or the fact that Rio Salado would provide a powerful magnet, focusing development back toward the center of the Valley and thus increasing inducements for productive use of empty lands.

With more activity turned toward the center, to the established cities, Valley taxpayers could save hundreds of millions, if not billions, of dollars through avoided expense—new roads, schools, fire stations that wouldn't have to be constructed out at the urban fringe.

As significant as all those gains would be, we would count another even greater: what Rio Salado might do for the spirit of the Valley. By moving forward with Rio Salado, the Valley's people would have undertaken what might be the most ambitious public project of this generation in any metropolitan region of the United States.

Rio Salado would be unique to the Valley—a grassy ribbon across the desert floor, an oasis with its lakes and drops and brief whitewater rapids. In time, it might become as much a trademark of the Phoenix region, spoken of and admired across the continent, as Central Park is for New York today. And it would be five times larger!

The point is that the Valley would gain what it now, with its immense geographic spread, so sorely lacks: a single focus. For that simple reason, many publicly oriented projects that don't appear feasible today would become real possibilities.

Above all, Rio Salado provides a glistening opportunity to overcome the Valley's greatest failure—its inability, save on rare occasions, to pull together for a common purpose. The spinoff benefits of such a break-through, for all aspects of the Valley's life, could be enormous.

Forging the Spirit of Cooperation

How shall the people of the Valley live together, grow together, to form a more cohesive, resilient area for the 1990s and into the next century?

It's only possible, we concluded, by purging two negative, dangerous stereotypes. We heard both with depressing frequency. Any Valleyite likely will find them familiar.

First there's the anti-Phoenix stereotype that seems to flourish in many of the suburbs:

The city of Phoenix is an aggrandizer, a pig. It's a population monster. It doesn't respect its neighbor cities; it lords it over them. It wants to capture all the sports, all the culture complexes, everything desirable for itself. Phoenix better learn the day's over when it can pull the chain and every other community will come obligingly along.

And what's more, Phoenix has these dirty little secrets. Its schools used to be OK, but now they're getting lousier all the time. It has lots of poor people, people of color. It has slums and winos and soup kitchens; small wonder the homeless congregate there. It's a dumping ground and a dangerous place. Steer clear of it—especially that dangerous downtown.

Then, with just a little less virulence, there's the negative stereotype looking from the big city outward:

We're the big city—in fact by sheer population, not to mention land size, we're the biggest capital city in America. Except maybe for Scottsdale, all those carping suburbs around us are led by unsophisticated types who don't understand how a metropolitan area works. They're petty little barons of their own fiefdoms. Small-town and small-minded—that's what they are. They want to dump the homeless, the runaways, the mentally disturbed and drug addicts (except maybe their own kids) on Phoenix.

And then, having damned us for being a big city, they want to duplicate all the facilities that rightfully belong in a center city, from sports stadiums to arts complexes to industrial parks to high-rise business cores. They'll do anything to keep downtown Phoenix from developing.

No single person we talked with reflected all those prejudices. But we did hear an extraordinary degree of rancor and distrust expressed by the champions of Phoenix and the "Other Cities" alike. We concluded that the stereotypes do immense disservice to the people of the Valley.

Too much of the region's energy appears to go into internecine strife—Phoenix versus Mesa versus Tempe versus Glendale. If that same energy could be rechanneled, away from "win-lose" to "win-win" scenarios, there could be long-term benefits.

Phoenix needs to understand that the constellation of rather large, independent cities surrounding it aren't typical of the suburbs of most metropolitan areas. Some, such as Tempe and Mesa, are almost as old as Phoenix. Early this century, when Denver, Los Angeles, and Salt Lake City already were mature regional centers, Phoenix was still a striving little city just struggling to outgrow its territorial status. Unlike the others, it was never a great rail and transportation terminus with a strongly developed central area. Its major growth came after World War II, after the train era, in the time when trucks were starting to rule transportation, encouraging development away from established center cities.

What's more, it is natural for the other Valley cities—located in one of the fastest-growing metropolitan regions of North America—to be feeling their oats, to be seeking their own identity, to be talking down their ties to the central city. And if sophistication and an urban aesthetic sense are the criteria under consideration, Scottsdale need make no apologies to Phoenix or any other place.

Phoenix also might be reminded that the form of urban growth its own planners devised—nine "urban villages," each with its own mix of residences, work places, and shopping opportunities—is being implemented more successfully outside the city limits than within. *Phoenix Gazette* reporter Tom Spratt observed last fall that Tempe, Mesa, and Scottsdale already have centers offering the mix of shops, offices, and homes envisioned in the urban village concept.

However, those outside of Phoenix who believe they can "go it alone" and operate successfully as if Phoenix didn't exist, are making a grave error. There is not a single great metropolis, in North America or anywhere around the globe, that does not have an acknowledged center by which it is identified. Some would say California's burgeoning Orange County is starting to break that mold—a fast growing urban agglomeration with its own airport, scores of shopping centers, multiple office complexes, yet no acknowledged center. But let no one doubt: for law, finance, corporate headquarters, or international identity, Orange County still defers to Los Angeles, its mother city.

The Valley has no mother city save Phoenix itself.

For every major opportunity the Valley can offer, Phoenix will remain the major port of entry. Any resident who travels elsewhere and then is asked his hometown likely will answer "Phoenix"—whether, in fact, it is Gilbert, Mesa, Wickenburg, or Peoria (Peoria, Arizona, that is).

Everyone in the Valley also should recall Phoenix's very special status. It is one of the few cities in America where the governmental, economic, and population center of a state coincide in one metropolis. The synergy that combination can produce is immense, as the success of the Minneapolis–St. Paul, Boston, and Salt Lake City areas prove. Should the Valley spurn Phoenix, it would be turning its back on one of the region's great inherent advantages.

As for potential industries, they aren't fools. They know political boundaries don't seal off problems of pollution, toxic substances, solid waste, transportation, schools, or adequate infrastructure. In the new international economy, only markets with regional scale and diversity likely will succeed.

Advertise a suburb alone and you might be able to offer a great labor force and housing stock, but no educational centers, no concentrations of financial and legal services. Advertise a center city alone and you might talk of great centralized facilities but expose poverty and lack of skilled labor. Mix the two together and their strengths are complementary—and you are in the ballpark of modern competition for trade and sophisticated new industries.

Nor is the talking point just "things." Do the political leaders, the CEOs, the civic leaders of a region talk to each other? Are they capable of facing problems in a timely fashion, and solving them? Does the regional civic culture work? If not, the word will get out: Watch out for that region, it's riding for a fall. If in time to come the word ever spread that Phoenix has become an urban disaster—whether through air pollution, crime, instant slums because it let its neighborhoods go to pot—who would then be flying into Sky Harbor?

Conversely, if the word is that Phoenix is a gem, a sparkling desert oasis, the world will continue to drop in. Newcomers and new investment will spread out from Phoenix to other communities of the Valley. The benefits will be felt by all. Everyone in the region should have a stake in the central city and be proud of it. Not just to be fair, but smart, too.

This is why we say it is time for the cities of the Valley to acknowledge the Valley might not be a traditional metro area—and that Phoenix's sister cities will continue to develop their own urban centers, their own strong characters and strengths. But it is also time to put a stop to the poor-mouthing of Phoenix.

There is no question that downtown Phoenix, among major U.S. cities, presents a most curious case, because, to put it bluntly, there is so little downtown there. Incredible amounts of land in the central area are simply vacant. One facile explanation offered to us was that "the market" simply hasn't found downtown Phoenix desirable, and that until it does, things won't change.

We kept inquiring: "Who owns those immense stretches of vacant downtown land?" Mostly speculators, some who bought it for as little as $10 a square foot, we heard. We heard, too, that the Phoenix newspapers held some center-city land. But the papers have been candid about their downtown landholdings, they insist.

That being the case, we believe the region would benefit if the papers undertook some tough investigative reporting to ferret out the truth. Who indeed owns all that land? How long have they held it? What are their plans? How much of the land lies fallow for speculation? How much is unused because of indifferent or incompetent ownership?

We stress the vacant lands issue because yawning empty lots in the center of a city are like a grotesque smile—with missing teeth. They breed fear and abhorrence. The center of a metropolitan region should be the property of everyone—the common meeting ground of all ages, classes, income groups, and races. If the center of the city is made inhospitable, if it becomes hostile territory, it is more than a question of private land owner-ship. The public trust has been violated.

A partial cure for this situation would be to enact what is known as "land value taxation," a property tax weighted heavily to the intrinsic value of property. "Tax downtown land at its true and proper value when it's surrounded by high rises, and you would force down land prices, discourage speculation, and encourage building in the center city," one of Arizona's leading experts on city affairs told us. "Any urban economist would tell you it works. You just have to have the guts to do it."

With the "guts" issue, of course, the critical question is raised: Who cares? "Even if they could make the City Council understand it, it would take a tough bunch to pass a land value tax," a former mayor of Phoenix told us. "It would cause an uproar, and well-wired people would kill it," warned one skeptic of downtown development.

All of which prompted us to think it might be a pretty good idea—a lot better, in fact, than the ridiculous proposal to build the world's tallest skyscraper at 114 stories in half-empty Phoenix.

We found it hard not to empathize with a county official who said: "Phoenix needs a downtown. I feel like I am living in a mass suburbia. There's no sense of community here unless you can say the sun—literally— is the symbol."

It is true that a huge amount of downtown development—some $1 billion worth, say the boosters—likely will spring up in the near future. Included would be a Mercado—traditional Mexican market; Square One, with the nationally famed John Jerde, designer of San Diego's Horton Plaza, signed on as architect; a so-called "Superblock"; a major theater complex; a festival marketplace. One recent planning document we saw set the goal of "a downtown of such quality and magnetic interest that it becomes the symbol of the entire metropolitan area and gains national recognition as the downtown of the future."

Phoenix needs much more of that kind of vision—a common and shared vision, not simply another private development. Folded into the plans are a major office district, a government mall and a professional sports complex, civic convention and retail district, preservation and promotion of historic neighborhoods, and a new housing district.

It is also fortuitous, we found, that the Phoenix Community Alliance and the city, rather than concentrating exclusively on the traditional downtown, are now targeting the entire Central Avenue corridor—"from Camelback to the railroad tracks."

The problems of making a vibrant center of the Valley are, of course, little less than daunting. The region's and city's vast spaces are a top reason. A recent study showed that Central Avenue might be the longest major avenue in the world. There might be, a leading official told us, 75 years of absorption ahead. Barry Goldwater, a Phoenix councilman 35 years ago, recently mused that the city has become so splintered by the distances from downtown to North Central to Camelback that one might have to wait until some future time, when Phoenix might become the fifth or sixth largest city in the world, for sufficient development to fill in the spaces.

Yet we see the excitement in a vision of downtown that includes the following components:

> A Central Avenue that becomes a true southwestern "theme" street
> More museums and cultural attractions
> Restaurants and inviting shops and the birth of street life where such a pitiful dearth exists today
> Better planning and development of the state capitol area
> Appealing transit systems—extension of the present center-city minibus system, perhaps—to link not just downtown and North Central but also, when it becomes a reality, Rio Salado a mile or so to the south.

Phoenix can and ought to have all that, as the lead city of the Valley and of Arizona. Yet its leaders must not forget: a mutually supportive community of Valley cities, concerted efforts to share and move with the other communities of the region, is the only way to build the spirit of cooperation that will make Phoenix the true center of Valley life, even when it's "completed."

One specific short-term way to achieve that spirit of cooperation might be to concede to Tempe, in advance, the location for a professional football team at the Arizona State University stadium, even though Phoenix ought to work assiduously to get a baseball and general-purpose sports stadium for itself.

Another big gain for cooperation would be to push vigorously the idea of a shopping mall near the geographic meeting point of Phoenix, Tempe, and Chandler that would share its tax yield with all three jurisdictions.

These are sample ideas only. The design of a Valley that avoids the mean stereotypes, that forms a shared civic vision, can evolve only in practice. It must come from a media with courage and wisdom, from a business community that looks further than the next quarter's ledger sheet, from citizens and public leaders who are capable of rising out of small and parochial ways to a vision of what this buoyant civilization, at its finest, might become.

It is not difficult to tote up all the reasons why the region's future will be one of continued stalemate and bickering, not the breakthroughs to new forms of cooperation. Yet we leave the Valley convinced more than ever of its incredible potential—*if* its people care enough.

Update

The Peirce Report for Phoenix had perhaps deeper and more lasting effects than its counterparts in any other city. The reason would seem simple enough: notwithstanding the Valley of the Sun's phenomenal population growth, the Phoenix community was still a primitive place in terms of government, slumbering in its primordial civic innocence. Power had always been in the hands of major economic powers; serious civic dissent was rarely heard; the population was so new, contained so many "snow birds" and other young "birds of passage," that hundreds of thousands of people felt they had little long-term stake in the community. No strong independent citizen organizations existed. The "great given" of local debate was that the economy of the Valley of the Sun (and the economy was generally seen as the only thing that mattered) had always grown at a robust pace. Assuredly, a few of our interviewees told us, it would continue to do so far into the future.

But bubbling underneath was growing concern that all was not well, that the foundations for a flexible, open, equitable society were not being built. Many of the leaders and would-be leaders we interviewed told us as much. We heard them, agreed with them, developed their thoughts and concerns in our report.

The message to the Phoenix community was that its old "Plan A," the idea of riding the horse of growth into every sunset, would not work forever, that the local economy and polity were vulnerable to the pressure of national and global fissures. The report instead called for a "Plan B," looking to economic diversification, more compact growth, and attending to such vital and shared assets as infrastructure, neighborhoods, and radically improved education and career training. Heard only in fragments before, those ideas, published in the region's leading papers and reaching 500,000 regional households on a single day, helped to change the terms of the debate.

Soon after the report's publication, Valley developers and associated industries formed "the Valley Partnership" to counter what they saw as the development community's increasingly negative image. The mayors of Phoenix, Scottsdale, Mesa, Glendale, and a Tempe city council member met before an audience of 400 at a forum sponsored by the Phoenix Together organization—the first time, *The Phoenix Gazette* reported, that such officials had "reached across city boundaries and agreed that while competition is healthy, cooperation is the key to the Valley of the Sun's future." At the meeting, Scottsdale Mayor Herb Drinkwater commented, "The real value of the Peirce Report is that it gave us a kick in the pants."

Dozens of other civic meetings later took place and two major organizational efforts emerged: formation of the Valley Citizens League, the region's first broad-based citizens organization; and the Phoenix Futures Forum, an ongoing strategic planning process for Phoenix sparked by Mayor Terry Goddard. These efforts differed from predecessors (such as the Arizona and Valley Town Halls) because they (1) were inclusive, inviting all interested citizens to join, encouraging openness and diversity; (2) spanned all areas of public policy and concern; and (3) encouraged regionwide and long-term perspectives. They quickly became the area's leading leadership training groups, with influence in key policy areas. They were supplemented by goal-setting/strategic planning activities in Glendale and Scottsdale, town hall meetings in Chandler, and numerous other civic projects.

Two major initiatives—funding for the Rio Salado project and a "ValTrans" effort to authorize and fund a full regional public rail transit system—were rejected by the voters by wide margins. One criticism was that they were conceived and presented to the public on a grand scale, with a high price tag, and involving little citizen participation in conception and development—contrary to the recommendations of the Peirce Report.

County home rule was the governance solution the report recommended for the region. After a protracted struggle, the Valley Citizens League and its allies were able to convince the state legislature to place a measure on the November 1992 ballot—which the voters then approved— authorizing a committee to write a home rule charter for Maricopa County. Neighborhood groups also received stronger support in public policy planning. In addition, aggressive development of Phoenix's downtown moved forward.

The Citistate in Brief

The Seattle citistate encompasses Seattle and King County at its heart,
Everett and Snohomish County to the north, and Tacoma and Pierce County
to the south. Across Lake Washington lies the fast-growing Eastside, with
such cities as Bellevue, Issaquah, and Redmond (home of Microsoft).
Renton to the south and Everett to the north are among operating sites of the
Boeing Company—the citistate's 800-pound gorilla. The population of the
three-county, 5,891-square-mile citistate grew by 22.3 percent during the
1980s, reaching 2,559,164 by 1990. The area has 65 cities and towns, 48
school districts, and 213 special districts; the counties provide direct
governance for large swaths of unincorporated territory.

The Peirce Report Glossary

Seattle's waterfront, the historic cradle of the city, boasts an active port.
Ferryboats crossing Puget Sound serve the nearby islands and Kitsap
County, where Bremerton and other communities are located. The *Pike
Place Market,* built largely on stilts over the edge of a bluff overlooking
Elliott Bay, almost fell to the wrecker's ball in the 1960s but was saved by
citizen protest; it offers local vegetables, fruits, and fresh fish, along with
hundreds of small shops and stalls. The 605-foot *Space Needle* dominates

the 1962 World's Fair site. The *Seattle Center,* also built for the fair, provides sports arenas, theaters, and a home for the Seattle Symphony and Opera. To the south lies *Denny Regrade,* once a high point of land and then leveled by engineers. It was filled for years with parking lots, but now is turning into a prime site for in-city housing, shops, and restaurants. *Westlake Mall* is a conglomeration of restaurants and shops under one roof. Well-established neighborhoods ring Seattle's historic center, ranging from *Rainier Valley* to the south, now home to growing numbers of Asians; through the *Central Area,* with the city's heaviest minority concentration; to *Capitol Hill, Montlake,* and the *University District* (home of the University of Washington); then such newer neighborhoods as *View Ridge* and *Lake City.*

Major governmental changes include a King County government merger with *METRO* (provider of countywide transportation and sewage services) and creation of a new *Puget Sound Regional Council* to replace the old *Puget Sound Council of Governments (PSCOG).* The regional council holds authority over transportation and growth decisions across the citistate.

Recapturing
Paradise Lost

(Originally published in The Seattle Times *on October 1–8, 1989.)*

Is Puget Sound Paradise Lost?

Nature set the stage for a memorable world civilization on the shores of the great sound. But only the imaginative power of farsighted citizens can make it happen—and they'd better hurry. The drumbeat of accelerating physical growth calls for a new urgency.

Here is a region so physically expansive that it was able to swallow big waves of growth, decade after decade, barely showing the strain. But now it's filling up fast. People who live here feel the impact every day: on more crowded freeways, in longer lines, in less breathable air. They look outward and see developers' bulldozers ripping apart more of the forests that had forever seemed to define the region's identity.

Jobs are easy to come by. The economy booms. Houses are suddenly worth a lot more money. Nobody wants to go back to the days of that sardonic early-1970s billboard: "Will the Last Person to Leave Seattle Please Turn Out the Lights?"

But as your net worth mounts, don't you have to ask yourself: Is this the same Pacific Northwest, the same fabled Puget Sound, that nurtured me as a child or beckoned me as an adult?

The new prosperity is breathtaking in the prospects it brings for better careers, housing, recreation. But it's also a ticking environmental clock. Time is running out on critical conservation decisions. Radical reform of the Puget Sound region's tangled and ineffective regional governments is 20 years overdue. A thousand delayed decisions are starting to take their toll.

The buffer of time and space, the elasticity of nature, and the patience of the citizenry are wearing thin.

Time's up.

For a quarter-century or so, we have been visiting and watching the region. For this report, we spent 10 days in intensive interviews with dozens of leaders—men and women from business, government, labor, environmental alliances, the neighborhoods, and minority and ethnic bases. The interviews were off-the-record; we found Northwesterners beguilingly candid. They love their region. They fear for its future. They bristle with frustration at the paralysis that holds hostage the region's most critical decisions.

We see a regional plate filled with exciting opportunities. There are a number of things the people of this region can—and should—do to control growth, preserve the environment, improve governance, nurture human resources, and develop leadership.

Paradise Lost might still be regained.

Facing the Threat of Sprawl

On a dazzling summer afternoon, our helicopter rises from Boeing Field and heads north over the thin isthmus of Seattle.

Quickly, there's the Kingdome below us; then to our left, the city's waterfront, remembered for its drama, its Skid Road roughness, its welcoming lights as one returns at night from the islands, Canada, Alaska. Today Puget Sound's waters sparkle, and on the horizon, snow glistens on Olympic peaks. Downtown's spine, directly below us, bristles with the 1980s' burgeoning crop of skyscrapers.

We sight the Seattle Center and Space Needle, then veer east, across boat-studded Lake Union and Lake Washington. Few cities anywhere offer such shockingly precipitous hills and ever-shifting city- and waterscapes.

Across the waters we sight Bellevue—skyscraper city of the 1980s. We are over Kirkland, the region's Sausalito, and fast-growing Redmond. Our route is along the Interstate 405 corridor, past spread-out, highway-oriented, high-tech plants such as Microsoft's. We whirr past forests, opulent subdivisions, car-packed shopping mall parking lots, preserved farmlands, the towns of Woodinville and Monroe.

Northward lies Everett; we swing east instead by way of the Avondale Bear Creek area. Before long we are above Snoqualmie Falls; a wondrous rainbow radiates from the billowing spray.

And suddenly it's clear: these are no "normal" American suburbs, no run-of-the-mill forest lands awaiting bulldozer and saw. To the contrary, these evergreen valleys and emerald streams and rivers constitute perhaps the most stunning natural treasure one would find close to a great metropolis anywhere on earth.

Almost a bonus: from behind the ridges Mount Rainier emerges in crystalline perfection.

We glance down among the evergreens and glimpse a few peaceful older villages and spots of careful, tasteful real estate development. But we also see scarred hilltops, raw cuts into the land. Bulldozed "progress," wrongly sited, wrongly executed. Most of it is very recent.

Nineteen-eighties development is stepping far too heavily onto these treasured lands. So far, the damage is relatively isolated. Unchecked, it could become an ecological, aesthetic tragedy sometime in the 1990s.

We fly down over Interstate 90, twin ribbons of concrete through the expanses of green, the highway's edges an obvious next target of the commercial strip promoters. There are more great ridges, Lake Sammamish off to our right. The flight takes us south, past Renton and Maple Valley, past a large Boeing plant, large homes, mobile home parks. Over a ridge lies Seattle-Tacoma International Airport. We are over the Kent Valley, Federal Way, glimpsing Tacoma from a distance.

A massive junkyard violates the broad, luscious valley of the Green River. We get a view of Weyerhaeuser's extraordinary corporate offices, layered architecture under greenery. South King County presents a jarring jumble of land uses.

There's the Sea Tac Mall area, the town of Auburn, Boeing's research and development center, the huge Southcenter shopping mall. As we started, we land at Boeing Field.

Our flight path has missed much: most of Puget Sound's waters and islands, Bremerton, closeup views of the Cascades or Olympics, and all but cameo views into Snohomish and Pierce counties. Yet, as we disembark, duck out from underneath the helicopter blades, and start to think of what we've seen, a strong conviction grips us: If all the people of the Puget Sound region could have shared that helicopter ride, seen the totality of their region from the air, they would not just share our exhilaration, our wonderment at the scope and beauty of this extraordinary territory. With rare exceptions, they would demand: *No matter the cost, save this land, for ourselves, our children, and our children's children.*

The clear fact is, the Puget Sound region's future is not assured.

Without early, determined action, hundreds of thousands of those gemlike, treed acres between the sound and the Cascades could fall victim to the most land-consumptive, thoughtless forms of development imaginable. Vast stretches of the region could become the Northwest's version of California's Los Angeles County or Orange County or Silicon Valley. Low-density office centers, shopping malls, strip commercial development, and housing tracts, the whole monotonous and unrelieved, could easily spread in a blanket over valley and ridge, eventually even pushing up against the slopes of the Cascades.

For a couple of years, the 1985 King County Comprehensive Plan, with its goal of channeling growth to established urban areas and keeping the eastern two-thirds of the county in forest and farm, might stem the outward march. But not for long; by its very nature, the spread pattern demands constant supplies of fresh land. No plan is any stronger than the newest change a council may approve. Indeed, growth's less scrupulous promoters, once they have a dominant hand, know how to work the system to get virtually all the zoning variances and permits they need to transform their plans into reality.

Thirty cities, anxious to maintain total local autonomy, still resist complying with the King County plan. Unchecked, the spread pattern obliterates natural features, destroys the greenbelts between towns, creates nightmarish traffic jams, spews forth incredible air pollution.

Puget Sounders might consider the environmental fate of Phoenix, Houston, and Los Angeles, regions that stand as the epitome of decentralized, sprawl development. Using an environmental "stress test" measuring air and water quality, sewage treatment, and hazardous waste, Zero Population Growth gave Phoenix its worst-in-U.S.A. rating. Houston was third-worst. Los Angeles has the nation's worst air quality.

Yet whatever the dangers, a number of astute observers told us, the Puget Sound region is destined to adopt the sprawl pattern. These were the reasons they offered:

➤ Citizens of the region's center cities appear to have all the growth they want. Witness Seattle's CAP vote, the effort to downzone Seattle neighborhoods, an antitraffic ordinance in Bellevue.

➤ Puget Sounders, like most Americans, are wedded to their private cars. They love the air conditioning, audio systems, phones, employer-provided free parking. They believe the private car represents on-demand, personal transportation, free of bus schedules or waiting in the rain. Notwithstanding heroic, years-long efforts to boost Metro, its buses still carry less than 10 percent of the area's employees to work.

➤ Rail transit, the heart of quality, denser development patterns like Portland's, might have made sense when it was offered as part of the Forward Thrust development proposals in the late 1960s. Now, despite resurgent citizen interest, the skeptics argue that the time for rail has come and gone. The pattern now is cross-suburb, not suburb-to-downtown, commutes. Big new employers such as Microsoft prefer campus-like suburban locations almost totally inaccessible to buses, not to mention rail. Anyway, the cost of rail could be astronomic, and there are no "Maggies" (the late and highly influential U.S. Sen. Warren Magnuson) to talk the feds into footing the bill.

➤ Environmental controls, including wetlands protection, have driven the cost of land up to 50 percent of the cost of developments. So growth goes where the land is relatively cheaper: the Issaquahs, Marysvilles, North Bends and beyond.

➤ Denser, concentrated growth sounds great; but spread growth creates lots of winners—not just the farmer hoping to sell out for a fortune, but the realtors, bankers, carpenters, and developers operating at the urban fringe. Many are set to make a killing on urban expansion. They form a powerful constituency against growth restraints.

➤ Suburban cities, bolstered by Washington State's strong home-rule tradition, seem to scorn the King County Comprehensive Plan as they annex more land and let it develop at sprawl densities.

The bottom line, by this reasoning, is not hard to figure out: Beyond some elementary environmental controls, don't get in the way of spread development. Let 'er rip.

But the region's people ought to have no illusions. The path of least resistance is to follow the siren song of unfettered, spread development. But if they go that way, they could fritter away their breathtaking natural birthright in less than a generation.

In the long run, dispersed settlement is unsustainable environmentally or fiscally. And it is socially unsustainable as well. This pattern, with its longer commutes, generates traffic that overwhelms existing roads. Demands for new highways escalate. As civic leader James Ellis has asked:

Where would the Seattle region locate its next I–90, I–5, I–405 without touching off a firestorm of homeowner and neighborhood protest, and absolutely staggering expense?

But putting the roads where the people aren't yet, as with the proposed East Sammamish arterial to connect the Issaquah and Woodinville areas, would just shift the sprawl eastward while doing nothing to relieve pressure on the older highways.

The spread pattern inevitably fills up the open spaces between the region's towns, submerging their identity, suffocating their green lungs. Public purchases to preserve choice pieces of land might help a little, yet boil down to tokenism in the face of the growth juggernaut.

Dispersed settlement fosters ugly social divisions by isolating less-skilled workers in declining city centers, while more-educated, mobile employees pursue jobs in the new suburban office parks. About half the Seattle region's population gain in the 1980s has been from outside the state. Overwhelmingly, these new residents are highly educated people who move to the Eastside. They represent a real economic plus for the region, but their lifestyle often epitomizes the car-captive, suburban office culture of the times.

We interviewed a number of outstanding Eastside officials acutely aware of the region's environmental and social problems. Yet we were left wondering: Will the new Eastsiders provide a progressive political base if they live totally disconnected from the region's cities and diverse populations, particularly minorities and the homeless? Ever-more-dispersed settlement translates into a less socially cohesive Puget Sound region.

In 1988, the L.A. 2000 Committee, appointed by Mayor Tom Bradley, painted a grim scenario of the Los Angeles Basin becoming "a Balkanized landscape of political fortresses, each guarding its own resources in the midst of divisiveness, overcrowded freeways, antiquated sewers, ineffective schools, inadequate human services, and a polluted environment." Such are the potential costs of constantly dispersed development, a form the Angelenos can claim to have practically invented.

Scattered settlement carries another cost: incredible waste, as older, inner-city infrastructure is abandoned before its time, even while the public gets stuck with the bill for replacing roads, fire stations, sewage treatment facilities on the urban fringe. As Washington State Gov. Booth Gardner says, "I find it difficult to accept closing good schools in Seattle while we have kids in portables out on Issaquah Ridge."

A big motive behind the legislature's 1989 vote for a state growth commission was concern that too much state money flows to new highways and other subsidies to cover the costs of urban fringe development. How can that be justified, ask some legislators, if older communities suffer and vital health, education, and human service needs go begging in the process?

We believe the people of the Puget Sound region have it within their power to reject decentralized growth and adopt a more compact form of settlement that safeguards the environment and provides sustainable, high-quality economic opportunity. There can and must be a vision and a way to grow that is worthy of this physically exquisite region.

Smart Growth

If the Puget Sound region had only one policy tool left in its bag to deal with the growth-propelled threat, what would it be?

Simple enough. Ban further residential and commercial development in all unincorporated areas of King County. Restrict all growth to recognized cities, new or old.

What would that mean?

We'd know, right away, where development may continue—in the incorporated cities, the Redmonds, Kirklands, Issaquahs, and the rest. Such cities would see the handwriting on the wall: zone more densely now, stop your silly downzoning games, and forget about adding and adding to your population through annexation. That game's up.

What about the region's unincorporated areas? That's simple, too. They would remain open to hiking trails, backpacking, farming, mining, fishing, and lumbering.

Clearly, a ban on development in unincorporated areas would have some exceptions. Chief among them would be tracts located immediately between already built housing and commercial developments. There's legal reason for such an exception. If government takes away all the value of anyone's property based on present or immediately prospective use, the owner can sue and probably win. But this applies to only a small portion of the unincorporated area in King County. For the most part, property rights are no real barrier to putting almost all unincorporated areas out of bounds.

Why is there a need for such a radical change in policy? Because, in the waning years of the 20th century, this physically vast region is the target of unprecedented population pressure. Puget Sound citizens, from the humblest to most powerful, wonder how they can preserve their region's quality in the face of a growth juggernaut.

This region needs to start thinking—and acting—for itself. The alternative is to relive the horrors of cities that came under the growth gun earlier—Los Angeles, Miami, Houston, San Jose, and others. These are the regions that agreed to build virtually all the housing tracts, all the shopping centers, all the office parks that one promoter or another demanded. What might have been great public decisions turned out to be piecemeal acquiescence to private projects. The bitter harvest is now apparent: dense air pollution, a desecrated physical environment, virtually unmanageable infrastructure costs, deep social divisions.

The bad news is that Puget Sound communities have begun to slide down the same slippery slope. The good news is that their slide can be stopped. It lies in the hands of the people of King and Snohomish, Pierce and Kitsap counties, to set the rules, lay the groundwork for less sprawl and more compact development.

To some degree, King County is already making that effort. It has already downzoned—lessened permissible building densities—for 1,500 of the 1,850 square miles of its unincorporated territory. Today's arguments over development, such as that proposed east of Lake Sammamish, are focused on the remaining 350 square miles.

It will take a lot of political courage for King County or any other county to hold the line. Yet if the people of this region insist, they can have it all: exemplary environmental protection, shared economic progress, and design of true international distinction.

But none of that will happen if they don't care, won't make decisions, won't accept some sacrifices.

Outside of a freeze on development in the unincorporated areas, here are some of the best ideas we've heard for shaping growth in the Puget Sound region:

Celebrate and undergird the cities of Seattle, Bellevue, Tacoma, and Everett as the critical urban centers of the Puget Sound region. These communities set the region's national and international image. They're strategically placed, north to south. They're gritty and cultured, historic and combative. They have what it takes to handle growth. They have most of the region's streams of minorities and immigrants, a reservoir of untapped human potential that will be critical to economic success in the 21st century.

All possible employment growth should be channeled into the downtowns and industrial areas of these cities. Compactness in town means open fields and forests out of town. One can't redo the past: Boeing is where

Boeing is, and Microsoft and its high-tech groupies are entrenched on the Interstate 405 corridor.

But future growth should be channeled to the places ready for it—the big cities. Those are the places that have—in addition to human capital—the highways, the water and sewer systems, the legal, accounting, and related services to handle major employment.

Vigorous center cities create diversity: in jobs, restaurants, theaters, museums, galleries, universities; in ethnic and racial groups of every description; in the stimulation of places like the Pike Place Market and Seattle Center. By contrast, sprawling business parks on the urban periphery are dull stuff.

Puget Sound cities must learn to work together. For starters, they might learn more about each other. Bellevue or Everett or Tacoma people, for example, know a lot more about Seattle than Seattleites know about them. Seattle should wise up and take far more interest in its big-town neighbors.

Sharing should enter the picture, too. Seattle, for example, has a remarkably varied and strong arts scene. But the time has come for Seattle, with some grace and magnanimity, to share cultural attractions with other lead cities. Example: Bellevue has aspirations for a performing-arts center. Perhaps the Puget Sound region's leading ballet should be based there. Or, for that matter, how about the Sonics moving to Bellevue?

Keep pushing for a great public transportation system. It is impossible to have great cities without mobility. Across the world, that means quality mass transit—rail included. One of the great tragedies of the Seattle region was its failure to approve the Forward Thrust rail proposal in the late 1960s. Had the outcome been different, today's Puget Sound cities would have more focus, more density, clustered along the rail corridors. A Bellevue connection would have come early. Everett and Tacoma might well have hooked on by now. And the region would be immersed in far less contention and confusion about land use and urban sprawl's consequences.

Los Angeles stalled and stalled before it went for rail transit. The horrendous results, in degraded air and nightmare traffic jams, are legendary. Will the Puget Sound region emulate that model? Will Seattle exit the 20th century without even trying to emulate the rail success of Portland, its allegedly junior partner to the south? Some people say rail is too expensive. But ask: If this region can spend $3.6 billion each year on new automobiles, as once calculated by *Seattle Times* traffic reporter Peyton Whitely, why can't it afford a couple of billion dollars, one-time, to build a rail system and start catching up with Portland?

The hourglass geography of the Puget Sound region, with its narrow land-passage points, is particularly well suited to rail transit. Rail has been repeatedly, unjustifiably poor-mouthed. Consider that just a single stop, for the University of Washington, might serve 65,000 people a day.

It is said that the multibillion-dollar bill for rail makes the idea prohibitive, especially without massive federal funding. Even James Ellis, the great civic leader and regional "Mr. Rail" for decades, now blanches at the bill. Ellis has suggested an interim strategy: install an areawide system of HOV (high occupancy vehicle) lanes, eventually "upgradable" to use by vans and buses only, and later, to a full rail system.

Another idea, coming out of a study done for the Port of Seattle, is regular ferry service on Lake Washington, recognizing it as a great natural right-of-way and center of "Pugetopolis." Buses could connect at each end.

People who insist on commuting alone in their private cars should pay for the congestion they create. David Brewster, in the *Seattle Weekly,* suggests that anyone who drives alone across the crowded floating bridges or takes an off-ramp into Bellevue or Seattle at rush hour ought to be shunted into a special lane. There the solo commuters should be privileged to pay a $3 fee, "suffering public indignity and waiting in a line while the virtuous poolers drive right on by."

We'd suggest a variation on Brewster's remedy: apply the levies in Seattle, but not in Everett or Tacoma, destinations eager for more growth and not yet overwhelmed by its consequences.

Perhaps the alternative strategies make the most sense in the short term. But we note the region's economy is at a historic high, with its lead employer sitting on years of back aircraft orders. So one has to ask: When, if not now, will Puget Sound ever be able to afford a rail system?

Encourage more in-town residential development, up and down the income scales. The Bellevues and Seattles, the Everetts and Tacomas, should work hard on low-income, affordable housing. More concerted effort is needed to save single-room-occupancy hotels and replace low-cost apartments lost to the inner-city office boom of the 1980s. But for a healthy tax base, it's essential that the cities have a fair share of middle- to upper-income housing, too. In the face of CAPs (named after Seattle's growth-limiting Citizens Alternative Plan) and downzoning movements, can the region's top cities welcome more people? The answer: to bolster their own finances, to remain vital centers, they *must.*

And, popular impression to the contrary, there *is* space for substantial new residential development in the older cities. Tacoma and Everett offer plentiful opportunities. Seattle's Denny Regrade could take a good chunk of rather dense housing.

Stand on top of one of Bellevue's high rises and you see dozens of potential housing sites around the downtown's periphery—land now vacant or used for parking. Leading developers tell us there is a market for in-town living in Bellevue. The political process ought to encourage, not discourage, it. And include moderate-to-lower-income housing.

What of citizen resistance to new in-town housing? Of course, Seattle's leafy, finely gardened, middle-class neighborhoods are a great asset; no one wants them destroyed. Ugly, out-of-scale apartment buildings have sprouted in Seattle neighborhoods since the 1970s and '80s; protection is needed.

Neighborhoods should have design review powers. The city might set quotas for additional housing for all neighborhoods and then negotiate the scale, the design, and other trade-offs necessary to move forward. Special city concessions to cooperating neighborhoods might include new parks or boat moorages. In some areas, "superblocks" might be created by eliminating alleys and returning to green some of the 40 percent of the city now devoted to streets.

All new housing need not go into the heart of established neighborhoods. One might look instead to the Aurora Avenue Norths and comparable strip developments about the region. Sometimes within a block of residential streets you find a line-up of the tawdry hamburger stands and used-car lots and video outlets we have all learned to know and sometimes hate. But this is developable land, for much higher purpose.

There are examples along California's once-famed, now jumbled and rundown El Camino Real, running south from San Francisco, through the Silicon Valley and into San Jose. On selected blocks, in place of low-grade commercial clutter, there are now mixed-use projects reflecting the best of modern design. Shops and restaurants line the streetfront. Then above and extending a block behind them in a setting of gardened courtyards, come hundreds of apartment units. Beauty and density, it turns out, can coexist.

While we're about it, here's another deceptively simple way to house more of today's small families: allow every single Puget Sound family home, city or suburban, to be a duplex. Within a few years hundreds of thousands of "mother-in-law" apartments would likely materialize—without a single developer laying out a single new subdivision plat.

Some people worry where all the extra cars could be parked. In some streets it could be a problem, but a minor one compared to building more high rises or gobbling up wilderness for housing tracts.

Restrain new development on the urban fringes. Short of the elegantly simple solution of stopping new development in unincorporated areas, the counties should set iron-clad rules to forbid new development on the outer fringes. One way to do that is to tighten the rules on land that cities can annex. The cities, in turn, need to restrain exurban growth within their borders. A new multicounty authority with regional land-use controls may be necessary.

There's a new-fangled word in land-use planning: *concurrency.* The simplest translation is "pay as you grow." It means that all the necessary public infrastructure—roads and sewers and water systems, fire stations and schools—must be in place *before* any new development comes on line. If a developer can't pay for infrastructure himself or talk the local government into it, the development shouldn't be built. Florida has made concurrency holy writ; Washington State should.

Today, state and local governments subsidize immense growth at the urban fringe by supporting huge utility and road extensions. That growth often creates neighborhoods for the well-to-do, even the wealthy, while we—all taxpayers—subsidize such development, year-in, year-out.

Government should stop subsidizing sprawl and switch to supporting affordable housing in and near the city and town centers. Growth restraints and super-heated downtown development, like Seattle's in the 1980s, drive up housing prices. Thousands of low-cost units have been lost in Seattle. Sound policy would support public subsidies for lower-income housing within cities instead of subsidies to the middle and upper classes on the urban periphery.

Puget Sound housing prices are already going through the roof. People claim they want quiet, old-style neighborhoods—as long as they can rake in a half-million dollars or so for their old Seattle bungalows as the Californians and their money roll north. So the logic seems irrefutable: government should tap some of the loose real estate money for the homeless, the poor, and other people not lucky enough to ever make it into the star-spangled American real-estate game.

The time has come for a 1 percent tax on all property transactions, with the money earmarked for low- to moderate-income housing subsidies; or a 2 percent tax, with the other half earmarked for the acquisition of open spaces.

Wherever and whenever there's new development, make it look good. Kitsap County Commissioner John Horsley said this best: "We believe view corridors and buffering are critical. What matters is what you see as you drive. So we try hard for visual buffers along our roadways, and keep them green—that's half the battle.

"In the Northwest, we're lucky to have started with a lot of evergreens. We try to have developers retain native vegetation. If not, we ask for berms and sometimes fencing. We try to get housing clustered. Our overall strategy is concentration—to get development in and around the towns that are there—and keep rural what's rural."

Right on, Mr. Commissioner. Respect for the natural environment and aesthetics do matter, for the shape, the form of a region, its quality of life.

Go for long growth. Whenever a metropolitan region grows at a topsy-turvy rate, the potentials for grievous aesthetic and social planning errors compound.

There are dozens of examples across the Sunbelt states. Developers, financiers, and construction interests inflate growth projections and land-supply problems to justify all manner of publicly subsidized infrastructure. Local government planners get overwhelmed. There's lots of profit taking but minimal public benefit.

The Puget Sound region's objective should be simple: Plan development first for its own sons and daughters. Put out a welcome mat for newcomers to the region. But don't hype the process. This isn't a time of massive unemployment around the Puget Sound. The economy already attracts more new businesses and families than the region can comfortably handle. The development that doesn't happen today can always come tomorrow.

Share the growth with the "other Washington." Rural and inland Washington has not shared in the spectacular job growth and prosperity of the metropolitan counties. World economic forces perversely dry up communities whose economies are based on timber and agriculture or, for that matter, any kind of natural resources, as opposed to information-based economic activity.

The contrasts could hardly be more dramatic. Jobless rates around the Puget Sound region have dropped as low as 4.4 percent. Demographers say King County could expand in population by as much as 20 percent in the next decade.

Yet in parts of rural Washington, community leaders agonize about empty storefronts, idle farms, lost population. Unemployment has been as high as 16 percent in Adams County, 16.3 percent in Okanogan and Columbia counties. As rural poverty mounts, many of the jobless head to the Puget Sound region. Not infrequently, they end up on welfare.

Clearly, spreading the heat of the Puget Sound boom to rural and inland Washington could result in huge mutual gains. A magnanimous Puget Sound is a smart one. It can reduce its problems with growth while it creates opportunities for growth where it's wanted. In the process, it seems less overbearing, gets more popular in Olympia.

And there are multiple opportunities, outlined by David Harrison, director of the University of Washington's Northwest Policy Center. Metropolitan-area firms with large white-collar employment can be encouraged to take advantage of telecommunications technology by locating "back office" functions (largely clerical) in rural communities. Innovative high-tech firms in the Puget Sound area could, as some of their manufacturing becomes more routinized, start moving assembly operations to inland Washington. The ports might be a "window on the world" for progressive inland enterprises, helping them gain a foothold in international trade.

There are already some hopeful straws in the wind—Boeing's decision to set up a manufacturing facility in Spokane, for example, and Seafirst's transfer of its credit-card center to the same city. We like David Brewster's idea of a cap on Boeing employment in the Seattle area, a move that would cool excess metropolitan growth and provide an opportunity for the company to do more in smaller communities.

The state's new growth commission should take on the issue of comparative growth in metropolitan and rural areas and recommend a statewide growth management plan with attention to job dispersal. A good model is a new Georgia state law that puts rural economic expansion on equal footing with containment of excessively "hot," land-consumptive growth around metropolitan Atlanta.

Washington State is already a generation behind Oregon, which has an exemplary statewide land-use law that has worked splendidly, like oil-spill containment booms, to put boundaries around urban sprawl. Perhaps the new issues of economic interdependence will bring related state action in Washington. But not automatically. Action on this and every other regional challenge will come only when people of the Puget Sound region stir themselves to fight for change. Never has the old adage been truer: Not to decide is to decide.

No One's in Charge

"All the things people are worked up over, they're 'governance' issues. But most folks don't know it yet." It seemed to us those words, from a longtime government insider, couldn't be truer. It's no secret what people of the region are worked up over:

Nightmare traffic. Polls prove it. The issue dominates public consciousness so much that *The Seattle Times* even started a column devoted exclusively to commuting and traffic.

The environment. People wonder why that orange haze outlines the vista of Mount Rainier. Disturbing news pours in about toxic wastes, landfills, and sewage. Scary predictions arise about how this region, its setting in the watery Northwest notwithstanding, could soon face a serious shortage of fresh water.

Rapid-fire physical growth. There's tangible fear that growth will destroy the special qualities that have always drawn people to the shores of Puget Sound in the first place.

All of the top issues are indeed governance issues. There's not a ghost of a chance any of them can be dealt with until the region has some kind of a mechanism to drive the hard choices. That means a regional governmental authority empowered to decide the critical regional issues, the ones that in fact span city and town lines.

The need, we submit, is overwhelmingly clear. Just in its central four counties, the Puget Sound region has 71 municipalities and more than 1,000 special service districts attending to every issue from schooling to parks to fire to transit to mosquitoes. No one's in charge. A private corporation that operated in this manner couldn't even manage its way into bankruptcy court.

Try to change any of this and you run into a mine field of past disappointments and present-day pessimism. One civic leader recalls leading a King County–Metro merger effort in the late 1970s and tells of "how we were ahead of our time—our proposal was an instant orphan, an unclaimed bundle on the doorstep, dying a horrible death." Today, one is told, local prerogatives, parochialism, and pettiness will still sink any regional restructuring effort that erodes full-bore local autonomy. And a strange belief lingers that if the city of Seattle is in the room, it will dominate the outcome.

"I'm not yet to the point where I'll take the quiche-eaters of downtown Seattle telling us meat-eaters out on the islands how we should run our show," said a Kitsap County official.

Maybe that's understandable. In any region the big central city has a history of overwhelming its neighbors. But Seattle no longer has that population weight or political power, and the leaders we interviewed agreed. The region had better realize no progress is possible until politicians get past the "Seattle versus Us" syndrome. Once they do, today's compelling reality is that virtually all the tough, critical issues are beyond any city's reach.

What single city is capable of controlling congestion on Interstate 5? Of safeguarding the quality of the air that hangs over the entire region? Of saying where major new development is environmentally feasible for the 1990s? Of redesigning the region's solid-waste disposal system?

Look at things a bit more closely and it's apparent that a raft of social issues—preparing the labor force for international competition, sheltering the homeless, building bridges between social classes and racial groups— go way beyond single-city solutions.

It's challenge enough for cities to take care of the basics—fixing the potholes, putting out fires, keeping neighborhoods safe. The cities' own welfare depends on regional structures and services backing them up. But those structures are now shaky, half-baked, or nonexistent.

Instead of intelligent, coordinated action to tackle regional problems, there's a yearly diet of substitutes—analyses and studies—normally followed by nothing. Who but the ultimate government junkie will follow reports from a King County Charter Review Commission, then a Local Governance Study Commission, then the King County 2000 Commission, then the King County Reorganization report, topped off by the latest PSCOG review? (For the uninitiated, PSCOG stands for Puget Sound Council of Governments. Actually the latest review of its purpose isn't a bad piece of work. It recommends that PSCOG be disbanded and its responsibilities handed off to some new super-regional body.)

As long as there's no sound regional structure, a thousand-and-one circumscribed authorities and commissions, generally overseen by no one, get created as stopgaps. In case you hadn't noticed, there's the Puget Sound Air Pollution Control Agency, the Solid Waste Interlocal Agreements, King County's Capital Review Commission, the Zoo Bond Oversight Committee, and many others.

The list is guaranteed to get a lot longer if the structure isn't changed. Puget Sound residents will have more and more governments in their hair. But they'll have less and less governance that ties the problems together, sets priorities, and comes up with solutions for the regional problems that concern people the most.

What the region needs is a new Puget Sound Council that puts every legitimate regionwide responsibility in one place. The big land-use planning issues, new highways, sewers, solid waste, water quality, air quality, planning and operating mass transit—all would come under the same roof.

The immense advantage of single, focused accountability is that all these issues are closely related. It is folly to try to deal with them one at a time. The way we dispose of garbage affects the quality of the water. Success with mass transit has everything to do with air quality. Failing to match new highways to new development is to ask for grief—and get it.

The council should have a single executive, elected by the people. By districts of equal populations, all the council members should also be chosen by the people. But it would be a bad idea if all this functioned too distant from the existing cities and towns. Each mayor should be invited to sit at the table with the council and participate in its deliberations, without actually having a vote.

Would the mayors show up without a vote? You bet, given the new council's high-stakes agenda.

The first question is how to purge the system of the more-or-less regional bodies already in place, all of which have run into serious difficulties, none of which now seems fully effective in dealing with the region's problems. The candidates for extinction would include PSCOG, Metro, and the King County government, as they currently function. One pleasure voters could take would be to truncate the present King County Council pay structure, topping out at an extraordinarily high $70,000 a year. Fine, someone may say. But how do we get from here to there?

Washington State law provides a method: the "freeholder" process. It would make sense to start it in King County. All a group of citizens has to do is get signatures of 10 percent of the voters in the last election. This triggers the election of 15 so-called "freeholders," who are empowered to write a new county charter. Except for abolishing the courts, the freeholders could recommend virtually any reforms and changes they chose. If the voters agreed, the new structure would become law.

It's an exciting, Jeffersonian idea: the people can remake their government. The time never seemed riper. And a lot of Puget Sound civic leaders relish the idea. As one told us: "A lot of us would sure like to get into the room. It could be a kind of Continental Congress on growth."

The Puget Sound Council would require a solid tax base of its own. And it should have a major responsibility for equity, too.

In the modern-day development game, some cities tend to win, others to lose. Some places, for example, attract a major base in revenue-fat shopping centers and office buildings. Others fail. Big fiscal disparities emerge between sister cities. Major land-use decisions of the new council could well have some of the same effects.

So the freeholders should instruct the council to enact a system of tax-base sharing, allowing a significant share of the tax base for all new commercial and industrial facilities to go into a common pool. Cities would receive a proportionate share back, depending on their population and their property wealth.

What of the other counties of the region? Clearly a freeholder process for King County wouldn't apply to them. But one needs to remember: counties would not disappear. They'd continue to carry on their traditional responsibilities—courts and social services, parks and open space, some land-use control, for example. Only truly regionwide matters would pass to the new Puget Sound Council. And if the new council were designed and conceived well enough, there could be a voluntary movement—perhaps through parallel freeholder processes—for Pierce, Snohomish, and perhaps Kitsap counties to join.

If that didn't work, Washington State could and should intervene. The state has an overriding interest in seeing efficient, accountable government in its largest metropolitan region, the region on which a huge portion of the state's economy, educational structure, and environmental future depend.

How could the state intervene? One choice would be to use its preeminent powers to literally force the other counties to join. The second would consist of a diet of carrots and sticks—offering the counties various inducements to join, various fiscal penalties (loss of highway funding, for example) if they didn't.

One can already hear a number of the city and county elected officials railing against the imperious state, howling about loss of their prerogatives, warning how big government is about to devour citizens' rights.

Balderdash. Remember where they're coming from. Monks never reformed any monastery. The problem isn't big government. It's bad government, which is what the system, however well intentioned the players may be, in fact now delivers.

If people don't like the state coming in to make some order of things, consider the alternative: the state continuing to react, in piecemeal, disjointed fashion, to the region's decision-making vacuum. What the people of the region don't do for themselves, the state will ultimately do for them in the form of unelected, single-purpose agencies.

It's said that regionalism is a boring, unsexy subject. But if there were ever an issue that people should start taking into their own hands, this is it.

Anyone who's tempted to tarry with the region's status quo might consider what one of its most powerful mayors told us about how things work today. "The biggest things people expect me to work on," he said, "are all beyond my official jurisdiction."

Little time should be lost in elevating the governance issue to the top of the region's agendas. But that will indeed require more assertive leadership.

Politics of Postponement

"Water, water, everywhere, nor any drop to drink," says the well-remembered line from "The Rime of the Ancient Mariner."

The same seems true of leadership in the Puget Sound region. One finds bright, articulate, extraordinarily talented individuals engaged in the region's commerce and civic activity. On first impression, we'd rank them among the country's finest—people with the stature, the depth, the commitment that ought to provide any community with vitality and vision.

But if there are leaders everywhere, where's the leadership? There's a void as perplexing as the mariner's lack of a drop to drink. Every Seattle-area problem seems to get studied to death. Meeting follows meeting follows meeting; study follows study follows study. A whole cadre of public-affairs professionals serves on task forces and commissions and produces recommendations.

But when it comes to leadership that translates into action, more often than not nothing happens.

"It's like Italian Renaissance politics," one of the more clever players told us. "Even when you think you've reached agreement, half the people are already plotting how to overthrow it, and the others are prepared to extract a price if it happens."

Such, it seems, are the politics of perennial postponement and nonstop special-interest maneuvering. The result is that the region fairly bristles with anger and resentment about lack of effective leadership. People sense a deterioration in the way public decisions are made and public enterprises are run. Their example list is depressingly long:

➤ Precipitous loss of confidence in key school districts and their ability to deliver a decent education.
➤ Deep pessimism about the prospects for better regional services, from transportation to air quality to more rational land use.
➤ Less and less public trust in the ability of government officials to

"do the right thing" in a fractious political environment.

➤ Fear that paralysis in public policy will lead to continuing pell-mell physical growth, imperiling the region's distinctiveness and quality of life.

There is special irony to this region feeling bereft of effective leadership. A generation ago, Seattle wrote the text for effective grassroots citizen leadership in America as attorney James Ellis and his friends conceived and won passage of the Forward Thrust bond issues. (Ellis, in fact, had a small army of allies: altogether 200 business people, lawyers, academicians, public servants, clergy, and conservationists coalesced to write the Forward Thrust proposals.) This extraordinary commitment of citizens who were not officeholders literally transformed the face of the region. Forward Thrust's lasting legacy tells the story: generous open spaces and parks (including one atop a freeway), public waterfront use, storm-water control, community centers, an aquarium, and more.

Ellis today remembers the costs of the Forward Thrust effort. He had to spend much more time away from his career and his family than he anticipated. With the triumphs came some bitter disappointments—the loss of a bond issue for rapid rail, for example. But there's no other way, Ellis believes, to move the society forward. A few individuals, he reasons, must get out in front, give massive chunks of their time to galvanize an immense planning and selling effort—and keep plugging away until they get results.

Ellis was not the sole civic entrepreneur of his time. There was Joseph Gandy, the car dealer who sparked the successful effort to make the Seattle World's Fair of 1962 a reality. Other "Mr. Seattles" included Eddie Carlson of the Westin Hotel and later United Airlines, and Lloyd Nordstrom of the famed department store. Such figures collectively embodied perhaps the best definition of ennobled community leadership: leadership so "big" that it doesn't seek its own reward.

Today it sounds elitist to say a downtown establishment could meet for lunch at the old Rainier Club when it was still a white male bastion and make farsighted decisions for the community. But in its time, that system often excelled.

Until the late 1960s and early '70s, for example, the Seattle public schools were governed by a strong board of prominent establishmentarians, people like Phil Swain, who commanded wide community respect and had the know-how to run the district successfully.

The old order could not, of course, endure. The surge and proliferation of ethnic, racial, and other interests have irrevocably splintered the old power base—around Puget Sound, around America. It is not a new experience in our national history—each reiteration of the American dream expands the player base and brings such dilemmas.

This time, no one quite yet knows how to put the egg back together again. Perhaps it will simply take time, as new leaders mature.

A best scenario to relieve the present agony of the Seattle schools, for example, would be that the parties become so alarmed that they determine, jointly, to settle on a new focus and consensus. Another desirable outcome would be if the May 1989 CAP initiative vote, so eloquently described by Seattle economist Glenn Pascall as "reality clearing its throat," were to lead to more community dialogue. Pascall paints a pretty grim alternative—CAP as "the progenitor of blunt-instrument politics in which an unresponsive officialdom is periodically clubbed by an inarticulate populace led by a handful of skilled organizers."

Few of the regional or city leaders we interviewed professed any desire for politics-by-shillelagh. Perhaps we are beguiled by the decency and thoughtfulness of these persons as individuals, ignoring their collective decision-making paralysis. Yet, in our interviews we were immensely impressed by some of city's and region's new leaders, people who would never have been invited into the old Rainier Club's paneled interiors. Some of those who today head Asian, black, and Hispanic organizations seem legitimately anxious to add a communitywide perspective to their more targeted advocacy.

And then the women! So clearly ignored today, they might well constitute the Puget Sound region's secret leadership weapon. We encountered so many outstanding women—in local government, business, unions, and advocacy groups—that we feel confident predicting they'll play a dramatically expanded role in the region's future. The talent is there, maybe waiting too patiently to be invited.

What of today's Seattle-region business community? Can it lead as Ellis and his peers once did? Here there's reason to worry, for the business game is played differently these days, and civic leadership suffers.

International competitive pressures beat down on practically all corporations now. Current stock value is held as a cudgel to clobber business executives with every quarter's bottom-line results. The neighborly old hometown firm has to think in increasingly demanding fiscal terms.

Meanwhile, the explosion of mergers and acquisitions removes critical decision making to disinterested boardrooms hundreds or thousands of miles away. That, in turn, means less business time and talent available for partnerships with the local community.

Then there's what many business leaders depict as a newly savage generation of reporters, born into cynicism from the Vietnams and Watergates of their youth, nurtured on a diet of Wall Street greed and the peccadilloes of politicians in high places. The new generation, it is alleged, looks across the civic landscape expecting to find evil anywhere and everywhere. Any civic figure who seeks to lead publicly on an issue may become an instant target. "Who needs it?" a respected business leader asked us. Even Ellis found his footsteps dogged during the debate about the new convention center in downtown Seattle. Eventually the reporter gave up, having discovered no evil.

But can business simply walk away from the civic game? Hardly.

To the contrary. Subpar schools, crumbling infrastructure, perils to air and water quality and the quality of life of their workers, require that business executives "get out there" and lead—the risks notwithstanding. The tragedy is that some top business leaders think they can have their profits and just let the community stew.

We asked a leading developer about his civic role and whether there's a growing need for business figures to approach and negotiate with their adversaries in society, and he shot back: "I'd love to be mayor for four years, but I'm not going to do the political B.S. it takes."

So, will lawyers lead where the corporate types can't, or won't? Not if one takes the recent example of a Seattle law firm that fired a whole bunch of its attorneys for not having enough billable hours. The discharged lawyers' apparent problem was too much pro bono civic service.

It's easy to be discouraged. Here's a region that talks ambitiously of an international future, but all too often opts for parochial politics. It's a region where elected officials, cowed by ferocious initiative campaigns, routinely hesitate to stick their heads above the parapet.

Yet as dreary as these scenarios sound, they are but half the story. People's love of this region remains simply stupendous. Sufficiently articulate, dedicated leadership may well work. Some impressive homework, comparing well with that done in any region across America, has already been completed.

Consider, for example, the Greater Seattle Chamber of Commerce's annual forays that take Seattle business leaders to see how other leading North American cities—from Boston to Toronto to San Diego—run their civic affairs. Or the chamber's yearly conference on regional leadership, now bringing in several hundred attendees, many invited from the community and distinctly not business's own. Or the work of the Washington Roundtable, made up of top private-sector executives, taking on thorny issues such as public education.

Increasing numbers of smart, informed business and civic leaders are getting to understand the stakes for the regional future. Quality political leadership, when and if it emerges, may find more followers than one would think.

Another regional plus is the bold commitment of the Municipal League of King County to take on the toughest political issues and arm citizens and officials with the facts they need to deal with them. Or, as self-serving as it might seem, the willingness of *The Seattle Times* to sponsor these prickly commentaries by outsiders. Even the CAP vote can be interpreted, on its bright side, as a show of ownership, a statement by some citizens that they want to play a role and not simply cede decisions to others.

Effective regional citizenship means more than voting, as important as that is. It means endorsing thoughtful change, seeking alternatives, supporting the risk-takers, rejecting parochialism. It does not mean a heavier hand of government. It does mean citizen empowerment.

How can the Puget Sound region reach closure on more of its pressing, shared problems? In today's fast-moving, heterogeneous society, that task will never be easy.

There's one experiment that might be worth a try. The public could be provided, on a regular basis (perhaps monthly), with a clearly explained list of the 5 or 10 most critical issues awaiting decisions before councils, mayors, businesses, or philanthropies. Will King County move on a critical open-space decision? Will United Way support community groups building or rehabilitating housing for the poor? Will Boeing, a hefty political player when it chooses to be, back, block, or ignore renewal of the Puget Sound Water Quality Authority? Clearly, there'd be no shortage of critical decisions to highlight.

The goal wouldn't be to dictate the decisions, but to make it clear for everyone what the stakes are, where the decisions lie, and the names of the leaders responsible for making them. Possible partners in such a venture might be the Municipal League, known for its objective, excellent research, and a newspaper such as *The Seattle Times*. Armed with information, the public ought to be better positioned than ever before to press for and get closure on issues critical to the region's future.

Critical Needs: Learning, Training—and Caring

As human beings, the people of Seattle and its sister communities are pretty decent folks.

The city's United Way can trace its roots back 67 years. A Human Services Roundtable, formed recently, tries to assure critical people-to-people services across King County. Historically, Seattle's per-capita charitable giving has ranked among the top 10 cities in the United States. But what used to be good enough, a quite acceptable record in serving "the deserving poor," misses the target for any region that hopes to excel in the toughly competitive national and international economy of the 1990s.

In times past, philanthropy used to be an "extra," an add-on, a cover for nice people doing nice things. Schooling was for the abler kids; we thought it OK if the failures dropped out around ninth grade and spent their lives hauling wood or waiting tables.

None of those old stereotypes works any more. Brains, not brawn, drive global economies. Successful metropolitan regions, across the nation and across the world, focus on their greatest resource: people. Their survival, they know, rests on a constantly refreshed supply of motivated, educated young people. Quality schools, quality universities are indispensable.

But government and business leaders in smart communities know it's equally critical to work with the also-rans and attack the root causes of poverty. Why? First, because child abuse, rotten schooling, drug abuse, teenage pregnancy, and delinquency are gruesomely expensive. Failed lives get translated into dependency, ill health, and, at worst, years of incarceration for crimes committed. The cumulative bill, for taxpaying businesses and citizens, is staggering.

Second, hobbled lives translate into a hobbled region. The dead weight of dependency erodes a community's productive and competitive power.

Consider the labor-force issue alone. Baby-boomers have stopped entering the labor force; today's new workers, born after the pill gained popularity, were born into a far less populous "baby dearth" generation. Labor shortages are a real peril—across America and in the superheated Puget Sound economy in particular. Half of all new workers from now to 2000 will be minorities or immigrants.

So any region has to ask: Are we doing a decent job of educating Hispanic, black, Asian, and poor white kids? If half the searing criticism we heard leveled against the Seattle public schools is correct, the answer for the lead Puget Sound city is a resounding no.

How about the record of King County and its neighbors on providing critical social services for children and youth? Multiple social-service agencies are working feverishly on the problems, we were told. Indeed, the region has so many single-purpose social-service groups, many born in the 1960s–'70s era of free-flowing federal aid, that critics complain about how entrenched and narrowly focused they are. A prominent regional leader told us: "We need desperately to get more order in human services, more efficiency in providing services for the un- and underemployed, single-parent families, minorities, and the mentally ill. This field cries out for serious attention."

Look into specific minority groups and critical problems leap to your attention. Drugs and gang activity, a leading Seattle black leader told us, "are devastating this city's African-American community. We have gangs like the Crips triggering family breakdown. More and more black youth are dropping out of school. The mortality rate for Seattle black babies is higher than in Trinidad. Our black community is more like a third world community than a part of a highly technical industrial Western nation."

Among Hispanics nationwide, the school dropout rate is a staggering 50 percent plus. Nor is all well on the Asian immigrant front, though Washington State can be proud of the substantial numbers of Southeast Asian refugees it helped settle. Many of those immigrants have prospered. But others face massive disabilities. Among the most severely impoverished people of the Puget Sound region today are Cambodians, Thais, Vietnamese, Hmongs, and Laotian tribesmen.

Some people believe the dire social problems belong overwhelmingly to Seattle. Twenty of King County's 28 emergency shelters for the homeless, for example, are in the city. But the problems of poverty, ignorance, and social isolation are hardly limited to the big city. They are fast moving regionwide.

Consider South King County, with its low-cost mobile-home parks, inadequate public transit, and catch-as-catch-can social services. The South County's low-income population is projected to soar from 26,000 households in 1980 to 73,000 in 2020. The Eastside will have three-quarters as many poor families: 55,000. By 2020 there will be more poor people living outside Seattle than inside it, a dramatic change from 1980, when the city had twice as many poor families as the rest of the county combined. Yet, while poverty mounts on one side, one hears of some Eastsiders so rich and removed that they've taken up residence in palatial homes built in walled-off enclaves.

Could this region be headed toward a two-class society—more poor, more rich, less middle-class? It would be a tragedy.

True, there's a hint of class division in Washington State history. Conditions were so wretched in the early company-owned lumber towns, for example, that radical unionism flowered, and the "Wobblies" (Industrial Workers of the World) gained a foothold.

Yet by and large, the Pacific Northwest has always seemed a region of the common man, a region without vast divisions of wealth or status in life. The grittiness of Seattle's working waterfront, overwhelmingly middle-class neighborhoods, closeness to the natural environment, the idea that anyone could go out and catch a 30-pound fish and lead a decent life—all that makes the idea of a split society, haves and have-nots, even more offensive here than it might be elsewhere.

The only way to avert deep social divisions is to keep the ladders of opportunity open—for everyone. It ought to go heavily against the grain when it's reported here that the Puget Sound region's new service and high-tech firms just can't find the engineers and skilled technical workers they need in the area, and must recruit from outside. That means rungs are missing from the opportunity ladder and points to a fundamental failure of the region's schools and universities. It means Washingtonians have simply failed to goad, fund, and motivate their educational establishments satisfactorily. It means the choice jobs of the new economy could go largely to outsiders, while Washingtonians' own kids do the tedious data-entry jobs and clean the latrines.

We heard that many Puget Sound employers, faced with minimal literacy on the part of their new local hires, simply throw up their hands in despair. Quite often, it appears, specific on-the-job skills training and literacy education, not to mention advanced training, don't exist.

We have a set of recommendations that are as urgent as they are elementary:

From Everett to Bellevue, Seattle to Tacoma, local government and business leadership needs to take a long, tough look at the social-service, school, and community-college systems. Are those systems up to the mark of modern managerial excellence? Do they operate with sufficient sense of the urgency of their mission—to protect and develop the human talent on which the community's future rests?

If the answers are no, some radical reorganization may be in order. One approach is to set realistic two- to five-year goals for lower dependency and school-dropout rates and higher school test scores, and then challenge the service professionals and educators: How do you propose we get there? Can real progress be made without radically changing how the social agencies and schools are managed? If business sees better education as critical, shouldn't business be a leader in this fight?

Experience coast to coast shows that unless the business community presses for basic system change, not much will happen. Elected officials have a tough time doing the job on their own; often they have political ties to the very system that needs to be changed. Even the most dedicated public officials can't achieve much without strong outside support.

Business leadership, with the respect it commands and the resources it wields, is indispensable. Business people simply cannot throw up their hands in despair and say it's someone else's concern when a Seattle public school system loses a big chunk of its middle-class enrollment, or when the school dropout plague continues unabated.

Another red flag: the vast sums of public money squandered as schools are closed down in Seattle and older suburban areas and have to be replaced in newer, far-flung suburbs.

The region offers some exemplary business-led efforts to improve schools. Sponsors include the Greater Seattle Chamber of Commerce, the Seattle King County Economic Development Council, and, statewide, the Washington Roundtable. Some business leaders are starting to see that the usual goodwill gestures—businesses adopting schools, providing mentors, contributing computers—won't cut the mustard.

But in general, Puget Sound businesses see a problem rather than a crisis in the schools. Unlike the thoroughly alarmed business establishments in such cities as Baltimore, Chicago, and Pittsburgh, they've yet to take on truly critical school issues, the ones that might lead to major change in the system.

Examples of the most critical issues include reducing central bureaucracies so they stop micromanaging the schools, shifting major authority and accountability to principals and teachers, joining with grassroots citizens groups determined to make their community schools accountable, and working with families to increase the motivation of students.

We are convinced that among the managers of such powerful, leading corporations as Boeing, Nordstrom, Weyerhaeuser, and Microsoft, and among the region's professionals, local governments, and university facilities, there *is* the talent to assure a farsighted human-resources policy for the region's future.

The time is especially ripe for the Microsofts and other high-tech firms to leave their relative isolation and plunge into civic leadership. As one former state and local official told us: "Leadership will default to the high-techers whether they want it or not. After you earn your first couple of hundred million, it's tough to find places to spend it, and people expect you to expend a lot in your community."

We'd only add: The high-tech and aircraft industries, above all others, have a direct economic interest in a superbly well-trained local labor force. If they want it, they'll have to provide dramatically increased catch-up help for today's more female, minority, and immigrant work force.

Foundations and community organizations must take the human resource issues as seriously as business and government. Ditto the churches. Despite the region's long history of charitable giving, its local foundations tend to have fairly shallow pockets. Just as seriously, few of them appear willing to risk backing some of the rough gems of our society—the original thinkers and fledgling organizations anxious to tackle social problems in new and inventive ways.

The Puget Sound region is seriously deficient in this area. It needs to remember that risk capital is just as critical for social innovation as it is for successful new technologies and products.

As for the region's community organizations, many are terrific at stirring up opposition to policies and trends they don't like. Witness the May 1989 CAP vote in Seattle. But there need to be more efforts like the Seattle-based Neighborhood Crime Center's imaginative work to combat the drug menace by forging connections between neighborhood crime-watch groups and the police.

In the competitive international economy of the 21st century, strong and mutually supportive interracial, intergroup relations will likely be a key to regional fortunes. The Puget Sound region can and should be a world model. The lives of many of this region's blacks, Hispanics, and Asians are characterized by harsh conditions of poverty, scant economic opportunity, even social disintegration. Yet if there's any place in the United States where the problems should be manageable, it's the Puget Sound region. There are no ghettoes or barrios on the scale of those in New York, Detroit, or Los Angeles. There's no history of deep conflict among the various groups. Racism never sank deep roots here. The regional standard of living is high.

Among leaders of the minority races and nationalities in the Puget Sound region, one still finds a sense of goodwill and belief in the larger society that's tragically been destroyed in many American cities. As one black leader said to us: "I love Seattle. It's a city that has a solid chance of keeping hope alive for all its citizens. We have to get on a more rapid course to that end."

At the same time, Seattle has an exciting opportunity to become by the next century one of the great meeting cities of the world. It is roughly equidistant between Europe and Tokyo, a capital of the emerging Pacific Rim. It has a superb natural setting that could draw international meetings. It has great international corporations to give it a measure of credibility. Its people relate to international opportunity: witness how many volunteered to open their homes for the 1990 Goodwill Games.

A future as an international meetingplace won't materialize automatically. The region, for example, would need hundreds of multilingual experts (again, the education issue). Thousands would have to master a smattering of the world's languages. New meeting facilities would probably be needed. But the payoff could be immense—in cultural diversity and richness, in economic gain, and in an "industry" as environmentally pure as any that exists.

We suggest, though, that the region can't seriously entertain such ambitions unless its own racial and ethnic house is in order—unless Asians, Africans, Europeans, and South Americans visiting here can see the Washingtonians who share their racial heritage leading decent and unoppressed lives.

The ways the region could seize this opportunity are legion: forming interpersonal linkages across racial lines; helping black entrepreneurs sell to white customers; helping Hispanic kids make it through school, get vital connections and jobs; assisting all Asians, not just the privileged ones, to make the transition to healthy, middle-class life.

Would such a policy strain the resources of local and state governments? Could it cause painful social adjustments as high-techers from Redmond or Mill Creek experimented with drawing educationally deprived black youth from the Central Area and Rainier Valley onto the high-tech track? Would it involve some initial failures, cause occasional political backlash? The answer to all the questions is yes.

Yet it is almost a sure bet: if the human-service and educational systems could be shifted from mediocrity to excellence, if ways were found to hand out figurative green cards of opportunity throughout the communities of Puget Sound, then virtually every resident of the region could experience palpable, positive benefits within half a generation or less.

Linking Conservation and Development

Open-space acquisition is a great idea.

Across America—in New York State, Bergen County (New Jersey), the suburbs of Chicago—a new land trust is being born every week. Green lungs for cities, places to hike, a touch of nature near home. Who could object?

Puget Sound and Washington State have not missed this train. King County voters approved their first farmlands-preservation ordinance in 1979. There have been repeated King County ballot bond issues for buying particularly imperiled parcels of forests and farms and transforming them into greenbelts and preserves for the people. The Washington Wildlife and Recreation Coalition is proposing a dramatic $450-million initiative for land purchases statewide.

But making sure that natural land is preserved is only half the answer to the pressures of growth. The equally critical challenge is to accommodate the waves of new people one *knows* will keep coming to the region. Along with its admirable push to purchase public space, the region must account for growth and human settlement—or simply be overwhelmed by both.

Therefore our new twist: take 25 or 30 percent of the open spaces the public buys and turn those lands into compact, European-style villages. These new settlements would simultaneously accommodate population growth and respect the Puget Sound region's majestic environment. And they would guarantee that the rest of the lands remain in their natural form in perpetuity.

This startling idea, using public-land purchase both for conservation and development, emerged from our conversations with dozens of Puget Sound leaders. Virtually all seemed eager to take the two elemental forces shaping the region today—population growth and environmental consciousness—and fuse them in a distinctively Northwestern way.

The conservation side of the idea already enjoys high popularity. The public has come to recognize that land purchases are critically important for two reasons: first, vastly enhancing the quality of life with close-in green space; second, creating a natural buffer between cities and villages so their identities aren't submerged in rolling waves of nonstop development.

We applaud the region's past and proposed future land purchases. We believe dramatically larger land acquisitions are in order, especially along the already disputed territory of evergreens, rivers, and hills that runs north and south of Issaquah and east from the environs of Woodinville, Redmond, and Lake Sammamish to the slopes of the Cascades.

Virtually all this land is beyond the urban growth boundary set down in the King County Comprehensive Plan. But the pressures to leap that line are already intense. Zoning protection, it appears, just isn't enough. Public ownership of the land is the only safe, totally reliable protection. Unquestionably, equally promising land acquisitions can be identified in the other counties of the region.

But with the high-velocity growth pressures the region is experiencing, some portion of these lands will be needed for human settlement. Thus our proposal to set aside a fraction for compact villages and cities. Here is an opportunity to assure new development of the highest conceivable standards in design, placement, and respect for the natural landscape. This would be possible because the public, not private landowners and developers hungry for maximum profit, would set the original terms and conditions for development.

We propose a Puget Sound Land Trust be authorized under state law and empowered to issue bonds to cover the cost of its land purchases. The trust's geographic scope might begin with King County and then, as citizens of Pierce, Snohomish, or other Puget Sound counties opted to join, become truly regional in character.

The Puget Sound Land Trust would have a board of trustees, organized perhaps along the lines of the Pike Place Market Preservation and Development Authority. The membership should include some of the most talented and respected citizens of the region.

Repayment of the land trust's bonds would be guaranteed by the taxpayers of each of the affected counties, as the trust increased its scope. One could hope for immense purchases—perhaps an initial target of $1 billion, conceivably as much as $2 billion worth of property acquisition in just a few years.

But we do not envision this as a significant hit on the region's taxpayers. We believe residents may indeed have to pay higher taxes if they expect their region to deliver decent human services and the improved education necessary for the 21st century.

But the land-development game is different. There's already plenty of money in it. Breathtaking profits are often registered by lucky landowners, speculators, and developers. (Not accidentally, we suggest, the land game is also the biggest source of questionable local government campaign contributions, under-the-table deals and actual corruption in fast-growth areas across the nation.)

What we propose is to take the windfall profits out of the game through public purchase of open lands before those lands are zoned for development and, ideally, before roads are even in place. The land trust would then decide which portions of the land could be reserved for development without uglifying the landscape, and with the least peril to the natural environment.

It would prenegotiate with local government the upzoning of those parcels to dense development standards. The trust would pay for a good chunk of the infrastructure—roads, sewers, and the like—necessary to make the development work. Then and only then, it would sell or lease back to developers the limited tracts for dense development.

With zoning, permits, and infrastructure in place, the price per acre would be dramatically higher than what the trust paid for the undeveloped land. This would be particularly true if the bold step we outlined earlier — forbidding virtually all new residential or commercial development in unincorporated areas—had already been taken.

That means the land trust would be receiving immense payments—enough, if carefully planned and executed, to pay all the principal and interest on the bonds it issued. This could be a win-win game for everyone, save the land speculators:

➤ The public, virtually cost-free, would get huge chunks of greenbelt, assured forever. The kind of ugly sprawl development that gobbles up open land would be stopped in its tracks.

➤ The environment would be served as new human settlement was limited to ecologically safe locations, such as the lower sides of valleys. The decision would be based on careful research and planning done in the public, not private, interest. There'd be none of the raw, scarred hillsides, the bulldozed cul-de-sacs on ridgelines, that you see when flying over the Eastside today. Land consumption would be minimized by creating truly compact villages and small cities. There would be fabulous views out onto the incomparable Northwest scene of green forests, flowing rivers, and ice-capped peaks. But these would be shared views from multiunit garden apartments and town houses, not private views into three- and four- and five-acre back yards of private residences.

➤ Developers would obviously have to compete for the trust's available land sales or leases—and a fiercely competitive bidding it might be. But developers also would be free of hostile environmental and citizen groups trying to head them off at the pass with zoning battles, lawsuits, and the threat of losing their investments.

➤ Social justice could be served by requiring developers to reserve a reasonable portion of the new housing for lower-income families. If the land trust leased rather than sold the land, it could guarantee that the designation for lower-income people stuck over time.

➤ Public transit could be planned as a major mode of access to these settlements—from the start, not as an afterthought. A light-rail line running through the hills to the new villages would be idyllic, but perhaps too expensive. Alternatively, bus service could be planned to connect the new villages to subregional transfer points.

Superior transit service, complete with on-board phones and other amenities, might be a trade-off for building two-lane roads that are less destructive of the environment than broader highways. There could be specialized van service to major corporate locations. To assure rapid transportation, even at rush hours, buses and vans might be allowed special passing zones, zipping past private autos every few thousand feet.

We recognize that there'd be an ocean of details to work out in making these ambitious scenarios come to life. For example: Should the new settlements be incorporated? Yes, we think they should be. Local self-government is the taproot of democracy. Would they be able to annex territory on their borders? No. That would defeat the whole purpose of closely contained communities that leave the natural landscape largely free of development.

Would the land trust's appearance on the market drive up already escalating land prices? Some, perhaps, though today landowners are in a crapshoot as to whether their property will ever get the zoning and permits for development. This is another reason to quickly prohibit development on unincorporated lands, because speculation reigns in markets of great uncertainty.

What fair-market value would the trust pay for land? Perhaps something more than the forest or agricultural value of the land, reflecting the fact that part of the publicly acquired lands would sooner or later go for development.

Would these villages have their own employment centers? Yes, we'd suggest some varieties of back-office (clerical) work might be ideally suited to facilities relatively close to, but not actually in, the region's larger cities.

Would people really want to live in compact villages? Don't Americans insist on suburbanization, with the standard one-acre plot? Developers often say yes; right now they're clamoring for more and more virgin Eastside land because it's cheaper. But the market has already taken a turn: we're seeing larger and larger portions of developments being used for multifamily housing. Unless you're willing to let cities crawl up the sides of the Cascades, the old suburban model will never accommodate the demand for growth.

Pedestrian-oriented villages stand for community, personal interaction, shared experience. Tested through centuries in Europe, they sound radical in America. We predict, though, that once a high-quality village were built by the Puget Sound Land Trust, demand would be simply immense for the personalized living style and unsurpassed natural setting it would offer.

Do we have specific sites in mind? Not precisely, though land-use experts note a few early possibilities. Among them is the East Sammamish Plateau Area, a vast territory with relatively few owners of massive holdings who might be willing to sell if they saw that private, piecemeal development of their land would never get government approval. Another possibility: buying out the massive, extraordinarily controversial Weyerhaeuser development on Snoqualmie Ridge and executing it with dramatically less consumption of open lands.

The east side of the Northshore area, not far from the high-tech corridor, could absorb some of the suburbanization pressure on Snohomish County. Another possible site is the Soos Creek Plateau, near Kent, Renton, and Auburn and already connected with transportation networks.

Other potential targets should open with time and investigation. Yet it would be vital for the Puget Sound Land Trust, at each turn, to bid for control of land before it was zoned, had roads built, or became a prime development target at all.

Today government is constantly whipsawed as it tries to control land development on the public's behalf. "When we upzone, somebody gets a killing. When we downzone, we get sued," a county planner told us. The Land Trust would provide a device to put the community as a whole on top for once.

What would be the targeted populations of the new communities? There's no pat answer. Given the region's growth today, some people suggested populations in the tens of thousands if the communities are to make a real long-term difference. Others suggested 3,000 or 4,000 residents, to maintain a rural quality.

For the first few experiments, our temptation would be to start small.

One of America's most ingenious ideas for a new "suburban topology," for example, has been developed by a group of leading American architectural experts. Among them is Doug Kelbaugh, chair of the University of Washington's architecture department. Though most grew up in the suburbs, these architects believe it's time to move well beyond the familiar model of the large, single-family suburban house on a curving cul-de-sac, automobile-dependent and land-consumptive.

Instead, the new architects' group has invented the idea of the "pedestrian pocket," a cluster of low-rise, high-density housing, retail space, computerized back-office space, and a shared central square, all within a quarter-mile of one another. (A quarter-mile is the maximum distance Americans will walk, says Kelbaugh.)

Ideally, the "pockets," with up to a few thousand residents, would be connected by light rail. There would be a cross section of residents, by income, age, and ethnic/racial background, including many of today's single-person or single-parent households. The goal is an old-fashioned village of all kinds of people, not just look-alike families.

The goal, as Kelbaugh sees it: "a new compelling suburban topology— one that takes the low-density, homogeneous net that has been thrown over the outskirts of our cities and gathers it into finite knots of culture and commerce that are bounded, contained, lively, and pedestrian."

We think that's a pretty exciting vision, and that Washingtonians should be proud someone at their own state university is a leading inventor and proponent of it. In a way it's utopian. But it comes close enough to the reality of the present-day American family, to the reality of 1980s-style back-office employment, and to so many people's yearning for old-style villages, it deserves serious experimentation. In times past, California was called the experiment station of American social form. Now, why not Washington State, particularly the Puget Sound region?

Another consideration: how to invent villages that show more life, more architectural and design variety, than the dull sameness of housing form and color in many recent condos and "planned unit developments" (agglomerations of houses, town houses, apartments, stores, and so on, in a single area, planned simultaneously and comprehensively.) One approach could be to allow several developers and designers to get a shot at portions of each new village or city.

We've described the villages as European to underscore their compactness and land-conserving style. But this is the Pacific Northwest; any and all communities should reflect that special character.

An idea sheet from the Friends of Snoqualmie Valley provides a smorgasbord of what that might embody: nearby "working" forest lands, with environmentally sound milling and logging; a guarantee that a body of water like the Snoqualmie River remain a "pure, free-flowing stream which supports farming, sports and commercial fishing, and boating, canoeing, and kayaking"; preservation of the area's "neighborly pitch-in-and-help-one another" values, including such events as Snoqualmie Railroad Days and exhibitions of home-grown products and arts, extending to Christmas tree farms, flower growing, and community festivals.

How large could new settlements be and still maintain such great Northwest qualities? How could some of the old local culture be transmitted to the new settlements? For starters, one might include in the early planning a good contingent of old-time residents of nearby villages. Let them leaven the counsel of design professionals, government "experts," and wilderness-hungry yuppies who might rush to the opportunity of defining new settlement patterns for the Pacific Northwest.

Would a Puget Sound Land Trust be limited to projects on the exurban fringe? Not necessarily. Projects around Puget Sound, from Kitsap County to the outskirts of Olympia, might eventually be considered. As long as the affected cities approved, the trust could be authorized to assemble large parcels of land for beneficial public purpose.

Consider, for example, the concept of a new Seattle park, three blocks or so wide, extending from Westlake Mall to Lake Union. Within easy walking distance of downtown, such a park could be Seattle's equivalent of New York's Central Park. The land along it would become immensely valuable. This would provide a major opportunity for diversified housing at the urban center.

Give the Land Trust enough power to assemble such a big land parcel, including the immediately adjacent blocks, and the eventual financial return, through smart real-estate management, could equal its exurban operations.

Similar golden opportunities might be found in and around Bellevue, Everett, and Tacoma. The constant, we suggest, would be to invite the regional leaders who sat on the Puget Sound Land Trust Board, together with those notorious socialist visionaries—the region's own people—to plan their future.

None of this would be an easy task. Nothing so complex, so important, ever was.

But consider the potential if the great American land use game can be altered so that the commonwealth, the people and leaders of the Puget Sound region, take charge, set the ground rules, and then let the private sector execute the actual development. Compactness, physical beauty, environmental protection, workable public transit, free-enterprise opportunity, social equity could all be achieved.

If it worked—and most of the regional leaders we talked with thought it could—the Pacific Northwest would have made a stunning contribution to American life.

Update

The Seattle Peirce Report grew out of the determination of *Seattle Times* executive editor Michael Fancher, editorial page editor Mindy Cameron, and other colleagues to give new context to problems their readers were experiencing firsthand, such as traffic jams, disappearing woodlands, and soaring house prices occasioned by the Puget Sound's economic boom of the late 1980s.

The report's impact seemed less dramatic than in Phoenix because this was a region with a mature civic process and focused public debate. Washington House Speaker Joe King had already won approval of a blue ribbon commission to study the impacts of uncoordinated and unplanned growth, and possible state growth management legislation.

The report tended to reinforce an existing growth debate, not ignite a new one, identifying the need for concerted action to preserve open space, clear up the regional transportation mess, and concentrate population growth in core urban areas. An avowed "no new growth" champion upset a veteran incumbent for the King County Council just a month after the report appeared. The Municipal League of King County began a series of "growth challenge" forums around King County. Demands for more discussion of the topic came from chambers of commerce around the sound, land trust groups on Bainbridge Island and in rural Snohomish County, League of Women Voters meetings, and others.

As a sequel to the Peirce Report, *The Seattle Times* teamed up with KING television to stage a televised debate on growth involving a dozen knowledgeable and outspoken residents, with Neal Peirce invited back to town to join the discussion moderated by Harvard law professor Arthur Miller (well-known for managing public broadcasting discussions on complex issues).

In 1990–91 the Washington legislature did pass the state's first-ever Growth Management Act, requiring counties and cities to come up with comprehensive plans sensitive to better use of land and concern for environmentally sensitive areas.

No broad-based, popularly elected Puget Sound Council, such as the report recommended, was created. But several significant steps were taken toward regional coherence. King County voters in November 1992 did agree to merge their Metro agency (responsible for transportation and sewage) into the overall county government. The county itself steered more toward general purpose governance and away from being so much a service supplier for unincorporated areas. The Puget Sound Council of Governments was allowed to die, and a new Puget Sound Regional Council was created. The new organization was still basically a council of governments but with expanded powers to get counties to agree on land use and transportation (including the critical issue of allocating transportation monies between highways, mass transit, greenways, and other improvements under ISTEA—the 1991 federal Intermodal Surface Transportation Efficiency Act).

By the end of 1992, exploitive suburban growth had yet to slow perceptibly. But the mechanisms to slow it were clearly being approved and coming on line. The Peirce Report's rather grandiose proposal for a series of compact, urban-oriented villages on the region's eastern growth corridor did not come to pass. But the Trust for Public Land drew partly on the report's vision to work closely with the Bullitt Foundation to create a Mountains to the Sound Greenway Trust. The redoubtable and irrepressible James Ellis, long a champion of acquiring valuable lands for the public, agreed to chair the trust, which focused on keeping green spaces between the cities of the east side and connecting greenways along the I-90 corridor from Ellensburg in central Washington to Seattle.

The Peirce Report picked up and expounded on the previously discussed idea of creating a grand public park, surrounded by diversified housing, from the Westlake Mall to Lake Union. In 1992 a new organization, Seattle Commons, was founded to make the idea a reality, moving rapidly to draw up plans and acquire land.

Two ideas imbedded in the report—urban villages and the thought that space for more residential development *can* be found within Seattle proper—

gained new credence when Seattle Mayor Norman Rice, in April 1992, called for a series of new urban villages—communities of small parks, schools, townhouses, and apartments—to be built in areas of Seattle now occupied by old warehouses and empty lots. Rice took a political risk: in some Seattle neighborhoods, there's knee-jerk opposition to adding any new residents. But Rice coupled his urban village idea with a challenge to the suburbs—that they create, in return, a buffer zone of parks and open spaces between Seattle and their existing communities.

Rice's offer represented precisely the citistatewide agreements, the constructive city-suburban dialogue urged in the reports for Seattle and all the other cities treated in this book. Yet it was uniquely Northwestern. He said he wanted Seattle children "to feel their linkages to water and weather, to sense the unfathomable power of salmon returning to spawn after years at sea, to have mountains and the forests as anchors to their souls."

The Citistate in Brief

The Census Bureau officially linked Baltimore and its environs to the Washington, D.C., metropolitan area in 1992. But the 1,609-square-mile Baltimore citistate remains fairly distinct, despite its peripheral suburban merge with Washington in such counties as Howard and Anne Arundel. The region's population grew 8.3 percent in the 1980s, to 2,382,172. Baltimore City had 751,380 people, suburban Baltimore County 689,300. Other counties in the citistate include Carroll and Harford; the principal communities are Aberdeen, Bel Air, Columbia, Fort Meade, Glen Burnie, Hunt Valley, Jessup, Owings Mills, Woodlawn, and, well to the south, the Maryland state capital at Annapolis. The region has 168 cities and towns, 96 school districts, and 88 special districts.

The Peirce Report Glossary

Union Square, surrounded by skyscrapers and aging office buildings, anchors old downtown Baltimore. Restaurants, museums, the National Aquarium, the Maryland Science Center, and ethnic fairs draw crowds to the downtown *Inner Harbor,* the Chesapeake Bay waterfront area revitalized during the 1970s. The Inner Harbor is also home to *Harborplace,* the Rouse Company's festival marketplace; and the *Power Plant,* once a functioning power facility, then an amusement center, most recently vacant. The *Fishmarket,* an upscale amusement center near the Inner Harbor, periodically goes bankrupt. Historic *Fort McHenry* sits on the south side of the harbor, several miles to the southeast.

Neighborhoods range from the elegant and historic *Mount Vernon, Mount Washington, Fells Point,* and *Ashburton;* to the working-class neighborhoods of *Canton, Highlandtown,* and *Hampden-Woodbury;* to distressed *Sandtown-Winchester.* Vendors hawk Chesapeake Bay seafood, meat, and produce at the *Lexington Market,* which dates from the 1850s. *Druid Hill Park* in central Baltimore features a zoo and wooded parkways.

The *Greater Baltimore Committee (GBC)* is made up of leaders of the region's top corporations and private foundations. The *Metropolitan Council,* formerly the *Baltimore Regional Council of Governments,* is composed of the mayor of Baltimore and executives of the surrounding counties. The *Citizens Planning and Housing Association (CPHA)* has been actively involved in the city's housing and urban planning issues for over a half century. *BUILD (Baltimoreans United in Leadership Development)* is based in some 30 inner-city churches, working on such issues as housing and public school performance. The *Black Community Council of 100* consists of leaders in business, industry, education, and the arts.

BALTIMORE

Breaking the Boundaries

(Originally published as a special section of The *(Baltimore)* Sun *on May 6, 1991.)*

Baltimore, from the air, presents a tableau rare among cities. The silvery surface of the Chesapeake Bay, one of the world's greatest protected estuaries, stretches past Fort McHenry, past great port facilities, straight to the city's front step at the Inner Harbor.

On a crisp autumn day, we toured the Baltimore region from a helicopter, looking down on the city and surrounding counties, above buildings and greenery and water.

The sight's intriguing. At the center there's not just renewed downtown Baltimore but also the old settlements rolling over the city's hills, church-and-steeple neighborhoods that evoke flavors of Old Europe. And out beyond, clusters of development emerge from the area's necklace of green spaces—the Owings Mills and Hunt Valleys and Columbias that have begun to define the new regional lifestyle and economy.

From an aircraft, you can imagine all the world is above average in income. You see no strife in the metropolis, no drug wars, no educational disparities, no race problem.

But two hours later, on the ground, in a van for a closer look, we pass through the dilapidated Sandtown-Winchester neighborhood, take a turn onto Argyle Avenue and see a drug deal in progress. Around the corner, we see public housing high rises, once a monument to society's outreach to the poor, now ravaged by wanton destruction, drug dealing, and fear.

We pass by the Lexington Terrace Elementary School, where we'll later learn the average age of the kindergarten children's mothers is 20. On corner after corner, hovering over bedraggled or boarded-up shops, are mini-billboards pushing booze, cigarettes, and sex—a display of capitalism's most exploitative side.

Yet, rounding another corner, we come upon a housing rehabilitation dedication sponsored by the New Song Community Church and attended by Baltimore Mayor Kurt L. Schmoke and Jack F. Kemp, then U.S. Secretary of Housing and Urban Development. We're reminded that Baltimore, during the years of William Donald Schaefer's mayoralty, registered more low-income housing renewal per capita than any other U.S. city. The good results, in spruced-up homes, are still to be seen, block by block across the inner-city neighborhoods.

Crisscrossing the city that afternoon, we found ourselves constantly shifting between neighborhoods burnished like old heirlooms—comfortable, well-maintained, even tony—and others where the paint was peeling, the masonry deteriorating, the curtains tattered.

For architecture and history, our favorite is Mount Vernon. From his perch atop Baltimore's own Washington Monument (older than the upstart obelisk in the nation's capital), the father of our country has been gazing down Charles Street toward the Inner Harbor since 1829. How many cities can match *that?*

Down by the waterside there now loom the behemoth office towers of the Signet Bank and Legg Mason. There's the new Gallery that adjoins Stouffer's Hotel, four floors of finery and boutiques and eateries, antiseptic ambience encapsulated.

Yet, a few blocks distant, the great old Lexington Market still displays fresh fruits and Chesapeake shellfish and meats, sold by merchants with stained white aprons and the smell of an old Baltimore no one in his right mind would want to lose.

Just north of the Inner Harbor is Baltimore's majestic City Hall—faced with brilliant white Baltimore County marble, adorned with a central dome and clock and belfry. Nearby is The Block, once a prime stop on the national burlesque tour, now a seedy strip of peep shows and sex shops, prostitutes and drug dealers.

It's a poignant contrast, the rich history and dangerous decline. Is this a city and region in disintegration? Or one awakening?

The next morning we began more than a week of intensive interviews of business leaders, county executives, the mayor of Baltimore and the governor of Maryland, neighborhood activists, environmentalists, philanthropists, and civic group leaders. So that they would be candid, we guaranteed that their comments would be used anonymously. We brought to Baltimore our perspective as outsiders, comparing this city and metropolitan region with others across the nation.

To each person, we posed fundamental questions: Are Baltimore City and the counties doomed to ever-deepening conflict, racial tensions, a cataclysmic parting of the ways? Or are there ways the city and counties can build on mutual interests, forge common agendas, find their way into the 21st century as a cohesive unit in the new world economy?

If the reader finds our series prickly or blatantly prescriptive, we plead guilty. Baltimore, city and county, are passing through some rough waters; worse may be coming. If we didn't like Baltimore so much, we might have shown more proper Baltimorean reserve.

Looking at the Future

Baltimore and its surrounding counties need to hurry to make a deal.

On the surface, things may look OK. The city boasts a glittering chain of big, attention-getting projects. Harborplace and the National Aquarium are known across the continent. The proposed Christopher Columbus Center might just become the world's premier research institution in the field of marine biology.

The counties—Howard, Carroll, Harford, Anne Arundel, and Baltimore County on the city's northern flank—have soared in population, jobs, income, so much so that growth itself is now the counties' most controversial public issue.

But dark clouds are rolling in. The city's brilliant downtown redevelopment notwithstanding, it is becoming poorer and poorer, losing more middle-class residents every year. Without some real help, Baltimore could one day be another Detroit or Newark.

Baltimore's surrounding counties have developed into economically independent jurisdictions, no longer slow-moving satellites of the big city. And some county residents, who rarely see a need to go to the city anymore, seem to feel that as long as Harborplace or the Orioles survive, the rest of Baltimore could slide into the bay.

If there isn't an early stop to the city's social free fall, plus the counties' rather constant withdrawal, economic prospects and the quality of life from Columbia to Bel Air, Glen Burnie to the Pennsylvania border, will be imperiled.

In the emerging world economy, the critical competitors are metropolitan regions. The Baltimore area already faces tough rivals as close as Norfolk/Hampton Roads in Virginia and as distant as Singapore or Rotterdam. Meanwhile the sheer economic weight of Washington and its Virginia and Maryland suburbs, home to the biggest federal facilities and thousands of businesses, grows yearly.

But so far, Baltimore City and its neighbors are failing to function cooperatively. They often exhibit sheer indifference toward each other—and, on occasion, outright hostility. A political hacksaw hovers over the neck of any county official who suggests meaningful assistance to the troubled inner city. A Baltimore politician will be pilloried for giving up an ounce of the city's autonomy now that blacks are finally in full control. The best defense is for Baltimore and its surrounding counties to strike a deal—a deal based on mutual respect, a deal in which all the players win.

At the heart of a deal must be enthusiastic county support for new state policies that will channel major tax revenue to Baltimore City. For all its attractions, Baltimore is among the poorest of U.S. cities. Its tax rate of $5.95 per $100 of assessed value—at least double that of any Maryland county, a huge burden on its businesses and remaining middle class—strikes us as terribly unfair and indefensible. In a truly cohesive region, the Baltimore-area counties would be leading the charge for tax reform designed to channel a fairer proportion of state revenues to the city and other especially needy jurisdictions in the state.

But there's an onus on Baltimore City to change, too. It must earn outsiders' support by radically improving its schools. Until that happens, there's not a chance the Baltimore region will have a high-quality work force in the next decades. Baltimore must also concentrate intense effort on human reconstruction in its most deeply deprived neighborhoods. The social turmoil convulsing those neighborhoods, from shattered families to drug dependency to vicious crime, is ruining too many lives and costing too much money to tolerate.

Baltimore City must sharpen its management practices, trim bureaucracies, and contract services to private companies when that would save money. The slate's not blank here. About 1,400 city jobs were eliminated in 1989–1990. And the city is experimenting with one of America's most advanced computerized geographic information systems. From planning street improvements to tracking school truancy to spotting gang activity, the system has fascinating potential.

Yet there's also serious bureaucratic lethargy. Baltimore has 736,000 people but a hangover bureaucracy large enough for its old population of 950,000.

And more than reduced payrolls are appropriate. Baltimore should follow the lead of Dianne Feinstein, the former mayor of San Francisco, who enlisted business executives to act as consultants to major departments. It isn't humbling when a city seeks business assistance; it's smart. The city manager of Bellevue, Washington, the most prosperous big suburb in the Seattle region, recently asked chief executive officers from the Pacific Northwest to provide regular reviews of the city's management. (The Greater Baltimore Committee has offered Baltimore City the same kind of cooperation. But City Hall's response, several business leaders told us, has been less than enthusiastic). Strong steps to tighten management would not only win Baltimore respect from Towson to Annapolis; they'd boost the city's reputation in national and international investment circles.

But the politics of a deal will be tough. County residents show increasing alienation toward a city that's become the region's catchment basin for poor families. Median family income in the city, once roughly comparable to the counties, is now just half. With the loss of so many middle-class people (first whites, now more and more blacks), Baltimore City faces abandonment and decay.

Not all city neighborhoods, of course, have those problems. But the news media dwell on them. Crime does breed fear. We sensed a raw contempt for the city by many people who don't live in it. This strikes us as particularly tragic because the city's assets are real. Walk the streets of Baltimore's exquisitely preserved Mount Vernon or Union Square, or stroll about Federal Hill, or visit Lexington Market, and you know you're in a city of rare culture and color and variety. More progress is coming in the 1990s, with a 7.5-mile waterside promenade reaching from South Baltimore to Canton. Baltimore has defined, for aspiring cities, what one town, by wit and grit, can achieve.

The barriers to a unified region, let us add, don't lie exclusively in county people disparaging the city. We ran into remnants of Baltimore City conceit, as if the counties hadn't developed into quite grown-up partners. A member of Baltimore's City Council told us: "We have a more formal structure than the counties. They have a ranch-style bureaucracy. We're more like a high rise." County officials must have the courage to tell constituents that Baltimore City's well-being is critical to the entire region, that if the city starts to sink economically, the ripples of decay will spread inexorably out.

County delegates to Annapolis ought to identify with city interests as one would with a close partner. Conversely, a Baltimore City that expects partnerships and support from its neighbor counties needs to reach out and realize it's no longer in a position to tell others what to do. A major business leader said it was time for Baltimore "to say thank you" to its county partners. What about a Howard County Day each spring at the Inner Harbor, featuring artists and performers from that county? Or a yearly appreciation dinner for the leading Anne Arundel and Baltimore County patrons of the city's cultural institutions?

There is also value in promoting the city's assets—whether in culture, entertainment, or attractive neighborhoods. Mayor Tommy D'Alesandro 3rd inaugurated the Baltimore City Fair, one of America's great civic celebrations, in the early 1970s. Under then-Mayor William Donald Schaefer in the late 1970s and early 1980s, the city hustled on a grand scale to celebrate neighborhoods and welcome business expansions.

A sound city/county "deal" should open the way for something more significant: reorganizing the governance of the Baltimore region for the century to come. We heard the usual competing "solutions"—merging Baltimore City and Baltimore County, sharing the property tax base across the region, creating some super-regional government. The truth is, few people want any of those proposals to become reality. None has a chance of flying politically soon.

But focus on interdependence and first steps occur. Indeed, many are already creeping in. We heard them called "metropolitanism by stealth"— cooperation that's discreet enough to avoid fire by flying under the political radar line. For example, the counties already share some costs for Baltimore's symphony and museums. A joint purchasing council exists. The city and Baltimore and Anne Arundel counties are contributing to the new light-rail system. Sheer necessity is likely to drive more and more regional accords on such issues as waste disposal, air quality control, and land-use policies. To save money, police and fire departments across the region could merge training, firing ranges, crime lab work, communications.

Or how about simple consideration of human needs? We were amazed to hear that residents of the Baltimore region are charged big tuitions if they pick a community college across their city or county boundary. Goodwill ought to solve that kind of problem.

But more is needed. Even if the Baltimore region today doesn't need full-blown regional government, it does need some form of arbiter—short of throwing every decision to the courts or to Annapolis. An arbiter could resolve differences on issues ranging from highways to waste recycling. The Baltimore Regional Council of Governments, already a state-created agency, could fill that role. Instead, the city and counties seem to be standing by listlessly as the General Assembly slashes the Regional Council's budget. There's concern the council might even be abolished. It would be hard to think of a more misguided decision, at the very moment that cooperation among the region's governments has become so vital to its well-being.

Down the corridor of time, perhaps by the mid-21st century, Baltimore and its neighbor counties may be ready for an arrangement close to true, direct, and popularly elected regional government. To ever get there, though, the initial city-county deal has to be made. The Baltimore region desperately needs a new set of trust relationships. Each year it delays putting them in place it diminishes its prospects of becoming a strong, cohesive region.

The Interdependence Imperative

Why do the counties need the city? Here are a few big reasons:

City image. Across the world, a region is known first and foremost by the physical image, the character and success of its center city. The counties' economic success of the 1980s rested heavily on the positive economic climate generated by the "Baltimore Renaissance." Conversely, when center cities float toward bankruptcy—Cleveland in the late 1970s, Philadelphia today—the entire region suffers worse things than cruel jokes on the "Tonight Show." It's able to attract fewer conventions and tourists. Skilled executives and engineers don't want to move there. Prospects for job-generating new research and technology are dimmed.

Work force. America faces a growing shortage of qualified workers—not just engineers and technicians, but all manner of service personnel. In suburban offices, employers find it tough to get able clerks, salespeople, and service workers. The inner cities are the likeliest labor pool.

"Pay me now or pay me later." Trouble in the cities isn't cost-free. Political boundaries do not, in the long run, seal off problems of ignorance, poverty, inferior child care, teenage pregnancies, crime. Fail to address inner-city social problems now and the bill—in higher welfare costs, failed schools, packed prisons—will come back to haunt everyone in higher taxes. Image, again, is related: few people want to visit a devastated inner city.

Physical safety. Significant pockets of high crime increase the danger that residents of the region—even people from the farthest suburbs—will suffer personal violence as the inner city becomes ever more desperate and criminals begin to roam far and wide.

Growth and the environment. An abused, depopulated center city forces growth farther and farther into suburbs and "exurbs." Splendid inner-city areas, with appealing architecture, fine parks, and enviable ambience, get underused as middle-class people, fearful of crime and bad schools, desert the city. More county land gets chewed up, the population is dispersed, and mass transit becomes impractical. With longer commutes, air pollution increases. And hundreds of millions of dollars worth of schools, water systems, and fire and police facilities have to be duplicated—at immense public cost—on the metropolitan fringe.

Why does the city need the counties? Again, several reasons:

Customers. County people are big customers for the city's shops, restaurants, stadiums, Inner Harbor, and entertainment offerings. Lose those customers and thousands of city people go jobless.

Workers. Hundreds of thousands of people from the counties (418,000 daily, by latest count) work in the city. The city might like to tax them more, but at least it has to value the disposable dollars they often spend in town after work.

Jobs. The counties are where most jobs are today being created. Many city people need those jobs.

Political clout. As Baltimore's population declines, the counties' population grows, and the suburbs become more and more powerful in the state legislature. The city needs the friendship of those legislators so it can get more state money to run its schools and grapple with its social problems.

Oomph. With their population, their economic expansiveness, the counties provide the muscle to make the Baltimore region a major player in the new world economy. That means new businesses and benefits for everyone.

Citizens: Heroes for a New Era

For far too long, the people of Baltimore City and the neighboring counties have looked to mayors and county executives to set the pace for change. If relying solely on elected leaders was ever a good idea, it's dangerously wrong today. Few people believe that Mayor Schmoke or any mayor in the foreseeable future will ever lead the city with the aggressiveness that William Donald Schaefer exemplified.

In the suburban counties, hero leadership has faded, too. The fall 1990 elections swept in new executives who ran more as protest candidates than as torchbearers of a new vision—such figures as Charles L. Ecker in Howard County and Roger B. Hayden in Baltimore County. Their energies have been quickly absorbed by the struggle to balance budgets during a difficult recession year.

Will any politician around the Baltimore region soon rise above stamping out brush fires? Is another Mayor Schaefer or Theodore Roosevelt McKeldin (famed and charismatic mayor in the 1940s and again in the 1960s) about to appear? Are the counties likely to see leaders who match the energy shown by Theodore Venetoulis and Dennis Rasmussen in Baltimore County, Habern Freeman in Harford, James Lighthizer in Anne Arundel?

Probably not. Not just here, but all across America, there are few communities where people gladly let *anyone*—government leaders, political organizations, business heavies—make decisions for everyone else. We seem to be in an era of what some call "the democratization of power." It's a time when one's likely to see more partnerships in place of government dictation, consensus building rather than order giving, collaborative rather than heavy-handed leadership.

The regions that succeed in the 1990s will be those with leaders who have learned to share power and to look for a diversity of talent: women as well as men, minorities as well as whites, county as well as city people.

If Baltimore area residents need any proof that politicians are failing to provide real leadership, they don't have to look far. No challenge facing the Baltimore region today is greater than growth management and protecting Maryland's most splendid asset—the Chesapeake Bay. The Maryland General Assembly flinched at the prospect of passing landmark growth management legislation, which resulted from a 1988 report on the bay's declining health and recommendations of a gubernatorial task force.

Yet polls on growth management have shown Marylanders—in the city, the counties, across the state—leagues ahead of the politicians. They want action. And there's nothing especially radical about the proposed law; it simply places mild restraints on sprawling development to reduce the heavy consumption of "raw" land that magnifies the silt-laden runoff and pollution of the bay.

The state wouldn't dictate precise land use: it would simply require counties and cities to develop their own plans to minimize sprawl, focus development in established towns and cities, and protect the natural environment.

Similar statutes in Oregon, Vermont, Georgia, New Jersey, and Florida haven't crippled development or caused anyone inordinate harm. Michael D. Barnes, the former congressman who chaired the bay task force, says moderate growth management could save 400,000 acres from development in Maryland. The state's rural scenery and quality of life would be protected. The program could save local governments millions of dollars they'd have to spend on new roads and sewers for new shopping strips and subdivisions.

As in other states, the proposal is opposed by county officials leery of any curbs on their powers. The parochial politicians are joined by farmers, developers, and land speculators who believe controls would impair their potential to sell off their lands for big profits. Yet if there were ever an issue on which the people of the Baltimore region need to educate themselves and then fight in unison for state action, this is it. Growth management legislation might not produce miracles. But it would contribute to a revived bay, one of Maryland's greatest assets and strongest economic tools.

And if rapid-fire growth were slowed at the urban periphery and encouraged in the center, Baltimore City would be better able to attract new residents—a win-win scenario for the counties and city alike.

A few years ago, Governor Schaefer's embrace might have been able to force a growth management plan through the legislature. No longer. He doesn't command that kind of power now. The politicians are defaulting. People power is needed to force action.

What's the way to create broad and powerful constituencies for change, alliances that neither government nor entrenched special interests can overlook?

One answer, but just a partial one, is through enlightened business leadership. It can be an immense assist—in demanding, for example, regional economic planning, in pushing for stem-to-stern school renewal, in supporting community development corporations.

The problem here is that Baltimore has been witnessing the fall of some of its most civic-minded business leaders—the result of failed business plans, bank buyouts, and the massive wave of corporate restructuring and takeovers of recent years.

Yet the prospect is not altogether dim. Among top business organizations across the United States, the Greater Baltimore Committee is greater than most of its counterparts. The GBC didn't earn its position in the top echelon, along with such groups as Cleveland Tomorrow and Pittsburgh's Allegheny Conference, just by signing up all the big CEOs in town. It did so by some farsighted economic thinking and by undertaking such efforts as the "Commonwealth" plan to improve the city's dysfunctional public schools, working with such unlikely partners as BUILD, the grassroots, church-based organization. That alliance is a signal to how other groups—neighborhood, civic, city, county, professional—need to be pulled into the leadership act.

Where will the leadership be found? A first source could be the several hundred graduates of programs sponsored by the GBC and the Howard and Baltimore County Chambers of Commerce. It's a process in which bankers get to learn about welfare, civil rights activists about job creation, journalists about the excruciating process of actually making things happen.

Neighborhoods also need to be in on the new leadership mix—not just the neighborhoods of Baltimore City, which have received more recognition in the past, but also the undeclared but potentially vital neighborhoods of the counties.

And we believe that foundations, which have grown dramatically in Baltimore over the past decade, should be major players, too. A great opportunity is lost when foundations just give to "safe" colleges or hospitals or arts groups. Foundations must also be ready to fund advocacy for the region's most pressing needs—better schools, children's health and welfare, neighborhood development, and protection of the environment.

A good example of how the new system needs to work is the Goldseker Foundation's gift of $250,000 to Baltimore's Citizens Planning and Housing Association so it could create a Neighborhood Resource Center. The gift was unusual because Baltimore's foundations have traditionally offered anemic support for community development. Foundations in such cities as Boston, Cleveland, and Chicago have provided many times more neighborhood support, creating a much stronger network of activist neighborhood organizations than Baltimore enjoys today.

Everyone's grand new hope, of course, is the Harry and Jeanette Weinberg Foundation, announced in 1990, with its astounding $900 million—overnight the 12th-largest foundation in the United States. If the Weinberg Foundation trustees target their funds into the city, and if they set up a professional staff that shares a vision of a revived Baltimore, there'd be a stunning opportunity to choke off endemic poverty.

Baltimore and the counties need a forum in which citizens can reach a consensus on public interest—rather than special interest—solutions. And the politicians need assurance that there'll be a constituency supporting them, that they won't be left twisting in the wind when they pick up the citizens' approaches and demonstrate courageous leadership.

A first step, we suggest, would be a one-time Civic Congress, a sort of constitutional convention for the Baltimore region. The delegates would be citizens from each of the five neighboring counties and Baltimore City. A top item ought to be forming a Baltimore Region Civic League. Such a civic league, open to all interested citizens, could form task forces that would focus on regional issues the political system handles poorly—from the environment to education to building regional governmental structures.

Citizen task forces might take on the issue of state and regional parks along the Patapsco and Severn rivers. Or look for ways to make Baltimore's lovely Druid Hill Park a safer place, so that people from across the region will again use the whole park, not just the zoo. Or consider possible expansions of the light-rail line—perhaps a spur into Howard County to the Columbia/Ellicott City area or directly to Baltimore-Washington International Airport.

Most important, citizen leadership is needed to prompt the politicians to rethink and redesign the ways government does things. Even in boom years, demands for services are rising much faster than taxpayers' willingness to pay more. The problem isn't just dividing up the pie differently (the way politicians normally think). It's fundamental redesign so we don't keep packing our jails, warehousing students, or building new roads and firehouses to feed our appetite for sprawl development.

Such metropolises as Minneapolis–St. Paul and Cleveland already provide examples of how a regional citizens organization can produce high-quality proposals on how to make government work. The idea isn't to produce "take it or leave it" policy stands, but rather to engage public officials and the media in ongoing conversation and debate.

Why, if this is such a sensible idea, hasn't it long since been launched? Probably because no group in the region feels it has the necessary "permission" to take the lead.

We suggest that the leadership program graduates would constitute an ideal group of conveners for the Civic Congress. In addition, people active in neighborhood organizations, academics, and heads of area foundations and nonprofit organizations might participate. Perhaps some of the region's most respected citizens might act as civic midwives, urging the leadership alumni to move ahead. Names that spring to mind: James Rouse, developer of Columbia and Harborplace; Otis Warren, a businessman; Martha Smith, president of Dundalk Community College; Sally Michel, the region's quintessential volunteer leader; and the venerable Walter Sondhelm, GBC board member and a key Baltimore leader for years.

Neither government officials nor business will quickly endorse "unprogrammed" convocations of citizens. But the GBC could make a critical difference. By trusting citizen leadership—even leadership with which it might occasionally differ—the GBC could register an act of imaginative statesmanship worthy of its own pioneering history. In the process, it would be demonstrating the visionary leadership Baltimore and the counties today so desperately need.

Growth Crisis: An Opportunity for Choice

As badly as the Baltimore region needs new citizen-based leadership, progress will be tough unless residents are presented with clear-cut alternatives for their future course. There are compelling examples in education, environmental control, public transit, and solid waste management. But let's take a single issue we know concerns the people of the Baltimore region: the way the region is growing.

State legislation to restrain and guide growth is just half the story. The public has to be trusted to think through alternatives. It's time to move past "the age of the experts" who tell everyone what their choices are. There needs to be a clear public debate: What would compact development, with new styles of housing and streets, really be like? Would it be feasible?

Example: More compact towns. Growth management doesn't mean everyone has to move into a high-rise apartment tower. Maryland's Columbia and Virginia's Reston both suggest how a community can achieve a lot of density, but not seem that way. Excellent design can create inviting environments with housing densities dramatically greater than the average subdivision.

Example: Reclaiming sterile malls and parking lots. On Cape Cod, two developers took a 1906 vintage suburban mall and transformed it into a three-block town center complete with streets, sidewalks, and traditional storefronts. The idea is to bulldoze the oceans of parking lots around old malls, create new streets and line them with pleasant buildings, and stack some of the lost parking in garages. Apartments, to add more human activity and physical attractiveness, can be built above the shops. The result: a newly humanized environment, where strolling can be fun.

Alternatively, to get people really close to work, developers could take parking lots around suburban office parks and convert them into attractive, compact housing areas with the parking buried below.

Example: Downsized residential streets. A generation ago engineers convinced planners to put ridiculously wide streets through subdivisions—sometimes up to 45 feet wide, when 22 to 24 feet will do nicely. Narrow the street and you slow down through traffic, create pedestrian-friendly walkways and a more pleasant visual setting for the community. Add a few planters and other deterrents to fast traffic and the street can become a new playground for kids.

Example: Alternatives to zoning. Fort Collins, Colorado, has tossed out traditional zoning. Instead, developers bring their proposals to a planning and zoning board. There's provision for neighborhood hearings, and only disputed cases go to the city council. Developers are in effect challenged to accommodate Fort Collins's goals: developments that include a mix of residential, commercial, and factory space in a square mile or so, so that more people can walk to work.

Example: Retaking the strips. Too many communities are blighted by miles of used-car lots, hamburger stands, and convenience stores. A visual cure is needed. Fort Collins, as well as Park City, Utah, and Scottsdale, Arizona, have learned to make commercial strips attractive. They require miniaturization of the signs—the McDonalds and Burger Kings and Pizza Huts. Then they add landscaping along median strips and insist that owners landscape their parking lots.

Problem: All that takes regulation—and money. How can citizens persuade Baltimore-area governments to take the plunge?

These ideas need a lot more public discussion. Indeed, the lack of full public debate is said to be the reason growth management legislation had trouble in the Maryland General Assembly.

We'd suggest the newspapers team up with local television stations for coverage that illustrates the different growth options the Baltimore region faces. People need to see alternative types of housing and design and how they might affect their lives, and then debate the pros and cons of setting rules and raising money for better public spaces.

Back in the early 1970s newspapers and television stations around New York City tried a fascinating experiment. The television stations aired documentaries on housing, the environment, poverty, and urban growth, each program coordinated with citizen feedback. Eighteen stations actually aired the "town meetings." Some 50 newspapers printed policy option "ballots" for citizens to fill out and mail in.

Similar experiments were later tried, on a smaller scale, in such cities as Chicago, Milwaukee, Roanoke (Virginia), and Hartford (Connecticut). It's one of the most promising ways we've ever seen to bring thousands of citizens into the decision-making process—not as most polls do, by simply reporting citizens' off-hand opinions, but after they've been candidly briefed on the benefits, costs, and trade-offs of each policy option.

Decade of Downtown Breakthroughs

Revive your downtown? Make it a national showplace? If any city ever pulled off the trick, it was Baltimore in the 1980s. If Baltimore City and its surrounding region entertain doubts about their prospects in the 1990s, they ought first to recall the historic investment and breakthroughs of the 1980s. *Almost every year,* there were landmark openings:

1980– Convention Center, Harborplace
1981– National Aquarium at Baltimore, Pier 6 Concert Pavilion
1982– Meyerhoff Concert Hall, Lyric Opera House renovations
1985– Theatre Project renovations, the Power Plant, Harborplace Movie Complex, Festival Hall, Maryland Science Center expansion
1986– Baltimore Arena renovation, Archeology Museum, Rash Field International Garden
1987– IMAX Theater at Science Center, Convention Center expansion, Museum Row
1988– Fishmarket, the Gallery at Harborplace, Harrison's Pier 5, Maryland Art Place

Everyone knows there were some flies in this ointment: the rather spectacular initial failures of the Power Plant and the Fishmarket, for example. But new formulas may still be worked out for each. What's more, the early 1990s promised to bring two spectacular additions: the Orioles' new ballpark at Camden Yards, and the $130-million Christopher Columbus Center of Marine Research and Exploration on the Inner Harbor.

No one, we believe, can doubt the bottom line of these achievements— a downtown Baltimore spectacularly renewed.

New Hope in Old Neighborhoods

The soul of Baltimore is in its neighborhoods. There's Fells Point by the water, where the city began. Tree-shaded Mount Washington. Ashburton, home to many prominent West Baltimore families. Or Highlandtown, a historic and present-day mélange of Germans and Italians, Greeks and Poles and West Virginians, where cobblestoned streets run beside infinities of white marble steps.

It's true, of course, that these neighborhoods have often been fiercely defensive enclaves, rigidly segregated by ethnicity or race. But they have also been cohesive and supportive places, offering a far stronger sense of community than American society typically does today.

The neighborhoods not only defined Baltimore. They helped open the city to successive waves of immigrants. And with their grit and character, they held the town together through good times and bad. It wasn't surprising that when community-based economic development organizations sprang up in U.S. cities in the late 1960s and early 1970s, Baltimore groups won national recognition. From the Southeast Community Organization to the Greater Homewood Corporation to COIL (Communities Organized to Improve Life), many showed remarkable spunk.

Even William Donald Schaefer, the man who'd eventually earn his national reputation remaking the Inner Harbor, began his mayoralty in the early 1970s seeking to restore the city's flagging confidence by rebuilding pride in neighborhoods across the city.

Sadly, the Schaefer embrace turned out to be an oppressive bear hug for a number of community organizations. As his mayoralty flourished, and surely with an eye to keeping as many influential people as he could in his own happy political family, Schaefer started putting neighborhood activists onto city payrolls. Many of the city's once-vaunted neighborhood organizations became co-opted, losing their spirit and ability to carry off entrepreneurial projects.

Today Baltimore neighborhood organizations almost never crop up in lists of the country's most active. Nor does Baltimore have strong networks of community development organizations comparable to those in such cities as Boston, Cleveland, and Chicago.

There's one notable exception. It is BUILD—Baltimoreans United in Leadership Development, a church-based group, part of the Saul Alinsky-inspired set of Industrial Areas Foundations across America. BUILD has taken the heritage of the late radical organizer Saul Alinsky and forged novel alliances. First it worked with the Greater Baltimore Committee to create a "Commonwealth Agreement." The goal: dramatic improvement in performance in the public schools. BUILD in 1989 also launched a massive "Nehemiah" development of 300 new housing units in the Sandtown-Winchester neighborhood.

Yet, while he was mayor, Schaefer found BUILD so independent that he'd have nothing to do with it. His difficulty in accepting and working with strong neighborhood organizations is a striking irony because Schaefer would top anyone's short list of American mayors who grew up in humble neighborhoods, never moved away, and for years seemed obsessed with neighborhood welfare.

We found it easy to get Schaefer to talk about the 600 block of Edgewood Street.

"I was on my block when I was the only person with an automobile," he told us. "I was there when low-income people moved in and there was broken glass all over. But then people started to take pride in it again. Now the house across from me is as pretty as any house in Roland Park. There are still some houses where nobody seems to care. Just rent them out. The neighbor on my right—he's dead now—worked himself until he died of exhaustion putting his kids through college. I saw another neighbor sweep the gutter every darn day of his life. Across the street was a prostitute. Drug addicts and murders. My street's where I learned about teenage pregnancy, saw 14-year-olds having babies and treating them like rag dolls. I've seen kids dumped out of the house at 7 a.m. and let back in at night. I saw chickens dumped out of second-story windows. I didn't read about urban life. I lived it."

The several dozen Baltimore region leaders we met were as quick to talk about the city's neighborhoods and speculate about their future as the former mayor was to reminisce about his own home street. And a clear difference of attitude struck us. On schools, Baltimore City's other compelling problem of the 1990s, virtually no one was optimistic. Instead we heard despair, sometimes disgust, never hope. Yet when talk turned to neighborhoods, and even if the diagnosis was just as serious, people started talking about the cure as if it could happen.

Why? A consensus, however fragile, has formed around a common-sense strategy to help the city's most troubled neighborhoods. Mayor Schmoke, BUILD, and James Rouse's Enterprise Foundation agree on the plan. The idea is to reach, in a very personal way, the neighborhood people who need help the most. Examples might include a mother and her two children who lose their apartment in a fire, a young woman who is routinely beaten by her boyfriend, a teenage dropout who knows there's no future in drugs but still sells crack because he likes the cash, or a young girl who sees no road to self-esteem other than an early demonstration of her fertility.

The consensus says that however daunting the obstacles, these imperiled lives and families must be saved. And second, that the problems, from poor housing to drug affliction to poor schooling, are interconnected. Third, that standard social service referrals won't do the trick, that only personal contact is likely to break through. And finally, that one needs a mediating institution—a church, social club, community center—to make the contact and then, through good days and bad, keep it up.

Eventually, it's suggested, community residents must figure out that they—not outside "providers"—have to look out for the people on their block, set the rules and standard for their neighborhood.

Baltimore's most concrete experiment along these lines is taking shape in the Sandtown-Winchester neighborhood in West Baltimore, a 20-block area that's home to 12,500 of the city's poorest residents. Much of the impetus for the Sandtown experiment came from James Rouse, the famed Marylander who pioneered the Harborplace development that made the Inner Harbor succeed spectacularly, and who later created the Enterprise Foundation, working across the United States to create new housing in America's poorest inner-city communities. BUILD added a strong grassroots element, cooperating with Rouse in the Nehemiah housing project in Sandtown. Kurt Schmoke became the first mayor in the United States to commit his city so wholeheartedly to a neighborhood self-help model. And he pledged to give Sandtown residents a major say in how their local school is run, as part of an experiment in school-based management.

A critical part of the Sandtown effort was a resident-controlled task force charged to write what amounts to a neighborhood charter, indicating how the community wants to be organized on issues ranging from health care to employment, schools to substance abuse. The examples of what might be achieved are pretty exciting: local schools managed by the principal, teachers, and parents—not a central school bureaucracy; tenant management teams to run public housing projects and develop citizenship centers; "enrichment centers" to provide job training that might lead to middle-class futures.

This grand plan shouldn't require a lot more money than what now flows into Sandtown for government functions ranging from welfare to Medicaid to food stamps. The problem is that the money often flows into the pockets of outside providers—middle-class social service agencies that all too easily, to local residents, resemble an occupying army.

But while the Sandtown-Winchester experiment might serve as a national model for more efficient use of public dollars in a poverty-plagued neighborhood, it remained very much an experiment, depending, for example, on a mayor's office hardly known for crisp efficiency.

Police on the Beat: A Way to Strengthen Communities

Using talent and resources they already have, Baltimore City and the counties could vastly improve their police services and create safer communities. The highly promising formula is called community-oriented policing.

It's as traditional as the old "cop on the beat." Officers get long-term assignments in single neighborhoods. They're expected to be out on the street, get to know residents and business people and analyze local problems, ranging from trash-strewn lots to rowdy taverns to drug markets, and then to work cooperatively with citizens to solve them. Especially in poor and disorganized neighborhoods, police officers become, in effect, community organizers.

Why return, just before we plunge into the high-tech 21st century, to the cop on the beat?

Because we've hit the limits of what the 911 emergency call system can ever achieve. Especially in high-crime areas, rapid emergency response is seriously deficient. When a call comes in, officers go roaring off, sirens wailing and lights flashing, to deal with disturbances in communities where they don't know the residents. After a few minutes they roar off again, perhaps with a suspect, more often not having addressed any of the root problems that led to the disturbance or crime.

The Baltimore region is lucky: one of its leading public safety officials, Baltimore County Police Chief Cornelius J. Behan, is recognized nationally as an expert on community policing. He has sought to implement it with a 45-person COPE (Community Oriented Police Enforcement) unit.

The COPE officers in Baltimore County focus first on reducing residents' fear, analyzing what causes crime, and then trying to do something about it. Example: in the Garden Village area, close to the Baltimore city line, antagonism between residents and police was chronic. In the early 1980s, unruly teenagers terrorized the neighborhood. Burglaries and drug abuse became common; a stabbing and shooting occurred. Police responded to 911 calls. They made a few arrests. But the gangs continued to hold sway over the neighborhood.

Two COPE officers then were sent in. They started talking to Garden Village residents. They analyzed crime statistics, photographed the area's dismal deterioration. They zeroed in on ringleaders in the crime spree. Arrests followed.

But the COPE unit went further. It persuaded the county highway department to pave the alleyways, the utility company to repair streetlights. The officers got the county recreation department to turn a rubble-strewn park into four basketball courts. End result: a neighborhood with sharply reduced crime, kids playing basketball, fear radically diminished.

Not all the improvements have held; the underlying reasons for instability in such neighborhoods as Garden Village remain. COPE units have to be redispatched from time to time. The Baltimore County police haven't felt they could maintain full-time community policing anywhere.

Could the money be found anywhere, in tight budget times, to spread community-based policing and then keep it in place? The answer is yes, if the police could curtail their responses to 911 calls.

And why not? A huge portion of 911 calls are for service, not crime. The answer is to retain "rapid response" capability for the 10 to 15 percent of calls that involve life-threatening situations or that might result in the arrest of a felon. But in less pressing cases, it makes sense to train 911 operators to delay response until less busy hours.

Community policing has lots working against it. Detractors can belittle it as social work inappropriate in times of soaring homicide and robbery rates. But society's need has changed. Huge numbers of people feel isolated. Many poor neighborhoods are hostile milieus of violence.

Community-oriented policing addresses these realities with a personalized law enforcement presence. It raises a new potential for crime prevention. The prospective long-term savings—cleaner neighborhoods, fewer crimes, less clogged courts, fewer overcrowded prisons—are stunning.

Community policing isn't a cure-all. Introduced in Baltimore City, it wouldn't correct the problem of hundreds of serious offenders—even in homicide cases—being released and out on the streets again.

But a community-policing orientation could attack another serious shortcoming of Baltimore's police—heavy centralization at headquarters. Since the early 1980s, the department has lost about 400 investigative and patrol officers, even while the headquarters' staff has enlarged. Detectives are no longer assigned to precincts; they're assigned cases almost randomly and have no chance to learn the people and dynamics of individual neighborhoods.

Maybe it's time to get the Baltimore force back out on the streets, in the neighborhoods, where it belongs.

The Imperative for School Change

There was sadness but not surprise in Baltimore recently when Maryland issued its school "report card," showing Baltimore City schools failing in all of the state's eight critical measures, from reading and math achievement to writing to dropout rates.

The counties surrounding Baltimore weren't perfect either. Howard County failed to equal the state standard in one area, Harford and Baltimore County schools in four, Anne Arundel in six. Even when the counties lagged, however, they weren't far off the state-set measures for "satisfactory" performance.

Baltimore City, by contrast, scored abysmally, far behind the state standard on almost every count. The report card seemed to substantiate what leaders already think of the city's schools. Here are some of the comments about the city schools we heard in our interviews with leaders from Baltimore businesses and civic groups:

"This school system is dead, but no one has buried it. There's no spirit in the organization."

"Of the 108,000 kids in the system, only 30,000 or so get a decent education."

"For several generations, the Baltimore school system was a wonderful enabling institution. But it's lost its way. Maybe we should declare Chapter 11. Frame it as a civil rights issue for the kids. It'd be easier to start over."

"There's a powerful school reform movement blowing through this country. But the educators are the last to realize it."

"The central administration here? It ought to be blown up. They're a bunch of dispirited people who come in late and make up for it by leaving early—and for that we're lucky."

"The school board hasn't been much of a player. The mayor appoints them and tells them who to make superintendent. Of course, it would be a step forward if you abolished it."

"The city schools are a disaster, but the Baltimore County schools aren't so terrific either."

In contrast to all of that, one high official of the system offered a shred of hope—tied to two critical "ifs."

"If we only had the money to run a decent system," he said, and "if we only had the guts to replace bad school people with good, then we could be damned close to being the best urban school system in the country."

Those challenges to an institution absolutely critical to Baltimore's future set us to thinking: What single step would telegraph the message that change *must* come, that there *is* a day of reckoning for schools that fail in their mission?

We concluded that Baltimore may be ripe for competition in education, that this community had to imagine what *might* be.

Imagine a group of teachers eager to get to work every morning, and a principal eager to see them because he chose them and enjoys working with them. Imagine students showing up enthusiastically because it's the school that they and their parents chose—not one that some distant bureaucrat assigned. Imagine an elementary school in which the lights of curiosity don't flicker out in kids' eyes by the fifth grade, a school whose teachers believe passionately that even children from the most disadvantaged families can learn. Imagine a group of new, smaller high schools in which every teacher knows every student. Perhaps one high school devoted to the new career front of biotechnology or communications. Or a school that prizes a traditional curriculum of Latin, English, literature. Or a school devoted to exploring African-American culture and producing the most talented young black leaders it can.

We believe those kinds of schools should be imagined—in Baltimore.

We propose giving permission to any qualified group—teachers, administrators, a university or social service or neighborhood organization— to form a public charter school.

Nearly everyone's heard of so-called voucher plans, allowing students to attend any school—public, private, religious—that their parents may choose. A public charter school would be similar. But public charter schools would have some special rules.

Religious training would be out.

Discrimination would be illegal. Schools could not screen for race or ethnic background.

"Creaming" would be forbidden. Charter schools would have to accept children first come, first served, without regard to their academic records. (In case of a surplus of applications, selection would be by lottery.)

Elitism based on wealth would be out, too—charter schools would not be able to charge tuition. Baltimore and its surrounding counties already offer lots of ways for people affluent or mobile enough to find the school they'd like best. With enough money, the choice is all yours. The public charter school is designed to bring choice and quality to students where they live—even students from the poorest families.

Instead of tuition, charter schools would operate with 100 percent public funding. We suggest they be financed by the state government and permitted in Baltimore or any county of the state. For each child they enroll, the charter schools should be paid the average total cost of educating a public school child in Maryland. The state and district of residence ought to share the cost.

To teach at a charter public school, teachers would have to be already certified in Maryland. Or a teacher would have to hold a bachelor's degree and successfully complete an intensive, three-month teacher training course.

Teachers now working in the public school system should be allowed leaves of absence, retaining all their health and retirement benefits, for a limited number of years. Why? Because there are hundreds of able people in the deeply troubled public school system. Charter schools would provide a once-in-a-lifetime opportunity for them.

If Baltimoreans would like a model for charter schools, a rather good one is already here: the Baltimore School for the Arts. Though it's officially under the school bureaucracy, it doesn't operate that way. The principal can hire and fire teachers as he deems best. Part-time teachers can be brought on board. The school is a place of warmth and color, perhaps the best integrated in the area. Not surprisingly, its motivated students do well in school and afterward.

Admittedly, the Baltimore School of the Arts has admissions discretion. But even schools open to all comers, problem children included, should be able to create positive learning environments.

Public charter schools should be free of the mountain of pedagogical micromanagement that's usually imposed on public schools. They should be able to function independently of the city school bureaucracy to assure public confidence and to prevent sabotage from the 600-person administrative staff on North Avenue.

Charter schools should be certified by an independent chartering board operated by the state. That board would assure that all charter schools report regularly on their enrollment and finances. Most important, it would assure that the schools test children on a schedule similar to that for the state's regular public schools. Nobody would tell charter schools *how* to get their results. But the state-ordered testing would *measure* their results—the achievement of their students. The test results would be public knowledge. If a charter school didn't show achievement, it couldn't expect to survive. Fail to offer a truly excellent, competitive school, and in time the student base would drift away.

Small schools should be encouraged, though not always required.

Why? So that students and staff can get to know each other; to tighten the bonds between teachers and students; to develop a sense of community.

Of course, an effort to win approval of charter schools would be a tough political battle. It's safe to predict monumental resistance from defenders of the educational status quo.

Would the struggle be worth it? We think so. We encountered, in our interviews, the avalanche of bitter complaint and damning criticism of Baltimore's school system cited above. A good part, but not all, of the complaint centered on the school system's central bureaucracy.

We believe it's worth remembering that Baltimore children lag a year and a half or more behind the rest of Maryland's youngsters. Their absentee rates are double the statewide average. Half drop out before graduation.

When public confidence in a public institution sinks so low, incremental reforms and improvements just won't do. Promises of improvements by political leaders won't do. A new school superintendent won't suffice. Basic structural change becomes imperative.

The first and predictable argument against charter schools will likely be that they'll be fine for smart kids from aware families, but that the less motivated, poorer, uninformed kids will be mired in the worst schools.

No! That criticism describes the situation we have today. Poor kids are already congregated in terribly deficient schools—schools so bad the children could hardly do any worse. We view it as intolerably patronizing to claim (as some educators do) that inner-city parents are so ill educated, so callous, that they don't care about their children, and that given the opportunity to switch their child to a new charter school, they wouldn't jump at the opportunity.

The market opportunities for charter schools would likely be the most compelling in depressed neighborhoods. That's where we see them first springing up. By contrast, where the public schools are of high quality, charter schools will be of less immediate appeal.

There are lots of questions about how to set up charter schools. What's critical are the underlying premises—the introduction of competition, terminating school boards' monopoly on starting schools, letting teachers teach in the kinds of schools they've always dreamed of, and giving poor kids and their families a chance to opt, for a change, for schools of caring and quality.

The existing Baltimore public schools, we discovered, do have some defenders. They acknowledge the schools' problems are severe, but then they offer up a whole range of explanations.

The first relates to money. Baltimore is a poor city, with half the tax base, per child, that the surrounding counties enjoy. The city is home to nearly half the disadvantaged children in the entire state.

When J. Edward Andrews came from nearby Montgomery County to become Baltimore's deputy superintendent, he decided to do something dramatic to illustrate how the city kids get shortchanged. He persuaded a bank to lend him $40,000 for a few hours. Then he went to a state hearing and threw the money on the table to show how much more, per classroom, other Maryland districts have and Baltimore doesn't, to run its schools.

The state of Maryland appears guilty of serious negligence in regard to Baltimore's schools. Legislators from such areas as Montgomery County, despite years of support for equalization formulas to help the city, claim their own taxpayers are so hard-pressed in hard economic times that more aid is out of the question.

We heard the arguments—that more money channeled to the Baltimore schools simply hasn't produced results, that the city gets lots of special state aid for every need from police to the Peabody Conservatory to the new baseball stadium. That still doesn't explain how Baltimore schools, even if they were brilliantly run, could produce the same results as affluent county school systems that have an extra $1,000 or more to spend on each child each year.

The money is, in fact, there to be had. Maryland is a wealthy state, 7th among the 50 states in per capita income. But it ranks an appallingly low 43rd on spending for schools related to personal income. Critics of higher spending for the city schools are on somewhat firmer ground when they ask whether extra school subsidies wouldn't simply be soaked up by Baltimore's school bureaucracy, resulting in little, if any, gain at the classroom level.

And what's the point, it's fair to ask, of pumping more money into classrooms where student peer pressure telegraphs the insane message that it's stupid to study too hard? Not far from Baltimore, there's the unhappy example of the District of Columbia public schools, which fail thousands of hard-to-teach children each year despite far more generous funding. No one we talked to, in fact, believed extra money should flow to Baltimore's schools without some dramatic quid pro quos designed to effect fundamental reform in the system.

There's a related excuse for the Baltimore schools' subpar performance. Call it the social overburden argument—the case that no school officials and teachers, however brilliant, can educate well in a culture where teenage pregnancies, poverty, and crime abound.

Said one administrator: "Kids run the streets. They come to school and only know the nickname people call them. It's terrible what these little children have to deal with. Kids talk in show-and-tell about seeing some kid get shot down in the street."

A Johns Hopkins University program to help students at Dunbar High prepare for health careers and get into college worked well—but only for girls. Few boys even make it to Dunbar; most have already dropped out.

Yet there are individual schools, scattered from inner-city New York to Chicago to Los Angeles, in which skilled principals and dedicated teaching staffs have found ways to fend off the downtown bureaucracies, establish order and stability, and give children a sense of excitement about learning. The evidence shows that creative teachers can succeed.

Nationally, there's growing impatience with the educators' social environment excuse. And in Baltimore, too. As one parent told us: "I know, dear teacher, the school is overcrowded; you have a tough job. But please, if you could find time to teach my kid to read, I'd appreciate it."

Over the years, reform experiments in Baltimore have been kicked off with great fanfare but then have been snuffed out by the school board or the central bureaucracy on the grounds there wasn't enough money in the system.

Mayor Schmoke appears to care deeply about Baltimore's system of public education, about school-based management and holding principals accountable. Those concerns led him, after much agonizing, to dismiss School Superintendent Richard C. Hunter, who clearly wasn't in sympathy. But we determined that fundamental school reform would depend on extraordinarily focused, tenacious, even ferocious Schmoke leadership. That could well mean, on occasion, offending the black adults who work in the public schools in favor of the black schoolchildren whose lives today hang in the balance because of the system's incompetence and indifference.

One test will be the school-based management pilot program begun in 1990. Starting in 15 schools, the program calls for basic management decisions to be turned over to the principals, teachers, and parents. Decisions on staff assignments and curriculum, for example, are to be made at the individual school sites with minimal interference from the central bureaucracy. It helped that the Baltimore Teachers Union supported the pilot project. The Baltimore business community, too, appeared hopeful and anxious to help. Yet we noticed that Mayor Schmoke's own appointed school board dragged its feet, and, given its druthers, wouldn't have approved the plan at all. The core problem is that support for school-based management is an institutionally unnatural act for the school sytems's central bureaucracy. Taken seriously, the very idea imperils North Avenue's reason for existing.

Color Line: Realities and Myths

Burned deep into the American consciousness, race remains a Baltimore obsession—aggravated by the divisions of a border state, rooted in a half-truth. The half-truth is that Baltimore is so black, the counties so white, that nothing else is much worth discussing.

Like any half-truth, some measure of fact lies behind it. Baltimore City is a lot blacker than any of the counties. The counties, in turn, are much whiter. Within Baltimore, there are neighborhoods where blackness, poverty, social ills, and high crime intertwine. Out in the counties, one stumbles on glades of white suburban affluence.

Some of the regional leaders we talked with danced around the race issue; a few could talk about little else. But whether they addressed it outright or not, we could see them thinking race-race-race as they touched on any topic from new subway lines to schools to who gets to work for mayors and county executives.

To hear some Baltimoreans talk, race is the catchall that explains everything—financial assistance for the city, for example, or city schools' problems with drugs and violence. Race is seen behind splintered families, teenage pregnancy, the middle-class fight from Baltimore.

But a half-truth is not the real truth, and it's dangerous to let it masquerade unchallenged. For one thing, what looks white is getting blacker, and what looks black is whiter than people think. The city may be 60 percent black, but it's also 40 percent white. As for the counties, they're fast losing their lily-whiteness.

Baltimore County's black community has grown from 3 percent of the total population in 1970 to more than 12 percent today. The Howard County black population was 8 percent; now it is almost 12 percent. Blacks in the counties are pocketed in a few places, but they are integrated in many more. Many hold important business or government or academic posts. Many earn excellent incomes. In one recent year, blacks in Howard County had higher average incomes than whites.

Anyone who sees only white when looking at the suburbs is colorblind. Blacks work for the Social Security Administration in Woodlawn, for state agencies in Jessup, in Fort Meade or Aberdeen, and at the new shopping malls in Owings Mills, Columbia, White Marsh, and Marley Station.

A second half-truth is that blacks lack strong institutions, that the Baltimore regional culture's only strengths are formed in the dominant, white-oriented, European-rooted community.

In fact, Baltimore and the counties have a rich panoply of black-led organizations. In higher education there's Morgan State University, Coppin State College, and Sojourner-Douglass College. Black-oriented bookstores, museums, theater companies, and choirs enrich the region's culture. On the civic scene one finds the Black Community Council of 100, a vibrant Urban League chapter, business and professional organizations for black accountants, nurses, government workers, and engineers. The national headquarters of the National Association for the Advancement of Colored People is in town.

The perception that blackness equals poverty, or whiteness affluence, is simply false. It's true that many middle-class blacks have left for the suburbs, leaving their old neighborhoods worse off. The migration has weakened the corner store, black newspapers, black inner-city churches. Sometimes one of the few vestiges of black middle-class life in urban neighborhoods is in "gathered churches," where former residents appear for worship but play little role in community life.

But notice: white flight has done the same thing to white inner-city neighborhoods. They've lost many of their role models, too. For proof, check out the struggle for survival going on among whites in such working-class neighborhoods as Hampden, Highlandtown, or South Baltimore, or even in the far reaches of affluent Howard County. Making poverty seem all black makes poor whites invisible. But they're there. There have been reports of growing homelessness in Harford County, which is overwhelmingly white.

Equating blackness with crime is another insidious half-truth. Popular image makes inner-city Baltimore into some kind of combat zone, a kind of Beirut by the Bay. Whites conjure up images of falling victim to muggings and rapes by roving bands of black youths.

Reality says it's not exactly that way. There is gruesome crime in the city. But blacks—not whites—are overwhelmingly the victims. Blacks are two to three times as likely to be crime victims as whites. Stolen purses, women assaulted, stores robbed at gunpoint—the odds are that blacks will be the victims.

Whites seem to believe they have a monopoly on fear. They should talk with more blacks, learn of the vivid, poignant fear of crime that many black families must live with practically every day of their lives.

What does it take to right half-truths, to let Baltimoreans shake the shibboleths and get on with the tough tasks the region faces? Recognizing a generation of top-notch black leaders should help. C. Vernon Gray, the only black on the Howard County Council, is its chairman. William Jews, chief executive officer of Health Dimensions, is a leader in his field. Freeman Hrabowski, executive vice president at the University of Maryland at Baltimore County, and Jerome Paige, associate provost at the University of Baltimore, are in high leadership posts in predominantly white university settings. Mayor Kurt Schmoke sets a standard of intelligence in high office.

Race differences run, of course, deep in our society. None of us can expect the tensions between Eurocentric and Afrocentric attitudes to disappear—now or perhaps ever.

That doesn't mean the region's leaders—black and white alike—can't address a shared agenda of initiatives to improve everyone's security, economic prospects, and quality of life. The items on the agenda can range from schools to community policing, growth management to metropolitan governance.

But should we have to select one goal above all others, it would be mutual respect.

Update

The Baltimore report—officially entitled "Baltimore and Beyond" by the Baltimore *Sun*—initially played to quite mixed reviews, with special reserve expressed by city political players close to Mayor Kurt Schmoke. They faulted the report for its negative portrayal of some conditions in this city. But Schmoke, Baltimore's first elected black mayor, was publicly warmer to some of the report's recommendations—especially community policing and looking for new ways to strike deals with the suburban counties—following his easy reelection victory in November 1991.

Suburban county executives and council members generally welcomed the report, agreeing that the city and the surrounding counties did indeed need to strike up some form of mutually beneficial deal. Other major players, such as the Greater Baltimore Committee, the editorial staff of *The*

Sun, and the Chesapeake Bay Foundation, thought that the report corroborated their views of the need for city-suburban cooperation, for regional economic development combined with regional growth management.

The Baltimore Regional Council of Governments, referred to several times in the report, was subsequently dismantled as a state agency and replaced with a Baltimore Metropolitan Council, a nonprofit organization operated by the mayor of Baltimore and executives of the surrounding counties. Though significantly restructured and downsized from its predecessor, the new council retained critical responsibilities for transportation, the federal Clean Air Act Amendments, and regional data collection and management. The shift to the new form followed an evaluation of the old regional council, performed for the Maryland Office of Planning by the William Donald Schaefer Center at the University of Baltimore under the direction of Lenneal Henderson. Henderson, a senior fellow of the center, had been a member of the "Baltimore and Beyond" interviewing team.

Almost two years after the report's publication, no action had yet occurred to fulfill its central recommendation—that some form of major accord, a pact for mutual assistance, be struck between Baltimore City and the suburban counties. Even if there had been political will, the extreme fiscal difficulties that Maryland experienced in the two years following the report's publication would have darkened the outlook for major change.

Maryland also failed, by 1993, to take any action on the growth management legislation that was recommended in the report as an urgent need for the Baltimore region.

Intense interest was privately expressed, however, among some major political leaders of the region, as well as regional foundations, in organizing the type of regionwide citizens' organization recommended in the report. By early 1993, however, no official announcement had been made.

Preparatory work on some of the major social initiatives described in the report, such as the partnership for the revival of the Sandtown-Winchester neighborhood, moved forward.

No move to establish public charter schools in Baltimore, as the report had proposed, took place. But a private corporation won a five-year contract from the Baltimore Public Schools to manage eight elementary and one middle school, starting in autumn 1992. Additionally, four elementary and ten middle schools that the city had allowed to experiment with site-based management were named "Challenge Schools" and seemed likely to receive state support of up to $500,000 under the Maryland School Performance Program.

On the community policing front, Mayor Schmoke hired a special consultant and was engaged, by late 1992, in discussions with officials of both Baltimore and Anne Arundel counties on joint programs targeted on "common problem areas" along their borders with the city.

The Citistate in Brief

Owensboro, with a 1990 population of 53,549, is Kentucky's third-largest city, located 100 miles south of Louisville on the Ohio River. It is the capital seat of Daviess County, which had a population of 87,189 in 1990, up 1.4 percent in a decade. The county covers 463 square miles in the western Kentucky coal field region. Except for Owensboro, the county has only one other incorporated town—Whitesville. There are separate city and county school districts, and six special districts.

The Peirce Report Glossary

Fiscal Court is the name assigned to the county government (a throwback to early days when territorial moneys flowed through it). *Griffith Avenue* is a major Owensboro residential street, known for its lovely dogwoods in the spring, a route on which many prominent citizens built their homes. One such citizen, shopping mall magnate David Hocker, has such a massive Griffith Avenue home that the text makes jocular reference to it as the *"House of Hocker."* *Stone Creek* is an area where homes are more properly identified as estates. *Thorobred Acres* is a typical middle-class housing development filled with a labyrinth of residential streets rather than anything like the straight-away racetrack its name suggests.

The *West End* historically housed Owensboro blacks, as well as a spare scattering of poor whites. The *East End* tended to be dominated by poor whites. *Smothers Park,* on the waterfront, has fountains, flags, and boat launching ramps. *English Park,* also on the waterfront, has an outdoor amphitheater capable of seating 10,000 to 15,000 people for music festivals and other activities. *Downtown Owensboro Inc.* promotes the downtown's business and commercial life. The *Campbell Club* is Owensboro's "establishment" social club. The *Owensboro Career Development Association* seeks to help young blacks, mainly in grades four to eight, raise their sights academically so that more will become interested in going to college and into business and professional lives.

OWENSBORO

Reforging Community

(Originally published in the Owensboro Messenger-Inquirer *on September 29–October 3, 1991.)*

On a perfect spring day, the little Cessna lifts off from Owensboro–Daviess County Regional Airport, quickly revealing to us three worlds: western Kentucky's fertile fields, the city of Owensboro, and that mighty lifeline and geologic creator, the Ohio River. We had come for several days of interviewing, to meet and talk with a broad cross section of the leaders, exalted and humble, of Owensboro and Daviess County. But first, to our delight, we were able to get this bird's-eye view of the Owensboro region.

In a broad semicircle, we flew west over the Audubon Parkway, sighted Alcoa's red and white smokestacks across the river, identified the future Scott Paper Company site.

Then our pilot picked up the tree-lined, meandering Green River, took us in a wide arc over McLean, Muhlenberg, Ohio, and Hancock counties, and finally, from a spot near the Cannelton locks, picked up the Ohio and flew us downriver to Owensboro again.

A thousand feet above the earth, an hour in a small plane, watching meadow and water, town and mine site, factory and forest and field roll out below you, makes it clear why so many people love this part of Kentucky—and why some worry, too, about its environmental future.

It was May, and the fields were being prepared for another season of corn and soybeans, wheat and tobacco. Tractors furrowed many fields, tiny clouds of dust rising in their wake.

On some pastures, planted even earlier, the tender and luminescent greens of first growth soothed the eye. And here and there, great splashes of

159

yellow sprang to view: canola, considered the new "health plant" because it has the right chemistry for more health-conscious diets—more monosaturated, less polysaturated fats.

Occasionally the air tour produces extraordinary surprises. Right in the midst of grassy farm country, for example, is Delbert Glenn's huge Diamond Lakes spread—breeding lakes for fish, laid out with geometric precision, together with a restaurant, country music theater, and campgrounds, miles from any settlement.

Over Muhlenberg and Ohio counties, the countryside gets a lot hillier, and suddenly more and more chunks of territory have been laid bare for strip mining. The vast gashes upon the earth, monstrous earth-moving machines astride them, are a visual shock. Far pleasanter to the eye are some of the green, recovered mine strips. Saddest of all are the "orphan mines" stripped before the reclamation laws came in.

Mighty industry greets us along the waterways, a muscular, raw presence, whether for power or aluminum or paper or brick, a reminder that this region's economy depends as much on making things as growing them. Companions to the gritty factories are the great barges moving up and down the Ohio—common-sense, cheap transport that holds on tenaciously in the age of the monster truck and interstate America.

As Owensboro looms into view again, multiple images rush before us: the lacy blue steel of the bridge spanning the river from Indiana, the town's orderly grid, church spires and the two hospitals, the massive Executive Inn Rivermont at the water's side, the great white silos of Owensboro Grain. White homes, modest and expansive alike, line many streets. There's Griffith Avenue, springtime's Dogwood and Azalea Trail, one corner anchored by the multiwinged House of Hocker.

Yet for all the beauty trees give to Owensboro, they don't shade the blotches of multiple downtown blocks that have lost their historic structures and now stand vacant for parking. On the periphery, asphalt seas surround the shopping centers. Owensboro has become car country and has paid a price for it.

But not everyone is encapsulated in two tons of steel. Kids are playing baseball on a green diamond. And down near the river, crews are getting ready for the yearly International Barbecue Festival. Some 50,000 people will pack the scene. We hear they'll consume beef and pork by the carload and 20 tons of mutton. Wow!

Central Challenges

If the community that consists of Owensboro and surrounding Daviess County is going to make itself a more desirable place to live and "hack it" in the harshly competitive economic world of the 1990s, it will have to face up to a challenging set of shifts—some psychic, some civic, some economic and social.

A new, broader concept of regional citizenship will have to be nurtured. Ugly and counterproductive city-rural antagonisms will have to be alleviated. Power sharing will have to be opened up. A dramatically enlarged role for women in local leadership must be created. The *Messenger-Inquirer*—and its critics—will have to reach some understandings.

On the economic front, the focus of job development will have to switch from fishing expeditions for the increasingly rare big catch to something closer to aquaculture—nourishing smaller, more numerous, homegrown fish. The environment will have to rise higher on peoples' lists of concerns. We will propose a "safe growth committee" to evaluate industrial deals on economic and environmental grounds. We'll suggest a stronger focus on agriculture as a base for economic growth. Owensboro must pledge itself to an intensive campaign to re-create a downtown with character and attractiveness, a true meeting place for the region's people and visitors from afar. Developing a fully accessible, lively waterfront must be a top priority.

On the social front, Owensboro–Daviess County can strengthen itself by reaching out more aggressively to support and "deal in" sometimes estranged communities, from the children and parents of troubled families to senior citizens to the area's small but significant African-American community. Finally, we'll suggest it's time to create a strong community foundation to support the multiple civic adventures of the coming years— first because "risk capital" is critical to community progress, second because strong corporate supporters (Texas Gas, for example) could be buffeted in an increasingly tumultuous international economy.

The reader may detect an undercurrent of sharp criticism as we make some points. We acknowledge that. On the other hand, there are a lot of things about Owensboro–Daviess County that strike a visitor very positively. Chief among these is the community's capacity to turn goals into reality. In the mid-1980s the Citizens Committee on Education sparked the creation of Owensboro Community College, opening opportunities for the region's residents to gain sophisticated new workplace skills. The creation wasn't easy. There were fears of negative impact on Brescia College and Kentucky Wesleyan; community leaders disagreed about the location; big state dollars had to be collared.

But the competing visions were resolved; a new institution was born; a handsome campus took shape. And college participation by Daviess County's young people has soared from 45 percent to 61 percent.

RiverPark Center, when it opens in 1992, won't merely be home to Owensboro's symphony, theater, dance group, and a new bluegrass museum. Nor will the 1,500-seat auditorium and 300-seat theater just be spaces for use. What the center will represent is the caring and commitment of Owensboro people to the distinctive shared culture of their community— Bach to Balanchine to bluegrass. The $9-million fund-raising effort to make it happen is simply extraordinary for a city of Owensboro's size. If Mayor David Adkisson thinks of the downtown riverfront district as the community's living room, then RiverPark Center's three-story atrium overlooking the Ohio River will indeed represent its picture window.

Of course, visitors have to be impressed by the immense outpouring of public support that complemented the industrial recruiters' work in landing the Scott Paper Company plant last year. The "We" in the newspaper's jubilant banner headline—"We Got Scott"—referred clearly to the whole community.

Could this be the same community that managed, in 1990, to rip itself apart on a city-county merger issue, revealing rather scary urban-rural animosities, a yawning gulf between political elites and regular folks?

As we listened to leaders from across the city and county—bankers and farmers, entertainment moguls and neighborhood activists, industrialists and environmentalists—a string of remarkable contrasts sprang into focus.

Take the familiar Owensboro–Daviess County lament about isolation: "The interstates don't come here. Our only bridge is on its last legs. The big planes don't fly in here any more. It takes hours to get to a big city. We're cut off. We need better and bigger roads and bridges."

The visitor hears a lot of those sentiments, and they sound like complaints. Yet in the next breath, the very same people will turn the tables and tell an astoundingly different-sounding story: "This is a safe community. We don't have to lock our doors. This is a family-oriented town, a churchgoing town. It's a terrific place to raise kids. There are no porn shops. No places to buy adult videos. No dangerous street types here. This is the way we want it."

Not everybody agrees; some (especially young singles) complain the community is too safe. They say there's not enough street life, diversity, excitement. Like all humans, Owensboro people may want the impossible—the advantages of quick connections with the world, but without the social consequences that come swirling in its wake.

Here's a town where one hears a lot of expressions of fierce independence—a community that many residents claim is the best place to live in North America. Back in the 1920s, when industrial might was prized above all else, Owensboro called itself "the Chicago of the South." Today its "Rooster Booster" events draw up to a thousand people for monthly breakfasts. Another side of the community is deeply suspicious of new ideas. Back in 1963, Owensboro voted not to accept federal money for urban renewal projects.

"'There's a sense around here that right or wrong isn't relevant, it's how we do it,'" one civic leader told us. "Owensboro," he continued, "is a very comfortable place to be, especially if you can ease into the feeling of the place, if you can accept what most of the people accept."

A veteran journalist in town reminded us that the statue on the Courthouse lawn memorializes a Civil War soldier who wore a gray, not a blue, uniform. Owensboro–Daviess County and its surrounding territory, he said, were Confederate then and remain basically conservative today.

From a leading entrepreneur in town we heard: "People around here get worked up over anything that's changing, and they get mad at the people who cause it." But all's not hopeless, he added. "Later on, they're proud of the result."

Owensboro–Daviess County's fundamental challenge, as we sensed it, is to meld its skepticism, its reluctance to change, with recognition that no city, anywhere in America, is going to be safe against buffeting economic and social change in the years ahead. Since the Scott announcement, the Owensboro–Daviess County area has lost more jobs in the aluminum industry alone than all the jobs that the Scott plant promises to bring.

The community college was a great accomplishment for the 1980s. But the acid test will be whether it can prepare constantly increasing numbers of people from the Owensboro–Daviess County region, the underprivileged as well as the affluent and senior-college bound, the rural as well as the urban, for the fearsomely tough job requirements of the years ahead.

The RiverPark Center could be a white elephant, not a center of community pride and accomplishment, if it's not managed as well as it was conceived, if bluegrass development isn't pushed forward with verve and imagination, and if the surrounding downtown can't be made a more

163

welcoming place. The center could become the cultural mecca of western Kentucky and southwestern Indiana—but only with the right leadership and foresight.

Strengthening the Home-Grown Economy

The echoes of "We Got Scott!" were still reverberating when we came to visit. And why not? Snaring the gigantic paper maker's manufacturing plant, with its cutting edge technology, represents a sensational industrial recruitment hit for the region as it approaches the 21st century.

Here is a firm nationally admired for civic interest and an acceptable environmental performance. The Owensboro–Daviess County area gets a state of-the-art new factory, set to roll out a near recession-proof product—paper tissue. And then there are the jobs—500 to start with, at high wages, and maybe more later. "Scott will be here for a hundred years," a bank president told us. "It's a massive investment they can't walk away from. In two years they'll be closing other plants and bringing those jobs here, too."

Owensboro–Daviess County would be very foolish, though, to think other Scott deals are out there waiting to be tapped. The community lucked out this time; to anticipate a similar future "hit" would be foolish. Footloose factories are getting to be as rare as buffalo on the range.

The way American communities first attracted industries, through the 19th century and until World War II, was by sitting in the right place—on rivers or beside great harbors, on top of mother lodes of such natural resources as coal and gold. In the 1920s, industries started moving from the North to the South for cheap labor alone. Then came the post–World War II era of active "smokestack chasing," as communities searched far and wide for factories, promised tax exemptions and low-interest bonds and sometimes outright grants to companies who'd succumb. Kentucky's catch of the Toyota plant was a sensational "smokestack win."

But the 1980s ushered in a dramatically different era. The number of potential catches kept growing smaller as more and more manufacturing facilities moved offshore. The Southern Growth Policies Board actually likened smokestack chasing to buffalo hunting—pursuing a constantly thinning herd.

Today most states and communities are pursuing a much more sophisticated strategy. States have set up venture capital funds and supported high-tech research laboratories tied to new industrial capacity. They've emphasized the training of a broadly capable work force.

Today education is a top economic development tool, as skills, not low wages, become the new magnet for growth. Smart states and localities now identify the encouragement of entrepreneurs and the growth of existing businesses as their most important economic development strategy. Indeed, the most dramatic growth of businesses in the Owensboro–Daviess County area itself has taken place in existing firms, manufacturing and service alike.

For some really significant numbers, take a look at the Owensboro–Daviess County Hospital, which has expanded its work force from 1,000 to 1,400 workers and today ranks as the county's largest single employer. The Owensboro–Daviess County Hospital is, to be sure, a not-for-profit operation. But it is also a major business, grown from 50 doctors in 1969 to 150 today. It offers a carefully selected, profitable group of treatment technologies such as a cardiac catheterization unit and laser gall bladder treatment. On every front from open-heart surgery to sophisticated cancer therapies, it's become a prime regional center, drawing patients from considerable distances. And in a time when most U.S. county hospitals depend on property taxes to cover their growing deficits, here's an institution that functions virtually free of local subsidy.

Or consider Terry Woodward's WaxWorks record and video operation. Here's an industry born and grown in Owensboro that expanded to $172 million in sales in 1990—the country's fifth-largest video distributor. Terry Woodward, with his 145 music stores in 35 states, has kept his operation in downtown Owensboro, constantly outgrowing his space. Today he has 1,500 employees nationwide, 220 in Owensboro.

It would be silly to ignore opportunities for good buffalo hunts—especially when an unusually fat critter gets sighted. But most importantly, the city and county need to plunge into a day-in, day-out, year-in, year-out effort to strengthen and expand the base of the area's existing firms, the industry and service partners already here. If job growth is the goal, then helping the Terry Woodwards, large or small, is a savvy strategy.

Looking at what's already on the ground must include what's growing out of it. Agriculture is a vitally important part of the local economy, but not taken seriously enough in many quarters. Tobacco, the area's traditional crop, is still a massive business but may be imperiled more and more by health concerns. Canola, the new crop, is on the opposite edge—a low-fat oil with immense potential.

And there are lots of other potentials for a community that keeps its antenna up. Consider tomatoes. Owensboro's Ragu plant needs them badly, but up to now has had to import all of them from points far distant. We wondered why a major local effort wasn't under way to see that Daviess County—an ideal tomato-growing area—produces the fruit that this processor needs so badly. It did seem good news when word came recently of a state-of-the-art tomato processing plant and warehouse to be constructed near Friendly Village in Daviess County. But the plant would eventually want commitments for 3,000 acres of tomatoes each year—12 times what Daviess County farmers have been producing. Some major readjustments are obviously in order.

And the challenges go well beyond production of a single crop. Today's agriculture is as much people operating computers and scientists working in laboratories as farmers plowing fields. With enough imagination, multiple new products and processes could be developed—right in Owensboro. Farm chiefs used to look for strong backs; now they want strong minds, too. "I need people with good math, biology, chemistry, microbiology backgrounds—and they're hard to find here," a leading local agribusiness leader told us. He made us wonder, in fact, why Owensboro Community College hadn't begun a special effort in agribusiness-related biotechnology.

We believe Owensboro–Daviess County needs a new way to think about economic development in the 1990s.

First comes understanding how critical education is to any and all growth—a subject that's already received intensive local attention, and for the right reasons. Without a trained and motivated work force, few other inducements the city and county have to offer are likely to cut much ice with prospective targets.

A second strategy must be protection of the region's environment. What, after all, is more important than the health and quality of life of the people who live here? With sound education and a quality environment, we argue, job expansion—whether internal or through industrial recruitment—will come almost naturally.

We recommend an independent Committee for Safe Growth for Daviess County and the city. This would be a specially constituted group to advise the public on the critical issues—environmental issues, plus potential economic deals or opportunities—that face the region. Such a group would have no official power. But we believe it could empower the region's people by obliging industry and government alike to share more critical decisions.

Let's face it. Typically, massive economic deals, like the Scott agreement, get made behind closed doors, with the public knowing little if anything about what's happening—even when vast sums of public money are getting committed. We think the public deserves to know more, and that progress wouldn't get stopped in its tracks if that happened.

The rigor of environmental debate in Owensboro–Daviess County lags well behind that in most American communities. One has to assume it was corporate responsibility—not retreat under ferocious criticism—behind Scott Paper's recent announcement that it would radically reduce the potentially dangerous emissions from its new plant by using new chemicals in the manufacturing process. Some credit belongs to local environmentalists who first raised the issue and to the *Messenger-Inquirer* for reporting and editorializing on the issue.

Yet it would be naive for Owensboro–Daviess County to believe that every corporate citizen will be as responsible, or indeed that some future generation of Scott executives might not chart a different course.

We're aware that in a job-hungry area of massive power plants, huge aluminum factories, and strip mining, relatively few people have wanted to rock the boat. Yet there is also some history of environmental activism in Owensboro–Daviess County, exhibited perhaps most strongly a dozen years ago when three massive "synfuels" plants, intended to create synthetic fuel by coal liquification, were proposed for the Owensboro area. As Lee and Aloma Dew write in *Owensboro: City on the Yellow Banks:*

> Owensboro became the center of a . . . battle over the environment and quality of life versus industry at any cost. It was a battle of esoteric arguments about clean air and water, floodplains and prime agricultural land, earthquake faults and cancer risks against the palpable promise of jobs and paychecks to a group of people frustrated by unemployment and underemployment.

As it turned out, the grand vision for synfuels collapsed on economic, not environmental, arguments. But the community had been awakened enough to reject the 1982 proposal for a hazardous waste treatment plant at the Owensboro Riverport. The safety of the technology was doubted; there was fear that Owensboro might get a name for drawing hazardous industry, driving away others.

But how, on any industry-related environmental question, does a community know how to make a judgment? How can people know if there is or isn't a potential threat to their family's health? How does the average citizen find out? Whom does he or she trust?

We believe the Owensboro–Daviess County area will be confronted with more and more debates of this type, related to new and existing industries, to business and government activity alike. We think it's insufficient to rely, as some local officials are prepared to do, on Kentucky's air and water quality regulations unless, of course, you believe government always stays clean itself, and of course makes the right decisions.)

Owensboro–Daviess County needs the capacity for thorough, independent analysis of all manner of environmental issues. There's some promise in the new local environmental organization—POLAR, or Protecting Our Lives and Resources. "Official" Owensboro's reaction to POLAR has been cool, but we advise the community to think twice. Experience across the country teaches us that environmental groups don't just fade away—they end up either screaming on the outside or talking at the table. We think the table makes more sense.

But environmental organizations, by their nature, are advocacy groups. What's missing is an independent voice, backed up by solid research, that hears all sides.

Industry, let us note, needs this dialogue, too. Its operations require a clean environment; its executives and workers drink the same water, breathe the same air as everyone else in town. And who would want all those children—for whom everyone claims Owensboro–Daviess County is such a great place to grow up—to be exposed to environmental hazards that could distort their lives, even subject some to premature death?

The Safe Growth Committee would be a good arena in which these issues could get aired. In addition to industry representatives and environmentalists, it would have a majority composed of citizens with no special ax to grind. We think of college presidents, clergy, a barbecue waiter, a farmer, a retired professional, college faculty with expertise in the environment. To provide some independent research to the group, an interdisciplinary environmental task force could be formed at one of the local colleges, or perhaps cooperatively among them.

We're aware that an environmental committee of sorts was formed, at Scott's request, to funnel community concerns back to the corporation. The members were appointed by local officials and told to report to the local economic development director.

That may have been a useful gesture, but it shouldn't depend on the goodwill or responsibility of any corporation. The process needs to be open, independent, recognized as the expected way of doing business in Owensboro–Daviess County.

Members of the Committee for Safe Growth might be appointed by the Daviess County judge-executive and the mayor of Owensboro. But multiple nominations should also be solicited from civic and business groups, urban and rural, across the region. And the appointments should be for enough years to give members time to learn and to speak independently. It's important not to have an automatically harmonious group. All points of view need to be represented, so that the right questions get raised. That kind of process may be tougher, but in the end, the committee's advisories will have far more credibility.

We can imagine such a committee attacked as a threat to the region's industry and economic development. We believe quite the opposite—that it would promote sound economic development by raising legitimate issues. Conversely, when a scare is raised over some environmental issue and there's no evidence it's truly serious, the public ought to be given a reassuring advisory.

Ninety-nine percent of Owensboro–Davies County residents endorsed the Scott deal in a poll in December 1990. The morale boost the big catch gave to the community was clearly enormous. But it was also a frightfully expensive agreement, all at taxpayers' expense. The city and county agreed to come up with $4 million in job training money for Scott's new workers. The firm was assured a $300 bonus for each worker it took on. The county said it would build and pay for a $3.5-million wastewater line from the new factory to the Ohio River. Free water lines would be constructed to the plant. The county would pay for any wetlands mitigation that might be needed. A series of industrial revenue bonds, locally and state-authorized, would provide Scott with well over $100 million in financing, the interest rate subsidized by the public.

The concession list leaves one almost breathless. The *Messenger-Inquirer* calculated the public cost at more than $300,000 per job—one of the most expensive deals, job for job, in American history.

But even if the public seems happy, one has to ask: Should agreements of this magnitude, with such vast sums of public expenditures involved, be signed before the public knows the terms?

Kentuckians seem to hate taxes with a passion. The idea that some people might pay marginally higher taxes helped send the city-county merger referendum down to defeat last year. But the Scott deal obligated the city, and especially the county, to vast financial obligations, a massive hit on taxpayers' pockets. And it all seemed to be accepted without a murmur.

What if a Committee on Safe Growth had been in existence and had a chance to take a look at the Scott agreement and evaluate it for the public before the official signing? Would it have made any difference? Would publicity have killed the deal and handed it to Indiana? Or would public attention have stiffened the back of the local negotiators, emboldened them to bargain from greater strength?

No one can answer for sure, but our guess is that a little sunlight on the negotiations would have won better terms for Owensboro–Daviess County and landed the Scott plant anyway.

Our suspicion, though we can't prove it, is that Scott had already settled on Daviess County and was out to get it on the best terms it could. Owensboro's problem—as in all such negotiations—is that it had to play a poker game in which the company could see all three hands—its own, Daviess County's, and the Indiana competitors'. It sounds like a funny analogy, but under those rules, the house always wins. And this time it was the local taxpayers' money on the gaming table.

We asked local political leaders if there was any price that would have been too high to offer Scott, if it had asked. We were shocked: they couldn't think of a limit!

We asked them if the city and county could entertain another Scott-type proposal. Would there be enough funds in the public treasuries, anytime soon, for another corporate payment demand? We must report that the answers we got to our questions seemed quite evasive, even from officials with otherwise exemplary records. We suggest that unless the residents of Owensboro–Daviess County like the idea of writing blank checks, they ought to blow the whistle on indiscriminate buffalo hunting.

There is a possible antidote, one that hit us after Owensboro financial leaders provided us with one of their pet ideas—to establish a dedicated revenue source (perhaps a payroll tax of 0.25 percent or so). The sole use of the cash, they suggested, would be financing infrastructure or other induce-ments to draw new corporations.

But we saw the potential a lot differently. First, we recommend that any such tax fund should be capped at a reasonable level, thus providing a clear giveaway limit—a point beyond which the taxpayer's wealth couldn't be placed in private corporate hands. Secondly, we'd suggest that at least 50 percent of the proceeds from any such tax be dedicated to holding and strengthening existing businesses—a fund for the county and city's own firms, to help them flourish and expand their work forces.

Leaders of existing firms told us they were pleased Scott had been recruited. But they felt the inducements offered the paper giant were discriminatory against the city's and county's own firms. We think they were right.

There's one thorny problem in imposing a countywide occupational tax. At the last moment in the Scott negotiations, the company's attorneys demanded that Daviess County agree not to adopt the same kind of payroll or occupational tax that's been in effect in Owensboro (but not outlying portions of Daviess County) since 1960. It was as if Scott, getting ready to come to town and use the local schools and roads and facilities, not only asked megabucks to move in and build its plant, but freedom for its executives and workers to escape a fair share of area costs.

Was the tax concession truly critical to the Scott deal? Some insiders we talked with thought not, that Scott's attorneys threw it in at the last minute and that county officials, paralyzed at the thought of losing the deal, crumbled. County officers even put it on paper: they'd plead with their successors not to pass such a tax.

It's hard to imagine Scott would want to let anything get in the way of its extraordinarily positive image in Daviess County–Owensboro. Our suggestion would be that Scott's senior executives, as an act of good corporate citizenship and commitment to a diversified, healthy regional economy, voluntarily relieve Daviess Fiscal Court from its pledge not to adopt the occupational tax. Then a countywide occupational tax for economic development could go into effect, creating not just a rush of goodwill but some dedicated dollars to build a strong and diversified future economy.

Education: The Foremost Challenge

As tough as new state and national goals for schools and higher education may seem, the Owensboro community hardly starts from ground zero in this area. It added a community college to its base of two fine independent four-year colleges in the 1980s. The Citizens Committee on Education, sparkplug of that effort, has lived on to push for constant improvement. The Daviess County and Owensboro school districts do so well, at least compared with the rest of the state, that they fear the 1990 Kentucky Education Reform Act will actually hold them back, while poor and deficient districts catch up.

Owensboro has a very high incidence of single-parent households—reportedly as high as 70 percent. Nearly half the kids qualify for free or reduced-price school lunches. Still, the city educates so well that no grade level falls below national averages on standardized tests.

Both the city and county schools have seen their college-going rates increase dramatically in recent years. There was evidence of long-term thinking in former Owensboro Superintendent J. Frank Yeager's tough challenges to invest early and often in the youngest children, especially those from troubled homes.

But just when you think Owensboro education is a success story, you hear of employer after employer who can't find qualified workers. When WorldSource came to Hancock County and started hiring, it was shocked to find 3,000 of the 4,500 applicants had to be ruled out because of insufficient skills. And clearly there's lots of underemployment, too. In 1989, when Pinkerton Tobacco advertised to fill 20 openings, more than 1,200 would-be workers applied.

Then there's the problem that more than 21,000 adults in Daviess County have less than a high school education. And we hear that a persistent anti-intellectualism holds on, especially in lower-income white families where education isn't taken seriously. School officials tell sadly of parents marching into school on their child's 16th birthday to remove the child from the classroom. That might once have been a rational act, given the lower-skilled employment needs of 1950. But today, parents who make that choice may condemn their kids to perpetual poverty.

Add to that the projection that of the 348,000 new jobs likely to be created in Kentucky by the year 2000, more than 90 percent will require at least two years of college.

All that suggests to us there's much for the Owensboro–Daviess community to address on the education front. This is no time for complacency.

Owensboro's Downtown "Living Room"

In renewal accomplished and grand things to come, Owensboro's waterfront and downtown are standouts. We doubt if the citizens of Owensboro and Daviess County fully appreciate the importance of what's occurred already—and what will happen soon—on their doorstep to the Ohio River.

Like most cities, Owensboro saw its downtown retailing flee to the shopping centers and Wal-Marts. The familiar, dreary story of so many cities was repeated here: mindless demolition of many fine, still serviceable old buildings, the appearance of gaping holes in the flow of a once-proud streetscape.

But during the last decade, the pattern of downtown decay in Owensboro has met its match. First came coal mine owner Bob Green, who stumbled into the hotel business in Evansville and liked it so much that he decided to build on the waterfront in Owensboro. By booking Las Vegas–quality shows into the Executive Inn Rivermont, Green not only captured a lot of hotel trade that used to go to other towns, he also encouraged people to come to Owensboro, stay overnight, spend their money. Green became the Father of Tourism for a city that had never known it.

Terry Woodward, by contrast, became Owensboro's Entrepreneur Extraordinaire. He was the man who carried off one of America's great business success stories of the times, right in downtown Owensboro, which virtually everyone else had declared dead.

Woodward took his father's business and parlayed it into one of America's leading music and video distribution firms—WaxWorks. (Sales soared from $200,000 in WaxWorks' first year to $172,000,000 in 1990.) Choosing Sears' old downtown store in Owensboro as his staging area, Woodward expanded almost constantly until he'd taken over the entire building. Today he owns all four corners at Second and Crittenden.

Bob Green and Terry Woodward are at least half the story of downtown's historic turnaround. But they aren't all of it. There's also the saga of the host of Owensboro leaders who got engaged in the process of planning for their city's future, decided downtown was critical to the city identity and well-being, and then went to work to make it happen.

In 1987 their thoughts and plans came together in a broadly representative "Strategies for Tomorrow" for Owensboro–Daviess County. The official players in the strategic planning effort ranged from the city and county governments to the Chamber of Commerce and Metropolitan Planning Commission. Three hundred private citizens took part. While the future of downtown and the riverfront was only one element of "Strategies," it was a critical one.

Here was the community's first official call to implement the long-held dream of a cultural/civic center, built directly on the riverfront. The center ought to be, said the "Strategies" committee, a new home and stage for Owensboro's leading performing arts groups, a civic gathering spot for speakers and special events; a place, in short, where the entire Owensboro–Daviess County community could come together. The facility also would be linked to a new Bluegrass Museum and Hall of Fame.

"Strategies" urged the building of a major corporate office center downtown—also directly on the river. It recommended public construction of downtown parking, which had been identified as a major barrier to further development. And on the existing riverfront, which they called "woefully underutilized, unsightly and unattractive," the "Strategies" planners called for a stem-to-stern clean-up, redoing all the riverfront property from Smothers Park to English Park.

Many cities' strategic plans go on the shelf, honored only in the breach. But in the last half decade, the steps that the "Strategies" report outlined for the downtown and waterfront have left the realm of abstract dreams to become very tangible brick, glass, concrete, and walkways. Today the corporate center, the waterfront cleanup, the parking facility are well advanced. And RiverPark, the name with which the new civic/cultural center got baptized, is to open in 1992, the crown jewel of Owensboro's downtown redevelopment.

A remarkable quotient of civic "imagineering," replete with all manner of citizen input, has been added to the new downtown formula in recent years. Take bluegrass. In the mid-1980s, Terry Woodward had the idea to launch an annual bluegrass festival on the riverfront at Owensboro. It was a compelling case. Bluegrass sprang from this area of Kentucky: father-of-the-art Bill Monroe was born 30 miles from Owensboro at Rosine. Jerusalem Ridge, of the bluegrass ballad, is nearby. The Bluegrass Festival started in 1985, culminating in a joint concert by the Osborne Brothers and the Owensboro Symphony—the first time a symphony orchestra anywhere had ever performed at a bluegrass festival.

But Woodward's mind already was racing ahead: Why not found an International Bluegrass Music Association and make sure its headquarters got located in Owensboro? How about a bluegrass awards show? Why not, by the fifth year or so, create the Bluegrass Museum and Hall of Fame and put it right beside Owensboro's new RiverPark Center?

So far, the Woodward timetable is working almost perfectly. And it would be tough to think of a better business move: 40 million Americans listen to bluegrass; 1 million call it their favorite music.

Or consider barbecue. The art is legendary to Owensboro, dating at least from the 1830s. We were amused when Mayor David Adkisson took the trouble to prepare a fully researched article for the *Messenger-Inquirer* to certify the community's standing as the barbecue capital of the world. (Adkisson's measure: more barbecue restaurants per capita than any other city. No competitor came even close.)

In the late 1970s, Ken Bosley, whose family owns Moonlite Bar-B-Que Inn, was one of a bunch of Chamber of Commerce members dreaming up new ideas to promote tourism in Owensboro. Recalling how big church barbecue picnics are, they settled on Bosley's idea—a barbecue festival. Soon Owensboro's International Barbecue Festival became an annual event, drawing tens of thousands of carnivores from far and wide to the barbecue pits around Smothers Park.

Bluegrass and barbecue, twin legends, demonstrate Owensboro's skill at capitalizing on longstanding local tradition, turning popular custom into stunning commercial success. They suggest the potential of turning Owensboro increasingly into a "celebration city," offering a year-round diet of events that attract hundreds of thousands of visitors every year.

Yet, however impressive the downtown and waterfront revival has been, it's too soon to celebrate, to rest on one's oars.

Take the challenge of Owensboro's looks. A downtown design review commission has been seeking to encourage owners to build with good taste, to preserve the integrity of historic buildings, to see to it that buildings and streets, old and new, work well together.

For the entire city, Mayor Adkisson has pushed a "Streetscape 2000" initiative to work year by year at improving the main arteries and central business district. The effort embraces planting trees and bushes along streets and in the medians, banishing ugly signs, sprucing up buildings with fresh paint.

These efforts are critical to Owensboro's future—critical to the way the town sees itself, vital to the image the city projects to the world. Looking at the community through the eyes of a prospective new business, one city official said, you "notice every bad sign, every sagging wire, every pole and weed. Fighting for good aesthetics isn't an interest in botany. It's a competitive thing."

And nowhere is the competitive challenge greater than downtown. People insist on top-level services in their neighborhoods, where they have major personal investment. But downtowns so often lose out. Their future is everyone's interest, but no one's in particular.

So one has to ask: What particular advantage do downtowns offer that suburbs can't? One answer is history, color, variety—rare commodities in the world of homogeneous subdivisions and shopping malls. But in today's world, there's an equal value to downtowns: compactness. Only in downtown do you have a chance to get where you want to go on foot, to shake dependence on the automobile for every move.

On this score, Owensboro's quite lucky: it has a remarkably compact downtown. The points of attraction—from English Park to RiverPark Center, Executive Inn to Courthouse and City Hall—are close enough to walk between (or, at most, to ride to on simple downtown shuttle buses). That's an asset to build on.

But downtown streets also have to be attractive and enjoyable—and lead somewhere interesting. Again, Owensboro is lucky. While some cities consider spending millions to create the waterfronts nature didn't give them, Owensboro has the banks of the Ohio River, which helped spawn the town in the first place.

During our stay in Owensboro, we found ourselves fascinated by the river, by the constantly moving panorama of mid-America's brawny commerce. The river constantly changes its face. At one moment its waters are roiled by the winds and churned by currents. And then, as if by magic, the powerful flow seems to dissolve into a placid pool.

Clearly, there's the potential for so much more use of this waterfront. It was a stroke of genius to pick this location for the new RiverPark Center. We predict the grand lobby, overlooking the Ohio, will become renowned among public places along the river's 700-mile span.

As Owensboro's planning goes forward, we'd keep a clear view to the water for every street and walkway possible. As Dick Rigby of the Washington, D.C.–based Waterfront Center said when he visited Owensboro, Owensboro people need "to go and get inspired" by what other cities—from Charleston (South Carolina) to Wilmington (North Carolina) to South Bend (Indiana)—have done with their waterfronts, in some cases with more difficult situations to start with than Owensboro.

For Owensboro, it makes sense to do everything possible to encourage lively recreational boating activity. Multiple restaurants, walkways, and viewing spots should be sited with river exposure. The Executive Inn should cooperate—gladly, voluntarily—to let the walkway from Smothers to English Park pass by its water side. Indeed, the Inn could benefit a great deal by reviewing and rebuilding its entire river exposure with promenades, open-air restaurants, and cafes all oriented to the city's expanded water and boating future. (Bob Green's entrepreneurial spirit has given a lot to Owensboro, but he also owes this hospitable host town a great deal.)

But what about street activity when downtown workers have gone home for the day, when the festivals take a holiday, when tourists aren't thronging the scene? Owensboro, like every other downtown in America, needs people who select the center city as their neighborhood and decide to live there full-time. We think there ought to be a market for downtown Owensboro housing—among office workers who'd just as soon be in the center of action near the river, among senior citizens who prize a walkable environment.

Downtown housing doesn't need to depend on a wave of upscale buyers willing to plunk down hundreds of thousands of dollars for a pricey condo with a river view. A successful downtown neighborhood encourages residents at all points along the income scale. Owensboro ought to think about multiple public-private incentives for a mix of people to live in and help create a lively downtown.

Housing, in turn, can be a big inducement to specialized retailing. When enough people live downtown, one can expect the retail landmarks of a strong community—hardware stores and beauty shops, newsstands and dry cleaners, grocers and florists—to return. Downtown living may not be everyone's choice in the age of the automobile and sprawling lawn culture. On the other hand, not everyone drives, or cares to, all the time. If a livable, walkable downtown environment is offered, more people than you'd think will snap up the opportunity.

To anyone who suggests downtown retailing is irrevocably dead, never to return, we'd suggest that the shopping patterns have always been volatile, always in flux. It's true many downtown retail stores became stagnant, forgot how to compete. But in some American cities today, the smart small retailers are discovering special niche markets and are competing successfully, on the turf they choose, with the Wal-Marts and other mass outlets.

Oftentimes, downtown retailers begin a comeback when they think anew about their potential customers—not the thousands following the red-tag or blue-light specials at a mall or outlying mass retailer, but the downtown resident who pursues quality at a reasonable price, or the tourist who isn't above impulse buying of memorabilia, or the downtown worker who squeezes in a purchase over the lunch hour.

Owensboro is fortunate to have Downtown Owensboro Inc. working on these issues. But all the downtown players will have to encourage some form of what's called "centralized retail management." The idea is for the downtown stores to collaborate and mimic some of the advantages of a mall. They could establish systems, for example, to recruit stores missing from the mix, survey customer preferences, standardize hours. (Why not set downtown store hours at 11 a.m. to 7 p.m., to catch both lunchtime and after-work customers? Then keep downtown stores open every night there's a special festival or event, so people can count on the opportunity for late shopping on those days.)

Successful retail management efforts in other cities have made the whole downtown environment predictable, accessible—and newly attractive—to customers. A prime example is Neenah, Wisconsin, an old manufacturing town of 35,000 people, so successful in marketing its downtown that the outlying mall last year took downtown's marketing theme as its own. Another is Oak Park, Illinois, which chalked up 20,000 square feet of new downtown leases over three recent months.

There is a lesson to be learned from all these towns: serious staff time and long-term commitment have to go into the process. Consider that the average shopping mall agent works 200 hours, or five weeks, to sign a single new merchant. Retail management won't work without a real commitment to outreach, organizing people, holding intensive meetings. But it is doable, and Owensboro could do it if it cared.

Sadly, we ran into some prominent Owensboro citizens who've effectively written off the downtown as a safe or attractive place to do business. But that judgment was the exception, not the rule. A refreshing majority of Owensboro leaders appeared not just to have hopes for, but to believe in, their downtown.

Communities across the country might copy the counsel of Mayor Adkisson:

> Downtown is the living room of our community. It's where we all
> come together to see each other. The suburbs are like the bedrooms. If
> you give a kid everything he needs in his room, you'll never see him
> again in the living room. We need to provide the arts, entertainment,
> restaurants, cultural celebrations. Downtown is our gathering place.
> It's our people place.

A Wider Role for Everyone—Including Women

We believe the people of Owensboro and Daviess County have a remarkable opportunity to define and practice a powerful, exemplary regional citizenship for the 1990s.

Every urban area in America faces a challenge to its old ways of doing things. Downtown power elites find their decisions don't get respected any more. Old-fashioned county politics is discredited. All sorts of groups can block any new idea; few can make things happen.

The successful communities of the 1990s will be those that transform splintered power into shared power. They'll be those that consciously include all groups, learn to be mutually supportive, work cooperatively on shared problems. They'll create all sorts of imaginative mechanisms (a countywide child support program, a downtown management district, for example). They'll have an open spirit about new ideas. Job recruitment will be important—but only as a means to the larger goal of developing the civic, spiritual, and economic potential of all the region's people.

Owensboro–Daviess County may have a better shot than many American communities at the new regional citizenship because its problems are of manageable scale. Another plus: despite what seemed a divisively bitter fight over city-county merger here in 1990, the best of the new city and county leadership that emerged in the 1980s has laid a foundation for creative regionwide approaches.

What about governmental reorganization issues of tax and spending fairness, efficiency of services? We heard a great deal of discussion about how government might be made more rational, tax bases distributed more fairly, services combined for delivery on a countywide basis.

And we heard some constructive short-term suggestions for building better city-county relationships. One example: joint sessions of the City Commission and Fiscal Court, perhaps monthly at first, and beginning with uncontroversial, "apple pie" issues. If that worked, touchier issues (taxes, for example) might be addressed later.

To us, such careful, incremental steps are the wise way to go. On merits alone, merger made a lot of sense. But the results proved the community wasn't ready. It's probably fruitless to try for changed systems of government until a sounder base of shared interests and mutual trust can be built. Merger or some variant may come some day, but only when the entire community sees it as a "win-win" scenario.

In the meantime, regional citizenship can be built by multiple strategies designed to create trust relationships across the city and county. Today's lack of trust is disturbing. So are the contradictory ways Owensborans talk about their community. On the one hand they boast about life in their prosperous, serene, comfortable, solid middle-class American community. "I wouldn't want to live any other place," person after person seemed to be saying. "This is a good community. I never moved anyone here who didn't love it or who wanted to leave," a prominent agribusiness leader told us.

But there's another Owensboro–Daviess County mind-set. It's rife with deeply held suspicions—urban-rural, white-black, privileged elites versus regular folks.

We heard that folks in Owensboro–Daviess County have great love for stability, resist any kind of unproven change. But a thin line separates what's stable from what's stale. Ask leaders of this community about its downside and they often reach for such words as *stubbornness, compla-*

cency, and *resignation.* We heard echoes of the all-American quotient of selfishness and shortsightedness—"I got mine, you get your own."

Yet in Owensboro today, there are ripples on the still waters—stirrings of outreach, the beginnings of new connections, such as shared leadership visits aimed at learning how other communities address their problems. They suggest to us that city and county people may be ready to grasp the strands of opportunity on every front.

Nearly everything the Owensboro–Daviess County community needs to do to achieve full regional cooperation and citizenship exists already, at least in fledgling form. The secret of the future is really quite simple. It is to take these efforts, broaden and diversify them, until they're stretched to their full potential and translate into major advantage from Whitesville to the West End, English Park to Thorobred Acres.

Working for its children is perhaps the best test of whether a community is looking forward, shaking off short-term expediency, concerned about its most critical resource—its people—in the 21st century. We were fascinated to hear of the variety and vigor of programs operating across the city and county to reach kids, especially very young ones.

The leadership seems to be coming from various organizations. Owensboro got on this wave length—well ahead of many communities—when then-Superintendent J. Frank Yeager addressed a meeting of community leaders to warn of an alarming rise of poverty among the Owensboro school district's children. Half the kids, he said, come from families eligible for subsidized lunches—more than twice the national average.

So a committee for children in need was created, with members appointed by Mayor Adkisson. A foundation for children was founded by Larry and Frankie Hager, with initial funding of $1 million. The Audubon Area Community Services is in on the act with a broadening of its services for children. The idea of creating a citywide preschool for all children— "Kiddy Tech"—has been raised. The Owensboro Citizens Committee on Education has a subcommittee discussing at-risk youth, alternative schools, mentoring, self-esteem efforts, and a community awareness effort targeting potential dropouts.

And a critical role has been played by the United Way, which has determined to provide "venture grants," to put a heavy emphasis on preventive programs and less, comparatively, on after-the-fact remedial efforts. (If you've watched other United Ways around America, you know that's a tough drill—risking heated reaction from existing agencies likely to receive less if a creative new strategy gets adopted.)

Yet with United Way encouragement, a consortium of 16 local agencies has agreed to work as a team on a pilot basis in a single school, coordinating a full range of services for children from kindergarten through the third grade. Critically important is the fact that the families are to be involved, too. United Way hopes it's developing with charitable dollars a program that public dollars can pick up and broaden, as the Kentucky Education Reform Act kicks in with a full program of parent resource centers and a dramatic broadening of early childhood education. (Right now Head Start is reaching just 21 percent of eligible children in Daviess County; if KERA money flows as planned, 50 percent could be covered.)

We see in all this an extraordinary start at getting special help to children—especially those from poor families—so that they'll be ready for school and able to succeed once they get there.

Experience around the country proves that quality, early help means that kids are much more apt to stay in school, less likely to get pregnant, more likely to end up in college than in jail. Eventually, kids who get this kind of an early lift stand a much better chance to live fulfilling rather than frustrating lives, to become taxpayers rather than tax-eaters.

It's hard to think of a more imaginative investment a community can make in its future. But the test for Owensboro–Daviess County remains: Can the early childhood/family programs cover the entire community, providing help to all families in need? Pilot programs and committee studies are great but don't accomplish much unless they lead to across-the-community action and results.

At the other end of the age spectrum, the community's most valuable untapped resource today may be its retired and elderly citizens. And they're an expanding resource. Statistics show that Daviess County people 65 and older are increasing in number more rapidly than any other segment of the population.

Most communities have programs to take care of senior citizens; what impressed us most in Owensboro was mention of programs to reach out to senior citizens, capture their skills and wisdom for multiple volunteer tasks waiting for attention across the community.

As a very senior citizen of Owensboro told us: "With company policies shoving people out at 65, or early retirement programs, we end up with people with vast experience and vast ability doing nothing but playing golf or—in the case of men—having their wives say, 'Get out of the house.'"

We suggest the mobilization of senior power needs to go a critical step further—to retirees themselves organizing to serve the community. Today's seniors are the most "helped" generation in our history on every front from Social Security to Medicare to Medicaid. Most enjoy a health and vigor no generation older than 65 ever has before.

And they represent a resource too valuable to waste. Nowhere is that resource so needed as in multiple efforts to help children—particularly in a time of shrinking public budgets for social service workers, teachers' aides, childcare workers, park and recreation workers and supervisors. Each seniors' organization in the community should decide on the role it could play and then start scheduling its members to work with the schools and parks and social agencies and neighborhood centers.

As seniors organize themselves, we believe respect for them will escalate. Reengaged in the community, they'll be more fulfilled as individuals and will add to the substance of the new regional citizenship. These kinds of dividends are already being recognized in Asheville, North Carolina, where 1,500 retirees are participating in multiple activities, ranging from career counseling for college students to helping hospitals to running discussion groups for adults in rural communities. There's a seven-week Leadership Asheville Seniors training course in which leaders from the schools, government, and education brief senior citizens about the community's needs. Work in the local schools has become a special focus of the Asheville program.

What about woman power—and potential? Owensboro–Daviess County has a dismal record in tapping it. We were shocked to hear that of the 47 elected positions in Owensboro and Daviess County, only one is held by a woman—the vice-chair of a school board.

"The political culture here is mostly good-ole-boy, male-dominated politics," one veteran—a male—noted. No woman, for example, has been elected to county office since 1961.

We found that record almost incomprehensible. Consider just cities in and around Kentucky that have elected women as mayors in recent years. The list includes Charlotte, North Carolina; West Lafayette, Indiana; Rock Hill, South Carolina; and Little Rock, Arkansas (which has actually elected two women as mayor). In big, manly Texas, the cities of Houston, Dallas, El Paso, Austin, and Fort Worth have all seen fit to elect women as mayors in recent years. Up near Washington, D.C., the chairman of the board of supervisors in Fairfax County is a woman. Both the mayor and city manager of Alexandria, Virginia, are women.

So why the virtual blackout of women in political posts in Owensboro and Daviess County? Why aren't women encouraged to run, given support when they do? We didn't get any clear answers. But one thing's clear. If a community fails to regard women as serious leaders, it writes off half its potential leadership pool. It loses the distinctive leadership qualities that only women may contribute. That may have been an affordable luxury in the 1920s or even the 1950s; it isn't in the 1990s.

Who's in Charge Here?

How do Owensboro and Daviess County get ready for an even more challenging future? Not, we'd suggest, by throwing their traditional caution and conservatism overboard. Nor by failing to honor the bursts of creativity and imagination that created the community college and RiverPark Center and went out to successfully land a "biggie" like Scott Paper. What Owensboro–Daviess County needs now, in our judgment, is a more expansive view of who can lead, who needs to be consulted and involved.

Take corporate leadership. In the 1960s, General Electric Company and Texas Gas Transmission Corporation were relied on for community leadership. Today Texas Gas carries on a sparkling array of civic outreach. Yet, as the GE experience reminds one, economic change generated outside a city's borders can destroy a business-city relationship that once looked like the Rock of Gibraltar.

Today, more corporations need to be asked to accept major responsibility. Some are more ready than you think. Corporations homegrown and still growing, like Terry Woodward's WaxWorks, are becoming as important on the local scene as any traditional utility or megaindustry.

Educators can also play a major role. Among the Owensboro area's colleges, substantial expertise is building in multiple fields—sometimes insufficiently appreciated in the community.

On the political front, voters are casting aside the old politics with the election of people such as David Adkisson as mayor of Owensboro, or Buzz Norris as Daviess County judge-executive. Each has a bagful of bright ideas. But neither of those two men seems to believe he's the whole show. As Adkisson himself said when he first ran, the community needs to unleash the talents and energies of more citizens: "We cannot afford any spectators."

Every community, to move forward, needs a vision. Cities without vision are all but certain to fail in the harshly competitive new national and international economy. But in today's world, when every civic group, every ethnic enclave, every geographic area believes it's entitled to a voice, building vision is tougher than ever. What's the secret? We suggest it's making an effort to include people, hear their concerns, and take their suggestions seriously.

The shots in Owensboro used to be called by a crusty old-boy network that met informally, oftentimes at the Campbell Club, to cut deals affecting everyone. As in cities across the country, that model—of "insider" leadership—no longer works.

The decisive change in Owensboro was signaled by the 1982 formation of Leadership Owensboro. The program has continued since, a deliberate effort to build a network of new leaders, within business, government agencies, and nonprofit organizations. The program's had 300 graduates and is still growing.

But Leadership Owensboro's outreach hasn't been perfect. Its alumni haven't reached out aggressively enough to stimulate community discussions of critical issues. Sign-ups among farmers, ministers, and grassroots groups have been too rare. If Leadership Owensboro is to build the region's leadership for the 21st century, it will need more of all those.

Even with broader leadership, there's danger that the good ship Owensboro, bearing down on certain critical issues, will find itself bogging down, scraping bottom, taking on water like a carelessly piloted sternwheeler of old. It's time for a wake-up call. Owensboro and Daviess County need to think much harder about their assets, their liabilities, and how to broaden leadership in the region.

Owensboro is unlikely to ever again be declared an All-America City, for example, until it clears some of the most dangerous rocks in the stream—the stereotypes various parts of the community have about each other.

The urban-rural stereotypes may be the most perilous of all. From rural interests, we heard: "People in Owensboro aren't interested in us at all—except when they want our money. City people don't work very hard. But they live pretty well. Agriculture has become just a stepchild."

City people sounded just as estranged: "Farmers still practice a barn-raising culture—they'll show up at the drop of a hat to help each other, but not anyone else. They're not members of the Chamber of Commerce. They're only concerned about being watchdogs."

The 1990 merger vote, we concluded, was less about the critically important issue of consolidation of services, taxes, and efficiency than it was about feelings of alienation, about power. Even merger proponents said not enough people had been brought into the thinking and planning process early on.

And from a leading opponent, we heard there wasn't that much actual disagreement about merging of services. The gut problem, he said, was that the "city crowd" was trying to put one over on rural Daviess County, to strip "county people" of "their" government. From that base, a whole range of antiestablishment feelings, in city and rural areas alike, rose to quash the merger proposal.

A passel of other stereotypes hobbles the Owensboro–Daviess County area—professional versus working class, black versus white, and especially in a community with one of America's slowest rates of population turnover, the few newcomers versus the big majority of lifetime residents. All too often, major community decisions in Owensboro–Daviess County "appear to turn less on what was said than who said it."

If truth be told, the stereotypes are probably less extreme and severe than a generation ago. But they're a massive barrier reef leaving no safe harbor for honest conversation and productive action. The challenge now is to carve a channel through those stereotypes, and probably not so much by frontal attack as by getting people to work together on all sorts of projects, building constructive interaction, building trust. Trust, in time, will drive out suspicion. Interaction softens the isolation.

We believe the *Messenger-Inquirer* needs to play a major role in this transition. Friends and critics alike, in our conversations, kept zeroing in on the paper's relationship to the community.

We need to confess, up front, our grounds for liking the paper. It invited us to town, gave us free rein to write an independent account, free of editorial direction. Not many newspapers in cities this size would take that risk. And it's accurate to say that not many newspapers in the *Messenger-Inquirer*'s circulation size are of comparable quality, from its appearance to the range of national and international news it covers. If one of the national newspaper chains bought up the paper, you could expect a strictly bottom-line mentality to take over and a lot of the paper's spunk to fade away.

But the relationship between a locally owned paper and its home community is intimate, fragile, as prone to misunderstandings as the ties among members of any family. A simple error can get read as a slight. And it's too easy to blame the paper for reporting unpopular or bad news when it's only doing its job.

In a single newspaper market, a town that even lacks its own television stations, a special burden of responsibility falls on the *Messenger-Inquirer*. What it fails to print won't get reported. The issues it fails to raise oftentimes won't get debated.

The paper may not have to do a lot of investigatory journalism, trying to prove scandals and wrongdoing in high places. But it has an obligation to do what we'd call exploratory journalism—looking carefully at trends, causes, and prospects on every front from the complexion of local industry to the quality of the local schools and colleges to environmental hazards. Based on that kind of thoughtful, quality reporting, the paper has a compelling opportunity to get people thinking harder, and more honestly, about the problems the community faces.

We heard legitimate complaints raised about the *Messenger-Inquirer*. Several interviewees said they'd like more coverage of state government and economic trends in other regions of Kentucky. They wanted to see the editorial page reflect more local opinion. Rural people felt the paper was simply not respecting their point of view. Others said the African-American community shouldn't be covered just when it starts to raise some modest hell—that ongoing events in black neighborhoods need coverage. And it was suggested that in a community where women rarely win office or get top business posts, the paper should be on a constant lookout for legitimate ways to give rising female leaders a clearer community profile.

The paper should respond to those kinds of criticism. If new, unconventional, different voices can't be heard on its pages, where can they be?

But the newspaper can't do it all itself. The community has to make a vigorous effort to overcome the old biases and stereotypes, to enable and empower more kinds of people to take part in spirited planning and action on topics ranging from downtown development to agricultural land protection. For better or worse, the *Messenger-Inquirer* will be the critical means of communication as the region learns to talk to itself far more effectively.

That's a tough challenge, but we see no reason it can't be met. Learning from its errors and building on its breakthroughs, the Owensboro area has every prospect, through the 1990s, to set a high standard of civic cohesion that works for city and countryside alike.

Learning from Others and Supporting Innovation

How do Owensboro and Daviess County build the new institutions they need to undergird an expanded regional citizenship for the 1990s?

A first and critical step for many communities is to learn—and keep on learning—from others. We were heartened to hear that Mayor Adkisson has organized community leadership visits to such other communities as Iowa City and Bloomington, Indiana. It may be even more important that the

Owensboro–Daviess County Chamber of Commerce has scheduled a three-day visit for 30 business and government officials to Augusta, Georgia. For a community in which 83 percent of the people were born in the county, there's special need—in Adkisson's words—"to put up the periscope and look around."

Chambers of commerce and other civic leadership groups in many of America's smartest cities—Seattle, Charlotte (North Carolina), Louisville, Jacksonville (Florida), Greenville (South Carolina) among them—believe there's important payoff from intercity visits in which dozens of city leaders plunge into two- to three-day briefing sessions in other communities. As Owensboro joins the cities undertaking intercity visits, it has a lot to gain.

And it's not just that an Augusta, for example, has an ambitious riverfront development project the Owensboro crowd can learn from. "In your own city," a Seattle government executive told us, "you have your facade, your place. Go to another place and you're all fellow travelers in a foreign land. A different bonding takes place."

The intercity visits have stimulated some of urban America's most candid "show and tell" sessions. A Charlotte leader explained that delegations get both challenge and reinforcement out of the visits, stimulation from other cities' superior models, comfort when they register the fact that other towns' problems may be worse than their own.

Intercity visit delegations get "turned on" by the experience. Their imaginations, their competitive spirits get aroused. And when they come home, their enthusiasm easily spreads through the entire community.

It may matter as much *who* goes as *where* the group goes. "Establishment" business and government executives need to be balanced with some of the council members, journalists, and civic activists with whom they may even be at odds back home. To make the project "click" for the Owensboro region, we'd add agribusiness leaders, educators, social service leaders, African-Americans, and—as we suggested earlier—a strong contingent of women. The more people who get included on an intercity visit, the more "co-conspirators" there'll be for getting some of the positive ideas implemented.

Blacks don't have much to celebrate in Owensboro. True, they get honored for top performance on championship basketball, baseball, and football teams. They can point with pride to some who made it all the way to the NFL and NBA. And it's true the premiere performance at the RiverPark Center will be about Josiah Henson, the famed liberator of thousands of black slaves who spent five years in Owensboro before his escape north. (We were impressed to hear local governments and businesses contributed $50,000 to commission the drama, designed to later become an outdoor drama—the only play with a black theme and principally black characters ever written for an outdoor stage.)

But overall, Owensboro's African-Americans are invisible people, nonparticipants in the mainstream life of the city and county. They're just 6 percent of the city population, and the evidence is that young blacks are increasingly leaving town. It's not hard to figure why.

Blacks in leadership roles are disappearing. Today there are none in public school administration, none on the faculties of either of the private colleges, only one in elected office. We heard there's not a single black doctor or lawyer in the community. The total number of black professionals appears to have fallen by half in the last dozen years.

Most black children are assigned to a public elementary school that's more than 40 years old, bounded by a grain company, the city's sanitation operation, and heavy industry. Its equipment looks worn and old.

The black community believes it does not receive a fair share of funds for road improvement, utility upgrading, park maintenance. Kendall Perkins, the only park in the west side neighborhood with the heaviest black population, has a long, tall, forbidding wall and deteriorating shrubbery. The condition of its play equipment isn't up to what's found in the other city parks. There's general neglect of the grounds and shelter. The only occasion when the park seems to become part of the city's larger culture is each July when it hosts its "Dust Bowl" summer basketball competition and players come from across the city.

One hears of a certain passivity, quiet desperation, a disinclination in the black community to question "the way things are done." There seems to be a matching cynicism in the larger community. When west side residents last summer complained they were being shortchanged in basic city services, the mayor and council and city manager did respond with special hearings, and the neighborhood's condition got several days of airing in the press. There seemed reason to believe the residents' concerns would receive a lot more attention than in the past—perhaps even that such basic changes as assignment of regular foot patrolmen would get on the city's agenda. (It's absurd, we'd suggest, to think it's sufficient just to send a patrol car through a troubled or neglected neighborhood, without having police become personally acquainted with the people on an intimate, daily basis.)

Yet ongoing attention is essential for such neighborhoods. We were a touch alarmed when a longtime observer remarked almost laconically that minor protests like those of the summer of 1991 do surface every few years, but quickly subside, not to be heard again for another decade or so.

It's certainly true the Owensboro community has been spared the racially charged turmoil other American cities have suffered. We were told Owensboro's public housing, located on the west side, was something to avoid, to steer around. Yet when we saw it, it resembled rather well-maintained, lower-cost market-rate housing anywhere else. Compared to public housing in a Chicago, New York, or Atlanta, the Owensboro public housing stock looks like Eden on earth.

But the challenge to Owensboro goes a lot deeper than providing decent-looking public housing. Basic respect has to be built. Owensboro must acknowledge it needs its African-American citizens as productive and participating members of its future society. To ignore them isn't fair; it's also not smart.

One answer can be a far more conscious effort to draw blacks into civic activities, to try to open multiple gates of opportunity. The community's new outreach to disadvantaged children ought to have a strong, positive effect in the black community. A black-based community organization, Owensboro Career Development, is trying to stem the flow of school dropouts and is having reasonable success. (In the Owensboro School District, the black dropout rate is *lower* than that for whites.)

But blacks themselves need to take their natural share of political power. As a local minister told the *Messenger-Inquirer* last July: "Blacks are overlooked because they have no political clout, because half don't register to vote, and half of those that register don't vote. Then when you want something, you complain to the city, but they know you can't hurt them because you don't vote."

Few of Owensboro's young blacks are going to college. We find that surprising, because in most cities where new community colleges start, there's a rush of enrollment by minority groups that previously never made it into higher education. Indeed, community colleges have been a powerful democratizing force in higher education, a bridge over which hundreds of thousands of young blacks and Hispanics and poor whites have made the journey to a world of wider opportunity.

Yet there's this perplexing fact: the minority enrollment in Owensboro Community College is only 2 percent, while blacks represent 5.9 percent of the city, 3.9 percent of the county population.

If the community cares enough about the quality of its future work force—and opportunities for all its citizens—this is a correctable situation.

If the problem is that young blacks don't see college as a place for them, then there could be a community effort to guarantee any graduate of its high schools at least one year of community college.

If transportation from the west and east sides of Owensboro is a problem—and of course it is, given the community college's outlying location—then a bus or van service has to be instituted, diligently promoted, and seen as more than a passing experiment. Having chosen quite consciously to locate the community college outside of the town center, in fact at a location quite inaccessible to heavily black neighborhoods, the community has a special obligation here. Dismissing the special bus line idea for lack of interest or low fare receipts without advertising it actively and promoting the entire community college opportunity for minorities strikes us as insincere.

If some potential students have already taken on family responsibilities, lack of day care may be the biggest barrier. There are some stirrings on this front. Owensboro Community College has been considering a contract with the vocational school Kentucky Tech's child care program, hailed as one of the country's best, to offer a care program on campus. We also heard talk of a communitywide center for child care, one that would be oriented to child development rather than mere warehousing of young kids while their parents work.

All the planning is encouraging, but the community has to recognize it has a near emergency on its hands. For a growing proportion of families, day care is no longer an option—it's a necessity. If Owensboro–Daviess County can foster a set of services that are available broadly and democratically, then a lot of closed doors to college and work will swing open, especially for young women.

The sum of the strategies we've touched on—a Committee for Safe Growth, downtown revitalization, expanded help for kids and families, a more active senior citizen corps, and a community college that moves minorities into the mainstream—ought surely to be a stronger, more resilient community. But even experimentation with new ideas—civic research and development work, so to speak—costs money. A community may be awash with new ideas but unable to try them for lack of even a modest amount of research money. Ask any civic entrepreneur: social innovation requires some walking-around money.

Owensboro has been uniquely fortunate in the presence of Texas Gas, with its imaginative giving to community causes and pacesetting commitment of 5 percent of pretax profits for charity. With luck, this company and the banks and other corporations that follow its lead will be a feature of Owensboro life for decades to come. But in the shark-infested waters of American corporate life, nothing's guaranteed. Across America, business giving to communities has flattened out or begun to decline. It's time for the community to think about a backup.

Across America, hundreds of cities and regions have created, and now nourish, what are known as "community foundations." People who may have money to give, but not enough to start a megafoundation on their own, make gifts and bequests. Indeed, a little shopping around may locate a national foundation willing to put up matching dollars to get a strong local community foundation up and running. The Mott Foundation, located in Flint, Michigan, started doing that a few years ago and since has been joined by such heavies as the Ford, MacArthur, McKnight, and Lilly foundations.

Lilly, in fact, has committed $47 million over the next 15 years to help Indiana communities get up and running on the community foundation front. It recently gave the Fort Wayne Community Foundation a challenge grant of $1.7 million. An appeal to spread a little of Lilly's megabucks across the Ohio River might conceivably work.

We asked about private wealth in the Owensboro region and heard more than enough names to start and maintain a healthy community foundation. The outpouring of contributions for the RiverPark Center proved the potential.

An Owensboro community foundation was begun some years ago, but it's essentially dormant. It needs to be revived or a new effort inaugurated. Such an organization could be immensely helpful in launching the new efforts critical for regional citizenship—in providing social services, in supporting open space and the environment, in inaugurating new educational efforts, in researching governmental improvement. Look around America and you find hundreds of examples of what community foundations can do. Indiana's Elkhart County Community Foundation, for example, is now the lead supporter of a new riverwalk project on the St. Joseph River. In Louisiana, the New Orleans Committee Foundation has a "good neighborhood fund" to provide timely interim aid for people about to become homeless. The community foundation serving both Duluth, Minnesota, and Superior, Wisconsin, sought to encourage cooperation between local governments by giving one county sheriff's office a computerized "identi-kit" program—but only on condition it would be shared with all the neighboring jurisdictions. In Trion, North Carolina, the Polk County Community Foundation put up money for clearly numbered and lettered green and white signs along rural county roads, so that crews responding to "911" calls can get to the scene of the emergency.

Within the next few years, we believe Owensboro may be ready to form a regional citizens organization that examines critical public issues, develops new policy directions, acts as a sounding board for sensible solutions. Such an organization could take a consistent, conscious, regionwide view—something it's hard for elected officials, under the drumbeat of parochial constituent pressures, to do.

It's for that kind of situation that a community foundation could be invaluable. Community foundations manage the loose change in American society. They don't hand out huge sums of money, but their funds are the most flexible, potentially creative money around.

If the Owensboro–Daviess County community has a single big institutional goal for the early 1990s, we suggest a community foundation ought to be it. With its resources, such a foundation could enable continuing and expanded initiatives to strengthen city and county, to make proud regional citizenship a reality. And it could work to develop the informed, imaginative leadership needed to make Owensboro a flagship city among the urban centers along the Ohio.

Update

In the year after the Peirce Report for Owensboro was published, the city could point to some advances, some disappointments, but on the whole a healthy report card—one that most American communities would be hard-pressed to match.

RiverPark Center, Owensboro's jewel on the Ohio, opened to rave reviews, energetic ticket sales, and gratified reactions by owners of downtown restaurants. Downtown renovation moved forward apace and there was a tentative first trickle of people selecting the city's center as a place to live as well as work.

Daviess County's important agricultural base was recognized in a big way for the first time by the Owensboro Chamber of Commerce—an important step not just for regional economics, but for healing the wounds of the 1990 merger fight. A Chamber-organized tour highlighted innovations in local agriculture, and agribusiness people began to play a greater role in Chamber planning activities.

The idea of a community foundation, which the Peirce Report identified as perhaps the most important civic step the city and county could take for the 1990s, generated positive response from community leaders and seemed likely to become reality in the 1990s.

The Kentucky Education Reform Act appeared to have a positive impact in the local schools—both in creating new and exciting learning environments for children, and in involving parents and teachers in important decisions.

The city and county governments came together for six joint meetings, skirting the more controversial issues but establishing a valuable precedent. In the immediate wake of the 1990 merger vote, few people would have thought this type of cooperation possible.

Owensboro officials listened to African-Americans' complaints about the decrepit condition of Kendall Perkins Park, inaugurating clean-up and fix-up measures there. In 1992 the city voted to create Martin Luther King Plaza along several blocks of Fifth Street. Yet the issue of low black enrollment at Owensboro Community College remained unresolved.

As far as improving Owensboro–Daviess County's dismal record on bringing more women into public life, the community appeared to make virtually no progress.

On the business front, there was expanded outreach to businesses already active in the city and county, especially on the part of the Owensboro–Daviess County Chamber of Commerce. Such business retention initiatives appeared to balance the multimillion-dollar subsidy expended to recruit Scott Paper. But there still seemed to be an inequity—that a footloose firm debating whether to move into the area could well get special financing or tax abatement inducements denied to home-grown Owensboro–Daviess County businesses.

The suggestion that the community form a Safe Growth Committee to monitor the public subsidy costs and environmental consequences of proposed major industrial developments annoyed some who feared such a committee would become a forbidding new level of regulation, a "no-growth" panel. The proposal never went beyond an advisory group.

In a guest piece published in the *Messenger-Inquirer* to accompany a "year later" series of articles its staff wrote on the Peirce Report in October 1992, Neal Peirce insisted that the Safe Growth Committee idea still deserved consideration. "Owensboro is a relative latecomer to the era of

environmental activism. Indeed, it's impressive how fast groups of concerned citizens have come onto the scene and started to develop expertise
and negotiate with industries and government.

"But a smart region doesn't let its environmental debates be dominated
by 'NIMBY-ism' and bitter stand-offs between industry and activists.
America's effective international competitors, such as Japan and Germany,
are way past that stage. They see the immense, emerging international
market in industrial products that control toxics and the advantages of
creating products without triggering harmful emissions at all. A smart
region and its industries should think the same way, to get *ahead* of the
curve, phasing out 'dirty' plants and equipment, retraining workers now
employed in low-skill, economically imperiled jobs that gobble up energy
and nonrenewable resources."

The Citistate in Brief

The Dallas citistate is part of an even greater one—the "metroplex" embracing Dallas, Fort Worth, and their environs. This 18,580-square-mile, eight-county area, as defined by the U.S. Census Bureau, grew 16 percent in population in the 1980s, to 3,885,415. In 1990 Dallas proper had 987,360 people, Dallas County a total of 1,854,700. Among other significant population centers in the Dallas orbit are Garland, Plano, Richardson, Irving, Mesquite, Duncanville, Grand Prairie, and Arlington. Overall, the Dallas–Fort Worth region comprises 168 cities and towns, 96 school districts, and 88 special districts.

The Peirce Report Glossary

Skyscraper-lined *Pacific Avenue* is home to several major financial institutions, including NationsBank Texas. *Union Station,* built in 1914, is serviced by Amtrak and provides space for offices, restaurants, and the Dallas Visitors Information Center. The *Reunion Arena Complex* includes Union Station, the landmark *Reunion Tower,* and a multipurpose sports and entertainment facility that seats up to 20,000. Property in *State-Thomas,* an inner-city area northeast of downtown historically populated by African-Americans, has been bought by developers who plan to construct upscale apartments for in-town living. *Bryan Place,* located just east of downtown, in the late 1970s and early '80s provided the first new inner-city sites for upper- and middle-income housing. North of downtown, brick-lined *McKinney Avenue* has a five-block stretch offering some of the city's finest restaurants, antique shops, and galleries. Electric trolleys link it to the city's *Arts District.* The *West End,* also known as the "Warehouse District," contains 1920s warehouses and small factories being restored and converted to new uses, including over 150 of Dallas's most popular boutiques, restaurants, and clubs. *Deep Ellum* is a former industrial neighborhood east of downtown, now the site of avant-garde nightclubs and galleries. *Dallas Parkway,* considered to be Dallas's second "downtown," contains large, upscale shopping centers and several large office complexes.

Lake Cliff Park is a visionary inner-city water park planned for the Trinity River just south of downtown Dallas. *Fair Park,* a national historic landmark originally designed for a World's Fair, is home to the Cotton Bowl, the African-American Museum of Life and Culture, the Museum of National History, the Aquarium, Science Place, the State Fair of Texas, and other attractions.

Top business officials with civic interests make up the *Dallas Citizens Council.* The *Central Dallas Association* focuses on revitalizing the downtown economy. The *North Central Texas Council of Governments* attempts coordination of regional planning and economic development. *DART* stands for Dallas Area Rapid Transit, the regional transportation authority that has been occupied since the late 1980s with construction of Dallas's light-rail system.

Defining the Future

(Originally published as a special section of The Dallas Morning News *on October 27, 1991.)*

In 2010, will the city of Dallas be dynamic or decaying?

Imagine that the date is January 10, 2010. The scene is Dallas City Hall, the occasion the swearing-in of Stephanie Wong, daughter of an immigrant family of the 1980s, as Dallas's first Asian-American mayor.

Long rays of winter sun filter into the great public spaces of the building, which was remodeled in 2008 to restore some of the elegance of the late 20th century, when it was known as a Taj Mahal among American municipal buildings. The lobby has been redesigned to celebrate the multiple cultures—African-American, Asian, Hispanic, white—that make up the new Dallas.

Ethnic politics has indeed become so important that the president of the United States, Colin Powell, has just arrived and joined the crowd for the inauguration. In a couple of hours he'll begin a fast trip around Texas cities on the "bullet train" system built under the administration of Gov. Henry Cisneros in the late 1990s.

The significance of the inauguration hasn't been lost on Japanese economic leaders. In fact, Takashi Karatsu, chairman of the gigantic Takei Corporation, which only last year absorbed the often-restructured IBM Corporation, is on hand. Rumor has it he's also in Dallas for serious talks with Texas Instruments.

A television commentator babbles before a camera about the apparent political miracle that propelled Ms. Wong into the mayoralty in a city in which Hispanics now make up 62 percent of the population. Ms. Wong did build broad respect in the Hispanic community as BankFour's financial wizard, pulling off a string of sensational, job-producing Dallas–Mexico City trade deals before her plunge into politics.

But stop. This fanciful future—which we suggest is as realistic as any—doesn't tell you where Dallas and the region will really stand in 2010.

Assume that Ms. Wong's first big crisis will be a meeting with mayors and business leaders from across the region to deal with a roaring energy emergency. Nine months after the latest outbreak of hostilities in the Middle East, all major oil fields there are either on fire or behind enemy lines. The United States has been drawing down its oil reserves at an alarming rate. Rumors fly of gas and oil hoarding. The price of gasoline has soared to $10 a gallon—the equivalent of $5 in 1991 prices.

A few Texas companies cash in. But the blow to Dallas commuters and businesses, in a region built on inexpensive energy and the open road, is severe. What's the response of a freeway and freon society when someone pulls the plug? Does the crisis set off new and more bitter discord along lines of class and race and geography? Or does it demonstrate potential for cooperation and inventive survival strategies?

Put another way, how will things be different in 2010 from the way they are in 1991? Will diversity have turned out to be a curse or a foundation for a more vibrant, colorful, interesting Dallas society? Will the carnival of discord in the City Council and school board chambers during the early 1990s have given way to political maturity, a capacity for compromise?

Will South Dallas still be an economic pariah, or will it have become a burgeoning investment zone, with fresh opportunities for its people? Will downtown's precipitous decline of recent years be reversed? Will the schools have prepared the people of low-income neighborhoods to be competent players in an economy that demands constantly higher levels of skill? Will citizens across the Dallas area be organized to demand that their leaders think regionally and strategically and reward them if they do?

No one can say, with certainty, what the answers will be to these questions in 2010. But we're convinced that those answers are being born in the 1990s. We present below alternative visions of what the Dallas region may be like in 2010.

Vision I assumes that the region bumbles along without any major change in the way it now does things.

Vision II reflects what might happen with some dramatic changes in course—shifts designed to make Dallas more resilient in the next century. Our interviews with more than 60 leaders of the region—from business, government, neighborhoods, and environmental groups—revealed a cornucopia of new ideas. We sensed a clear capacity to make Vision II, a stronger and more equitable and more livable Dallas, a reality.

Our visit to Dallas came in a crisis-packed year, with dilemmas ranging from the bitter City Council redistricting dispute to the Dallas Independent School District's public relations debacle that occurred when it fired and then rehired teachers to adjust to a $47-million budget loss.

Yet behind it all, we found that enormous strengths remain in place: the Dallas region's "can-do" spirit, its positive long-term economic prospects, its immense reservoirs of talent in business and civic organizations, academia, and nonprofit groups. The real question isn't whether the Dallas region has the capacity to mobilize its resources to rise confidently— economically and socially—toward the 21st century. It's whether it has the will.

Vision I: Opportunity Lost

The path of least resistance for any community is to keep on making decisions the way it always has made them. Dallas and its surrounding cities can make that choice. If they do, here's a vision of how life might be in 2010.

Twenty years ago, during the early 1990s, a 20-ton tractor-trailer would have to jackknife on Stemmons Freeway to slow traffic to a crawl. Today, crawling is about the best one can hope for any time from 5 a.m. to late evening on most Dallas-area freeways.

Freeways don't seem so free anymore. Laws passed between 2000 and 2005 required that pavement meters keep track of freeway use through bar code devices on cars' underbellies. The roads are clogged despite heavy extra charges for drivers who add to peak-hour traffic.

There's the story of the European Community official from Brussels, Belgium, who swore never to return after a three-hour traffic snarl on the supposedly improved North Central Expressway made him miss his transoceanic flight. Earlier, he'd been asking about a rapid-rail link between the city and Dallas/Fort Worth International Airport, but locals had to tell him it had never been built. Then there was the hot August afternoon when the westbound traffic on LBJ Freeway came to a total halt from 2 to 7 p.m. while police helicopters were sent in to try to untangle the mess. Even 21st-century cars, it turns out, can boil over after a couple of hours in the sun, soon disabling the batteries powering their drivers' portable phones and fax machines. About the only place free of frightful traffic these days is downtown. At what was once called the center of the Dallas area, there's an eerie stillness. The wind whistles betwixt the towers of the architects' ego manifestations of the 1980s. City Hall is still here. So are the Federal Reserve Bank, the public library, and a couple of imposing but forlorn structures that had once been foreseen as the center of a lively Arts District of performance halls and artists' quarters.

But not a single downtown private building project has been commissioned since the 1980s. Except for a couple of convenience stores, all retailing has fled. Neiman Marcus, the last holdout retailer, finally abandoned its mother store in 1995. By 2018, downtown employment dwindled to half of what it was in 1991. Buildings stand abandoned, boarded at street level. Corporations no longer expect employees to get from car to office except by guarded tunnel or walkway.

A downtown circulator never got moving. The proposal for a light-rail corridor down Pacific Avenue collapsed with the disappearance of the regional transit agency—DART—that had hoped to put it in place.

Dallas has maintained its centrifugal march. Development has moved outward, outward, outward, forever in search of cheap land. Workplaces spread ever farther apart.

During the 1990s and the first decade of the 21st century, the number of vehicle miles traveled in Dallas rose 70 percent, although the area's population rose only 16 percent. The increase in auto miles traveled, plus the thousands of added trucks on the roads, paralyzed one Dallas-area freeway after another. Too late, the region's people realized that their northward and westward development surges, to Las Colinas, to Plano, across mile after mile of the North Texas plain, were not simply a glittering succession of commercial successes.

Another ugly bill came due on the air pollution front. The cumulative emissions of thousands upon thousands of added vehicles produced a perpetual smelly haze from Duncanville to Denton. Although the newer cars were more efficient, their sheer numbers overwhelmed technological advances. Aging baby boomers, average age now 60, complained of mounting health problems. Frequent pollution alerts cast a pall over the region's once-vaunted high quality of life.

Another consequence, perhaps even more alarming, sprang up on the social front. The Dallas area's economically advantaged North moved farther ahead of its depressed South. The area south of the Trinity River became an ever-worsening economic disaster zone. Old jobs disappeared, new ones failed to replace them. Restaurants, small shops, and manufacturing plants closed their doors. Almost total social breakdown ensued, centered in South Dallas but spreading at an alarming rate into once-stable Oak Cliff neighborhoods. During the 1990s, Dallas police were still trying to quash drug deals and close crack houses. By 2000, the physical danger to officers became so severe that the department was reluctant to enter South Dallas unless actual riots erupted. The area became so bad that Paul Quinn College left the area when land in Fort Worth became available.

Marauding gangs of disillusioned youths ruled the streets. They'd gotten the clear message that their lives were considered worthless, so they figured other people's lives were worthless, too. By 2004, Dallas had a murder rate three times what it had been in 1991.

Usually the gangs from poor parts of the city stayed close to home. But one summer evening in 2009, one group rode out, invaded a suburban shopping center, and vandalized cars ranging from Mercedes and Porsches to Novas. Customers in the stores were terrified. Afterward, gun shop owners sold out their stocks almost overnight, and private security companies picked up hundreds of new customers. Strip malls became favorite targets, as random violence ricocheted around the region.

Over time, Dallas's environmental and social crises began to deal the regional economy an even more dire hit than the banking and real estate collapses of the 1980s. The decline in property value, which people had first assumed was just part of the early 1990s recession, continued and accelerated. A shrinking tax base across Dallas County triggered cuts in services and deferred maintenance of critical infrastructure. The flow of office workers out of downtown, and out of Dallas, could no longer be covered up.

For years, many suburbanites thought that economic decline in the city really wouldn't affect them. As late as 1997, when Motorola moved to Plano from Chicago, people continued to believe that. But after Motorola, no one else came. Industrial locators carried stories far and wide of the Dallas region's environmental decay and mounting social discord. Slowly, the smugness subsided.

A decisive blow came in 2006 when the British Broadcasting Corporation did a comprehensive report on the Dallas region as it competed to be the site of the 2012 Olympics. Dallas's dire air pollution, the crime waves, the near-desertion of downtown, got full play. Fair Park, which was already reeling from the loss of the State Fair to San Antonio in 2002, was a big loser in the failed bid. The Olympic Search Committee laughed at the decaying Cotton Bowl and its tawdry surroundings.

KERA-TV, one of the few concerns still operating near the downtown core, caused an uproar by broadcasting the full BBC report and then inviting the mayor, the governor, and the corporate executive who headed the Dallas Citizens Council to comment on the fairness of the reportage.

There was special outrage over the BBC's assertion that Dallas's North-South split, whites moving northward, minorities stuck south of the Trinity, represented a new form of apartheid. BBC called it the equivalent of the homelands policy imposed by South Africa before its reform of the 1990s.

A spokeswoman for the Dallas Citizens Council accused the British of fouling up their facts. For 30 years, she said, there'd been a substantial movement of middle-class blacks out of southern Dallas to a variety of neighborhoods ranging from the area around Redbird and the Oak Cliff Country Club in the southwest to Carrollton, north of the LBJ Freeway. And Hispanics, she noted, were living all across the city and region.

But when an enterprising *Wall Street Journal* reporter got Mayor Stephanie Wong to agree to an interview on the BBC-generated furor, she admitted that if class rather than race were used as one's measuring stick, then the Trinity River was as deep a dividing line as ever.

At about the same time, a team of senior writers at *The Dallas Morning News* was analyzing just what had gone wrong, how Dallas had squandered its immense advantages and economic momentum of the glory years and reached such a sad state. The more they looked into the question, the more their answer came back to a failure of public leadership. The late 1980s and early 1990s had seen the Dallas City Council immersed in a deeply divisive battle over representation. Blacks and Hispanics were saying they'd been shortchanged for decades, that the time for equity was finally at hand. A court case, carried through many battles, finally forced a complete single-member-district system, doing away entirely with the at-large seats that had seemed for decades to favor the city's old white majority.

That decision, which coincided with dramatic Hispanic and modest black population growth in the city, should have been sufficient, at last, to put the matter to rest. But it wasn't. The expanded African-American contingent on the council ran into especially severe problems. Black council members found themselves torn between black "retributionists" in their ranks, who tried to make sure whites felt the sting of new black power, and black "pragmatists," who were eager to find middle ground.

But by 2004, Hispanics were taking away council seats blacks had gained during the 1980s and '90s, rubbing raw the very real Hispanic-black tensions in many neighborhoods.

The ethnic infighting sealed the city government's paralysis. The council failed to tackle the vital long-term issues that demanded its attention, from the North-South division to neighborhood deterioration to mass transit systems that might have reduced the region's mounting clouds of air pollution. The council stuck with the city manager form of government but rendered it ineffectual by making working conditions unbearable for a quick succession of city managers who left Dallas one after another in disillusionment.

On the education front, Dallas's quarrelsome school board remained mired in disputes about finances, staffing, facilities, and the increasingly hot issue of multicultural curriculum. Marches by teachers, parents, and students on the Ross Avenue headquarters of the Dallas Independent School District produced short-term reactions but little long-term change. The board eventually approved the dramatic school site-based management recommendations made by the Kress Commission it had created. A few pilot projects appeared, but the education administrators dismissed them as insufficiently impressive. By 2000, it was fair to say the system had succeeded in suffocating reform.

And when a group of civic entrepreneurs from Dallas and the suburbs tried to organize a regional citizens organization to press the politicians for positive change, for some kind of broader vision, they were quickly quashed. Politicos scoffed at the idea, saying it wasn't needed. Businesses turned a cold shoulder, refusing to support anything they couldn't control. Every camp, in fact, looked out aggressively for its special interest, virtually no one for the *common* interest. Dallas lost.

Vision II: A 21st-Century City

With vision and courage, any city and metropolitan area can take action to improve, often by dramatic measure, its future prospects. Here is a vision of how things might be in 2010, if Dallas started making the right moves now.

Dallas is on a roll again.

A wave of euphoria has swept over the region in the wake of the International Olympic Committee's announcement that the Summer Games will come to Dallas in 2016. The victory followed tough competition against such contenders as Rome, Tokyo, and San Diego and was the culmination of a business-citizen task force's concerted efforts to tie down strong local financial guarantees and showcase the city's advantages.

The committee was wowed by the state-of-the-art sports complex at the remodeled Cotton Bowl, along with the refurbishment of the neighborhoods surrounding Fair Park. Committee members said the facilities were world class.

For Dallas residents with any kind of memory, the Olympic "victory" was a tribute to the way the city and region had gotten their act together over the last 20 years. On the city hall front, the mayor and council elected in autumn 1991, the first election after all-district elections went into effect, tried hard to put behind them the ferocious internecine and racial conflicts of the prior years. People agreed that the new amity made it easier for Dallas to elect, with minimal controversy, its first black mayor in 1995 and its first Hispanic chief executive in 2003. Candidates able to suggest a common vision for the city tended to attract larger ethnic crossover votes than their counterparts in such cities as Atlanta, Philadelphia, and Miami.

And as Dallas looked forward to the 2016 Olympics, people would say policies established during the early 1990s had set the stage:

The council decided to make a frontal attack on the decline of poor neighborhoods. Multipurpose service centers were created in neighborhoods across the city, aimed at lifting needy residents toward self-sufficiency in a number of ways. Many of the centers were in school facilities that remained open to the public from morning through evening, seven days a week. Almost all provided health clinics, job preparation counseling, adult education, and connections to police officers permanently assigned to the same neighborhoods. The police became, in effect, allies and ombudsmen for residents.

Government services became friendlier, less bureaucratic—and began to work better. Through neighborhood boards directing multiple functions, Dallas became America's lead city in neighborhood self-governance. Thousands of troubled families started to get on their feet. By 2000, levels of welfare dependency, school dropouts, teenage pregnancy, arrests, and prison sentences were declining. Dallas made a welcome exit from the top of national murder and robbery charts.

Among the revived neighborhoods was West Dallas, where the council finally came up with the commitment from the city necessary to uncork $70 million in federal funds for a stem-to-stern revitalization—and humanization—of America's largest low-rise public housing project. Tenants were given a strong role in managing and shaping the social services and police support, which slowly but surely restored safety and stability. In the early 1990s, one of the West Dallas tenant leaders was elected to the City Council.

Between 1992 and 1994, four large local corporations started making good on the corporate rhetoric about the need for the renewal of southern Dallas. Putting their money where their mouths were, They opened substantial branch operations south of the Trinity. They demanded that the city first substantially upgrade public infrastructure and guarantee quality police protection—and got satisfaction on both counts.

Combined with the Southern Dallas Development Corporation's aggressive job and factory hunts and tied into training programs at the Bill J. Priest Institute and Mountain View College, the new corporate investments helped ignite a flurry of complementary business investments in the city's most neglected area. Each new job created as a result helped buttress neighborhood revival efforts.

And as the sinews of neighborhood life strengthened, Dallas belatedly began to form a significant number of community development corporations. These indigenous efforts to build housing and spawn grass-roots businesses, which had burgeoned from Boston to Chicago to Los Angeles during the 1970s and '80s, for some unknown reason had never taken root in Dallas.

In 1996, the New York–based Local Initiatives Support Corporation finally concluded that the powers in Dallas were no longer treating troubled neighborhoods with studied indifference. LISC formed a partnership with local corporations, the Meadows Foundation, and the Communities Foundation of Texas, flooding millions of dollars into community development projects in some of Dallas's poorest neighborhoods.

The new council decided that Dallas couldn't risk the quality of schools declining any further. So when the Dallas Independent School District board started scuttling some key recommendations made by the Commission on Educational Excellence headed by Sandy Kress, the council threatened to employ a rarely used state law permitting a city to declare a school system functionally bankrupt and take it over.

That broadside got the DISD's attention. School-based management and performance-based accountability, the heart of the Kress recommendations, were implemented. By 2002, the school board enthusiastically supported parent/staff-led schools as well as their circle of complementary social services.

It was finally time, the council decided, to transform the Trinity River ditch that had so long symbolized the deep divisions—psychic, social, and physical—between downtown/North Dallas and southern Dallas. Dramatically invoking the city's vaunted but overly protected bonding capacity, the council voted to start construction of a stunning new amenity—the long-discussed, decades-overdue Town Lake.

The initiative worked. By the late 1990s, downtown Dallas had a sparkling new doorstep. Investors and developers scrambled to meet the new demand for offices, apartments, restaurants, and cafes with vistas overlooking the water. New apartment buildings constructed on the bluffs of the Gateway Area, just across from downtown in southern Dallas, provided choice residences for young professionals who wanted to work downtown and enjoy spectacular views of the lake and downtown skyline. Each morning, the residents could stroll down to the ferry, cruise across the lake, and ride the new downtown light-rail circulator to their offices.

The lake didn't get built without spirited debate. Some people said its waters would be too stagnant. Others feared that it would be a threat to wildlife. Fears weren't put to rest until an independent environmental assessment gave the project a stamp of approval.

Others said it was outrageous for the city to go ahead with a project as expensive as Town Lake without a public referendum. No way, said council members; the accelerating disinvestment in downtown proved that it was time to get moving—and quickly. "For years, people have been asking us to show a little leadership," said one council member. "If anyone doesn't like it, they can replace us in the next election. I don't believe they will." (The next election results, interestingly, proved that he was right. All the Town Lake supporters won new terms.)

The council pledged itself to reverse downtown's drift toward an increasingly sterile, sometimes hostile, environment. They agreed that Dallas needed a friendly downtown, one that provided common ground for the people of the city and region. A multiple set of strategies crystallized: an interesting configuration of new sidewalks, fountains, and steps; construction of the downtown circulator; artists' studios and shops and cafes in the vicinity of the Arts District; street-level beautification; rewriting of tax laws to discourage speculators holding downtown parcels as empty lots.

A nationally renowned urban planner was brought on board to implement a number of the approaches developed by James Pratt for the Dallas Institute of Humanities and Culture. Top among them: the revival of Fair Park and turning Haskell Avenue into a tree-lined jewel of Dallas life, linking Fair Park, downtown, and Oak Lawn.

By 1996 it turned out that the "soft" approach to quality of life in the downtown had some "hard" business results. About 20,000 people were living in downtown, office employment had halted its alarming slump and began to creep upward again. From the West End to Deep Ellum, street life in downtown Dallas revived.

Another big boost for downtown materialized in 1995, when virtually all the region's colleges and universities coalesced to form a Dallas University Center, with facilities in one of downtown's abandoned department store buildings. Suddenly, all manner of research facilities were being shared. Students, allowed to take courses at sister institutions, enriched their curriculums and future job prospects. Dallas's stature as a center of higher education was enhanced. And for the first time, the University of Texas's Dallas branch, located well to the north in Richardson, was directly linked to the city's diversity.

In 1998, the state surprisingly agreed to take over Paul Quinn College in southern Dallas. Heavy lobbying by the City Council and enthusiastic support by Dallas's legislative delegation were credited. Because UT-Dallas had been located miles north of the region's center, supporters said, it was high time to put hard state dollars behind a major institution on the city's near-south flank, directly on bus lines. Paul Quinn's academic distinction grew. And Paul Quinn attempted a rare breakthrough on the cultural front. On the one hand, it became the region's premier college for African-Americans, enhancing the growth of a solid, middle-class black culture that Dallas had always lacked. ("Dallas's Morehouse," some called it.) Yet at the same time, Paul Quinn drew a significant number of Hispanics and whites and provided students who started at one of the Dallas community colleges with an opportunity to obtain a bachelor's degree.

Yet, for all the advances Dallas was registering during the 1990s, all was not well. The region's traffic nightmare was worsening. Citizens were increasingly enraged by snarled highways, air pollution, diminishing accessibility. A kind of gut fear developed: "No one's in charge here; there may be no solution." Metropolitan coordination remained as anemic as ever. And the local politicians threw up their hands in despair and said there was virtually nothing they, alone, could do.

In 1992, a group of concerned citizens from across the Dallas metropolitan area—neighborhood activists, academics, planners, business executives, environmentalists—began to meet. They quickly agreed that their central problem was how to attain the regional focus that the transportation and air quality issues required. ("Whose City Council do you blame for a brown cloud?" one person at the meetings quipped.)

After checking out the best regional approaches being tried around the country, the group developed a list of recommendations—HOV lanes, metered access, and peak-hour fees for the most congested corridors; "balanced" job and residence locations to reduce long auto trips; making development projects more compact, and thus, transit accessible; plus pressure on DART to complete its initial light-rail lines. The blueprint generated such interest that it ended up on the agenda of city councils across the region.

But the citizens recognized that their blueprint was just a first step, that continued research and friendly pressure on the politicians would be critical. They turned to business, including leadership of the once-dominating Dallas Citizens Council, for some significant financial support—and got it. In January 1993, the Metropolitan Civic League, independent of government and seeking members and support from citizens of every community of the region, was launched.

By 2010, the Metropolitan Civic League had become a critical regionwide player on every front from land use to solid waste, regional parks to mass transit. Its pressure on local governments sparked a regional consciousness and an agenda more ambitious than most had ever thought possible. It persuaded one community after another to save open spaces and build homes, offices, and commercial centers more compactly. It goaded DART to perform efficiently and helped accelerate mass transit development.

But where the rubber literally meets the road—on Dallas's freeways—progress seemed painfully slow in relieving the acute congestion. Road congestion and air quality problems seemed to peak around 2005. But by 2010, everyone was holding his or her breath. To snare the Olympics, the Dallas task force felt obliged to guarantee a significant reduction of pollutants in the air the Olympic athletes would breathe when the games opened in 2016. The promise meant, among other things, that freewheeling Dallas would have to put the brakes on its escalation in vehicle-miles traveled and even show the first steps toward a rollback.

Now, in the eyes of the whole world, "Big D" had to prove whether its promises were for real.

(Following the two visions of Dallas's future, the Peirce Report continued with discussions of individual aspects of the city's and region's civic challenges.)

Culture Shock: Changing Ways for Changing Times

Dallas seems poised, eager to become a great international city, a major player in a new world economic order in which citistates become the globe's arenas of critical action. What's more, it has strong assets—a mix of such industries as electronics, telecommunications, health care, transportation services, wholesale and retail merchandising—that are expected to grow in the years ahead.

Economist Bernard L. Weinstein of the University of North Texas classifies Dallas as one of the six American metropolises—the others on his list are New York, Los Angeles, Seattle, Chicago, and Atlanta—that carry international weight and serve as transportation and financial centers for multistate areas. But whatever the promise, the business style and collective decision-making culture of cities can make all the difference for their futures.

What about the Dallas culture?

We think there may be a problem.

The fabled Dallas of the past was a bit like a '57 Chevy. Dallas was America's car, the sleekest vehicle of the horsepower age. Its raw, muscular power made it a kind of legend in its time. It offered a spectacular economic success story, the stuff of TV legend.

Today, though, an unmodified '57 Chevy can be a peril on the road. It guzzles gas and can't compete with its modern technological rivals. Replacement parts are expensive.

To us, Dallas's legendary culture, the way of doing things that got it a nationwide reputation of being the smooth-running "city that works," resembles the '57 Chevy.

And there are some real questions about obsolescence. The curtain has come down on J. R. The once-omnipotent banks and real estate operators who made Dallas globally famous have hit the rocks. Today about 5 percent of Dallas real estate is owned by the Resolution Trust Corporation, the federally chartered overseer of failed savings and loans.

In the city where decisions used to be made quietly and efficiently behind the scenes, a carnival of political name-calling and shouting often seems to dominate City Council and school board sessions. Racial tensions, once suppressed, erupt everywhere. A federal judge declares the council districts illegal. Dallas's crime rate soars.

The only big city in America with a triple-A bond rating clings to it so timorously that it fails to make critical investments. West Dallas residents who inhabit America's largest low-rise public housing project, carefully segregated away from downtown on the other side of the Trinity, had to sue to force the city to provide the most elemental services. Fears mount of a "hollowing-out" of central Dallas, the city becoming—like a Detroit or

Hartford, Connecticut—the "hole in the doughnut" of an otherwise viable regional economy.

What's going on here? Did someone bury the plans for the future in the trunk of the '57 Chevy?

No way, some Dallas politicians and business leaders told us. The city is simply maturing. The disappearance of locally owned and controlled businesses, they explain, is happening all over America. The suburbs are outshining the center cities everywhere. The schools are just victims of a bad news media rap. Racial tensions are a temporary annoyance.

Don't worry, one top elected leader told us: "I'm bullish on Dallas."

We don't buy it. We believe that Dallas's problems run a lot deeper, that the changes under way challenge the city's very culture.

The city's task is tougher than simply opening the door to widened leadership. It has to change its ways. A fundamental change in cultures has to happen. A new paradigm, a new way of thinking, is struggling to be born. It needs many midwives.

The old Dallas culture celebrated the self-made man. Its prototype was the oilman or financier who hit it rich, left his competitors in the dust, and then bought enough space along Turtle Creek to show off his wealth.

That lifestyle may have been the stuff of legends (and great fiction), but it won't carry Dallas far during the 1990s. There'll still be an occasional buccaneer winner. But the people needed today, in business and public life alike, are collaborators, consensus-makers, people who have the skill to do things together.

Even corporate leaders who climbed to the top the old way are the first to agree that succeeding in business now depends on spreading decision making and responsibility for results.

The old culture said "I." The new culture says "we." It talks about interdependence.

The old culture said "private" works and "public" doesn't, unless "private" is calling the tune behind the scenes.

In fairness to the old culture, it conceived and perfected the idea of public-private partnerships that scored some great achievements. Examples abound, including Dallas/Fort Worth International Airport, the Morton H. Meyerson Symphony Center, and Reunion Arena complex. Dallas hotels and restaurants integrated voluntarily during the late 1950s. (An insider from that era told us that the admission of blacks came because it was feared that holding out would "be bad for business." Then he added, to our amazement: "We integrated hotels and restaurants before schools, on the theory it wouldn't have been fair to ask children to bear the brunt of integration.")

The new culture says that partnerships are great but that the process has to be open, frank, fully inclusive, and entirely public before it gets its private value added. Examples: building quality infrastructure in southern as well as North Dallas, excellence in education for all children, sensitive social outreach for troubled communities.

But note: the Dallas Citizens Council, the "heavy" behind the scenes of virtually every significant Dallas decision from the 1930s through the '70s, is starting to sound like the new culture itself. Its most recent strategic agenda acknowledges how much has changed and reaches out for partners. It outlines, in fact, an extraordinarily progressive social blueprint.

A critical difference, of course, is that in the old culture, the Dallas Citizens Council program would automatically become government's marching orders. No longer. The new culture respects the need for extensive community debate.

The new process can be protracted, discouraging, at worst paralyzing. But if trust can be developed, then a community can reach conclusions on tough issues, even if the process isn't as tidy or prompt as people might like.

The old culture seemed so simple—elites decided, others went along. Going along meant you might get a seat on a board or commission. There was a facade of participation. But legitimate consultation and sharing were carefully confined within groups.

The manipulative ways prevalent in Dallas's yesteryears stoked deep fires of anger among blacks and Hispanics. During the last half-decade, that anger, like a long bottled-up volcano, has finally erupted. The sparks and ashes of the 1991 council wars are simply the visible fallout from the fire stoked by a city's longstanding denial of diversity.

Today it may matter little that many people in the dominant culture meant no offense to others. Even deeply religious whites inadvertently fed the fires by failing to reach out when they could have. Even now, in business and often in politics, there's evidence of foot-dragging—at least from the African-Americans' perspective. High-profile black business leaders told us that they had rediscovered elements of seemingly intractable racism at the highest levels of Dallas's official and business leadership.

We found, by exciting contrast, that most of the city leaders we interviewed embrace the diverse culture that characterizes the 1990s. Yet to the degree that powerful elements in white Dallas deny the problem and prefer to denounce the messengers for their unruly manners, the result may only be more eruptions. Even the self-interest of the white community suggests that this is a time to correct old injustices and look forward, not backward.

When volcanic ash settles, it makes more fertile soil. The fallout in Dallas can, in fact, become the civic turf of a city that works again. What's more, in an international order of infinite cultural diversity, a world shrunk by electronic technology, the idea of a closely held Dallas has lost its allure and practicality.

Challenges remain, of course, especially in social life. A savvy Dallas observer told us: "I'll know a new culture's dawned when the president of Ghana visits and gets to play golf at our finest country club, with a woman, in the prime of the morning."

There are elements of Dallas's old culture that no one in his right mind would want to jettison. There is an exceptional volunteer spirit, including corporations' expectations that their employees will contribute to civic causes. One also thinks of the city's inherent optimism, its can-do spirit, its ability to dream and then galvanize for action. Those are qualities cities across the continent have envied—and may again envy.

But Dallas now needs to pick up cultural skills it never honed before: mutual respect, working with diversity, honoring the commonweal as much as the privateweal.

Some Dallas institutions are starting to do that, in imaginative ways. The Meadows Foundation and Communities Foundation of Texas are quietly but effectively working to redevelop whole neighborhoods, assimilating new populations of Asians and Hispanics and focusing on social services for multiple groups, African-Americans included. Meadows' Center for Nonprofit Management has helped more than 2,000 organizations extend services to people with more needs than cash. Parkland Memorial Hospital is a leader among America's hospitals in reaching out to neighborhoods across the income and ethnic rainbows to make health care relate to people's full life needs.

With pressure mounting on the Dallas Independent School District board to implement the Kress Commission reform proposals, a group of Dallas business leaders led by Tom Luce already has pledged to raise more than $1 million to help reward schools for better performance.

There remain massive challenges for Dallas citizens, churches, businesses, and civic groups in nurturing a more cohesive and accepting society. But at least the seedlings of the new culture are starting to sprout, an indication that the soil is ready.

Creating an Area Citizens Forum

Governing Dallas in the 1990s is—and will remain—a perplexing challenge.

Among America's city governments, Dallas has traditionally seemed the leanest—a kind of minimalist service approach run by a city manager attuned to the efficiency standards the business community espoused. The city manager was hired by the City Council; mayors led, if at all, by charisma, because they had minimal legal powers.

Now the very legitimacy of Dallas city government is under attack.

The 14–1 representation plan (all 14 council members elected by district, the mayor at-large) has arrived, culminating more than a decade of strife. The newly empowered voices of color—African-American and Hispanic in particular—aren't just searching for numeric equity. They want a city government that promises and delivers a much fuller range of services than ever before.

Meanwhile, Dallas's "old guard," having witnessed the turmoil of the City Council, questions whether city government has lost its head. Sorting out these strands is going to take exceptional political leadership—from both the mayor and from the newly representative City Council.

The council's African-American and Hispanic members may celebrate their election under the finally approved 14–1 plan. But bigger victories lie ahead if they can bring the same energies and determination to the process of governing. The all-district system, 14 wards structured to maximize minority group representation, should lead to much more attention for long-neglected neighborhoods, to business development in southern Dallas, and to other legitimate goals. Recreation, parks, and housing may all get more attention.

But if the new council becomes the same theater of confrontation the old one was, at least as it was popularly perceived to have been, no one will win. The challenge now is to move from racial polarization to the practice of interracial politics, a process of fair give-and-take and a search for a set of common priorities for the city's future. There is a danger that the 14–1 system districts may simply "embalm ethnic divisions," as University of Texas dean of social sciences Royce Hanson has warned.

There's a practical reason, too, for council statesmanship. Public consensus, and possibly more taxes, will be needed for a city government that provides fuller service. But bitter tax revolts and popular resistance are inevitable if voters get the idea that the new council is out to spend the public's money on a patronage, pork-barrel basis. The council's nightmare scenario could be snarling fights over pieces of a shrinking public pie in a city beset by discord and distrust.

The new mayor also will have to show statesmanship—first to deal with the new council, and just as importantly, to give the city a broader vision of where it can and should be headed. We agree with those who say the Dallas mayor's position should be enhanced with a four-year term, a proposal that's now pending, and with substantive authority to appoint all major department heads.

What's the reason for giving the mayor more substantive power? Is it simply to counterbalance a more black and Hispanic council? No way. Dallas residents of color will probably see one of their own elected mayor in the next several years. It would be tragic if the mayor found that he or she had climbed the mountain only to become a figurehead.

Does a stronger mayor mean throwing away professional management? We don't think so. It should be possible to add political leadership—some real clout for the mayor—even while maintaining Dallas's tradition of a highly efficient manager. If the mayor gets a four-year term, perhaps he or she would have the power to appoint (or reappoint) the city manager, subject to council confirmation. The manager would have substantive management responsibility. The City Charter could guarantee that.

Even at best, Dallas city government is going to have a tough time of it during the 1990s. The city tax base has shrunk 10 percent during the last three years. Unpleasant service cuts have just begun. And extra aid from the state or federal governments is about as likely as having the Dallas Cowboys' rivals voluntarily hand over all their first-round draft choices.

And there's another problem. What happens at the county level, or regionwide, is just as critical. Although other cities in the Dallas area haven't had the same intensity of racial divisions to address, they're all being challenged to make tougher choices about services and taxes. Then there's the huge set of problems that pay no respect to any municipal or county boundaries: air and water quality, solid waste disposal, spreading congestion, land use. Furthermore, problems of family breakdown, school failure, teenage pregnancies, crime and dependency, inevitably spill out across city boundaries.

The city of Dallas, in this game, can't dictate much at all. The harsh fact is that the city, the legendary "Big D," is becoming just another letter in a regional alphabet. The new and growing communities, from Richardson to Carrollton, Irving to Mesquite, Plano to Las Colinas, have monopolized regional economic growth for the last two decades. A large share of new high-wage service and manufacturing jobs has gone to the suburbs. Significant employment continues to move outward.

Yet no matter how vital the new-growth communities, it would be foolish for them to ignore Dallas, the city. Dallas proper sets the Dallas image for the state, the nation, the world. In London, they've never heard of Plano. The city and the suburbs are in the same boat, and there's no escaping. What's more, there's not a single problem of the 1990s that doesn't need at least some regionwide attention. Every local official with whom we talked agreed with that.

But none of them even entertained the idea of metropolitan government. The suburban cities are fiercely protective of their powers and historically have seen amalgamation ideas as faintly communistic. The one significant regional experiment of late, DART, serves an indispensable role even if, so far, it's been a public relations disaster. The minorities in Dallas, just now attaining power, aren't eager to see their new voice diluted. Texas's 254 counties, a powerful force in Austin, would probably thrust a spoke in the gears of any metropolitan government enabling legislation.

Yet the region *does* need some system of regional governance. At a minimum it needs some mechanism to resolve differences between its cities and counties. If the region had zero governments now and one had to devise a structure that fits, there'd undoubtedly be a clear regionwide authority, complete with mechanisms to share tax bases among the more and less affluent cities, counties, or towns.

But that's not politically realistic right now—even if one can speculate that the courts may, in the next decade or two, drive more equity-setting agendas than they do now.

The most to hope for now—and it could be extraordinarily helpful to plan for a fast-shifting future—may be to vest citizens, as opposed to governments, with a way to think about and plan for the Dallas region of the coming century.

A regionally oriented citizen voice could introduce a new, much-needed dimension. Local political leaders are in a box. If they start to think and act more regionally, parochial forces in their jurisdiction can rise up to swat them down. Act like a statesman and you may not get reelected. So even when they sit on a regional council of governments, local politicos practice a very safe, not a very courageous or effective, brand of politics.

So who'll think about a strong regional program to develop 21st-century work-force skills? Who's to decide on shared solid waste plants and programs? Who outside government (or the beleaguered DART board) is prepared to sort out the right mix of transit and highway strategies to stop the region from choking on its own congestion? Who can develop a sensible program to get affordable as well as upscale housing built close to—not miles from—new employment opportunities?

Right now, outside of the North Central Texas Council of Governments, there's no effective place to even argue about what the region's housing policies ought to be. And with the rising demand for more parks and open space, where's the regional thinking to come from?

We believe that the Dallas area needs a new grassroots forum that spans city and suburbs, reflects the region's emerging population patterns, and is about government, but not part of government itself.

It might be called the Metropolitan Civic League. (We'd say a citizens association, but that is easily confused with the business-run Dallas Citizens Council). Such an organization should be open to any citizen of the Dallas area, regardless of race, gender, or political orientation, or whether a person holds a blue-collar or professional job. The only requirements would be that a person is turned on by public issues and sees the value of viewing the region—rather than any single city or suburb—as the critical community of the future.

The Metropolitan Civic League could become the mechanism that best reflects the new culture: open, pragmatic, committed to hearing all sides of issues, willing to tackle the agendas that splintered governments find too hot to touch.

There are existing citizens leagues in such cities as Kansas City, Minneapolis–St. Paul, Seattle, Cleveland, Phoenix, and St. Louis. But we envision for Dallas a citizens alliance of fundamentally greater magnitude and impact than any of these possess. The need is greater in Dallas; but so is the potential to make a powerful impact on the way regional issues are defined, debated, and eventually resolved politically.

We believe that there are thousands of Dallas-area citizens who would like to view issues regionally rather than just locally, would like to be involved—but right now have no civic option other than voting in local elections. Dallas-area residents often work, play, and shop in different localities, but they never get a chance to talk about public issues on a truly regional scale. The variety of specific-issue task forces of the civic league would give residents that opportunity.

We don't offer the civic league model as the only way the Dallas area could coalesce regionally. The important point, whatever the mechanism, is that the principal actors must be not just residents, not just voters, but shareholders in the common civic enterprise. The league should be the place each participant acts as a *citizen*, not as a corporate executive or United Way advocate or eastsider. Members must be *free* to act so that their positions can have independence and impact.

A Metropolitan Civic League should set itself clearly apart—in function and practice—from what exists today. The league has to be irrevocably committed to objectivity, to look at every side of each issue it examines, whether it be light rail or radical school reform or curbing teenage pregnancy. Its task force members must pledge themselves to start with questions, not answers. Few other groups in our society want to make that pledge. But it's critical to a civic league's credibility.

The league has to make an impact. Its studies must pay off in useful ideas and sensible solutions that challenge and empower officeholders who are willing to be innovators, the first birds off the political wire in dealing with perplexing issues.

Usually politicians hear from citizens with strong feelings but insufficient information. Or they hear from "experts" who provide them with information but no passion for action. The league process would be different. By the time a report reaches a council or legislature, it would have been road-tested through hard debate and consensus searching by a task force of citizens who've worked out their disagreements.

Three guiding principles should be kept in mind as the league gets off the ground:

The league must be independent, not owned by anyone or any organization. It may get money or logistical support, but not its marching orders, from businesses or foundations. City councils and county commissions will dismiss it as another interest group if it can't lay claim to full independence.

It should be nonpartisan, not apart from the fray but consciously above party loyalties. Partisan guns need to be checked at the door at every league meeting.

The league must strive to be representative. It should look like the community does, incorporating the differences in cultural heritage, gender, political preferences, regional geography, and occupations that make up the mosaic of the region.

Because a community's elites are more given to policy analysis than Joe Six-packs are, a conscious effort needs to be made to assure broad representation. The civic leagues in other regions haven't done that well enough;

Dallas, recognizing the imperatives of the new culture, could do it better.

These are some of the principles for a civic league. But principles don't start organizations; people do. And Dallas is not bereft of organizations that provide natural stepping-stones toward a regional civic league. Many of them are women's organizations, and not by accident. Women are often ahead of men in recognizing cultural change. In today's setting, they take their own aspirations for equal treatment and fair opportunities and extend them to other groups that are also carrying oversized loads of frustration.

Or as one of the region's female leaders told us: "Women can think across boundaries more easily. By our nature, we're more comfortable with sharing of power. And we're more cause-oriented." For support and backing, it might then make sense to turn to some of the Dallas area's leading women's organizations, starting with the Women's Center of Dallas County or the Women's Council (a network of women's organizations that's already dealing with broad needs assessment, especially on social issues).

But the civic league would benefit from a convening committee of men and women whose citizenship is already held in high regard. Examples of some Dallas-area names that emerged from our interviews: such leaders as attorney Tom Luce; former City Manager Richard Knight; Plano writer/consultant James A. Crupi; W. R. Howell, chairman of Plano-based J. C. Penney; former Garland mayor Charles Matthews; Dallas Alliance leader Tom Dunning; attorney Sandy Kress; attorney Regina Montoya; attorney Ron Mankoff; Women's Council president Eleanor Conrad; civic leader Jack Miller; foundation chief Curtis Meadows.

A potential core of early organizers could be the young and middle-aged professionals who've gone through the formal community orientation offered by Leadership Dallas. Their appetites for civic activity whetted, many of them want to keep on growing and practice what they've learned.

The first announcement that a convening group should be able to make is that a start-up grant—enough for at least two to three years of operation—is already in place. It could come from corporations, law firms, foundations, or best of all, a consortium of sources.

The fact is that not much happens without money. Some communities try to start a league, banking entirely on volunteer energies, goodwill, and good luck. Those are valuable commodities, but not enough. Achieving credibility and influence in the political marketplace is daunting enough without trying to succeed on the cheap.

What's more, a civic league needs staff to lift the administrative detail off the backs of volunteers, freeing them to do the vital "citizen" work. If staff members do all the things volunteers often get saddled with—finding places to meet, sending notices, keeping records of meetings, chasing down facts for reports, drafting, revising and publishing quality reports—then the citizens who show up to do the learning and thinking can make much bigger contributions.

Experience in other cities says citizen task force members also get turned on to the process. Attorneys, CPAs, state patrol officers, hospital intake workers, and students—all will tell you how much they look forward to a weekly citizens league meeting, that it's often the most interesting thing going on in their lives.

A league can operate that way if it has staff. But it can't hire the staff if it has no money. Citizens league budgets around the country currently run between $150,000 and $650,000 a year. We suggest that Dallas launch the first million-dollar citizens league, with a goal of at least $1 million for each year's budget.

A good chunk of that support should come from businesses and foundations generous and farsighted enough to give the citizens league the capacity to work—but with the understanding that they will not call the tune on the league's policy recommendations. Businesses need to recognize that independent, civic allies are vital to business's long-term interests—a sound infrastructure, a well-educated work force, a quality environment.

But citizens themselves also should support a citizens league, paying a reasonable share of operating costs through membership fees and contributions. A long-term goal could be for citizens to match dollar-for-dollar the support the league receives from business.

With a million-dollar budget, the Metropolitan Civic League wouldn't just be able to hire a competent staff. It would also be positioned to plan some first-class outreach. One should envision, in fact, using many political tools, perhaps even the advice of campaign consultants, for the nonpolitical purpose of recruiting a broad base of citizen members.

A bottom-line goal should be attracting a coterie of active members from every community that makes up the region—a feat none of the country's existing citizen organizations has yet accomplished. What's more, we can see significant policy recommendations taking on multimedia form. The league might use video, for example, to get complex messages out to the public, complete with a campaign for dissemination to schools and civic and business organizations.

A regional civic league would be no guarantor of a superior regional future. But it might make it more likely.

Reviving the Downtown Core

Circling downtown Dallas by air is awesome. We felt ourselves, like moths sighting light, drawn strongly to this brilliantly sun-swathed forest of steel and glass towers rising over the North Texas prairie.

Indeed, the additions of the late 1970s and early '80s—the daring geometric shapes, the audacious strips of color—have given Dallas's skyline something of the complexity of a great mountain range, wrapped in ribbons of freeway. The image exudes rare energy, motion, and financial power. The bankruptcies of the late 1980s are invisible from the sky. We found it tough to take our eyes off the downtown scene, asking our helicopter pilot to swing around it repeatedly.

An hour later, at ground level, on the streets of Dallas, the glow faded, our enthusiasm evaporated.

With too few exceptions, the streets of downtown Dallas have that neutron bomb look—buildings intact, the civilian population somehow vanished. Of course there's a pedestrian here or there, perhaps a clump of people waiting at a bus stop. Yet across the United States, we have not seen a metropolitan downtown as devoid of street-level activity, of tone and texture and interest. Even such oft-maligned cities as Cleveland and Newark seem far more active and full of people.

Dallas is so off the mark in fostering downtown life that its city government gives street vendors a hard time. Instead it ought to make a 180-degree turn: advertise for street vendors, maybe offer them some start-up venture capital.

The shock of a street-dead Dallas is especially jarring because this city, by reputation, represents dynamism and commercial success. Yet what you see, in disturbing quantities, are big, boarded-up buildings. Some are haunted by such ghosts of yesteryear's retailing as Joske's and Sanger-Harris. Even as we visited town, Brooks Brothers, the last large downtown retailer other than Neiman Marcus, was closing its Field Street doors and consolidating operations into the Galleria.

Downtown Dallas has an unkempt feeling—yet without the people and activity that redeem the trashiness of a New York. It's surrounded by acre after acre of seedy parking lots and land that stands mysteriously vacant, even as people agonize about a lack of housing close to the core. It's a city with a brand new Arts District that people are sometimes fearful to walk through at night.

There's a pathos in all this. One hears of multiple efforts over the past few years to invigorate downtown. Not all of them failed. The depressing series of first impressions lightens up somewhat when you discover some of the assets in and around downtown Dallas.

The West End and McKinney Avenue have become major centers of urban activity, even on weekends. There's apparently spontaneous redevelopment, the seeds of a Soho-like culture, in Deep Ellum. The Dallas Museum of Art and Morton H. Meyerson Symphony Center represent impressive investments. Everyone still loves the Farmer's Market. Light rail should soon be coming down Pacific Avenue, adding a modicum of street activity. And crime statistics indicate that image notwithstanding, downtown Dallas is actually one of the safer spots in the city.

Yet from the Farmer's Market to the Arts District to Union Station, few of downtown Dallas's real attractions are close enough together to be mutually reinforcing. Or where they might be reached by foot, there are no inviting miniparks, plazas, bikeways, retail streets, or landscaping efforts to guide a person from one to the next. The McKinney Avenue trolley is a promising start, but only a fragment of the downtown circulator system that ought to exist. Today, the only way people can get pleasantly from one place to another is by car.

It's small wonder that the people of Dallas disparage the downtown area, asking why they need to go there at all. An academic at the University of Texas at Dallas (which is really in Richardson) asked us: "Why go downtown after you've seen the Kennedy assassination site? What the hell do you do there?"

Ironically, Dallas does have a pedestrian circulatory system. It operates mostly underground, with a few sky bridges. And it's no accident. It was designed for Dallas by international city planner Vincent Ponti, starting during the 1960s under the instructions of then-Mayor J. Eric Jonsson to separate auto and pedestrian traffic. Now scores of Dallas buildings make it a place that's easy: you can park, walk to your office building, and never set foot on the street. There are dozens of underground stores.

Yet what Mayor Jonsson thought would serve the best interests of the City Efficient has returned, in time, to plague the city he loved by making it a place that's coldly utilitarian, implicitly antiperson at the all-important level of the street.

We heard a number of people say the tunnels are a good thing because Dallas's climate is so boiling hot in summer—or chilling cold in winter—that the streets aren't habitable. We suggest the problem lies with Dallas-area residents' attitudes, not the weather. If cold and heat drive people inside or underground, why do chilly Boston and steamy New Orleans, both intensely street-oriented, have two of America's most successful downtowns?

If the underground circulators were expected to attract companies downtown, they're rank failures. Not a single corporate headquarters has gone to downtown Dallas since Diamond Shamrock in 1979. The suburbs continue to lure large tenants away. We heard of fears raised that downtown might lose 10,000 to 20,000 workers in the 1991–94 period, among them Mobil's thousands of downtown employees. Confidence in downtown has plummeted. A leading business figure told us that he signed a long-term lease on downtown property during the mid-1980s but wouldn't dare risk that kind of commitment today.

One doesn't need to be a soothsayer to grasp where this is leading. Downtown Dallas, during the 1990s, could face a spiral of disinvestment.

Would that matter? There are some people who think that downtown Dallas is just one of a growing number of "activity centers" scattered about the region. If it failed, so what?

There'd still be Las Colinas, Plano, the LBJ corridor, Park Central, Dallas Parkway, and the like. In today's wheeled society, goes this reasoning, downtowns may be obsolete anyway. So why agonize about downtown Dallas? So what if it ends up a suitable backdrop for a 2020 rendition of *On the Beach?*

We suggest that talk's as dangerous as it is facile.

Take taxes. Presently, downtown Dallas, with only a half of 1 percent of the city's land mass, collects 20 percent of its revenues. Without downtown, neighborhoods would have to pick up that slack. Are downtown's detractors ready for that?

Or take transit. More than half of downtown Dallas's 120,000 daytime workers use mass transit. Force them into autos for commuting, and massive traffic snarls would trap every driver in sputtering traffic jams. And air pollution would get worse fast. Consider Dallas's ambition to be a true international city. Europeans and Asians are going to be making decisions about where to locate U.S. trade offices, where to attend conventions, where to set up branch operations. Far more than Americans, they expect a vibrant center city atmosphere replete with sights, good ethnic restaurants, and sometimes a little sin. Try explaining to a sophisticated foreigner that Dallas has become some sort of multinodal, polynucleated, centerless city. In the new world economy, to borrow a Texas expression, that dog won't hunt.

Houston, San Antonio, and Austin all have strengthened, not weakened, their downtowns. So have Portland (Oregon), Seattle, and even Phoenix—despite the fact that each has been subject to the same centrifugal, "off to the suburbs" pressures that Dallas has experienced. What do they know that Dallas doesn't? Should Dallas become the first large American city to abandon its downtown it would likely become a laughingstock among business travelers and financiers from Denver to Dhahran. We recognize that no one in Dallas is making a conscious decision to junk the downtown. But without decisive, farsighted action, that's precisely what could happen.

The crisis of Dallas's downtown can't be solved by the private sector acting alone. The old pattern of a bunch of business leaders sitting around and concocting a solution won't work. Why do we say that, when we know that there are some business leaders—prominent figures in the Dallas Citizens Council and Central Dallas Association among them—who care desperately about downtown?

The first reason is that with Dallas's new multiracial politics, business leaders have lost their exclusive leadership franchise and are never likely to regain it. Business may sound a trumpet, but it can't count on an army ready to respond.

The second is that many business leaders are inherently schizophrenic on the downtown issue. Some who care about downtown also have megabucks invested in directly competing suburban locations. The city-suburban conflict recently surfaced in the Greater Dallas Chamber of Commerce's internal debate over how to focus its business recruitment efforts and respond to concerns that the city proper, and downtown in particular, were being shortchanged.

The future of Dallas's downtown, we are convinced, depends on courageous, assertive government leadership. Business may be a partner, but not the lead partner. That goes against the Dallas culture, the way it's always done things. Dallas doesn't have a strong mayor form of government. But there's a tremendous amount that a forceful mayor, demonstrating sufficient vision to command support from his or her council and administration, could push:

Hire an imaginative, nationally respected planner. Dallas hasn't had a strong planning voice since Weiming Lu left for St. Paul, Minnesota, in 1978. A planner should comprehend the fabric and potentials and shortcomings of cities and know how to work with neighborhoods and business leaders alike. He or she should develop a vision of how the disparate elements of downtown Dallas could be reshaped into a coherent whole.

A lead planner, in Mr. Lu's words, should be a "designer-servant," sensitive to the sounds and sights and customs of the city's varied cultures, a person who then can suggest how to reflect and amplify those cultures on the street level.

Clean up the wastelands. The ugly lots in and circling downtown present an awful city image; they breed fear of crime. Because it's in the shadow of skyscrapers, this land was held by speculators hoping to make a killing with a megastructure. With the bust of recent years, most of the land has shifted through foreclosure into lenders' hands.

There's talk of progressive downtown-based corporations trying to get control of these land parcels, maybe turn some into baseball diamonds or soccer fields to help generate more downtown activity. That's fine and good. But now is the time for the city to engage the owners in some serious conversation about the future of this land. It may be years until the market justifies big buildings on these sites. A proactive City Hall should be encouraging the lenders to think of more modest use as soon as the market begins to perk up at all. What's probably feasible is middle-scale development—two- or three-story offices and shops or perhaps townhouses and apartments. Dallas desperately needs, architect-critic James Pratt has noted, some middle scale, something between the massive skyscraper and the 7-Eleven. A tax code change ought to invite it.

A complementary strategy is to set stiff requirements, full landscaping included, for vacant pieces of land. The owners may be reluctant, but how this land looks is critical to Dallas's appearance, an inescapable element of how downtown looks. Building codes require homeowners in residential neighborhoods to maintain their properties; why not require that downtown? If Dallas public policy were as protective of downtown as it is of neighborhoods, downtown might start looking better.

Stress that downtown is for everyone. It's wrong to think that the only winners from a strong downtown are the big businesses there, or the people from North Dallas or Highland Park who hold executive jobs in its highrises. African-Americans, Hispanics, and Asians need downtown, now and in the future, as a work site.

Downtown provides the only major employment center close to South Dallas or southern Dallas as a whole. Shut up the downtown area and there'd be a disastrous loss of livelihood for low-income people, especially those of color.

What of downtown as a metropolitan area's legitimately shared ground? Writers such as ourselves can be dismissed as incurable romantics about street life, yearning for San Francisco or Paris archetypes in a nation in which people have been opting for decades for a spread-out, suburban, and ex-urban model. Joel Garreau, in his new book, *Edge City,* notes that Americans "have not built a single old-style downtown from raw dirt in 75 years." But if Dallas had no downtown, no recognized center among its multiplying suburban office centers, it would need one. The definition of a city, from the dawn of time, has been a meeting place of peoples. The cultural streetscape is a more powerful signature of a city than any skyline could ever be.

And in the multiethnic, multiracial world now dawning, in which we're all minorities, downtown does provide a region's only logical gathering place for everyone. We appreciate the appeal of full-scale, climate-controlled megamalls or corporate campuses in the suburbs. It's easy to find lots of substitutes for being on city streets. Suburbanites will find a good slice of entertainment opportunities closer to home. Downtown executives may find it more comfortable to hang out in their private clubs in the clouds. Downtown office workers may find the company cafeteria the path of least lunchtime resistance. The office-to-parking-ramp tunnels keep people off the streets.

Yet a downtown that is properly planned and promoted, with lively and welcoming streets and squares and plazas, still has a vital role to play as the shared, symbolically uniting space of an entire citistate.

There's one specific project we'd encourage as a way to dramatically signal the renaissance of downtown, to transform Dallas from a city that is park-poor and amenity-poor into one with an outstanding outdoor life. The Town Lake idea has been around since 1911, and it still makes sense: to create a lake (or perhaps a ribbon of lakes) along the bed of the Trinity River as it loops around the southern and western sides of downtown.

It's tough for us to understand why Town Lake has never been built. It would bring water to an arid scene. It would transform a ditch into an object of beauty. It would create a splendid recreational opportunity. Sharing shores with Oak Cliff and South Dallas, it would help wash away what's been called a "Berlin Wall" of psychological and physical division between those areas and downtown.

Town Lake's cost would be substantial but quite affordable for Dallas. New Orleans, in fact, spent more on its Superdome. We heard that recent breakthroughs in hydrology would make it less expensive than before to keep the lake's water quality acceptable.

And we heard that unless Dallas acts quickly, negative and competing developments could materialize—a high-power electric line right up the middle of the Trinity River, for example. Dallas has to decide if it wants a community resource or just another corridor for industrial use.

We like what Rena Pederson, *The Dallas Morning News* editorial page editor, has written: "Wouldn't it be a treat to be able to look out over the Trinity and see long, graceful racing sculls skimming along an expanse of water instead of a weed-lined ditch?"

Or consider the counsel of Stanley Marcus, who is a hard-boiled realist about downtown: "Build that lake; it would revolutionize downtown as a place to live. With a shoreline on both sides of the lake, you'd automatically develop a reason for people to live downtown."

Marcus's statements about making downtown a place to *live* are definitely worth taking seriously. Until downtown's a neighborhood for people, retailing will remain dormant, the streets will remain forbidding.

The new upscale housing at the Meridian apartments in the State-Thomas area created a lot of excitement. There's hope that it could open a wedge for substantial new downtown housing. Similar hopes were placed on the Bryan Place single home/town house development on downtown's northeast flank during the 1980s. Both the State-Thomas and Bryan Place developments had the negative effect of displacing some lower-income people. And although some might question whether Bryan Place can be considered a success, it did prove that Dallas residents, even affluent ones, could sleep in their own homes near downtown without turning into Kafkaesque beetles.

Dallas city government needs to develop an aggressive downtown housing policy, whether the tools are tax-increment financing, write-downs of mortgages for lower-income people, or partnerships with banks and foundations. Like such cities as Portland, Oregon, it needs to encourage housing in each income niche, from homeless shelters to luxury condominiums. Portland's rich variety of residents has helped create an exciting, livable downtown. Creating the same for Dallas would be a legitimate public goal. An unguided private sector can't and won't deliver it.

Downtown U.

The great cities of America either have great downtown universities or have created centers of higher education to play that role. Dallas, despite the excellent reputation of El Centro College, lacks a downtown university center. We hear there's talk of creating one. It makes all sorts of sense.

The situation may, in fact, be an extraordinary convergence of need and opportunity. Downtown needs to be used, thousands more people enriching its life daily. Dallas-area residents need continuing education. In the new world, the norm is for a person to anticipate at least four career changes in a lifetime. Furthermore, downtown has what the colleges and universities need. It's common ground, a location that may soften the turf barriers that normally separate competing institutions. It has space available. (One possibility would be now-empty structures such as the old Sanger-Harris building, just two blocks from El Centro. Another would be constructing a university facility to bring around-the-clock life to the Arts District.)

Participants in a downtown university center could range from El Centro to the University of Texas at Dallas, Southern Methodist University to Paul Quinn College. The University of North Texas and Dallas Baptist University already have a downtown presence and could be partners.

We heard that individual institutions have tried downtown Dallas operations and then pulled back for lack of enrollment. The downtown university center could start more cautiously, but nevertheless satisfy an immense need by opening its doors as a consumer-oriented higher education information center for the entire Dallas region. Would-be students of all ages would be offered full, impartial information on which institutions offer which varieties of programs, continuing education, and professional development opportunities. The center also would pioneer agreements between the universities so that a student could register once but take courses at several different institutions. All course offerings would be centrally listed.

Then, as market needs were clearly identified, downtown courses and programs could be offered as joint undertakings of the colleges. An urban affairs center could be created, perhaps building on the excellent effort already begun at UT-Dallas. The Dallas Institute of the Humanities might be housed at such a center, providing a place for studying what it takes to make cities work better.

What about outreach, to encourage Dallasites to move up the education ladder, to advance the quality of the future work force? A coalition of institutions could perform that outreach more easily than any one college or university. The center could even focus on a reach *back* into the schools, to encourage more youngsters to give higher education a try.

Other opportunities spring to mind: an electronic library to tap the resources of all the region's institutions, for example, or a special program to encourage and coordinate community service programs in the schools and universities.

Done right, a university center could add up to a lot more than miscellaneous efforts of the various colleges. It could create new educational excitement and make Dallas a stronger city.

Mending the North-South Division

For a generation the Berlin Wall stood, a monument to a society's bitter division, to hate, jealousy, and paranoia. More than 200 people were shot trying to scale it.

Dallas, we discovered, has its own Berlin Wall. It may be more subtle than the German version; some people even described it to us as "that fuzzy line." But on the map, the line of the Dallas "wall" is real enough. It runs on an east-west axis along the flood plain of the Trinity River and then farther eastward along Interstate 30. No one ever decreed this Dallas wall in law or mounted guard posts along it. But it has had profound psychological and economic repercussions over the years, repressing the spirit and opportunities of people on one side, channeling the vast bulk of new wealth and prosperity to the other.

Above the line are North Dallas, the city's downtown, Highland Park, and University Park. North Dallas's burgeoning commercial and residential sector has marched as far northward as Plano, where national megacorporations are opening world headquarters on fields where cotton grew not long ago. Some people believe that this onrush of growth may one day reach the Red River. Below the fuzzy line is southern Dallas. One asks about this "other Dallas" and learns that it encompasses 45 percent of the city's land area and is home to 45 percent of Dallas's people.

Southern Dallas is, in fact, an area of many great assets. Its rolling hills and chalk cliffs provide virtually the only interesting topography in the Dallas area. It has great oaks, a greenery rare to North Dallas. And here is Fair Park, chosen by Dallas leaders to be the city's grandest public place, the site of Texas's major centennial celebration in 1936.

From the bluffs of Oak Cliff, the view of downtown's soaring towers, burnished by the afternoon sun, ranks among the most dramatic scenes of a great city skyline anywhere in the world. It is a real estate site developers in most cities would kill for.

But in palpable form, all of southern Dallas is somehow considered inferior, dangerous, unworthy of investment, the pariah territory south of the Trinity. Despite having 45 percent of the city population, southern Dallas has only 25 percent of its jobs. Today it is scandalously underdeveloped, with 75 percent of Dallas's vacant land.

The region's yawning North-South shift began to take dramatic form, we learned, about the time the freeways were built. Before that, downtown maintained its dominance, and there was a rough geographic balance in Dallas's development. But afterward, the center of growth shifted radically northward, taking with it businesses large and small, hospitals, shopping malls, and new freeways. Today, some ads talk of the LBJ and Stemmons freeways as the center of the region.

Public investment followed the same path. The bulk of the city's dollars for new and better parks and libraries and sewer systems went north. And a thousand and one messages—"you're inferior, you matter less"—were telegraphed.

If you're coming from Fort Worth and want to get to southern Dallas, an Oak Cliff leader noted, "you can't there. You have to get off the freeway and wind around through industrial areas and then get on another road to go south." Needless to say, the vast majority of the economic wealth thrown off by Dallas/Fort Worth International Airport was enjoyed by northern, not southern, Dallas.

Race, let it be said, began to play an increasing role in Dallas's division and perceptions. By 1990, an overwhelming 83 percent of Dallas's 296,994 African-Americans lived in southern Dallas. A reported 53 percent of the city's 210,139 Hispanics, including a high proportion of the city's recent immigrants from Mexico and South America, lived there, too.

Reports of crime and unrest in South Dallas made the area infamous. One of Dallas's top black leaders described the area to us as a "powder keg."

We found South Dallas to be a neighborhood of startling contrast. We noted a "hot sheet motel" just down the street from a $9-million community college facility. Often, there are gutted and empty residences, burned-out crack houses on one street and modest, well-tended bungalows on the next. South Dallas has a high share of boarded-up stores and warehouses, tenement apartment houses filled with poor blacks or recent Hispanic immigrants. Yet, here, too, is the South Boulevard–Park Row historic district, once Jewish and now home to middle-class blacks living in architecturally distinguished homes behind deep lawns. And one notes what would seem proof positive of studied city neglect: Lake Cliff Park, whose lake was left for several years without water—or explanation from the city government.

The Oak Cliff secession movement of the late 1980s broke many peoples' stereotypes about southern Dallas. It was like a psychological break in the Berlin Wall, the people on the "other side" crying out their demands for equal city treatment, respect, and understanding. Suddenly, council member Charles Tandy was heard when he proclaimed, "Everyone assumes that Oak Cliff is one large black ghetto. But actually we are an integrated neighborhood that works."

The 1990 U.S. census showed that southern Dallas had the city's heaviest concentration of lower-valued homes and a large contingent of households headed by single women with children. But it also had a greater number than North Dallas of traditional families, couples with children living at home. The census also suggested that southern Dallas might be representative of Dallas's demographic future, with its much higher share of young people.

As we visited Dallas, we noted a number of other small holes punched in Dallas's wall of indifference toward southern Dallas. Candidates in the 1991 mayor's race, even those with their primary electoral bases in North Dallas, were spending significant time and expressing interest in southern Dallas. In Bill Rathburn, the new police chief, southern Dallas has a man dedicated to working far more closely with the black and Hispanic communities, decentralizing crime prevention and making it more sensitive to individual neighborhoods' needs.

On the economic front, Dallas released Jim Reid, a former assistant city manager, to form the new Southern Dallas Development Corporation, with a broadly representative 15-member board. The corporation in turn created Texas's first multibank community development corporation, designed to tap into government and bank funds to make loans to growing enterprises, many of them minority-owned.

In a part of the city traditionally starved for capital, the SDDC seemed to open the area, at least on the critical small-business side, to more traditional banking, plus other hardheaded business counseling small firms need. Based on our exposure to parallel efforts in other cities, we concluded that the effort, pushed forward with Mr. Reid's personal enthusiasm, was state-of-the-art and could hold real promise.

Reinforcing Mr. Reid's effort is the Bill J. Priest Institute, a one-stop center to support development of new businesses and help existing ones overcome all manner of technical and management problems.

Yet, as promising as these developments seem, southern Dallas probably won't experience anything more than peripheral improvement until the broad Dallas community makes an unprecedented commitment to the territory south of the Trinity.

The first commitment has to be made by City Hall, which has to give southern Dallas its first equal break in a generation in improved streets, parks, street lighting, sanitation, and basic maintenance.

The second commitment, once the city's is in place, has to come from the megacorporations of the Dallas region. All need to become players. Some, such as Texas Instruments, already have social programs focused on South Dallas. But now much more will be needed. Dallas's megacorporations must put their own investment and facilities into southern Dallas.

It was a leading private-sector leader who described the first need to us most vividly: "The city has to put its muscle together to build streets, to clean up what is clearly the most naturally beautiful part of the city. You'll have to lead with public-sector action. The next mayor has to make a public commitment and bring the council along politically. It will require a lot of public investment." The old corporate-first model just won't work, he warned: "Corporations will follow the public sector's lead if they think it's making farsighted decisions about its land mass, with substantial investments. No corporation is going to volunteer for arrows in the back. A lot of people want the private sector to solve the southern problem; it's just not going to happen that way."

Virtually every other business leader with whom we spoke made the same point—that the city government has to take the first big step. What we could not sense, from our interviews, was any kind of clear-cut corporate commitment to invest seriously once the public involvement is credible and moving.

There is some business community interest in southern Dallas. Frito-Lay has a small operation there; Texas Instruments is supporting a child-development program. The Dallas Citizens Council's strategic agenda refers to southern Dallas development needs.

We believe that a great deal more has to come out of the business community—openly, dramatically, forcefully—to demonstrate that it considers southern Dallas a frontier of opportunity and will put its stockholders' dollars behind concrete investment in the area.

In the Dallas culture, the voice and actions of the big corporations are of immense import. When Dallas's massive telecommunications, retailing, and energy firms say, "Yes, we'll establish a significant business presence in southern Dallas," then the entire region will know that the commitment is serious. And the actual prospects for southern Dallas will soar.

We talked with some corporate chiefs about the problems in doing this. They worried about the quality of local schools for their employees. They wondered how they could attract sufficiently trained people to that part of the city. They were clearly concerned about crime and infrastructure.

Each of those objections is surmountable. The Dallas Independent School District could be encouraged to start up new, integrated, high-quality schools in the area. (The district has promised for years to build a supermagnet school in southern Dallas.) To entice trained workers, southern Dallas actually has a stock of handsome homes, many old and historic, all available for dramatically lower prices than anything comparable in the Garlands or Irvings of the region. And if there are crime and infrastructure concerns after corporations and their employees move into southern Dallas, they'll be met with the city's commitment to clean up the area, as well as a new group of heavy hitters with a stake in southern Dallas who'll insist that the city act.

A high degree of corporate peer pressure will have to be exerted to get all the region's major corporations to make commitments to southern Dallas. And it won't do for corporations located miles to the north within the Dallas area to say they're really global outfits, only incidentally located here. Balderdash.

It occurs to us that the megacorporations ought to have a choice: press to make Texas a higher-tax, higher-public-service state or recognize that the private sector has a critical role, that corporations share tangible responsibility for the regional community they have joined.

We'd go a step further and suggest that the Dallas community at large, through its civic organizations, through its newspapers and television stations, through its political structure, make it abundantly and repeatedly clear to the big corporate citizens that this commitment is expected of them—and that the idea will stick around to bug them until they act, that "maybe later" or "when the recession's gone" won't do.

Corporate operations in southern Dallas should not be charity; they should be good economics. If these corporations are smart enough to be star performers on the national and international scene, surely they're sufficiently clever to make a major distribution or assembly operation work profitably in southern Dallas.

The day the public and corporate commitments to southern Dallas come firmly into place will be for Dallas the equivalent of November 9, 1989, in Berlin, when the infamous wall was finally breached.

As the Germans are learning, more years of tough struggle are necessary to bring a benighted area such as East Berlin back into the city's spiritual and economic mainstream. In order for unification to succeed, vast infrastructure improvements and the retraining of thousands of workers in the ways of a free-market economy must take place. But now, in Berlin, the question is not whether the eastern sector of the newly united city will recover fully, but how soon?

Dallas needs to make the same kind of commitment to its territory south of the Trinity.

People Power: Redefining Government

In Washington, Chicago, Seattle, or Peoria, few people would believe that Dallas, Texas, might prove itself a lead city in advanced neighborhood-based social experiments. Tell outsiders that tough, swashbuckling Dallas is poised to tie together for troubled neighborhoods such advanced concepts as community-based health care, community-based policing, and family-responsive social counseling, and they'd probably scratch their heads in disbelief.

It's a disbelief most Dallas-area residents would share. On the crime front, they're used to headlines that scream such messages as "Violent crime in Dallas is up 13% this year" and "Dallas 4th in U.S. in slayings," or alarmed editorials that proclaim, "Police brutality—time to get tough with bad officers."

Social statistics aren't much better. Dallas has a disturbingly high rate of teenage pregnancy. The Lisbon neighborhood in southern Dallas has an infant mortality rate higher than those of some third world nations. The city's yearly count of crack babies has soared to 1,300.

However depressing all these indexes are, our team was more intrigued by a story that hasn't reached the headline stage. It's the aggressive community health center effort Parkland Memorial Hospital has mounted. It's several years of community-oriented policing experiments by the Dallas Police Department, now being championed and expanded by the new chief, Bill Rathburn.

There's more evidence in a variety of promising social service programs sponsored by foundations and women's groups. For example, the Lemmon Avenue Bridge program at the multiracial North Dallas High School offers kids about 20 services, ranging from drug-abuse treatment and dental care to teen pregnancy counseling.

Some of the same dynamics may be emerging in Dallas's proposed "school-centered education" experiment, which would free schools from tight central control, giving parents and school staffs much greater authority over a variety of matters.

Whether Dallas fully realizes it yet or not, all these approaches add up to a new definition of how government relates to ordinary citizens in the communities where they live. For want of a better phrase, we'll call the new approach a "people paradigm," a grassroots, citizen-oriented way of viewing city life. The people paradigm changes the way government deals with neighborhoods in practically every city across America today:

> It says big bureaucratic systems—police headquarters, health authorities, citywide school administrations—have to change from being dictators to serving as enablers and facilitators of what happens locally.

> It places confidence in people on the firing line—local police, local teachers, neighborhood residents themselves—to devise ways to improve services and quality of life. They, not "central," get to control most of the resources.

> It rejects the "one best way" of doing things that credentialed professionals so routinely advance. Instead, it celebrates innovation and creativity in multiple, grassroots-designed approaches. It insists on accountability, but for results, not for compliance with procedures.

> Instead of talking about neighborhood people as "clients," it views them as customers—and partners. It's not about doing things to people, it's helping them do for themselves.

> It fits rather than fights the new multiethnic, multiracial society fast emerging in Dallas and other cities. By saying everyone counts, it gets emerging communities past a clamor for rights to positive experiences in self-determination and self-government.

> It's holistic. It says community police officers have to be concerned about graffiti cleanup and code violations, teachers about family life and neighborhood security, health care personnel about the entire family, not just the patient sitting in a clinic. It raises the possibility of close coordination, perhaps even merger, of some of these services. And it creates the potential for dramatic breakthroughs, with families and entire neighborhoods becoming less welfare-dependent, healthier, less crime-prone, and more self-sufficient.

As radical as all this sounds, it may fit Dallas better than it would New York, San Francisco, or Minneapolis. A people paradigm rejects the idea of big or bossy government interfering in people's lives and dictating neighborhood decisions. It's in line with Dallas's historic aversion to wasting money on big government programs.

And in a city that's always valued business acumen, a people paradigm can also lead to smart investment. The idea is that the money, training, and logistical backup made available to neighborhoods will pay long-term dividends, ranging from lower crime and prison costs to higher community confidence, a more competent work force, more taxpaying rather than tax-eating citizens.

Parkland's impressive system of neighborhood health centers may be the premier working example of a people paradigm, the new decentralized, accountability-based approach. The centers are spread from East Dallas to West Dallas, with a hope for additions from Oak Cliff on the south to Garland on the north. Each year they receive 110,000 patient visits, and with expansion could siphon off a massive chunk of the 500,000 visits made by patients at the hospital itself each year.

There's a special strength to centers dealing with people in their own neighborhoods. Center staffs look first and foremost at prevention, such issues as prenatal care and counseling young people on pregnancy prevention and drugs. For young women who are pregnant, it's claimed that every dollar spent on prenatal care saves, within a year of the child's birth, $3.78 in public health costs.

The centers are also a model of the new accountability approach. Physicians working in them get a base salary, but the rest of their compensation depends on specific health outcomes. Center employees get a 10 percent bonus if the community's health shows clear results-based improvement. These incentives, developed in Dallas's centers, are revolutionary in U.S. medicine today.

To visit one of these centers is to sense an enthusiasm about neighborhood service that's also rare in modern-day medicine. Each of the centers has a local advisory board, and many employees—young minority men and women included—live in the neighborhoods the centers serve. Some are being introduced to possible careers in the medical field.

The same people paradigm principles are just as clear, if not quite as well advanced, in Dallas's approach to crime control. An early breakthrough came in 1985, when the police department, with Meadows Foundation aid, set up a storefront operation serving the Asian refugees in East Dallas. Officers working on the project found most crime going unreported, multiple families crowded into single apartments, people who didn't know how to use plumbing filling bathtubs to hoard water. Residents couldn't report trouble because they couldn't speak English.

The storefront provided every necessity from food and clothing to blankets and fans. It sponsored English courses, scout troops, sports teams, and citizenship classes. It helped with job referrals and mediated domestic disputes. A community that clearly needed social services more than it needed a hard-nosed crackdown received crime prevention as it is most broadly defined.

Storefront police operations have since spread to 10 Dallas neighborhoods. Not everything's gone smoothly. Resistance has been strong among some police officers who dismiss the approach as just "baby-sitting a community." To them, neighborhood-oriented policing, or NOP, stands for "nobody on patrol."

But the hard fact is that Dallas's traditional police strategy is an abject failure. As a leading officer of the department described it: "Our officers have evolved into a very reactive mode. They're run ragged responding to calls. They don't solve problems. You just see them after the fact."

Officers' most frequent complaint is that criminals, when they are caught, are soon let loose again. But even keeping all the wrongdoers behind bars, in a state and nation already setting international records for the portion of the adult population held in jail, is hardly a solution. Jail, in any event, has become the nation's leading school of crime.

Community-oriented policing—the long-term presence of officers in neighborhoods where they get to know the people and can focus on preventing crime in the first place—is the best alternative to emerge in the United States in decades. Dallas did well to start some of the first experiments; it's lucky to have a chief today who understands community policing and wants to spread it across his entire department.

Without broad neighborhood support, there's very little a police officer can do, according to Patrick Murphy, director of the Police Policy Board and a former police chief in New York and other large cities. "She or he accomplishes the mission by mobilizing the eyes, ears, information, and influence of as many as possible of the parents, neighbors, teachers, students, clergy, employers, volunteer and community leaders. The fundamental role of the police is to assist every small neighborhood community to exercise social control."

Neighborhood-based police also provide an extraordinary intelligence system for the city. They get to know gang members by more than labels, can connect them back to their families. They're the first to see that a house has been abandoned, a park has been vandalized, or a street light has burned out. They let other city agencies know what's happened; they help get corrective action; they become a neighborhood's friend and champion, rather than its enemy.

Community-oriented policing has a special advantage in a city such as Dallas, with its difficult history of police-neighborhood tensions and abuse cases. After an officer has spent months getting to know a neighborhood's residents personally, the likelihood of the officer's verbally and physically abusing citizens, even under provocation, ought to drop dramatically.

Chief Rathburn believes that there has to be radical change in how police officers' performance is evaluated—from numbers of cases investigated or arrests made to how many things *don't* happen, how safe a neighborhood becomes. Maybe Dallas's police department should use the system Parkland does and give employees extra pay if a neighborhood becomes safer.

But no step on the road to community-based policing is likely to be easy. It means pervasive change in police culture; it's a hard pill to swallow for traditionalists who hold many of the department's key middle-management slots. The chief will need strong community and City Council support for it to happen.

The department is fortunate that the new officers it's recruiting have at least two years of college. Future recruitment and training will have to shun would-be macho crime fighters and focus on skills such as negotiation, mediation, communicating with neighborhood people, and forging partnerships with residents and businesses.

Could the schools also become a link in the people paradigm, in the chain of new responsiveness to neighborhoods and citizens that seems to lie within Dallas's grasp during the 1990s?

The answer's clearly yes. Schools are the most visible public institutions in every neighborhood. Historically, they've symbolized our commitment to a shared culture, to equality of opportunity. Schools come into daily contact with the children and families of the new demographics, the African-Americans, Asians, and Hispanics who will comprise a growing share of the community's future work force.

And if one reads the report of the school board's Commission for Educational Excellence, written by a 26-member panel led by lawyer Sandy

Kress, there's reason to be highly optimistic. Why? The report endorses school superintendent Marvin Edwards's idea of site-based management ("school-centered education"), a plan to give parents and educators dramatically enhanced control of the budget, staff, and instructional methods at their individual schools. But then the report goes further, saying site-based management is such a good idea that it should be expanded rapidly from the 10 pilot schools to encompass all DISD schools within four years.

No concept in American education governance today packs a more powerful punch than school-based management. It seeks to remove a good chunk of the burden of centralized school rules and mandates. It lodges the authority and the responsibility with the parents and the educators who are closest to the students. It builds psychological ownership. And it makes it possible to do what educators have always said is vital—to acknowledge the differences between neighborhoods and student groups.

The Kress report also stresses results and accountability. Results are to be measured school by school, with financial rewards for those that show clear improvement. Some of the financial gain will go to teachers, based on how their school's educational team performs. On the other hand, teachers who don't perform will be reassigned or removed. There's a proposal that all schools develop a strategy for multicultural understanding, including pride in one's own culture and respect for others.

Finally, to tie school efforts more closely to related community services, the Kress Commission urges that clusters of schools hammer out an "enabling compact" with the various public and private agencies responsible for social services in their community. All the services, in one form or another, would be available in the schools. It's easy to envision all-day schools, the hours expanded to entertain and instruct children until their parents finish work, woven into that kind of approach. Schools could also be open evenings for adult education and community activities. The Kress Commission suggests, along the same lines, a citywide case management system that's oriented to families.

We have to say this is as good a blueprint for school reform, for broadening school opportunities and futures for children, as we've seen in any American city.

Kress and his commission also demonstrated some smarts in following up their work by creating their own watchdog organization to push for adoption of the report. As a politician, Kress understands the need for constituency building and constant pressure to achieve change.

That's the good news. The bad news is that the district seems to be imploding from financial disarray and public distrust. And even if the district regains its balance, there's the sad fact that school reform programs rarely go according to plan. Education establishments—school boards and central administrations alike—are masters of crib murder. Apparently anxious to please, they'll agree to adopt a reform, but then they'll restrict it, purportedly to evaluate its workability, to a pilot initiative. Then, if the new idea doesn't suit their fancy, they'll slowly suffocate it. Later, if anyone remembers the innovation at all, it's classified as another idea that was tried but didn't work. Which will be the fate of the Kress Commission—a breakthrough in American school governance or another suffocated report?

The school board voted, 9–0, to approve the full plan. That may have been the easy part. The critical test will be follow-through, and the clearest test will be the rate at which the school-based management opportunity is expanded systemwide. If there's any material delay in the Kress Commission timetable, citizens can figure that the school board has become the problem rather than the solution.

That indeed raises an interesting question. What's the democratic legitimacy of a school board that garners less than 10 percent voter turnout each time it's up for election? Across America, people are questioning the usefulness of school boards. Many urban boards are in political turmoil that makes Dallas's bitterly divided sessions seem tame. Boston recently went so far as to abolish its elected board and empower the mayor to appoint his own. Part of the reasoning is that if the schools are the most important institution determining a city's future, then the top elected official of the city ought to exercise control of them.

Dallas might, in the event the DISD board were to deep-six the landmark Kress Commission proposals, think of adopting the Boston model. We've rarely seen so much community consensus around such a far-ranging set of reform proposals. If the board tries to withhold oxygen from the ideas, maybe it's the board itself that ought to be cut off.

And should the Dallas city government decide, in time, to take command of the city's own school system, the new people paradigm of community-based empowerment and self-determination suggests an interesting model. To replace the public input the school board purportedly now furnishes, the city could authorize each group of 10 or so school-based management teams to nominate a candidate for a new committee that would advise the city on critical school policy issues.

Such a grassroots group might lack the full legal powers today's school board enjoys. But it would be far more representative of the parents and educators who are on the front lines of efforts to improve school and student performance. Indeed, in each neighborhood, the local school groups could merge with citizen advisory committees focused on health, policing, and various other functions. The result could be a new neighborhood-by-neighborhood form of self-governance—a frontier of social innovation on which Dallas could blaze a trail for other cities to follow.

Update

The Dallas Peirce Report struck as many response chords as one would imagine in a big, complex metropolitan region stuck in a rather deep economic recession. The report spurred broad community debate and flavored many policy discussions in the region, especially adding credence to the idea of interdependence across the region's multiple communities. A number of top civic and business leaders agreed the city and region had to think and act more cohesively, though several complained the report had failed to place enough stress on their own particular interest (police, schools, the role of elected officials, and so on.)

Some attitudes, predictably, remained pretty much as they were beforehand. When the "Plano Vision 2015 Project" came before that city's council in May 1992—immediately following the Los Angeles riots—the document included all manner of high-tech communications concepts, talked of Plano's connection to the so-called "Trinity Commons" of North Dallas and territory up to the Oklahoma border, and suggested Plano build its own opera house and theater (as if downtown Dallas did not already offer full cultural opportunities). When asked about the elitist cast of the Plano plan, one of its consultants said, "We can't be plagued by greed or guilt."

But the broader trend, supported by some of the region's leading business figures, seemed to be in the direction of closer intraregional ties. John Carpenter, president of the Las Colinas Corporation, was quoted as saying, "The suburbs have to support the downtown, not fight against it. Long-term, the central core of Dallas has to work for the whole region. If Dallas gets a bad image across the country, it's going to be because of the core, and people are not even going to look at other parts of the region."

Downtown's appearance and morale seemed to pick up in 1992, with more cleanup efforts, successful policing on foot and by bicycle, increased acceptance of upper-income living in the adjacent State-Thomas area, and finally, the creation of a Downtown Improvement District. Property owners in the district agreed to let themselves be taxed, with revenues going to enhance security, keep the area clean, and finance needed capital improvements. Mobil, in late 1992, announced it would keep its major offices and most of its current employees in the downtown. The decision was an immense relief for downtown leaders, who had pressured the corporation heavily to maintain its center city presence.

The new Dallas City Council, elected in autumn 1991 with increased minority representation and all seats filled by individual district elections, avoided some of the rancor of its predecessor. But it had a number of rather explosive meetings and after a year was still struggling to achieve substantial harmony.

On the school front, attorney Sandy Kress, author of the major 1991 reform report, was elected president of the Dallas Independent School District board. A new bond issue for the schools was passed and site-based management instituted in selected schools, along with cutbacks in the central school bureaucracy.

The Dallas Downtown Association and others began efforts to implement the proposal for a downtown university center. Substantial planning went into the effort during 1992, but cutbacks at virtually all Texas public universities threw something of a cloud over its prospects.

The Citizens Council and other elements of the city's traditional white business leadership continued to move toward increased inclusiveness and a surprisingly strong focus on social and educational issues. Younger, more aggressive and regionally oriented leadership took over the Greater Dallas Chamber of Commerce. The South Dallas economic development process seemed to attract broadening mainstream support (albeit no commitments for major corporate presences). Paul Quinn College, with aspirations to fill for Dallas's aspiring young blacks the role played by Morehouse in Atlanta, went through a major financial and leadership crisis, but appeared to be stabilizing, with increased public support, by the end of 1992.

Observers noted a somewhat friendlier climate for a number of the Peirce Report's recommendations. On the other hand, despite interest by many individual citizens, no one in the city's leadership circles moved to implement the recommendations for a metropolitan partnership or regional citizens organization.

The Citistate in Brief

The St. Paul citistate is part of the larger Minneapolis–St. Paul citistate, with the Mississippi River separating the two major cities. St. Paul City, the capital of Minnesota, is the center of a so-called Metro East area covering the portion of the Minneapolis–St. Paul metropolitan region that starts more or less at the Mississippi River and runs to the Wisconsin line. (Metro East actually includes St. Croix County, Wisconsin). St. Paul City had a 1990 population of 259,110; the figure for the entire Minneapolis–St. Paul citistate was 2,464,124, up 16 percent since 1980. The combined citistate covers 5,052 square miles. Metro East accounts for less than half that total. Ramsey County, with a 1990 population of 478,000, encompasses St. Paul and is the largest jurisdiction in Metro East. Major suburban counties include Dakota to the south, Anoka to the north, and Washington to the east. Altogether, the Twin Cities region has 10 counties, 253 cities and towns, 65 school districts, and 168 special districts.

The Peirce Report Glossary

Summit Avenue is America's best-preserved Victorian residential boulevard, stretching several miles westward from a spot near the *Cathedral*— the Beaux Arts structure completed in 1917 that stands on a hill with a commanding view of the State Capitol and downtown St. Paul. *Grand Avenue* is the Twin Cities' best example of an old commercial district, once served by streetcar, a lineal neighborhood prospering through a century of continuous development. *University Avenue* is the primary pre-freeway link between downtown St. Paul and the Mississippi River where it borders downtown Minneapolis. The *Landmark Center* is St. Paul's old federal court building, remodeled during the 1970s into a multiple cultural center. The *Space Center* is a cluster of 19th-century warehouses converted to offices. *Town Square* is a downtown mall developed in the late 1970s.

Lowertown is a former warehouse district in downtown St. Paul, redeveloped in the 1970s and '80s with major McKnight Foundation support and now an urban area of shops, offices, and residential space. *Harriet Island,* actually part of the mainland since the 1930s, provides a major civic park area on the Mississippi directly adjacent to downtown St. Paul. *Frogtown* is a blue-collar neighborhood spreading out northwest from the downtown district. It was developed in the 1880s, when frogs were still heard nightly in nearby swamps; today it is an integrated, polyglot residential area with many Asian immigrants. *Lake Como* is an isolated glacial lake in the north area of St. Paul, its surrounding area developed for residential use in the 1870s.

The *Citizens League* is a Twin Cities–based public policy research organization with a large membership and a nationally known record for influencing lawmaking in Minnesota.

Building a New Vision on the Old

(Originally published in the St. Paul Pioneer Press in November 1991.)

Like civic sleuths, we came to St. Paul to discover the city's civic vision. We talked with dozens of interesting people and heard lots of exciting ideas.

But we found the grandest vision of all lying around in the city's archives. It's a 1906-vintage report by St. Paul's "Capitol Approaches Commission." It has Cass Gilbert's fingerprints all over it.

In 1905, Gilbert's white marble and domed Minnesota Capitol had been finished. It would be the model for all American state capitols for the next two decades.

But Gilbert was not satisfied with the achievement of a great capitol. Even before it was finished, he was agitating to create grand and majestic boulevards and malls that would connect the Capitol, on its dramatic hilltop setting, with the central business area of St. Paul.

The 1906 report spares no effort to associate St. Paul's potential with the expansive avenues around the U.S. Capitol in Washington, with such city planning triumphs as Berlin's Unter den Linden, Paris's Champs Elysées, and Philadelphia's spacious Benjamin Franklin Parkway. But Gilbert was so distressed by the jumble of scruffy buildings and squalid housing he found within a stone's throw of the Capitol grounds that he said his grand design was "a diamond in a garbage pail."

Gilbert's vision did not stop with dramatic vistas and urban cleanup. The master architect envisioned a close association of government and culture. He referred specifically to St. Paul's public library, the city's museum of art, and the state historical society. He believed the combination of all these amenities would serve as a magnet, drawing rivers of people to the city.

Add all this together, he proclaimed in the 1906 report, and "the first result" would be a proclamation to the world of Minnesota's "enterprise and foresight, its culture and the development of its public spirit." And the second result, Gilbert predicted confidently, "would be more swarms of visitors from all over this country and from foreign lands who would stop in the Twin Cities."

We believe the Cass Gilbert vision provides a wonderful base on which to build St. Paul's vision for the 1990s and beyond. The vision for this time must also enhance the physical grandeur—present and potential—of St. Paul. It would prize, as Gilbert did, the city's magnificent physical connections—Capitol and Cathedral and city center, Summit and Grand avenues, streetscape and river.

As a matter of critical importance, today's vision would look to heal and reconnect the severed parts of the city. St. Paul is still plagued by the butchery inflicted on Gilbert's dream by the interstate highway builders 30 years ago. In place of his commodious mall linking the capitol and the commercial center of the city, they threw down a canyon of concrete. It may be too late to remove that deep scar. But the more the freeway can be bridged and covered, the more St. Paul's grand physical unity will reappear.

The vision for today must embrace not only St. Paul's grand vistas and government buildings, but also its remarkable and growing collection of great houses of culture and arts and history and science. Indigenous architecture must play a role, too, from the dramatic restoration of the Landmark Center to the impressive variety of stately homes that line Summit Avenue.

We believe Mayor Jim Scheibel showed foresight in defining a "cultural corridor" of museums and concert halls, well beyond the general discussion about making St. Paul an arts city, and in talking of a "capital city strategy." Even as we worked on this report, many St. Paul citizens were coming up with ingenious ideas to make a new cultural vision work.

We believe they're on to something. It's time for St. Paul to recognize and proclaim itself the Cultural Capital of Minnesota, a place "owned" by every citizen of the state by virtue of its history, its architecture, its creativity, its warmth.

We believe that aggressive marketing of the Cultural Capital would draw millions of Minnesotans and out-of-state visitors each year. We believe the Cultural Capital concept could be the backbone of a recovery strategy for a city (and especially a downtown) that many citizens worry, with good reason, is in serious economic trouble today. St. Paul could well become a cultural mecca for the whole Upper Midwest. Let Minneapolis be the New York of the region, the focal point of high-intensity commerce. St. Paul could be Minnesota's Washington. It could well imitate the explosion of tourist interest and influx of capital that followed the opening of the Kennedy Center and dramatic expansion of the Smithsonian Institution starting in the 1960s.

St. Paul can be multicultural in its approach to its new role. It can agree that Cass Gilbert was indeed a rather Edwardian gentleman, that his vision was vividly Eurocentric decades before multicultural sensitivity developed in America. But then St. Paul can proclaim its desire to embrace the spectrum of cultures of its people today, not only Caucasian but also African-American and Asian and Hispanic and American Indian. Welcoming these voices needn't mean rejection of the cultural accomplishments of another order. The city of the 1990s needs to think of many roots to cherish and honor.

St. Paul is already taking steps in this direction. The city's Festival of Nations each spring celebrates and shares the arts and cultures of many peoples. There's an Asian New Year's celebration held at the Civic Center. The Minnesota Museum of Art has not only moved to define itself as "an approachable, intimate art museum with strong roots in the community and a great deal of public involvement." It has also, quite deliberately, redefined itself as a museum of American art and then defined *American* to include the cultural roots and achievements of all Americans, women and people of color specifically included.

Two St. Paul residents sent us a suggestion that the cultural corridor for downtown be supplemented with "a multicultural corridor along University Avenue to the State Capitol." This cultural corridor would build on the variety of ethnic restaurants and shops that have already sprouted along University Avenue and look for economic incentives for unified storefront designs and marketing so that "these stores could attract other Minnesotans and tourists."

A parallel idea from the same citizens: proclaiming Grand Avenue a "small home-based business corridor," celebrating the multiplicity of home-based businesses that have already sprung up there. Grand Avenue, it is suggested, could be proclaimed "an American prototype and resource center for people all over the world who are interested in starting their own small businesses."

We found both the University and Grand Avenue strategies promising, natural complements to a Cultural Capital strategy. They remind one that "culture" needs the broadest definition. Discussion about "arts," for example, shouldn't focus just on mainstream institutions, but also on small galleries, artists' lofts, cafes with live performers, and experimental theater.

And then there's a traditional St. Paul advantage, one that stands out on Cass Gilbert's maps: the Como Avenue corridor as it heads out from the State Capitol, ending up in the splendid parklike setting around Lake Como, with the city's zoo and conservatory.

We were stunned by the variety and strength of major arts, scientific, and history-related institutions operating in St. Paul today. We believe they constitute the first building block of a new vision and economic base for the city. As first proof one need only consider the popularity they've achieved as stand-alone attractions:

➤ The Ordway Music Theatre, with 492,000 patrons last year, is the architecturally exquisite home of the Minnesota Opera, the St. Paul Chamber Orchestra, and the Schubert Club. Despite year-to-year budget problems common to many arts organizations, the Ordway is so successful on the capital front that it recently paid off its mortgage four years in advance.

➤ The Science Museum of Minnesota, with 980,000 visitors, is a special hit with kids, second only to the Smithsonian in the production of Omnitheater films.

➤ The Penumbra Theater, with 235,000 visitors, is dedicated exclusively to the artistic interpretation of the African-American experience since the 1970s.

➤ The Minnesota Museum of Art, drawing 138,000 visitors, is now searching for a larger home in St. Paul.

➤ Cafesjian's Carousel at Town Square was enjoyed by 163,000 children of all ages in its first year.

➤ Minnesota History Center, with 300,000 visitors in its old quarters, is set to move in spring 1992 into a massive and architecturally striking $74-million building between the capitol and the cathedral. With its multiple new exhibits and attractions, the History Center will likely become one of Minnesota's leading attractions.

➤ Landmark Center drew 190,000 visitors to a cultural center that was a turn-of-the-century post office and federal courthouse.

➤ The Children's Museum attracted 233,000 visitors last year to its crowded site in Bandana Square. The recent decision of this inventive and highly successful museum to move to and build in downtown St. Paul—close to the Science Museum—means it should be able to draw at least 400,000 visitors annually, after its move in 1994.

➤ The World Theater, restored to its former elegance under the leadership of Minnesota Public Radio, was made famous world-wide by Garrison Keillor's "A Prairie Home Companion."

➤ The St. Paul Public Library attracted 424,000 people in one of America's most literate cities.

If any midsize American city has a cultural complex approaching "critical mass," with the potential to fuel significant local economic growth, we believe St. Paul is it. What's more, few cities St. Paul's size have a dynamic neighbor like Minneapolis, plus its booming suburbs, as a source of customers and visitors.

Some business leaders worry about the tax-exempt status of the arts institutions. Culture's nice, they say, but no substitute for tax-paying firms with big payrolls. The problem is that St. Paul today is suffering very serious losses on the business competition front, having trouble attracting offices and plants, nurturing and holding the ones it has.

The situation is in no way uniformly dark. St. Paul and its nearby Metro East neighbors are still home to several quite healthy titans of American commerce. The St. Paul Companies, 3M Corporation, Ecolab, Minnesota Mutual, H. B. Fuller, and even upstart ZEOS—recently the nation's fastest-growing Fortune 500 firm—are all located here. Few metropolitan regions are so favored.

But it's also true that St. Paul has suffered severe losses. Burlington Northern left for Seattle (and then Fort Worth). Amhoist went to Denver and then the oblivion of Chapter 11. Citing union problems, the Schmidt Brewery had to close its doors, although it has recently won a fresh lease on life under new ownership. The St. Paul Athletic Club is holding on by its fingernails.

A steady succession of law and accounting firms have closed their St. Paul offices, consolidating their Twin Cities operation into the more robust Minneapolis market. First Bank System and Norwest Banks turned their operations in St. Paul into mere branches of main banks in the late 1980s.

Today, downtown St. Paul suffers a 21.9 percent office vacancy rate, with numbers still headed in the wrong direction. The World Trade Center, captured in an exciting mid-1980s competition with Minneapolis and supposedly St. Paul's ticket into the new international economy, has turned out to be a well-designed if oversized building, sold on the state's political promises about a big trade program. Now, apparently abandoned by state interests, it's just another unfilled office structure (with a vacancy rate pushing 40 percent).

St. Paul's economic strategy for the 1990s can't be full steam ahead on standard business promotion. It just isn't working. Minneapolis is outscoring St. Paul every time in that competition, and no one told us a reason that could or would change.

Smart money says it's time for St. Paul to change the rules of the game to invite success. And this is where the Cultural Capital strategy comes in.

Instead of settling for isolated, random visits to its museums and performance halls, St. Paul needs a sweeping market plan to get Twin Cities visitors to spend a day and maybe an evening, to get out-of-towners to visit for two or more days.

It shouldn't be possible to go to any one attraction in St. Paul without being informed of all the others. And state government, in partnership with the city, should have the same kind of information available at the Capitol and its other offices.

We believe a massive culture and arts development and promotion campaign would first fire up the tourist economy. Restaurants, hotels, and all manner of travel-oriented businesses would prosper. But more than that, the Cultural Capital message could be expected to give St. Paul such a glowing image as a livable, interesting, desirable place to be, that in time it would experience a significant rise in professional offices and new residents eager to live in its downtown. On that base, still more future economic strategies could be built.

No standard promotional effort, whether by business or government, will ever get St. Paul to where it needs to be with a Cultural Capital campaign. A civic effort of rare scope will be required, and one can speculate about some of the elements that would have to be included.

For starters, the city needs a series of attractive, informative, and easy-to-see signs showing the way among all its attractions—a constant series of friendly reminders of where things are. St. Paul could try a variant of Boston's Freedom Trail, with its footstep marks embedded in the pavement, together with helpful signs. And signs ought to show up on the buildings, too. Right now, for example, there's no way to find the carousel in Town Square without insider information.

The task won't be easy. We've never seen a city with signs that are sufficiently informative, especially none that would reflect the historic, artistic bent of St. Paul's Cultural Capital theme. Hiring a standard sign company won't do. The first step could be a design symposium, perhaps a full design competition, bringing out the best talent the region has. And decisions about which designs to embrace shouldn't be made quickly by some small group. A big swath of St. Paul and Metro East people, including many from individual neighborhoods, should somehow be brought in to the process.

St. Paul will have to think much harder than it often has about excellence in urban design. It does have some jewels—Rice, Kellogg, and Mears parks, for example, places of beauty and warmth. Though Mears Park has been mostly a mudhole recently, it's finally getting its million-dollar renovation. The city needs more parks like these.

Perhaps it should think about tearing down a couple of its uglier unused buildings and putting new vest-pocket parks in their place. Every blank and rebuffing wall, every unlandscaped parking lot, make the city less attractive. Each change in the urban landscape is an opportunity to think about better design.

An immediate example: St. Paul made precisely the right move by insisting on superior decoration for its new freeway bridges and entrances. Equipping the bridges with antique-style lights instead of sodium vapor horrors and insisting on decorative wrought iron instead of chain link fence have made a real difference. It may take years, but in time, the whole city center, from the Capitol to the Mississippi, ought to have the same feel.

Our feeling is that St. Paul has enough skyways. We heard a lot of people complain about their maintenance and worry about their safety. They may be fine for office workers and a few shoppers, but won't help visitors much.

St. Paul's planning and design emphasis, for the next years, should return to the street. Why not think of St. Paul as a great "walking capital," emphasize pedestrian and biking opportunities, proclaim the city's streets "an urban health club" for employees, students, visitors?

It is true that asking people to walk from one cultural attraction to another will only work for some of the people and some of the year in the harsh Minnesota climate. For the Cultural Capital plan to work, a user-friendly St. Paul must fill that gap with another way to get around. The compellingly logical solution: a regular bus service linking the Capitol, the History Center, the Cathedral, and all the major cultural points. The buses don't need to be big and lumbering. Smaller jitneys would do, or better still, old trolleys on rubber wheels (fitted with appropriate double-pane glass and powerful heaters for winter). If the St. Paul community could find any way to do it, rides ought to be free. An economy version of a free service has been priced at under $500,000 a year. But it might be worth spending considerably more.

The trolleys could be tastefully painted. By virtue of being trolleys they'd harken back to St. Paul's olden days. But they shouldn't be gross billboards on wheels; instead they should be designed to reflect affection for the city's history and culture. A touch of whimsy, particularly in changing display space on their sides, could be part of the plan.

Each trolley would have information on attractions at each stop. People who know the city's history and culture could often ride along; nothing makes a city visit more enjoyable than an informed, running commentary. Senior citizens might be tapped for this role. Indeed, why not invite a coalition of senior citizen groups to try designing and running the entire trolley system? Many are history buffs. We bet some of them would take on this job with a wisdom and enthusiasm few others could. Minnesota is one of the two states in which people live the longest. (Hawaii is the other.) A community needs to look to its special assets and build on them.

There could be lots of variations on the trolley or jitney system. It might serve not just visitors but state government workers—there are 7,000 of them—and also thousands more people working for the county and city governments. Government workers represent a neglected market for downtown. One idea: ask state offices to allow workers who take longer lunch hours to visit the city's museums and restaurants and shops to make up the time at the end of the work day.

Trolleys might, in addition to the Capitol area, serve the complex of state offices at the Space Center on Lafayette Boulevard and on the south side of the Mississippi. Others might make "tourist runs" linking Summit and Grand avenues with the Capitol and downtown attractions.

Regular service and reliable schedules would be critical. And why not some ingenious planning? Patrons could be spared waiting outside in freezing weather, for example, by being invited to stand inside museum or government office lobbies until an electronic light flashed the approach of a trolley. One can even imagine St. Paul's friendly, free trolley buses ranging out to the hotels at Bloomington to snare shopping-jaded megamall visitors for a day. The possibilities are almost endless if the right planning, the right financing, the right execution, go into the project.

A natural complement would be a new multimedia visitor center for St. Paul—a one-stop information center with maps, informative displays, maybe a lively videotape introduction to the town. It might offer books of tickets to multiple attractions at discounted rates. Friendly senior staff, screen-sensitive information computers, tape rental for walking tours could all be part of the mix.

Hotel and bed-and-breakfast referrals into some of St. Paul's most interesting neighborhoods could be offered. Coffee and hot chocolate could be served on cold winter days. The visitor center should exude the kind of warm Minnesota welcome that might be memorialized in a Garrison Keillor monologue.

The visitor center needs to be easy to find, with guiding signs visible from the moment anyone comes into town. It should offer ample parking, in a location that itself symbolizes St. Paul's special character. We can't think of a better location than Lowertown. With its restored 19th-century buildings, Lowertown is a permanent monument to old St. Paul. The decision by the McKnight Foundation and city government to give Lowertown permanent staff for long-term planning and follow-through is a national model. We can imagine the Lowertown Development Corporation working well with a broad civic coalition to design and implement a visitor center.

The visitor center should also be home base for the trolley fleet. It should be a first stopping point for busloads of high school kids, arts organizations, history clubs, and seniors' clubs coming in from all over Minnesota and the Upper Midwest to visit St. Paul.

And consider what the new Minnesota History Center could do to capitalize on its commanding sight over the city. How about a series of slides showing what the city looked like, from the same hilltop site, in 1900, 1930, 1950, and 1970—all designed on a scale to permit a visual overlay of the same scene today? We believe a vigorous effort to make the Cultural Capital work—using a blueprint as meticulously planned as any Disney theme park—would have multiple, positive spinoffs.

Consider St. Paul's riverfront. Here's a part of the city historic St. Paul did not treat well. The city allowed industrial facilities, grain elevators, railroad lines, a power plant, and a winding, wreck-prone, four-lane highway to crowd into what had been a physically exquisite valley with high bluffs and groves of trees. It turned it into an industrial sewer.

Water cleanup has been under way for a couple of decades now. There's been ample waterfront planning. Much of the industrial wreckage has been cleared away. With federal help, some $50 million is being spent to construct retaining walls on both sides of the river—setting the stage for attractive walkways and development. Shepard Road is supposed to be set back from the water's edge.

We found St. Paul leaders and citizens impatient to get on with the riverfront job. The walkways, a top-notch landing and marina at Harriet Island, and opportunities for housing all spring to people's minds. We looked down at the river flats area directly opposite downtown and wondered if a Tivoli Garden–style entertainment center could be built there. But we believe it will take the driving energy of the Cultural Capital concept to create the enthusiasm and civic confidence, and with that confidence the capital, to transform riverfront plans from futuristic dreams to on-the-ground reality for the 1990s.

Yet another grand undertaking would involve major freeway improvements, designed with the ultimate goal of reuniting the Capitol and downtown. The improved bridges built on the stretch of freeway beside the State Capitol are a first step. But the freeway needs to be decked, put out of eyeshot and earshot still more, especially along the stretch between the Cedar and Wabasha bridges.

Skeptics say that would be too expensive. In Seattle some 20 years ago, civic leader James Ellis was told the same when he proposed putting a park atop a section of Interstate 5 where it cuts through central Seattle. Ellis didn't listen. He enlisted allies, got studies done, pulled off a couple of deals with adjacent property owners. Today Seattle not only has a lushly vegetated Freeway Park astride I-5 near the middle of town, equipped with walkways and fountains. It's gone on to build the entire Washington State Convention Center atop the same eight lanes of roaring traffic.

A bridged freeway park in St. Paul could well be named after Cass Gilbert. Or even better, it might be named after George Herrold.

Herrold was St. Paul's chief planning engineer from the early 1920s onward. A civil engineering graduate, class of 1896, he fought tirelessly to protect the streetscape, the architectural integrity of St. Paul. He was irascible, opinionated, and not very effective in dealing with the City Council—one of those brilliant people who might have persuaded more people if his personality skills had matched his passion.

But Herrold was Cass Gilbert's spiritual successor and even in his 80s waged a grand battle. Herrold was concerned that a freeway plunging through the city would become a gigantic, unshaded, unsightly, noisy ditch and concentrator of exhaust fumes. He was especially horrified by the highway planners' choice of the "St. Anthony" corridor for the St. Paul–Minneapolis Interstate 94 link.

So even in his 80s, Herrold went to work and produced a more northerly alternative. Herrold's route would have avoided displacing hundreds of citizens of the Rondo neighborhood—then St. Paul's largest black community. It would have averted the necessity of the freeway separating the Capitol from the heart of the capital city.

The highway engineers would have none of this, and the City Council wouldn't give him the time of day. Herrold's objections and alternatives went unheeded.

But we suggest that—along with the great Cass Gilbert—this stubborn and caring man deserves a special place in the hearts of St. Paul's people.

Promoting a Center for Higher Learning

With its seasoned and stellar collection of private colleges, with the University of Minnesota on its southwestern flank, with its community and technical colleges and Metro State as a growing force in the community, St. Paul already serves as a major center of higher learning. But this Cultural Capital of Minnesota, city and suburb alike, might be even stronger if it focused its educational offerings through a St. Paul University Center, located downtown.

Such a center wouldn't have to start out offering courses on-site. Perhaps it never would. But it could and should be the preeminent higher education consumer information center for St. Paul and all of Metro East.

A center would have two important markets to serve. One is obvious: young people examining college opportunities as they leave high school or look to graduate work. The other market, though, is actually larger: adults interested in upgrading their skills. Continuing education has become critical for people who want to stay "up to speed" in the fast-changing and highly competitive new international economy. The new norm, say education experts, will be for a person to anticipate at least four career changes in his or her lifetime. Already, 60 percent of enrollees in higher education are working adults.

At the university center, would-be students of all ages would be offered full, impartial information on which institutions offer which varieties of programs, continuing education, and professional development opportunities. The center would also pioneer agreements among the colleges and universities so that a student could register once but take courses at several institutions. All course offerings would be centrally listed.

Higher education is a bulwark of St. Paul's economy: 44,000 students, 8,000 employees, $350 million in annual operating budgets. But education is even more than that: it's the city's and region's ticket to a strong economic future. A university information center in the center of St. Paul would be tangible proof for the region's citizens that Metro East not only has immense strength at the college and university level, but cares about its people's educational future.

We detected strong enthusiasm for a university center, both among Metro East community leaders and the citizen panel we interviewed. Indeed, the Chamber of Commerce had a task force a while ago that strongly recommended treating higher education like an industry. One of the leaders of the task force is still enthusiastic about the idea and told us: "If the cumulative enrollments get bigger, think of how the rental market would expand, think of the surge in pizza deliveries. We should be jumping on this idea—it's the perfect nonpolluting industry. And it fits just right with St. Paul's cultural focus."

We also learned Minnesota already has a strong model that the St. Paul community could, at least in part, emulate. It's called the Greater Rochester Area University Center, and it was founded in the late 1980s on the basis of educational needs spelled out by the Rochester region's FutureScan 2000 project.

The Rochester Center has a board made up of prominent business leaders, city and county officials, and state legislators. Working with it is a "board of providers" composed of the leaders of Rochester's eight higher education institutions, ranging from the Rochester Community College and University of Minnesota Rochester Center to the Mayo Medical School.

The distinction betweeen the two boards is vital. The board of providers introduces each institution's point of view; it's the professional educators' voice, and it does encourage the institutions to work more cooperatively than they ever did in the past. But the overall governing board has an even broader mandate—to speak for the larger Rochester community and to think first of the education consumer's needs.

The Rochester board publishes the best directory to a region's higher education opportunities we've seen. Career education ladders from nursing to engineering to business management to computer science are shown, with a guide to which institutions provide which niche of training, from starting courses to the graduate level. Then, for each institution, there's a crisp rundown of its history, size, major programs of study, degrees granted, financial aid, admissions procedures, and more. An accompanying booklet lists virtually every course available in the Rochester colleges. This is the kind of relevant, highly usable information that a St. Paul University Center could make its first area of business.

Downtown St. Paul would be the right physical location for such a center because it's the heart of the Minnesota Cultural Capital, because it's convenient to everyone, and because it's common ground—a location that ought to soften any turf barriers among separate and sometimes competing institutions.

The Rochester University Center has encouraged the addition of nearly 200 courses and a number of new programs leading to bachelor's and master's degrees. And it's gone on, exploiting its close links with the area's state legislators, to get authorization for a new $17-million building on the grounds of the Rochester Community College. The facility will be shared by the University of Minnesota, Winona State University, and the community college. Construction began in May 1991.

St. Paul's needs aren't likely to include a new physical facility. But a university center could be a proactive force on multiple fronts beyond "customer" information. As in Rochester, the center could mobilize state legislative support. It might try to organize an electronic library to tap the resources of all the region's colleges and universities and museums. It could launch an effort to encourage and coordinate community service programs in local schools and colleges alike. The St. Paul University Center might even focus on a reach back into the schools to make sure that youngsters get encouragement at critical times in their development to give higher education a try. We know the work force of the future will be more female, more Asian and black and Hispanic than ever before. The education and competence of that work force may make the critical difference for a region's economic success.

But there are serious problems—an especially high dropout rate for minority students attending community college, for example. Every city and region needs to plan strategically, not just to open educational doors but to see to it that every reasonable means of support and encouragement is offered to make the "system" work for everyone.

The long-term payoffs—in building a well-paid, skilled, regional work force, in increasing a region's ranks of productive taxpayers, in attracting and holding corporations—can be stunning.

Who Will Lead the Way?

How can St. Paul organize its civic life for some of the immense challenges of the 1990s and the 21st century? Everyone can list the challenges—reviving downtown, making a single and strong economy of all of Metro East, stopping social or race divisions from taking the same toll they have in other areas. And now there's the possibility of developing a Cultural Capital strategy.

But who's going to lead? Who could make it all happen? Until a few years ago, everyone would have said, "Let's ask our business titans to take the lead." The problem with that approach now was summed up during the town meeting our panel held with a panel of local citizens. "We have no strong businessmen leading this community now," said one of the citizens. "They've all gone with the wind."

It's easy to critique the criticism. The civic concern of St. Paul executives is still impressive compared with that in most American communities. But there's an element of truth in the criticism. In a shockingly short period of time, a big share of power and business activity shifted away, as though borne by the wind itself. The galloping "Minneapolization" of Twin Cities economic power has drastically reduced the number of business leaders prominent in St. Paul civic life. When George Latimer became mayor in 1976, a local executive noted "there were 17 or 18 people in the city to whom he could turn—and who'd deliver. By the time he left office, the figure was down to 3 or 4."

This is serious stuff in a city whose most memorable leaders had been businessmen, including Pierre "Pig's Eye" Parrant, James J. Hill, and Phil Nason, who represented whiskey, lumber and railroads, and banking, respectively.

Agonizing about lost or nonexistent leadership echoed through our St. Paul interviews. The newspaper and television station and philanthropies that sponsored this report told us they had some of the same concerns.

But judging from the people we met, apathy is not St. Paul's problem. There remains a powerful local culture of civic involvement. (Some people even jokingly suggest there's too much—that Twin Cities organizations call more meetings per capita than any other place in America.)

What we heard repeatedly was that people are waiting for a signal. "Citizens are ready to make a commitment—they just don't know what to make it to," one local political leader told us.

Maybe, we concluded, the people of St. Paul are just too smart to go off in a dozen ill-defined directions. Maybe there's no mystery why they seemed to be waiting on the sidelines. They may be waiting for a vision that's worth pursuing.

That brings us back to the Cultural Capital. If people do decide it's the vision and goal St. Paul needs, how do they organize to make it a reality?

The wrong move would be to wait for the appearance of some charismatic leader to pick up the Cultural Capital banner and try to assemble a civic band of followers. Today there are few American communities with that kind of cheerleader and spear carrier available. Our business people are largely preoccupied with staying afloat and competing internationally; our politicians get knocked down if they get too far in front. In the 1990s, neither groups of business leaders nor politicians nor neighborhood interests will be heeded much unless they work assiduously to cross some boundaries and get a broad constituency behind them. That's why, for the Cultural Capital mobilization, it would be necessary to *start* with a broad coalition—business, government, citizen groups, neighborhoods in the act together. We could imagine St. Paul Mayor Jim Scheibel, a man known for his modesty and attentiveness to process, being a first convener in such a process.

Why not, for example, kick off a Cultural Capital campaign with a daylong community conference? It might start with architects and arts executives, urban geographers and tourism marketing experts who address the core idea. Then there could be break-out sessions focusing on some of the critical themes—pathway design, a trolley circulator system, a visitors center, and ways to reach out to markets across the state and Upper Midwest. At the day's end a permanent steering committee could emerge. Broad participation, drawing on the skills and diversity of St. Paul today, would be the key.

And let's ask: Why should the participants be limited exclusively to St. Paul people or St. Paul interests? St. Paul is Minnesota's capital. The start-up conference and continuing process should include people from the state and other Metro East governments, as well as citizens from communities across Metro East. And why not include, too, interested and sympathetic people from Minneapolis and the western suburbs? An attractive feature of the Cultural Capital idea is that it endangers no entrenched interests. It's as close to a win-win strategy as one could imagine.

Consider the issue for Metro East's suburban communities, for example. A healthy St. Paul is fiscal good news for them all. A safe and attractive St. Paul can improve the quality of life for people across the region. Today the suburbs have many middle-aged people—baby-boomers "graying in place," as it were. For them, a friendly city of multiple cultural offerings could be a real plus. Inclusion of Metro East people in the planning process could also bring out new, as yet unforeseen ways for city and suburban people to work together.

A question arises: Even if Scheibel played official "convener," who'd put together the resources, do the careful staff work to make sure the Cultural Capital effort had broad representation from its inception? Our suggestion would be to turn to those very foundations that owe their existence to past business success in St. Paul—the Wilder, St. Paul, McKnight, Bush, and Northwest Area foundations. The Citizens League might organize a special process and provide staffing. More than one of our interviewees said foundations have taken over the role that banks used to play, as catalysts for change in St. Paul.

We suspect the foundations would find the Cultural Capital idea extraordinarily attractive. It's a way to strengthen the long-term capacity of the community to control its own destiny. By drawing so many new patrons to St. Paul, it could come close to an insurance policy for the future of often fragile arts institutions. And it would represent an opportunity to celebrate the increasingly multicultural complexion of St. Paul.

We were startled to discover how rapidly people of color are climbing as a share of St. Paul's population—nearly 18 percent by the 1990 census, with Asians some 7 percent, African-Americans 7 percent, Hispanics 4 percent. While the numbers aren't yet overwhelming, they've literally doubled in the last decade.

New infusions of people of color and of different cultures are rapidly changing the city's image as an overwhelmingly white capital. While most people are aware of the fast Asian expansion, not so many know there's a significant influx of Russian Jews, only less visible in the schools because they have fewer school-aged children.

The shift has dramatic implications for St. Paul's future leadership. One senior corporate executive suggested a visual image. Let the whole student body of the St. Paul schools assemble on the broad stage of the Civic Center, he suggested. And then let the business leadership of the city assemble in the gallery. The business people would suddenly see the city's demographic future. Children of color today constitute almost half the school population.

A drive around St. Paul quickly destroys one's old stereotypes of the city. Of course there are still strong middle-class neighborhoods with stable parishes. But then, one suddenly sees the sign for Morgan's Mexican and Lebanese bakery—run by a German family! One comes across all manner of Asian-run enterprises—even the Hmong Auto Service. There's a delicious proliferation of ethnic restaurants all along University Avenue. And for a visual image of the new St. Paul, the scene of black and Hmong kids playing together on a lawn in Frogtown sticks with us.

Of course there are some tensions among the ethnic groups—we heard especially of resentment between Asians and African-Americans. But let no one doubt that a multihued St. Paul is here to stay and grow.

A Cultural Capital focus could help make diversity fun and natural. All manner of ethnic celebrations could be featured. One thinks of the outpouring of neighborhood and ethnic groups, each with its own booth or theatrical performance, that turn out for the Baltimore City Fair on that city's Inner Harbor. The smells alone, from calzone to chitlings, souvlaki to stuffed cabbage, metaphorically suggest what diversity has brought elsewhere—and could bring now, even in vanilla Minnesota.

"Value diversity rather than just tolerating it," one black leader told us eloquently. "Just being tolerated isn't good enough; people need to be accepted and valued. St. Paul once seemed homogeneous. Today that's changed. It's almost as if Minnesota wants to be nice and pretend you're not colored. Let's get real. If color is OK, then people will be OK."

The 1990s are going to demand multiple dialogues, not just across barriers of race but across class and municipal lines, too. However advanced the reputation of Minnesota's "civics," other American communities have been leaping ahead in initiating new dialogues between groups that had rarely talked before. Examples are to be found from Charlotte (North Carolina) to Portland (Oregon), Westchester County (New York) to Phoenix (Arizona).

Some leaders feel it's been too long since St. Paul had an energetic discussion about where the community is and ought to be headed—a way to engage people to see what kind of commitments they're willing to make for the city and region's overall benefit.

Some of the commitments need to be very concrete. A corporation that's felt alienated from local decision making might lend some of its talented employees to work on a complex government problem for a few months, with the tacit assurance it won't be blindsided with quick regulatory or tax changes. A poor community, in return for a community center or scholarships for its children, could agree to bring the truancy rate down dramatically.

All these kinds of commitments require trust. Trust requires familiarity and shared purpose—person to person, group to group. And the only way to build shared purpose is through some form of capacity-building process that brings citizens' and groups' common goals into clear focus.

Even the organizing of a Cultural Capital concept could pay powerful dividends. First, the Cultural Capital idea could demonstrate that St. Paul, its neighborhoods and sister cities of the region—communities for which so many people profess such deep affection—have a lot more going for them than sentiment. The Cultural Capital project could in fact prove that the collective communities of St. Paul and Metro East have the capacity to coalesce, to think cooperatively and strategically, to break their economic drift, to start taking command of their own future.

Shedding the "Second-Best" Mind-set

Consciousness of St. Paul's decadence is never mentioned aloud by her citizens. But the consciousness is there. It lies in an unmistakable inferiority complex betrayed by a scorn of bustling Minneapolis. That feeling is more than conventional intercity rivalry. It is the tight-lipped contempt of an embittered invalid for a twin who insists on having a hell of a time. — *Fortune*, April 1936

It's nothing new that St. Paul wonders wistfully, jealously, sometimes unhappily, about her big, booming sister across the Mississippi River.

But things are different than they were in 1936. People may worry about Minneapolis, how it's picked up most of the marbles in the intercity economic rivalry of the past decade or more. But today St. Paul leaders no longer—at least in the confines of the off-the-record interviews we conducted—make any bones about it.

If you want a quick picture of the difference between the business climate in St. Paul and Minneapolis, one of our interviewees suggested, just take a look at the largely empty cavern of St. Paul's Minnesota Club. Then go over to the Minneapolis Club and take in the bustling scene of deals in progress. No contest.

Even harsher characterizations came from a St. Paul leader who arrived on the scene in the early 1980s. He claimed the power shift has left St. Paul a wholly owned subsidiary, an urban appendage.

We found we couldn't get through conversations with many people without Minneapolis coming up, time and again. And we had to wonder why. Is the lingering preoccupation simply a reflection of St. Paul's spate of business losses during the late 1980s, combined with the consolidation of so many financial and legal institutions into downtown Minneapolis? Or is it just letdown from what now seem like glory days of the early- to mid-1980s, when St. Paul built its magnificent Ordway Music Theatre, won the World Trade Center competition, and saw its downtown take on a dramatic new look?

The odd thing to us was the almost excessive deprecation of the St. Paul of the 1990s. Sometimes it seemed like a time warp, as if it had been this spring, not more than 50 years ago, that the caustic *Fortune* writer noted:

> The Panama Canal killed St. Paul (by ending the transcontinental railroad monopoly on shipping goods). Larger, more strategically located, with a good deal more gumption, Minneapolis began feeding upon the carcass. Its wholesale houses outgrew St. Paul's and Minneapolis became the great jobbing town of the Northwest. . . . St. Paul's only big lumbermen, the Weyerhaeusers, moved more and more of their operations to the coast. . . . St. Paul society [saw] that no new wealth was being created. . . . Social and industrial rigor mortis set in.

Great analysis, except that a half century of very good years for St. Paul followed the proclamation of rigor mortis!

Yet the poor-mouthing, home-grown or imposed by smart-alecky outsiders, seems never to end. When we noted that downtown St. Paul, its office vacancies notwithstanding, has more retailing than most American medium-sized cities, a business leader responded, "Yeah, downtown's a good place to buy underwear."

Visitors, like us, find St. Paul a city of gracious, stable neighborhoods, friendly and well-educated people in the midst of a growing region. Yet one of St. Paul's own told us it's a community "that doesn't seem to like itself very much. It doesn't have good perspective on its strengths. And that's somehow related to Minneapolis."

St. Paul, said another, was always "old money." It didn't have "to show off" for anybody. "Of course, we also pretended we didn't have any diversity."

But buried in this barrage of bad karma were, we think, the seeds of a growing conviction—a new attitude that says, in the words of one longtime observer: "Don't even worry about Minneapolis. That's like the fur merchant worrying about the leather merchant. They're selling different stuff, entirely different."

A leading businessman seemed to agree when he told us that "St. Paul has tried to be Minneapolis, and it should try to be St. Paul."

Another businessman was more blunt: "Just quit talking about Minneapolis. Find what we do better. And focus, focus, focus!"

Or, in the words of a former city official, "The real question's not how to compare ourselves with Minneapolis, but how to distance ourselves."

Recapturing the Magic of the Minnesota Model

What is "Metro East"? A bus route? A marketing invention to fight off the westward tumble of population, jobs, and money? A code word for the more relaxed, non-Minneapolitan lifestyle that St. Paul and its sister communities prize?

Right now, the Metro East name sticks to nothing. Many officials of the growing new suburban cities who ought to be in its orbit blink at mention of the notion and report that their constituents relate as much to Minneapolis as St. Paul.

Could Metro East mean something positive? Could it stand not just for a less hectic lifestyle, but rather a compelling vision of excellence in public life, linked to productive economic growth? Could Metro East become a powerful concept, the best of what modern Minnesota offers its people and the country? Today that seems a distant dream. Minnesota may once have been the hotbed of governmental innovation in America. But visit today and you quickly get a feeling it's time to change the sheets. Rather than spearheading innovation, the state seems stuck on the shoals of indecision and ineffectiveness.

Minnesotans' confidence in public officials has plummeted. Many officeholders and government administrators are depicted as weary, worn out, increasingly timid about taking on the tough issues.

Like the rest of the state, St. Paul and its Metro East neighbors seem to have lost the magic of the old Minnesota model—the idea of government that conceives and provides quality services, and in turn earns the support of an active, interested citizenry. A corporate official told us he sensed in St. Paul today "a sort of learned helplessness," a feeling that problems ranging from growing ethnic tensions to loss of downtown businesses are just too daunting to overcome.

The mayoralty of George Latimer, say many, brought a series of fascinating projects—from district heating (a system of steam pipes serving a whole set of city blocks from a single heating plant) to the "homegrown economy" to Lowertown development—but little systemic change in a tradition-bound bureaucracy.

And no one should expect change to get any easier in the 1990s. In state after state across America, the story's the same—severely curtailed public revenues, unwillingness to raise taxes, dismissals of public employees, big cutbacks in services. St. Paul's city revenues, for example, rest on property taxes, state aid, and taxes on utility bills. None is expected to increase much if at all in the next years. "If state aid stays flat or declines," a close observer of the city's finances told us, "we go to double-digit tax increases."

The 1990s are bringing state and local governments under the same kinds of severe pressure corporate America suffered in the 1980s. The federal government is burdened by mountains of debt. States' finances are strung out tighter than ever. And waiting at the bottom of the fiscal food chain are fierce taxpayer revolts.

Cities and counties, more on their own than ever, have to ask themselves tough questions: Why are we providing the services we do? Which functions could we eliminate, which ones should we hand off to private business to furnish on a fee-for-services basis? How do our personnel systems, our incentives for our own employees, need to be reformed? Could we save substantial chunks of money and improve service by combining functions with neighboring cities and counties? The challenge for Metro East governments and citizens is to look those questions squarely in the eye and then start acting on them.

The task won't be easy. St. Paul is no longer simply a city of safe, prim and proper neighborhoods of unfailingly white Roman Catholic parishes. It's increasingly complex, home to thousands of Hmong, Koreans, Vietnamese, Laotians, Thai, Japanese, Chinese, African-Americans, American Indians, Central- and Mexican-Americans.

The numbers (18 percent nonwhite) aren't great by California or East Coast standards. But the new hues stand out vividly on St. Paul's traditionally white canvas. And already, children of color constitute close to half the student body of the city's public schools.

Government "service as usual" for these populations just won't do. Asian immigrants bring vastly different histories of disease susceptibility and health problems, for example. African-American young women may not seek prenatal care they need because the clinics represent, to them, an entirely white culture.

And St. Paul's own government is in danger of wandering into a fiscal fairyland. As one expert on the city's finances told us: "It's going to get a lot more tense as downtown property values decline. We've gotten by for some time leaning on tax-base sharing. But it's turned into a crutch for a cripple."

Then there's the profound physical change that's rolled across the lands of meadows, farm fields, lakes and bogs and forests that stretch out north and south and eastward to the St. Croix River. The suburban population growth may not have been as explosive as that of Minneapolis to the west. But dozens of new communities have emerged, and county governments are being faced with challenges of urbanization they never dreamed would be theirs.

With federal subsidies cut away and state support dwindling, how is government to afford the extraordinarily expensive demands of sprawl development—new roads and water and sewer systems, schools and firehouses spread far and wide across the once-rural landscape?

There is a growing belief around America that government will have to be fundamentally redesigned in the 1990s. It's clear there will never be enough money for social services if we just focus on after-the-fact remediation and don't get to kids and families before trouble starts. We'll never have enough tax money to pay for police and courts and prisons unless crime can be stopped before it occurs.

Likewise, the issue of overlapping, redundant government services, one jurisdiction duplicating what the next does often just to safeguard its own government workers' jobs, can no longer be swept under the rug. And we have to see that government itself will never be affordable if constant pressure can't be brought to train and advance its workers and reform its operations, just as private business must pare, reform, cut, adjust, reorganize to continue existing. It's something of a shock to hear—especially in Minnesota, with its civic mecca reputation—people speaking intensely, even angrily, about ill-functioning government, about insiders taking everyone else for a ride.

And then there's the palpable failure to come to grips with obvious challenges. We were amazed to hear that a proposal to merge the St. Paul and Ramsey County health departments, which carry out substantially the same functions and serve mostly the same populations, has been hanging around unresolved for 35 years.

The St. Paul Fire Department, despite years of demands and litigation, hasn't managed to hire even one female firefighter! The process to deal with the problem, now belatedly in place, is scant excuse for years of posturing and postponement.

The St. Paul Police Department has 15 captains supervising 25 lieutenants—and the same top-heavy (and exceedingly expensive) organizational structure reportedly pervades many of the city's other departments. A *St. Paul Pioneer Press* report shows that 500 St. Paul municipal employees earn over $50,000 a year—and people remember the story months after its publication.

Despite St. Paul's gargantuan office vacancy rate, the city is constructing a three-story addition to City Hall—when office space across the street can be had at a fire-sale rate.

Not so many juicy anecdotes get told about the suburbs. But have Metro East suburban officials coalesced across city and county lines to require compact, land-conserving, energy-efficient growth? The answer, unfortunately, is no. In the 21st century, when Metro East's people wake up to find virtually all their woods and wetlands and farms have fallen prey to highways, houses, and commercial strips, failure to protect the region's natural birthright may look more scandalous than old-fashioned government waste and inefficiency.

To be fair, there are some promising experiments in St. Paul and across the region to improve government's efficiency in the 1990s. The most significant among these may be the legislatively directed Ramsey County study commission looking for new efficiencies and shared-service arrangements across municipal and school district lines.

The Ramsey County cities of Arden Hills, Mounds View, New Brighton, St. Anthony, and Shoreview have been talking about service mergers, tagging 33 of 43 services they looked at as good candidates for consolidation. These northern suburbs, we heard, are starting to recognize they're a *community,* with common geography, cultural, and transportation connections. Building inspections, cable TV, even policing, are among the areas where they're starting to think joint operations might be more efficient. They're talking broadly and imaginatively about "right-sizing" services to the scale that works best, substituting sensible scale for the usual political jurisdictions. Dakota County officials—city and county—are discussing cost-cutting mergers in such areas as police and fire dispatching, health and environmental inspections, and ambulance and other emergency training.

There *ought* to be a lot more suburban cooperation in the 1990s, especially as so-called urban problems—emergency services, child protection, drugs, and affordable low-to-moderate-income housing—spread from town to town.

But we heard it said of the Metro East governments that they generally fall into one of two principal models: a management model or a political model. The management-model towns and cities already have long, successful, albeit usually quiet histories of cooperation. Today you can find them sharing computing services or buying their fire hose by the mile. In the political-model towns, by contrast, parochialism and a premium on contracts for friends and contacts dominate the culture. Such towns are likely to be bricks in the path of efficiency efforts—until and unless their own citizens, who are obliged to pay the taxes for the inefficiencies, demand something different.

So it's tough to say, right now, how many of the budding conversations about increasing government affordability and responsiveness for the 1990s will result in concrete change. For the moment, it's probably premature to clap with more than a single hand. If there is a shared view throughout Metro East regarding the fundamental need to literally reinvent government's ways of operation, it's pretty well hidden. Bare government cupboards and forced staff reductions in the coming years will likely propel the conversation forward.

But why wait until tensions and tempers rise, and constituencies are left snapping over the pieces of a shrinking pie? We believe there's a dramatic opportunity for rapid, forward action now—action that could give St. Paul–Metro East a leg up on reorganization that saves money, delivers services more efficiently, and restores citizens' confidence in government. In the process, the region also becomes more competitive economically—a tangible payoff for both citizens and business.

Since the late 1980s, some of the country's most advanced thinkers about government have been borrowing a number of the ideas of modern, flexible management structure expounded in Tom Peters's *In Search of Excellence* and Edward Deming's "Total Quality Management" concept and applying them to the public sector. One of the most enthusiastic experimenters is Gov. Lawton Chiles of Florida, who has set up a "Governor's Commission for Government by the People." Two top state-local government analysts, David Osborne and Ted Gaebler, have written a book on the subject, called *Reinventing Government.*

The leading Twin Cities expert on the new approach may be Peter Hutchinson, a former foundation chief and public affairs executive of Dayton Hudson Corporation and Minnesota finance commissioner in 1989–90. Says Hutchinson: "Only through the redesign of public services as if the customer really mattered can we get all the government we want, need, and can afford."

In Florida, Chiles got so impatient with the state's outmoded personnel practices that he persuaded the legislature to "sunset" Florida's entire salary classification system, the whole career system, effective at the end of the 1992 legislative session. His lieutenant governor, Buddy McKay, asserts it's possible "to bring into Florida a state-of-the-art system, which allows managers to manage, which allows managers to reward high productivity employees and to discipline, retrain, counsel, and, if necessary, discharge those employees who do not produce."

Florida's new idea is to give government managers a mission to accomplish, along with almost total freedom to run their operations, pretty much like a private business, as long as they produce the needed results. The director of the Workers Compensation Division of the Labor Department, for example, was given that freedom and used it to merge more than 70 job classifications into 14 and eliminate about 10 middle-manager positions. With the savings, a series of incentive bonuses ($50 to $200 a month) were set up for data entry and other clerks in the department. The system caught on fast; the number of workers receiving productivity bonuses doubled (from 102 to 203) over the first two months.

Giving government managers discretion to try these kinds of experiments is truly revolutionary stuff in government. It goes against the penchant of legislatures and councils to exert close control. But it may be the only way to reinvent systems and get clear results.

The new approach tries to introduce choice and competition into government. It rejects the "one best way" of doing things so routinely advanced by credentialed professionals. Instead it celebrates innovation and creativity in various locally designed approaches. It expects to see multiple services tied together for the benefit of (and often with the advice of) citizens and businesses at the grassroots level.

The ultimate goal, says the Florida governor's commission, is "to enlighten our government to see its people as a customer to win, not merely a citizen to tax." Needless to say, that's 180 degrees from government agencies that seem to exist for the convenience, pay, and perks of the providers, the people who work there.

Obviously it's a shift that won't come easily, without wrenching change. Typically, a myriad of special interests, from status-quo medicine to social service bureaucracies to assorted real estate and developer groups to unions of teachers and police, stand ready to scuttle major change.

In the private sector, our American free enterprise system seems to drive us to continued experimentation, probing, testing, and change. An executive of the St. Paul Companies mentioned that a customer service survey a few years ago showed the firm near the bottom in its industry. "We did something about it, and in the process cut our payroll. Today we are near the top," he noted. In a fiercely competitive environment, 3M has survived and prospered by sustaining a culture of mutual support—and accountability for performance results.

What these corporations know is that sole providers, monopoly sources, can wreak havoc with any organization's balance sheet. Even winning a sole-provider contract is not a permanent assurance. What companies are doing all the time is seeking competition among their suppliers, not just to cut costs, but also to improve quality.

By contrast, in St. Paul and its more unionized suburbs, contracting for government services seems like anathema. One Metro East union leader told us: "The people in government shouldn't be so shy as not to mention the words ['contracting for services']. But we beat 'em up every time they do." He argued that contracting is usually "a simplistic solution to problems that can be dealt with by a city work force with much more accountability." The practice, he said, reeks of union busting, of using underpaid private labor and breaking faith with government workers after they have a contract. "We can demonstrate," he said, "that it's not a cost-effective way of delivering the public services."

In one sense the union leader is right: contracting has to be disturbing to public employees because it introduces competition, performance standards, and risks to job security. But for the public, it seems to carry major rewards. Los Angeles County, since 1979, has documented 407 separate contracts producing more than $50 million in savings. A federal study covering 20 cities found savings ranging from 37 to 96 percent in contracting for seven of eight generic public services. In Chicago, Mayor Richard Daley has achieved tangible savings by contracting out such services as cleaning, auto towing, drug and alcohol treatment, tree stump removal, and parking garage operation. Northwestern University's Donald Haider reports that the most critical gain is that contracting "redirects mayors and public officials to dealing with constituents as consumers and service beneficiaries as customers."

The real question ought not to be the *whether,* but the *how* of contracting. One pitfall is to let a sole contractor get a stranglehold on a service, so that a private monopoly provider replaces the public monopoly provider. In a number of cities, government agencies themselves have bid for government contracts and won them against private competitors.

But contracting is *not,* by definition, antigovernment. Indeed, it makes it more critical than ever that government have officials of the highest skill and capacity to oversee contracts. There's always the peril of graft and kickbacks to be defended against. The job demands highly qualified government managers to evaluate bids, oversee contracts, and consider citizen complaints and expressions of satisfaction. Entrust contracting to untrained people and you can count on the private business folks taking government—and the taxpayers—to the cleaners every time. Contracting is but one method that ought to emerge when the serious, root questions are posed about what government does, for whom, how well, and at what price. Ask those questions honestly, repeatedly, and an exciting prospect emerges: government that's far more responsive and accountable—and for its more qualified employees, a much more stimulating, exciting place to work.

There's a thorny political problem here, though. Any public official who has the courage to ask the tough questions, to explore contracting, civil service reform, unconventional approaches, easily courts being isolated, cut off, faced with a phalanx of political enemies. In politics, boat rockers are rarely welcome.

The biggest ally of the fresh thinkers ought to be the public itself. And the public ought to understand that getting any change in government is tremendously difficult, that some false starts and errors are inevitable. Elected officials who show imagination and courage merit strong, continuing public support.

The media have a massive role to play here, too. Even while maintaining their objectivity, newspapers, television, and radio have an immense responsibility to track how government systems are working, to look at government operations not in the headlines. Reporters need to "hear the dog that doesn't bark," to give visibility and sustained coverage to public servants who are courageous enough to venture out into the quicksand of innovation.

Could Metro East be a pioneer, a testing ground for new ideas of governance—not just government and contracting and sharing services, but the most adventurous experiments in improved social services, land use planning, environmental protection, breakthroughs in education? The answer may be yes, providing there's some experimentation outside government to help it happen.

The two sponsors of this report, the *St. Paul Pioneer Press* and KCTA-TV, could play a critical role. Each could take up the challenge of examining and reporting on how all the communities of the Metro East region are grappling with vital issues. Not only are they the most visible media outlets in Metro East; each has a clear commitment as well as a direct interest.

One can imagine periodic full pages or even double spreads in the *Pioneer Press,* taking on a single critical issue—for example, school improvement, growth management, garbage incinerators and landfills, creation of moderate-income housing. The focus would be on how people and governments from Stillwater to St. Anthony Park, Hastings to Hugo, are trying to deal with that single issue. Not only would the coverage give credibility to innovators; it would also underscore the commonality of problems and interests across the region.

Public television's focus embraces Minneapolis and the western suburbs as well, but one can still imagine issue-based programming that shows how questions of improved governance arch across municipal lines.

Imagine, for example, newspaper surveys or television programs showing how multiple communities are trying to bring the Twin Cities' new racial minorities into the public process, into debate about their own communities' futures. Coverage of emerging neighborhood-based self-government, as well as human interest stories about individuals trying to make their neighborhoods safer and more livable, helps to expand people's consciousness of reform and improvement efforts across the region.

The Citizens League of the Twin Cities, possibly with the support of the Humphrey Institute, also might be called on to take a careful look at Metro East communities' governance and identify ways independent cities and counties might cooperate far more fully than their politicians will admit.

Without the perspective of organized but independent citizens, there will be neither sufficient research into what might be possible in a strengthened Metro East nor a credible citizen voice to counteract vested interests. To get the Citizens League moving on such an initiative, a committee of its Metro East members might organize to request a major league commitment.

With the newspaper as monitor-watchdog-prod, with public television underscoring the regionwide potentials, with the Citizens League and grassroots organizations in the individual cities and counties joining in, there could be a powerful groundswell of support for fresh thinking. Government up to the challenges of excellence in the 1990s, public service cast in consumer terms, communities learning to cooperate and share services, could fill the Metro East concept with substance based on commonality of effort and interests.

If that happened, the payoffs for St. Paul, for Ramsey and Washington and Dakota counties and their communities, could be impressive. Not only would their governments move toward the cutting edge; their image and desirability as a place to do business, to draw corporate activity, also would increase. It would take immense effort to make Metro East a new Minnesota model, using government as the vehicle. But it would be a perfectly Minnesotan device.

Organized Labor: Blessing and Malediction

"Organized labor has been one of our greatest strengths. But now we have to take a hard look, because our town now lives and dies by labor."

That voice of a citizen, at a forum to solicit people's ideas for this report, is just the tip of the iceberg. We found, among St. Paul business and government and neighborhood leaders, a crescendo of concern and growing hostility about government unions and their impact on the city. The only other American city where the union issue is so hot, we'd guess, would be New York City, or perhaps Philadelphia.

One thing is sure: the union movement has been fabulously successful in St. Paul. The AFL-CIO constellation of 110 unions has 36,000 members. School teaching staffs, city and suburban, are thoroughly unionized, and so are the janitors, lunchroom workers, clerks, and grounds people.

The American Federation of State, County and Municipal Employees has about 900 members in St. Paul and an additional 1,500 in Ramsey County. Indeed, through a variety of operating units, including several that represent supervisors, virtually everyone who works for government in and around St. Paul is a union member.

"The only people not unionized," said a leading officeholder, "are department heads." There are instances in which unionized managers find themselves across the bargaining table from representatives of other unions. Even the city's own attorneys have organized a bargaining unit.

Then there's the array of prolabor features the Democratic-Farmer-Labor Party has written into state law, guaranteeing public workers collective bargaining rights, guaranteeing pension rights, guaranteeing police and firefighters the right of mandatory, binding arbitration (no matter how tough a city's fiscal condition may be).

Yet with corporations and individuals having to batten down their fiscal hatches for the 1990s, there's growing resentment about labor's consistent success, about the reports of some St. Paul city workers earning thousands of dollars more than counterparts in other cities, or than equally talented people in private business.

Here's a sampler of what we heard in our interviews:

The unions have a stranglehold on this city.

The unions and the DFL, state and city, are intertwined, producing resistance to change.

One of the big obstacles to restructuring city and county government is that the legislature always agrees with the unions.

There's lots of inertia in city departments—people there a long time, supported by the union structure. You have to work around those people— around the dead wood.

City Council members have gone out picketing with public employees to show solidarity.

Labor laws and contracts drive the system in city government. Personnel rules make it tough for managers to operate in efficient fashion. Each time a reform gets proposed, the unions block it, or they turn it to protect their turf.

A lot of the city's high wages flow out to the suburbs. A majority of city workers live outside the city.

City union pay scales are the big barrier to merging city and county departments. The talks always collapse because city unions think they'll get less, and the county's afraid of having to pay more.

The school board's been bought and paid for by the union. Most of the board members are public employees themselves.

Labor's mainly focused on pension benefits, retirements. Most labor leaders are in their 50s. Older workers get protected. St. Paul wouldn't have had to lay off so many teachers if it hadn't been locked into seniority, salary, and benefits schedules.

The cost of administrative support in the schools is outrageous: clerical salaries 42 percent over the market, janitors 67 percent, food workers 100 percent. When budgets get cut, that easily leads to 35 students in one classroom.

Contract for services in the schools? That's absolutely politically unfeasible. The school board would figure it could never be reelected.

A school health program could be delivered without licensed nurses at $35,000 a year. But the unions insist.

The unions hamstring us. They're very self-protective, not interested in the bigger picture. Jobs is it to them. They'll push to build a new building even if we don't need it, just because it provides some construction jobs.

The construction and trade unions are also very strong in St. Paul. They scare off business.

As visitors, we couldn't evaluate the fairness of each of these charges.

But where there's this much smoke, and it's billowing through a historically prolabor town such as St. Paul, you have to figure there are some flames.

Defenders of St. Paul city government do argue there's no big problem here—that labor hasn't driven overall city costs too high. Neither St. Paul's per capita costs of delivering services nor its property taxes are out of line with comparable cities, they argue.

One could also say St. Paul's fiscal stability is fostered by its high number of middle-class neighborhoods, and that things would be calamitously worse without Minnesota's tax-base sharing laws (which are funneling $38 million to the city this year).

Even so, we sensed mounting worry about the high union wages the city's paying and a fear that with less federal and state aid, city property taxes could start a fast ascent and trigger an exodus by the city's prized middle-class constituency.

We found union leaders and critics alike saying that the unions' political clout is beginning to slip, that there's occasionally election-time apathy in labor ranks, that it's becoming possible to raise campaign funds without union endorsement. Unions have run into unusually stiff council resistance in their effort to get wages increased in the face of a prospective 1992 deficit and Mayor Jim Scheibel's call for a wage freeze. One of the union critics we interviewed actually sympathized with the unions a bit, noting that they're getting associated, fairly or unfairly, with the growing antigovernment tenor of the times.

But it doesn't take clairvoyance to see, right now, the seeds of a populist uprising against union power in St. Paul and Ramsey County in the 1990s. Part of it could come from small-business operators complaining they have bigger responsibilities and carry a much more demanding work load than a bunch of civil-service-protected assistant city inspectors living off public tax payments and earning tens of thousands of dollars more each year.

It's also easy to imagine rhetoric aimed at people of less means, residents of hard-pressed neighborhoods where there are few well-paid government workers. Such rhetoric might run like this: *Why work your tail off, pay a huge property tax, to support $80,000-a-year assistant city attorneys, $79,000-a-year engineers, $70,000-a-year deputy planning directors, $65,000-a-year building code officers, most of whom don't even live in St. Paul themselves? Why should these folks enjoy lifetime civil service protection, while you earn a fraction as much and have to worry about layoffs every week of your life?*

We're not endorsing that kind of political pitch; we're just saying that as the fiscal noose tightens on local government, it becomes increasingly likely. St. Paul has apparently tried, over the years, to hold down its overall payroll while attracting higher-than-average-quality city employees and paying them more than average. When a city is lucky enough to find exceptional people—and St. Paul has some of those—this is a good strategy. But in a civil service system, unfortunately it's not just cream that rises to the top.

What's more, no one contemplated the impact of the city's rush to embrace the "comparable worth" doctrine, even dropping comparisons to private sector wages. Female or male, if you work for St. Paul, and you think you're doing work similar to someone else but know you're getting paid less, you can easily file a challenge and fatten your paycheck.

One labor leader made it quite clear to us that when it's a choice between cutting payroll and cutting services, government employees' "standard of living" ought to be preserved and services put on the chopping block. Reduced services, he suggested, would make the public supportive of more taxes.

Employee costs get driven up by generous pension benefits. And civil service rules seem to boost city workers' pay while making it almost impossible to discharge an inefficient employee.

Clearly there's danger of losing the support of a less lucky electorate. There's already evidence of some outrage about the hundreds of city workers pulling down $50,000-plus a year.

How will the unions respond? One can see two strategies. One would be familiar enough—to deny there's any need for change, to attack opponents as union-bashers. But there could be an alternative—a deliberate decision, by the unions themselves, to embrace some big changes in labor-management relations.

Under the alternative, the unions wouldn't just grudgingly go along with some more flexible pay structures and work rules. They would initiate the discussions about how to start them. Government unions would press hard themselves for enhanced government efficiency, responsiveness, customer orientation. They'd talk straight to their own members—warning of the political firestorm that may be coming and urging early, preventive action. There's some evidence that union leaders already grasp the need for change, that they see the mounting fiscal problems and understand they may be far better off helping to shape solutions rather than waiting for a political firestorm.

A "total quality improvement plan" is beginning in St. Paul city government, with the unions promising to join an effort to improve the quality of services. Some tough discussions on health benefits have begun, and a less controversial repolishing of existing civil service rules is in the works. So far the conversations seem cooperative, nonconfrontational; and some of the unions, even over the objections of others, have sided with a lower-cost but nonunionized health care provider.

But to be progressive partners in the 1990s, the unions will have to go much further—demanding that their political allies, the people in control of the city and county governments, push forward aggressively on the new management frontiers and keep the unions in on the conversations.

A signal of real change would be union abandonment of automatic opposition to any and all forms of government contracting out. Instead of running from the idea of competition, unions ought to insist their members can be the most efficient, economical service providers and want to bid for the work. In such cities as Phoenix, the city's own public works department has bid for and won garbage contracts over private competitors. Another signal would be union agreement to salary reforms under which top administrators and department heads would be paid competitive salaries, leaving regular civil service salaries capped at ranges more in line with those of the citizens who pay the taxes.

Seniority rights in government employment ought to have the same sanctity they do in private industry—minimal. Managers need to have full responsibility and accountability; workers need training, counsel, motivation—but not lifetime security. Historically, civil service was adopted as a protection for government workers against corrupt political influence, not to create sinecures.

Unions should also lead the charge to throw out archaic civil service "bumping" rules, which create good, protected jobs for veteran workers, while younger, sometimes more productive, city employees get axed in budget squeezes.

Today's new management techniques don't denigrate workers; they make the overdue discovery that workers know more about improving the organization's performance than anyone else. The new order will say treat employees as partners, not subordinates.

The St. Paul unions have an opportunity to seize the leadership: not to wait and react as the fiscal noose tightens, but to persuade government managers to open up planning and decision and personnel processes, to substitute incentives for rigid guarantees.

That's a tough challenge, of course—even assuming sensitive leadership in Minnesota's AFL-CIO and AFSCME in St. Paul. It's a model of labor-management relations waiting to be born, but not yet reality anywhere. Abandoning old adversarial relations, championing a new opportunity track for workers based on skill and not seniority, is a dramatic idea.

But across the United States, there may be no better laboratory to give the new model a try than in Minnesota, and particularly in St. Paul, where the tough politics of the 1990s still haven't destroyed the foundation of popular support for government, where most citizens still feel affection for the public work force.

Vision Begins at Home: Strengthening the Neighborhoods

St. Paul stands out among all American cities as a place to live, a city of attractive and affordable neighborhoods, a place of fine parks and strong churches, a community in which to raise kids and put them through school.

Admittedly, there's some irony in the history. This city of modern-day middle-class propriety traces its historic taproot to none other than Pierre Parrant—that raw opportunist and brawling whiskey merchant whose shack and saloon constituted the new settlement until Father Lucien Galtier arrived to bring a holier spirit, converting Pig's Eye to St. Paul. And in a quiet St. Paul parish today, who'd ever dream that this city in the 1920s and '30s was a haven for the likes of John Dillinger and Baby Face Nelson and the Ma Barker Gang, that during those years the town tolerated a corrupt political machine and police force?

Today St. Paul has incipient problems of poverty and crime and racial tension, focused in what former Mayor George Latimer defined as an "arc of hardship" in neighborhoods circling the downtown.

But this is a city of happy endings. Even today, all you have to do is check around the cities of North America to find that St. Paul stands out as a kind of Rock of Gibraltar in neighborhood and family stability.

Consider families. It's true that the problems of divorce, separation, desertion, and single parenthood have begun to nip at St. Paul. Yet on the key index of family stability—the share of households with two parents present—St. Paul's figure of 40 percent is far ahead of Minneapolis's 33 percent. The figures for most American cities tumble downward from there.

Take the issue of middle-class flight to the suburbs. One does hear anecdotes of young families leaving their St. Paul "home parishes" for the surrounding counties. But compared with other cities, St. Paul has a tiny number of families succumbing to the urge to flee. There's a lot more talk than flight.

Indeed, there appears to be a small but steady stream of people returning to St. Paul from the suburbs—often middle-aged people yearning for the city's rich diversity of place and architecture and parks, ethnic restaurants, theaters and museums and excitement.

St. Paul's public schools are a striking—and rare—exception among American city schools. St. Paul offers what seems to be the nation's premier example of using magnet schools (latest count 36) to maintain racial balance, even as the ranks of children of color expand. The number of white children in the system has held constant at about 20,000. Test scores have been increasing since the mid-1980s. When statewide choice in school selection became state policy in the late 1980s, St. Paul actually gained some students from the suburbs.

Today the St. Paul school system is discussing with the neighboring Roseville school district a voluntary integration plan including shared enrollment and a new school. The Roseville board believes that its mostly white student body will be enriched by increased contact with the city's children of color. In the racially charged America of the early 1990s, it's a stupendous fact that such a discussion could be taking place at all.

It is true that the once-quiescent St. Paul crime scene has begun to turn scary, with gang activity and rising indexes of violent crime. Even so, in the face of a soaring national murder arrest rate among teenagers, not a single St. Paul teenager was arrested for murder in 1990 or was a victim of murder. There's no way anyone can feel good about 1990's 27 percent increase in St. Paul homicides. But it's also true that if St. Paul had a murder rate equivalent to Washington, D.C.'s, it would have had 202 murders in 1990 instead of the 19 it did.

Another measure of a city's success is the number of jobs it has to offer. At last count, 191,000 people were employed in St. Paul—not bad for a city of 272,000 people. What's most astounding, though, is that 60,000 St. Paul residents actually commute to work elsewhere, either in Minneapolis or one of the suburbs.

The message of those 60,000 jobs, one of St. Paul's most fervid exponents told us, is St. Paul's continuing desirability as a place to live. It means, he said, "that St. Paul's a suburb, and a superior one." The city may never have thought of itself that way, but it's time, this civic booster suggested, "to get more relaxed about who we are."

One does, in fact, hear of lots of Twin Cities people who find their professional opportunity in Minneapolis or the western suburbs, but deliberately choose St. Paul to live in. They're quick to assert St. Paul is simply the best place to live in the region.

Even for young people, the St. Paul advantage is clear. A student told us: "If you have purple hair and a pierced nose you should go to Minneapolis. That's not what you'll find at Central High School. Minneapolis is more fast pace, get down. St. Paul is more easygoing, more courteous."

The conclusion seems crystal clear: Neighborhood life is the essence of what St. Paul is. Neighborhood building needs to be the cornerstone of its future vision.

But the neighborhoods of St. Paul are not static. The early 1990s are a time of volatility in St. Paul neighborhoods. Neither the Neighborhood Partnership Program, instituted during the Latimer years, nor the elaborate "district council" system seems up to the challenges.

Gnawing worry about erosion of the city's stability and consensus echoed through our conversations. The theme of uncertainty surfaced whether we were talking with neighborhoods' residents, or professionals engaged in corporate or foundation or government services, or a group of St. Paul citizens who cared enough to show up at a town meeting to talk with us about the community's future. Neighborhood people feel increasingly powerless in the face of undisciplined youth, drug activity, violence on their streets. Racial tensions—differences between whites and blacks, Asians and Native Americans—come up again and again. And the police admit they've lost large measures of psychological control.

A community organizer in the Dayton's Bluff area wrote to us:

We're the cross-burning area. We experience all the fears of poverty and racial tension encroaching on us. Our business owners feel "immobile"—they fear failure as the community weakens. There are many caring and involved citizens doing their best to beat the odds. Some of them we lose as they give up, sell their homes, take a loss, and move to the suburbs. Some stay on and keep trying.

How, asked the Dayton's Bluff organizer, can people be assured "a peaceful, safe, nonviolent neighborhood?"

In stable St. Paul, one's amazed to hear complaints about "nomadism"—growing numbers of people wandering from one neighborhood to another, just a step ahead of the bill collectors. People blame these nomads for the nightmarish frustration of schools coping with yearly student turnover rates of 75 percent or worse.

We heard that migrants from such cities as St. Louis, Gary (Indiana), and Chicago have moved into St. Paul, lured by welfare benefits. The adults typically work a fast-food job for a few days at a time, then move on. One of the city's grassroots leaders described their attitudes as disruptive and disrespectful, "values that really hurt our neighborhoods."

Indeed, in a city where people always felt safe walking around neighborhoods night or day, rising crime has emerged as a dangerous virus. Gangs have been forming since the mid-1980s. At first they were mostly black; now some are Asian as more children of immigrant families reach their teenage years. In some neighborhoods, the word's out among youth: "If you don't have a gun, you better get one."

In 1990 the city saw a 50-percent-plus increase in aggravated assault using handguns. And St. Paul citizens watch with horror as crimes they thought belonged to "other" cities, murder and rape, grow most rapidly.

The crime specter can't be dismissed lightly. If there's a growing feeling that community safety sets with the sun, suburban flight will become inevitable. You can tell people it's worse in other cities. But they don't care about comparative statistics. They care about feeling safe.

Is St. Paul mobilizing to do something about these problems? Does it need to do more? The answer to both questions is yes.

One has to be impressed by the degree of neighborhood organization under way in St. Paul at this very moment. There are innumerable block clubs. There's continuing strong community life surrounding St. Paul's 495 churches, many of them vivid presences in their neighborhoods. What's more, every neighborhood seems to have at least one civic organization that's a rallying point for citizens voicing common concerns. And in recent years, a rising tide of new neighborhood-based organizations has begun to enrich St. Paul's traditional neighborhood scene, creating impressive new grassroots capacity.

Some of the grassroots activity has merited national attention. When the Ford Foundation and Harvard's Kennedy School of Government made their first sweep of the United States in 1986 to pick the nation's most innovative state and local governments, St. Paul's St. Anthony Block Nurse Program emerged as one of the top 10. Nurses and community volunteers work together in the program to provide personal care and companionship for elderly people, helping them avoid premature commitment to nursing homes.

The Mortgage Bankers Association of America cited Westminster, an affiliate of the Archdiocese of St. Paul and Minneapolis, for its development of more than $60 million worth of housing for the poor. Westminster targets specific neighborhoods where it can work in depth, providing not just housing but a variety of social services to help people become self-suffi-cient. The average income of families in Westminster projects is under $10,000. Residents have to vote on a plan for services—a way, say the sponsors, to give them "ownership."

Westminster screens tenants carefully, trying to telegraph the message that sleazy behavior won't be tolerated, that "the bad boys won't get control." Consider its work at the Torre de San Miguel Homes, on St. Paul's West Side, a squalid, failing cooperative housing project until Westminster mounted a $3-million rehabilitation project.

Even with various new tenant services, Westminster found fights were frequent among Torre de San Miguel's children, who come from 11 differ-ent ethnic groups. So a project called "Just Kid-ing Around" was launched. It's focused on the racial-ethnic barriers, slowly turning them into cultural celebrations. "Once you work or play with someone, they aren't black, Hispanic, or low-income; they're Pedro or Bob," said the project's youth services director.

One neighborhood area where St. Paul initially lagged behind Minne-apolis was creation of community development corporations, or CDCs, America's most powerful tool of the last quarter-century to push housing and business activity in depressed neighborhoods. But right now, there's a rather breathtaking effort to make CDCs a mainstay of St. Paul neighbor-hood revitalization. The biggest single player is St. Paul's Local Initiatives Support Corporation, or LISC, begun in 1988 with major contributions from two of the area's most forward-thinking sources of development capital, the St. Paul Companies and the Minneapolis–St. Paul Family Housing Fund. Since then the Norwest and Western banks, Honeywell, Northern States Power, and the United Way have lined up additional support. The corpora-tion also received a $2.3-million boost from the National Community Development Initiative, whose supporters include the Rockefeller Founda-tion, the Knight Foundation, and the Pew Charitable Trusts.

It's hard to believe LISC's impact in St. Paul neighborhoods won't be tangible and important. So far it has approved $1 million in 35 investments for 13 CDCs, leveraging $20 million in other project financing. Some 750 low-income apartments are being financed by LISC's National Equity Fund, at a cost of $19 million. And LISC is reaching out to the CDCs with $1.4 million in grants for critical core operating support.

Western Bank has plunged deeply, and with lots of savvy, into the community development game. It created a bank CDC that's busy creating new CDCs, developing joint projects with neighborhood groups, putting together finance packages, focusing on "micro" business development.

Western is one of a handful of banks in the country that has received a top rating under the federal Community Reinvestment Act. And it's not just into lending; one of Western's most interesting projects tries to help founders of neighborhood businesses find successors to take over and keep their operations running when they decide to retire. That effort, implemented for Western by the Northside Redevelopment Council, is emblematic of the inventive approaches that have to be used to keep neighborhoods healthy.

In some cases block clubs are turning into full-fledged CDCs. For example, the Aurora–St. Anthony Block Club in a neighborhood adjacent to University Avenue and Frogtown has fought crime and tried hard to sustain the area's remarkable home-ownership rate of more than 70 percent. One strategy: assisting young buyers to take over big houses that otherwise might turn into cheap rental properties when their owners die.

On the social front, St. Paul was a national leader in opening high school health clinics—not just as a way to curb teenage pregnancies, but to provide other critically needed health services and referrals for young people. Interviewing at one of the clinics, we were touched to hear of the number of young people from broken homes, or homes plagued by alcohol or drug abuse or worse, who come to find solace and substitute parenting at the clinics.

Then we heard of concerned law enforcement officers anxious to reach kids 5 to 15 with social programs, to put them on a sound course before the temptations of the street begin to threaten them.

In 1991 the St. Paul Ecumenical Alliance of Churches announced jointly with the First Banks system a $50-million program of loans to homeowners for rehabilitation in old and fraying neighborhoods. Mortgage applications would be taken from people whose loans would normally be unbankable—in exchange for a sophisticated preloan counseling program run by the alliance. There's also a $5-million venture capital fund, again with First Bank's money, to launch 50 new small enterprises in the inner city. Technical assistance will be provided by the entrepreneurial center at the University of St. Thomas business school. A third part of the project will train 120 teachers from St. Paul's public and private schools to deal more effectively with the new languages, cultures, and traditions of the emerging St. Paul.

The compelling challenge for St. Paul neighborhoods in the 1990s is getting it all together—redeveloping housing, shoring up businesses, helping residents define services, seeing to it that the pieces fit together for families. Some of the best examples are in Frogtown. On the East Side, the Payne-Phalen Family Resource Center, a collaboration of school people and nurses put together with McKnight Foundation support, helps at-risk families learn parenting techniques and gain access to the social services they need.

St. Paul is blessed with the largest operating foundation of its kind in the nation, the Wilder Foundation. Each year, Wilder spends $40 million on services ranging from child development to housing to in-home services for the elderly. Executives of both Wilder and the area's strong United Way talk of enabling neighborhoods to build on their own capacities, rather than depending on social workers. Some very positive steps have been under way recently, for example, combining two existing programs to form the Neighborhood Revitalization Program, focusing combined resources of nearly $10 million on issues ranging from family stability to community safety to low-income housing needs.

Compared with what most American communities have at their command, all this ought to add up to a dynamite combination. And this review hasn't even touched on dozens of other exemplary groups and efforts, ranging from the North End Area Revitalization to Chicanos, Latinos Unidos en Servicio (Chicanos, Latinos United in Service).

What, one asks, stops all these organizations from making St. Paul into a national model of neighborhood self-sufficiency?

One answer is that many neighborhood leaders, highly motivated but without broad outside experience, can be trapped in their own turf and fail to see the potential partnerships and connections they need.

But surprise! Even for that, there's a St. Paul program. It's called the Leadership Initiative in Neighborhoods program, the invention of Polly Nyberg, community affairs manager for the St. Paul Companies. Individual neighborhood leaders get grants to help them sharpen their skills with formal or informal study, site visits, travel, whatever seems indicated.

Anywhere in the United States, that kind of corporate grant making would be groundbreaking. Even for the usually progressive St. Paul Companies, Nyberg had to go against a corporate culture suspicious of giving to individuals or financing public advocacy. But graduates of the program are already getting broad recognition in the city. Nyberg recently won the prestigious Scrivner Award of the National Council on Foundations, the jury noting her pioneering work in developing indigenous neighborhood leadership and suggesting such endeavors will be vital to cities' survival in the 1990s.

What, then, needs to happen, that isn't happening, for St. Paul neighborhoods to succeed today?

We suggest the media ought to give greater weight to neighborhoods' needs and sensitivities—and not just report the sensational news when crime incidents erupt. Frogtown, for example, has received lots of newspaper and television attention for eruptions of violent crime. No one is saying that legitimate news be suppressed. But many Frogtown residents feel powerless. A steady torrent of "bad" news in the media reinforces their suspicion that the "system" doesn't really care what happens to them or their neighborhood.

A corrective course, for television and the newspaper alike, could be stories about neighborhood people making it—sometimes against immense odds. Such stories may be less sensational, but they're just as compelling. There probably are hundreds of these stories in such places as Frogtown, the West Side, or the Rice Street corridor.

A more intimate *Pioneer Press*–neighborhood tie was suggested by several of our interviewees. Sample ideas: The paper could concentrate on a more extensive stringer network. It might focus on developing news sources in neighborhoods just as it does in government or business. It might offer technical assistance to neighborhood newspapers, with reporters building some personal relationships with local people.

On the crime front, the St. Paul police department shouldn't satisfy itself with periodic saturation raids in drug-infested areas. Nor should it believe it can do the job without continuing community support. Recently, 750 residents of Frogtown dutifully filled out index cards identifying drug houses and abandoned houses. St. Paul's police chief then dropped by to tell them they'd done the easy part. But "the people who are going to get the job done," the chief announced, "are the men and women of the police department."

That approach (though the chief later said the press misconstrued the thrust of his remarks) is dead wrong. Residents, not cops cruising randomly by, have to be the first line of defense to make any neighborhood safe. The most progressive departments around the nation—New York City's now included—are embracing community-based policing. The new approach means officers get out of their cruisers, walk the streets, become acquainted with residents and business people on a personal basis. Officers get rated not by their arrest count, but by whether their beat becomes a safer place.

There is, to the credit of the St. Paul Police Department, a prototype community-policing effort in predominantly Hmong housing developments. It's called ACOP, the Asian Community Outreach Program. Funding comes from the federal Department of Housing and Urban Development. Early reports indicate some good results.

But pilot efforts aren't enough. The typical argument is that community policing is tough to pay for out of regular budgets in tight times. But you have to think a police department top-heavy with brass, a force in which the average patrol officer earns $15,000 more than his or her counterpart in big, bad Minneapolis, hasn't exhausted its budget choices.

Community policing, knitting social services together at the neighborhood level, building community development corporations so that economic development is an extension of the neighborhood's capacities—all these add up to quite a new way of looking at urban neighborhoods.

It may be that the whole community development movement is at a strategic turning point. In the 1960s and '70s, the entire idea seemed to be neighborhood organizing, often to stop some feared highway or building project. Then the focus turned to housing and commercial development, and those remain important.

But today it's clear that schools, social services, and much more have to be woven into the fabric. St. Paul neighborhoods, we heard, are tired of being told what to do, what they should look like. They want to define themselves and not have politicians, business leaders, police headquarters, or outside social service workers tell them how.

The 17 district councils, with their taxpayer-paid staffs, are supposed to represent the neighborhoods. Many of the people we talked with viewed the councils more as the problem than the solution. We heard them described as "a bureaucracy that wants to perpetuate itself," an apparatus much better at blocking ideas than furthering change in the neighborhoods.

"Real citizen organizations aren't on the take from government," one insider said to us. "It's almost the antithesis of grassroots community to pay somebody to do the job," said another. A lot of people suggested that doing away with the district councils might be a cathartic cleansing, leading to a new wave of entrepreneurial neighborhood creativity.

However it's done, the key is to focus on the neighborhoods. Historically, they've made St. Paul a distinctively livable community. A community strategy centered on empowered, supported, successful neighborhoods is the smartest thing St. Paul could do.

Preserving Nature and Farmland

The preservation and care of "natural" Metro East is just as critical a challenge to St. Paul and its sister communities as the nurturing and strengthening of city neighborhoods. We were deeply impressed by the beauty of the sections of fields and rolling meadows, forests, bogs, and lakes that lie still undeveloped in the arc of land stretching north and south and east of St. Paul and eastward to the St. Croix River.

True, development here has not been quite as intense as in the Twin Cities' western suburbs. But sit in a helicopter, as we did, and fly low over Washington, Anoka, and Dakota counties, and it's hard not to wish that development in the 1990s and beyond could be dramatically more sparing of the natural landscape.

One hears of heavy population pressures. (Dakota, for instance, now one of America's fastest-growing counties, lost 21,000 acres of farmland just between 1982 and 1987.) But still, why must shopping centers and strip malls, designed with dull monotony, devour so much land? Why build hundreds of miles of roads, even four-laners, where there aren't even people yet? Which law of economics dictates spreading development so thinly along the highways, when concentrated and compact development would be so much more land- and energy-conserving? What's the rationale for ostentatious "executive-home" developments, each house devouring several acres of land? Judging from sprawl-tolerant local comprehensive plans, few local officials in Metro East see much of a problem. The attitude in such communities as Shoreview and Eagan, we heard, is the more development the merrier.

Yet in such Washington County communities as Lake Elmo and Afton, many people would like to preserve the rural ambience and lifestyle. People in historic Stillwater are fighting a large bridge over the St. Croix River. There's talk of more malls, on Minnesota 36, for example. Our team heard citizens pleading to preserve farmlands and open spaces and rustic roads, save woodlots, encourage meadowlike yards, preserve oak trees during construction, promote natural species, protect wetlands. Monotonous new developments, one citizen wrote to us, destroy "secret" rural places and "create a sterile atmosphere for our children." A distraught citizen wrote to the *White Bear Press* that the building of a new Target store would "forever diminish the view of the sunset."

The 1990s may be the last chance, some Washington and Dakota county officials suggest, to acquire significant chunks of land for future park use. (St. Paul may have a lot of park land, but most of Metro East's open spaces, one hears, are privately held—and thus in future jeopardy.) The Land Stewardship Project, based in Marine on St. Croix, is pushing a "sustainable farming" effort in Washington County and considering formation of a land trust there. In Dakota County, the project encouraged Inver Grove Heights to pass what is being called "a groundbreaking ordinance" to prevent the taking of cropland by eminent domain for residential, industrial, or commercial use.

The central problem is that each community decides its own land uses, with little attention to what a thousand helter-skelter development decisions may do to destroy the very rural character that induced so many people to move to these towns. Countywide land-use planning seems almost nonexistent. And the Metropolitan Council finds itself under constant developer pressure to expand the urban service line.

We heard defeatist sentiments, even from some exponents of farmland preservation, about future prospects. Experience across America does show that single-minded antigrowth campaigns rarely post anything more than temporary victories. The political clout of the development community and its allies—from bankers and builders to farmers hoping to cash in on the new "urban" value of their land—simply is too great.

But the time could now be ripe for a quite dramatic land-use experiment that permits and even fosters growth—but only growth in concentrated nodes, compact new villages, leaving most of the landscape free, rustic, and open.

The prime candidate appears to be the I-94 corridor, as it moves east through Ramsey and Washington counties on its way to the St. Croix River and Wisconsin. A major part of the territory along that corridor is today still devoted to agriculture and other open-space uses. It represents some of the loveliest landscape anywhere in the Twin Cities region.

And it could remain lovely if a careful zoning plan were devised, coordinated between Ramsey and Washington counties and their constituent towns. Minnesota law allows any two or more local governments wide "joint powers"—the authority to do almost anything they wish if they reach a formal accord. Joint powers might be an ideal way to coordinate the zoning of all the communities along the corridor.

The new villages along I-94 wouldn't need to be filled with massive high rises. Among land-use planners and architects there's been lively discussion of "pedestrian pocket" development—a cluster of low-rise, high-density housing, retail and service space and a shared central square, all within a walkable quarter-mile of one another. Several thousand people can live in a single village.

With the right planning, the villages could draw a cross section of residents by income, age, and ethnic background, including a fair share of today's single-person or single-parent households. The goal is an old-fashioned village of all kinds of people, not just look-alike families.

Would there be sufficient demand for life in a village in which people can look out onto lovely rural landscapes—but not chop it into little pieces for personal possession? Our guess is yes—if not for every family in Metro East, surely for a big enough portion to represent a healthy market for the new, convenient, high-quality, village-in-the-countryside lifestyle. The pedestrian pocket could be very much like something as American as apple pie—our traditional small towns.

The highway link between the villages obviously would be I-94. But the region could think more expansively: Why not experiment here with a light-rail line, running out from St. Paul and along the interstate right-of-way? Advocates have long said that light rail would draw development along its spine. The Twin Cities have been terribly slow to allow as much as an experiment with that theory. The I-94 corridor, with compact villages, could be a good way to start, presumably extending a line that links downtown Minneapolis to downtown St. Paul as well.

A bold experiment with compact villages along I-94 could represent a big contribution to all of Metro East and the Twin Cities region. It could show whether there is a way to develop new communities without trampling the rural landscape, without destroying the open space that ought to be everyone's to enjoy.

Update

The St. Paul Peirce Report enjoyed a favorable reception from numerous sources, including foundation officials, the Chamber of Commerce, and Mayor James Scheibel. Public forums, television discussions, and other outgrowths of the report indicated it was an important catalyst for discussion and action. The *St. Paul Pioneer Press* announced editorially in January 1992, "We'll focus this year on Peirce Report ideas for community."

Predictably less positive reactions, given the report's challenge to organized labor to refocus its approaches to deal with the government reform issue, came from union leaders. Jerry Serfling, assistant director of AFSCME Council 14, said: "I'm bothered by the fact that of all the scape-goats Peirce could find in St. Paul, labor was the only one he singled out." What the report had to suggest about the role of public employee unions in government, said Serfling, "is simply not true. AFSCME and a number of unions in St. Paul have been very progressive."

Indeed, if there was a negative spinoff from the report, it was the general stonewalling by municipal labor unions. The city's planning direc-tor departed in summer 1992, telling confidants that his department could perform efficiently with about half its authorized staff. The region's sub-urbs, mostly professionally managed, continued to pioneer new service-sharing arrangements, while the city government was politically restrained from appreciable restructuring.

The Chamber of Commerce established a task force to make creation of the downtown university information center, as recommended in the report, one of its priorities. It received a special grant from the St. Paul Foundation to push the project forward. The center, as plans developed, was seen as having the following aspects: (1) an information clearinghouse/data base on academic and advanced educational programs in the region; (2) career counseling services; (3) a joint business/government training center, filling voids in available training; (4) connections among other networks, such as libraries and adult learning centers; and (5) integration of the education elements of each of the downtown's cultural attractions.

Most public interest, however, swirled around the idea of a St. Paul "cultural corridor" or "cultural capital." Consensus solidified around the concept as the right strategy for St. Paul's urban center. Several groups went to work on developing and promoting the corridor, helped by a $50,000 grant from the Knight Foundation.

The October 1992 grand opening of the Minnesota History Center lent added credence to the "cultural capital" idea, as did a test run (financed by 3M) of the proposed trolley shuttle connecting the attractions in and near the center of historic St. Paul. Design of signs for the trolley route, as well as the walking routes, was begun. The chamber hoped that regular trolley service could be inaugurated by sometime in 1993.

Citistate Guideposts

How should American citistates steel themselves to compete and work directly and effectively with world citistates spread from Seoul to Singapore, Oslo to Osaka, Berlin to Barcelona?

We have developed a list of guideposts, formulas for citistate cohesiveness and strength drawn from our experience with the six urban regions covered in this book, as well as our observations of hundreds of metropolitan centers in the United States and internationally.

Recognize the indivisibility of the citistate.

What would a visitor from another planet, approaching the dark side of planet Earth, first discern? Obviously, it would be the clusters of light where humans congregate in great numbers. And approaching any one of them, the visitor would see, as soon as dawn came, a fully integrated organism: a concentration of human development, of roads and rivers and bridges and masses of buildings, all arrayed together, people and vehicles, air, water, and energy, information and commerce, interacting in seemingly infinite ways. This is, of course, the citistate, the *true city* of our time, the closely interrelated, geographic, economic, environmental entity that chiefly defines late 20th-century civilization.

Some of the features one *can't* see from the air are as significant as those one can. Consider nation-state boundaries. Unless they fall along river lines or abut oceans, they are not to be seen from "up there." The same phenomenon applies within metropolitan areas. All those dividing lines between center cities, suburbs, counties, townships, and urban villages—the dividing lines politicians tell us are so utterly significant—are not to be seen from above. Indeed, between work and home, for errand and entertainment and shopping, the Earth's people cross such municipal lines billions of times each day.

The inescapable oneness of each citistate covers a breathtaking range. Environmental protection, economic promotion, work force preparedness, health care, social services, advanced scientific research and development, philanthropy—success or failure on any one of those fronts ricochets among *all* the communities of a metropolitan region. No man, woman, family, or neighborhood is an island.

There are compelling reasons why center cities, for example, need and depend on their suburbs, and equally compelling reasons why the suburbs need a healthy center city. We made a list of the salient interdependencies, city to suburb, suburb to city, in our Baltimore chapter.

In the new international economy, Theodore Hershberg of the University of Pennsylvania notes, only markets with scale and diversity are likely to succeed. A citistate divided against itself will prove weak and ineffectual. Political boundaries do *not* seal off problems of pollution, solid waste disposal, transportation, schools, inadequate infrastructure. Advertise a suburb by itself and you may be able to offer an above-average labor force and housing stock, but probably fewer educational centers and no really significant concentrations of financial and legal services. Advertise a center city alone and you may talk of great centralized facilities but end up exposing to your potential catch conditions of severe poverty and lack of a skilled labor force. But mix the two together and there is at least a possibility that the strengths will prove complementary and the citistate will be in the ballpark of competition for trade and sophisticated new industries.

Plan the regional economy to marshall internal strength and find a profitable niche in the new world economy.

Citistates that hope to prosper in the international economy need to plan as carefully as the smartest corporations. They need to decide what they're good at and seize their comparative advantages. They have to keep on strategizing to stay afloat in the volatile global economy.

Citistates can be differentiated by type. The National Research Council in the early 1980s made a stab at a division.[1] The waning of manufacturing, the concentration of large corporations and banks and law and accounting firms, the council said, are creating powerful "command and control" centers of which the United States has four: New York, Los Angeles, Chicago, and San Francisco. Houston and Miami were noted as potential early additions to the group. The Big Four, the analysis said, outshine such regional command and control centers as Philadelphia, Boston, Dallas, Baltimore, Minneapolis, Cleveland, Denver, Seattle, Indianapolis, New Orleans, and Portland, Oregon. The cities most subject to forces they can't control were said to be manufacturing centers—Youngstown, Flint, Erie, and the like—and such "industrial-military centers" as San Antonio and Norfolk, Virginia.

Another set of defining roles has been provided by urbanists John Logan and Harvey Molotch, though they are quick to note the categories are neither perfect models nor exhaustive listings:

1. Headquarters—for example, New York, Los Angeles, Chicago.
2. Innovation Centers—for example, Austin, Texas; Cambridge, Massachusetts; Silicon Valley of Northern California; Research Triangle of North Carolina.
3. Module Production Places—for example, Baltimore, Omaha, Houston, the Tri-Cities region of Hanford, Washington. The authors define these as urban centers that perform "routine economic tasks" that could be performed elsewhere; they are also said to be dependent on outside control centers. "They are not sustained by any of the unique organizational constellations that make up control or innovation centers." (We can imagine leaders of such cities as Baltimore and Houston taking hot exception to the characterization, pointing to special economic roles those cities play. But there is at least a grain of truth to the theory.)
4. Third World Entrepot—for example, Miami, San Antonio, San Diego. In the United States, Logan and Molotch observe, these places are linked primarily to Latin America, with which they have many social and organizational ties, and are home to substantial immigrant populations.
5. Retirement Centers—for example, Tampa, St. Petersburg, Tucson.[2]

We have also seen checklists of what it takes to be "an international city" today.[3] First comes international transportation capability—an international airport, great water ports. The city must be an active trade partner; it must be open to foreign capital. Its own firms must be competitive in the international arena. It must have convention and exhibition facilities, ample hotel space, research parks, tourist and student exchange with the wider world.

This list closely parallels the characteristics found by Peter Hall to differentiate "world cities" from other great centers of wealth and population in his classic book on the topic written in 1977.[4] But what has changed from that time to this are the demands of the new global economy. As Scott Fosler, president of the National Academy of Public Administration, has expressed it:

> Regions have become the primary units of economic geography in the new global economy. In the past, southern California, southeast Michigan, and New England traded and competed with one another. Today, they and the other regions of the United States trade and compete with the rest of the world.[5]

To compete in this new ball game requires parallel restructuring of economics and governance at the regional level. According to Fosler, regions must move beyond narrowly defined business promotion activities to integrate and build key economic foundations, including the following:

> ➤ A capable and motivated work force (primary, secondary, and higher education; training; employment security; labor relations)
> ➤ Sound physical infrastructure (transportation, water supply, energy, waste disposal)
> ➤ Knowledge and technology (universities, research institutions, public information systems)
> ➤ Enterprise development (capital, regulation, technical assistance, financial assistance, export promotion, recruitment)
> ➤ Quality of life (public services, environmental quality, amenities, aesthetics, social and political institutions)
> ➤ Fiscal soundness (tax structure and levels, user charges and fees, spending policy, transfer payments)[6]

Theodore Hershberg and Joseph Duckworth lay out a complementary set of requirements:

> Successful firms must have access to a competent labor force, a satisfactory system of transportation to move people and goods cost effectively, an adequate infrastructure to meet their basic water and sanitation needs, and finally, effective control over the environment, including solid, toxic and hazardous waste disposal, water quality, and given the penalties of the new (1990) Clean Air Act, especially air

quality. The most cost-effective means of managing these resources are regional in scope. Regional cooperation becomes vastly more important in the global economy because it is the key to controlling these external costs.[7]

All this makes it obvious that more than business smarts and capital availability is important, that the performance of the public sector, and regionally cooperating governments, are critical. The idea that business can get along well if government just keeps out if its hair was dubious in times past; in today's world, it is preposterous.

That should not be taken as a license for overregulating, overtaxing, burdensome government; rather it is an argument for creative business-government partnerships working on a broad set of common agendas. It is out of that type of partnership—the Metro Denver Network mentioned in the first chapter of this book, for example, or the Greater Baltimore Committee's alliances with Maryland's city and county and state governments—that the strategizing to develop a citistate's special economic niche can be developed.

The idea, according to Harvard Business School Professor Michael Porter, is to think locally and win globally. Porter contends that public policymakers should study the geography of such emerging regional economic clusters as Dallas (national building companies), Silicon Valley (microelectronics), or Rochester, N.Y. (photography, optics, imaging). In *The Competitive Advantage of Nations,* Porter suggests that the growth of regionally concentrated industries usually depends more on local factors— concentration of entrepreneurs, aware local universities, specialized infrastructure, a growing network of local suppliers—than on national industrial policy and targeted federal assistance.[8]

It's sometimes said, especially by industrial policy experts, that other countries are outperforming and outcompeting the United States because of their cultural comfort with extraordinarily close alliances of government, business, and education. The classic two-word summary is "Japan Inc." But Europe often excels in the right collaborations, too: witness the close government-industry ties in apprenticing and work force training that has been a key to Germany's enormous economic success.

What's essential, it seems to us, is to insert *clarity, accountability, and clear public purpose* into government-business partnerships. The major agendas of how that ought to be done at the federal and state level are beyond our scope here. But the potentialities at the metropolitan, citistate level have emerged repeatedly in the communities examined in this book. A common denominator is business looking beyond its immediate, short-term commercial advantage to the strengthening of the entire community for the long haul—even while government takes into account legitimate business interests. That's what occurs when a region's major corporations move to place branch operations in hard-hit areas, offering jobs for residents. "Rebuild L.A.," begun in Los Angeles after the 1992 riots, employed precisely such a strategy for south-central Los Angeles. Our 1991 report for Dallas suggested the megacorporations of that region place significant operations in troubled South Dallas.

The strategy to make St. Paul a "cultural capital" for Minnesota and the Upper Midwest, outlined in our report for that city, included suggestions for extensive public-private partnerships, drawing talent from corporations, neighborhoods, and city government alike to strengthen the economic core of a grand old state capital.

On the education front, examples would include the strategies to improve troubled inner-city schools developed by the Pittsburgh region's Allegheny Conference on Community Development and the Greater Baltimore Committee. Both aim to create a better-trained regional work force for the future while addressing challenges of human development in socially chaotic neighborhoods.

A common challenge for citistates is to assure that the public gets a fair financial shake when government guarantees or tax breaks are offered to lure new industries and to assure careful environmental protections when new factories are sited. A device to accomplish those "checks" on the public's behalf would be a safe growth committee such as we recommended in our report for the Owensboro, Kentucky, region.

It may be tough for citistate economic planning to avoid the scourge of predatory industrial recruitment—the practice, especially popular with U.S. state governments, of offering lower wages, or public subsidies and tax concessions, or perhaps a wink and a nod on the environmental regulatory front, in the hope of luring industries that are already operating quite successfully in other states or regions. The communities about to lose out in such zero-sum games of industrial recruitment have no on-site representation at all. Perhaps a safe growth committee or the media or independent citizen groups could try to blow the whistle. The bottom line is that a citistate will benefit far more consistently if it learns to nurture its *own* resources—human and fiscal and managerial—as the spur of new economic development.

Business-government partnerships should work at developing regional labor market policies closely related to the technology and skill needs of the citistate's existing and prospective industries. Some specialties will be glamorous high-tech type activities, but mid-tech industries definitely need inclusion—as suppliers for other industries and as potential employment generators in and near inner-city areas in particular.

In both our Dallas and St. Paul reports, we focused on the potential of downtown university centers, not just to coordinate a region's far-flung higher education offerings but also to act as a consumer reference/information center to help both first-time students and mid-career employees receive the training they need to get and keep competitive jobs.

On top of that, the leadership of a citistate needs to assess and more fully exploit the capacities of the universities within its region. With the vast public and private resources being poured into them, universities represent one of society's most important investments. They can and should act as partners in developing critical technologies for the citistate's global economic niche.

But that's not sufficient. They and their faculties should also be under friendly and persistent outside pressure to volunteer their skills in addressing the city's and region's various problems. Typically, the senior faculty who control today's highly specialized academic departments reward and promote their clones—people who publish copiously, however arcane the material. But society's problems—from toxic wastes to AIDS to traffic congestion to poverty to failing schools—are not compartmentalized; they are closely interrelated. Holistic, cross-departmental initiatives are unlikely unless partnerships of the citistate's business and government leaders literally demand—and keep on demanding—them.

We believe that the more such broad-gauged strategies and alliances become commonplace, the easier it will be for business and government to garner public interest and active support when it comes to devising specific strategies to define a citistate's global economic niche. Citistates need many new forms of alliances in which the public and private partners alike bring their special strengths to the table, in which the region's citizenry is kept informed, in which there is constant exploration for mutually supportive regional strategies.

The United States' private sector has always been a powerful inventive force—witness the nation's global lead in patents, copyrights, inventions, technology breakthroughs, and Nobel Prizes. Given American culture, government will never be quite as powerful a player as it is in most nations.

But partnerships and a sensible navigational role for government hold great potential. And it is at the regional level that partnerships are most desperately needed to make sense of educational competence, transportation, environmental protection, economic planning, and much more.

If American citistates can make themselves the fulcrum of that type of forward-looking planning and action, then we believe they can be the match and more for their competitors in the Far East, Europe, or any other place actively involved in the new world economy.

Reaffirm the critical importance of the citistate's heart—its historic center city and neighborhoods.

Center cities continue to define a citistate to the world. The mere words *Paris, Moscow, Hong Kong, New York, San Francisco, Chicago, New Orleans,* evoke powerful images. This means urban design, waterfront planning, streetscapes, and historic preservation are important issues for a citistate's presentation to the world. By contrast, a trashy, graffiti-laden, uncared-for center city landscape heralds decline and telegraphs a negative message worldwide. Every citizen of a citistate has a long-term stake in the appearance, the success of the center city. Even if the center has lost much of its manufacturing backbone, even if a number of technical and legal and financial services have found refuge in suburban areas, the center remains critical to the well-being of the entire region. Strategies to maintain the citistate's center for culture, sports, entertainment, and conventions, as well as for financial-legal-service needs that demand regional centralization, are immensely important.

Clearwater, Florida, architect Sam Casella, president of the American Planning Association, suggests another priority for citistate centers. It is *economic reformation*, recognizing that a center of high-rise towers and "retail toys for the rich" echoes institutions of a dying industrial age and tolerance of vast chasms between the rich and poor. Casella offers different counsel:

> To reinvent itself economically the center has to become a community marked by diversity, opportunity, creative production, learning and safety. Think of the liveliest college town you have ever known, and think of the most robust ethnic neighborhood you've ever seen. Now combine the two, and you can get a feel for the new city.[9]

And as an example of how fresh our thinking has to be, Eugene Grigsby of the University of California at Los Angeles suggests cities need to be a lot more open to the informal sector burgeoning on their doorsteps—street vendors, hawkers, or start-up merchants in a single low-cost building. City codes—health, business fees, licenses—inhibit these entrepreneurs. But their enterprise, says Grigsby, absorbs excess labor and "at least provides dignity and self-worth" for immigrants and low-income Americans.[10]

Focus on the growing link between social deprivation and work force preparedness, and go to work to fix the problem.

It is true that virtually all the world's citistates face serious social problems. As an international team of observers noted in a "1992 European–North American State-of-the-Cities Report" prepared for the German Marshall Fund of the U.S., two societies now exist side-by-side in many of the cities of the North Atlantic community: a mainstream population, able to access, adapt to, and take advantage of opportunities in the new global economy; and growing concentrations of alienated, poverty-stricken, chronically unemployed people in the shadow of the new offices, laboratories, and glitter, who are "out of sight and out of mind."[11]

The team noted that in such cities as Frankfurt, Rotterdam, and Toronto, many of the jobless, the poor, the underskilled, the school dropouts, and the perpetrators and victims of urban crime were from immigrant minority families. But the issue is by no means simply one of ethnic or racial divisions. In Glasgow, Scotland, a city plagued by deep and long-term unemployment with a quarter of the population living in poverty, the jobless are whites whose families have lived in Scotland for generations. The hard fact is that the population groups that are the least well-educated, the least prepared for the demanding jobs of the new world economy, are precisely those with the highest growth rates. They have more children; they account for most of the masses of migrants moving into citistates in our time. In the meantime, population levels of middle-class natives, in the United States and even more so in Europe, are stagnant or even in decline.

What this means is a massive crisis for citistate work forces. Employers have reason to be deeply concerned about where they will find qualified workers in the years ahead. And a citistate without a qualified work force will, by definition, be a citistate in serious economic trouble.

Remedial education programs may work best in traditional working-class neighborhoods. But the work force preparedness crisis cannot be addressed fully unless there's attention to desperate slum areas, too. This is an area in which American cities, in particular, harbor the most grievous conditions. The European members of that same German Marshall Fund team told us they were "particularly shocked" by the human and physical devastation they saw in the inner-city neighborhoods of such cities as Chicago and Atlanta. They witnessed conditions "to be expected in a poverty-stricken Third World country, not one of the earth's richest nations." The team heard it said across America that neighborhoods most afflicted by crime, by poverty, by hopelessness and violence and drug abuse, suffer their own riot, not every 20 years, but every night. Nothing they had seen in Europe, the team memberts reported, "was even remotely comparable."

Such human and physical conditions are a virulent disease that American citistates ignore at their peril. Wretched conditions cannot be kept secret. News of dangerous criminality, for example, travels instantly around the world. New York Mayor David Dinkins, on a trip to Europe in 1992, was repeatedly hit with questions about crime on the streets of America's greatest city. The potential for crime to eclipse New York's tourism, as well as the city's acceptability as an international business center, was painfully apparent.

We perceive a critical message for the community of each American citistate. Take the social challenge seriously, recognizing its implications both for work force preparedness and social peace. Carry the message to residents of affluent suburbs that *their* economic future is imperiled by social decline. Reach for every piece of assistance (federal, state, local) you can get. And, especially, formulate a coherent strategy to make the efforts of the citistate's thousands of individuals and public and private agencies and neighborhood organizations mesh together to help create a society with less poverty, less violence, and greatly improved educational opportunities.

Mobilizing the citistate's energies for that task may be incredibly difficult. Yet the price of inaction, in failed schools, work force illiteracy, packed jails, higher and higher taxes, and ultimately a failed citistate, will be simply enormous.

Spurn defeatism; dismiss the big social engineering solutions; focus on the re-creation of community at the grassroots.

Their historic and inherent optimism notwithstanding, many Americans seem willing to throw up their hands at the thought of restoring stability and safety to ravaged inner cities and troubled older suburbs. In the 1970s, people who ought to have known better talked of reducing the destruction-plagued South Bronx to a field of rubble, removing all its people, and starting all over again. Some urban experts suggest the only hope for families who want to improve their lot is *to leave* their barrio and ghetto communities, as fast as they can.

Ira Harkavy, Vice Dean of the University of Pennsylvania, has spearheaded a remarkable university-based outreach, through the schools, to poverty-ravaged West Philadelphia. And he quite perceptively notes that the deepest problem of such areas "is not housing, or education, or health care—it's the collapse of community." To suggest simply dispersing the population of a troubled area begs the question: what will happen to the poor single mothers, the undisciplined teenagers, the crack babies left behind? The real task, says Harkavy, "is to build humane, caring communities where individuals see themselves as having a responsibility to their neighbors as well as to themselves." The record shows, he adds, that "the strategy of hopelessness—assuming ghettoes will somehow disappear—just doesn't work."[12]

Indeed, while one may talk—as we do in this book—about coordination and dispute-resolution measures at the level of the citistate, there is an equally important agenda of devolution, pushing multiple policy decisions right down to the neighborhood level where community organizations can act as mediators with large social service bureaucracies. The alienation between poor communities and the middle-class service providers has become so vast that a rebuilding from the grassroots, employing community development corporations, churches, and other organizations to work person-to-person and family-to-family, is clearly a wise way to go. The need is for agendas that push tenant-managed housing, intensive neighborhood-based counseling for troubled young parents, peer-to-peer drug education and recovery programs, neighborhood-run schools, and neighborhood control of crime.

Asking people to take responsibility for their own neighborhoods without some special assistance is clearly too much to ask in a world of drugs and guns. But assistance offered in a way that lets people re-create community and self-responsibility can hold immense promise. A prescription for the right approach might focus on radical *decentralization* and radical *personalization* of outreach by the greater society.

Such an agenda is neither left nor right politically. The impulse to help troubled neighborhoods often comes from the liberal side. But the idea of *mediating structures* that intervene between poor people and government service bureaucracies was first highlighted by Peter L. Berger and Richard John Neuhaus in a book popularized by the conservative American Enterprise Institute in 1977.[13]

These new approaches are not even unique to American citistates; they are, in fact, starting to make headway even in Europe, with its far stronger tradition of centralized bureaucracy and elaborate, centrally directed social services. Rotterdam developed an ambitious "social innovation" program designed to foster self-reliance by returning responsibility from the bureaucracy to individuals. The idea behind the Rotterdam program is to decentralize service delivery to the community level, simplify regulations, and bring those being served into direct participation in designing and implementing each initiative. There is also an active outreach to poor Rotterdammers to opt *in* rather than *out*.[14]

It was encouraging to see these fundamental approaches implemented in the United States in 1992, when former President Jimmy Carter inaugurated his "Atlanta Project" to address problems of deep poverty and social dissolution facing 450,000 people living in Atlanta and the adjacent suburban areas. The plan was clearly conceived from the top down—what else could one expect in an effort sparked by a former president? And the gathering of some $15 million to make the project work, the money provided by some of the biggest corporations and foundations of the Atlanta region, was also an outreach from "outside" into the city's ghettoes.

But it was decided early on that the initiatives of the Atlanta Project would all have to be instigated and formulated by residents *within* each of the 20 geographic cluster areas identified for the project. A coordinator was designated for each cluster, but that person was told to pay first heed to the wishes of the community. And it was the coordinating committee in each cluster that was asked to determine how the multiplicity of services already pouring in, and the new ones to be invented, could be focused to work harmoniously and effectively.

No American community has ever faced a more complex challenge— not just to create a pilot community here or there, but to devise a multitiered system that harnesses resources, makes alliances, and focuses ultimate responsibility at the grassroots.

Yet Atlanta is not alone. In the South Bronx, the SURDNA Foundation in 1992 lined up Citibank, the Bankers Trust Company Foundation, and several other leading foundations to launch a $5-million, three-year comprehensive community revitalization program. The idea, as in Atlanta, was to "fill the gaps"—to bring primary health care to neighborhoods without doctors, supermarkets and drugstores to areas bereft of basic retailing outlets, and day-care facilities to single mothers seeking to pursue educational and job opportunities.

But the South Bronx initiative had one advantage over Atlanta's: it could tap the grassroots infrastructure of strong community development corporations that had grown up over the years since our first South Bronx visit in the mid-1970s. The CDCs were strong enough to be made the chief planning *and* delivery agents for the program.

Pessimists typically put down promising CDC and neighborhood revitalization efforts as isolated achievements of charismatic individuals, unlikely to be replicated or spread. But the point is not to replicate precisely; it is to transfer the core ideas and some of the skills of human and economic revitalization under the toughest of circumstances. Today the forces of revitalization are approaching critical scale. *Every* American citistate that expects to avoid dire social problems and stay in the competitive race of the 1990s must take note.

Plan for a multicultural future.

Throughout American history, the great cities have been ports of entry for massive waves of foreign immigrants. Despite early decades of serious tensions, immigrant groups including Germans, Irish, Poles, Italians, and East European Jews moved into the cities and in time became remarkably well assimilated into white, English America. Then, into our northern cities, in a great crescendo between and after the two world wars, came a massive internal migration of blacks from the American South. Close on their heels were millions of Puerto Ricans and Mexican-Americans.

Notwithstanding those historic folk movements, the present-day growth of multiethnic, multiracial America is beyond anything we have ever before witnessed. The 1980s brought the most immigrants of any decade in the nation's history. The United States added—through births and immigration—8 million Hispanics, 4 million Asians, and 3.5 million African-Americans to its population base. Ellis Island, at the zenith of the great European immigration waves of the early 20th century, never processed numbers like these. By some projections, the United States will receive 15 million legal and illegal immigrants during the 1990s, with a similar trend continuing until at least 2020.[15]

Future American citistates are destined, for all time to come, to have a distinctly and deeply altered ethnic complexion. Nationwide over the 1980s, white America grew by 6 percent, compared with 53 percent for Hispanics, 108 percent for Asians, 13 percent for blacks, 39 percent for Native Americans. Already, the nation is one-fourth black, Hispanic, Asian, and Native American. From the late 1970s to the year 2000, the total immigration flow into the United States is expected to rise from 1.1 million to 1.8 million persons a year, 98 percent from developing countries.[16] Within a decade or so, a majority of the population of California, home to an eighth of all Americans, will be minorities—and an overwhelming proportion of them will live in its citistates.

New York City, traditional magnet for immigrants, absorbed 854,000 foreigners during the 1980s—the sole reason the city's population grew slightly, even while white flight to the suburbs continued. By the end of the 1980s, racial-ethnic minorities accounted for 57 percent of the population in New York, 62 percent in Chicago, 63 percent in Los Angeles, 70 percent in Atlanta, 79 percent in Detroit, 88 percent in Miami.

But the immigrant boom is turning suburban, too. Along the Jersey Palisades, Korean, Chinese, and Japanese now make up some 20 percent of the population. In Fairfax County, Virginia, outside Washington, D.C., Asians outnumber blacks. In the studies for this book, we found such surprises as Hispanics spread across the Dallas citistate (not just in South Dallas); Baltimore suburbs veering toward a racial polyglot; and in supposedly Irish and middle-class St. Paul, one of America's greatest concentrations of Hmong.

Many believe immigrant ingenuity will "save" America's cities, bringing entrepreneurial energy to remake ravaged slum areas. But we know the transition will not come without pain. Miami, with its disturbances in the early 1980s, was a signal of black-Hispanic conflict to come. So severe were the interracial clashes in the Los Angeles riots of 1992—blacks versus Koreans versus Hispanics versus whites—that some people called it a "rainbow riot."

There are pieces of very good news. Thorny racial issues notwithstanding, a substantial black middle class has arisen. Many Hispanics are rising high in business and culture. Asian children are often star performers in our schools and universities.

And what we may be seeing in our citistates is the appearance of increasingly skilled, globally connected tribes, or transnational ethnic groups, as economic analyst Joel Kotkin describes them. Among Kotkin's prime "tribal" examples are British, Chinese, Indian, Japanese, and Jewish peoples, living in significant numbers in citistates across the globe. No longer are they isolated and cut off when they live far from "home," notes Kotkin. They "can find in most major world cities easy access to everything from their own language broadcasts and newspapers to shops selling videotapes in Japanese, Mandarin, Hebrew or Hindi." And in many instances, Kotkin insists, the tribes can make immense contributions to the great cities and their regions:

> For global tribes, the current weakening of traditional Nation States and the trend towards transnational "tribal" identities represent a unique opportunity. Indeed even as officials in Washington, Paris and elsewhere rail against Asian, and particularly Japanese investment, local communities—embracing what Kenichi Ohmae has called "global regionalism"—actively court the presence of those groups who can bring new technology, skills and capital. A region such as Puget Sound in Washington depends heavily on trade and investment from the Far East; it naturally opposes, even ridicules, the crude anti-Asian biases of the national elite in the distant District of Columbia. There, and elsewhere, commercial opportunism increasingly overwhelms the narrower economic nationalism of the past as the cosmopolitan global City State takes precedence and even supplants the nation.[17]

One wonders: Can American citistates truly benefit from the enormously varied and rich human skills a multicultural society brings? Look at America's corporate board rooms, its managerial ranks, its university faculties, its cadres of lawyers and accountants and doctors, and any face that's not white stands out in the crowd. The Anglo-Saxon hegemony in America is operating on borrowed time (as we witnessed in vivid ways in the politics of Seattle, Baltimore, Dallas, and St. Paul). The time was never riper for some forward-looking strategic thought. Major long-term benefits may accrue to citistates that welcome into circles of power and influence members of the global tribes as well as traditional American minorities.

Literally thousands of efforts toward inclusion must be made. One payoff should be a lessening of the brand of raw confrontation that Los Angeles, to its sorrow, learned can besmirch a citistate's international reputation. Another advantage may be to create the scene that will enable a citistate's businesses to fare better in the new world economy. According to Gene DePrez, formerly of PHH Fantus:

> A firm's customer base, as it becomes more and more global, becomes more diverse. If you're developing a consumer product or specialized equipment to sell all over the world, it has to be made in a way that meets cultural needs of Asia, Africa, North America alike. Your employee base can't have a white middle-class western bias—that will affect marketing, product development. Corporate America is moving

to discussions on cultural diversity; firms are becoming very aware of the demographic changes and need to prepare for them. A multicultural base is especially important for employees who interact with customers, but it's important too in people like engineers in manufacturing firms who have to work in plants and at sites all over the world.[18]

When multicultural accord and acceptance can translate both into greater peace in the inner city *and* enhanced capacity to do business globally, who's to say it doesn't deserve focused and strategic attention by a citistate's leaders?

Build a sense of regional citizenship.

This is no mean task. Americans are already encouraged to have some loyalty to their nation, their state, their local community. Adding yet another, the citistate, seems a daunting challenge. Yet, as we have tried to show in this book, a citistate's residents may have a greater interdependence and commonality of interests, in many respects, than do residents of geographically dispersed states and nation-states.

There may also be openings for regional citizenship absent in generations past. At a conference on regional transportation planning in the Pittsburgh/Southeastern Pennsylvania region in 1991, we noted that residents both of inner-city neighborhoods and of the small, often desperately depressed steel mill towns of the Monongahela Valley had a strong sense of identity with their communities. But residents of post–World War II suburbs—typically places that are physically spread out and lacking town centers, places of constantly shifting populations—felt much less geographic rootedness. Suburbanites in particular tend to live, work, and go to school or college in different municipalities. For such people, the county or a citistate may be a natural point of identity.

Political scientist Norton Long notes that the sense of community does exist and can be evoked when a common peril is clearly perceived. And on occasion that sense of community appears where one would *least* expect it. We remember vividly the Sunday afternoon after Los Angeles's fearsome riots of spring 1992. The charred and smoldering ruins of South Central L.A.'s stores and shopping strips clearly represented a cataclysmic loss of investment—and jobs. City Hall was sealed off with high fences and surrounded by National Guard troops. The *Los Angeles Times*'s windows were boarded up. The National Guardsmen patrolling the streets with M-16s suggested an urban America uncontrollable without military force.

We were reminded of the future the L.A. 2000 Committee had warned of in 1988: "a Balkanized landscape of political fortresses, each guarding its own resources in the midst of divisiveness, overcrowded freeways, antiquated sewers, ineffective schools, inadequate human services and a polluted environment."[19]

Yet on that Sunday after the Los Angeles riots, tens of thousands of volunteers—Anglos and Asians and Hispanics and African-Americans—had converged on riot-torn neighborhoods with shovels, brooms, and pitchforks. They came from communities across the Los Angeles citistate. They cared in ways that familiar political analysis rarely considers. The outpouring of volunteer help was also a reminder of how injurious it is to classify individuals solely by their ethnic status, when even first-generation Americans may differ so widely in character, class, and attitude within their "group."

The test of a truly successful city, Norton Long suggests, is whether people will feel sufficient attachment to stay there, even if they might earn more money elsewhere. Urban economists, he notes, intimate that cities have no more value than the wealth or wages they may offer at the moment. The economists regard people as free-floating factors of production, combining and recombining across the landscape as the market forces dictate. In this view, any idea of loyalty, of noneconomic value that might hold a miner or worker to the factory town, is seen as perverse, hampering beneficent operation of the market. Yet the same economist who sees such loyalties as perverse, notes Long, can see the natural amenities of sunshine, seashore, lakes, and mountains as appropriate locational advantages justifying an otherwise irrational preference for such locations.[20]

We suggest that Americans, notwithstanding the proclivity of many of them to change residences as easily as they might change a suit of clothes, have a yearning for communities they can call their own. A citistate that develops a regional labor policy, seeking through industrial promotion, inventive trade relationships, and apprentice and worker training programs to create fulfilling work for all its occupants, can start to build such loyalties. The gospel that Tony Hiss spelled out in his splendid book, *The Experience of Place,* is another means to the same end: creating and protecting connective greenways and open spaces and familiar landscapes, some intensely urban places and even some quite rural, yet located physically within great cities.[21]

A citistate's newspapers and television stations, whose circulation and viewing areas are often synonymous with the true region, owe it to themselves and their audiences to treat the region as an autonomous whole. Newspapers' regional editions often feed the parochial myopia; coverage underscoring the commonality of interests across the region is needed as a counterbalance, and it can even highlight how citizens across many communities—but within one region—are addressing common problems (a case we made in our St. Paul, Seattle, and Owensboro reports.)

Remember quality of life issues. Pay special attention to the environment, its quality and protection, and to the physical form of the region.

Once upon a time, quality of life may have been thought of solely as an aesthetic or social issue. No more. Today it is a critical *economic* factor profoundly affecting the future prospects of a citistate. As Dallas consultant James Crupi notes, there is a very real and increasingly recognized "symbiotic relationship between arts, culture, health care, crime, the environment and economic strength."[22]

In that mix, the arts do still matter, along with sports, parks, and quality recreation areas. Peter Karl Kresl, an expert on citistates' competitive strategies, writes that "an aspiring corporate headquarters city such as Toronto simply must have a first rate orchestra, a full range of galleries and museums, and a busy schedule of performances."[23] Indianapolis unquestionably benefits from the variety of amateur sports events available there now. Cities fight for big league sports teams and too often get taken to the cleaners in negotiations with their owners; yet the image of being a big league town *is* very important.

Traffic conditions are a critical factor in attracting—or repelling—firms, notes Gene DePrez. And the issue isn't just having an adequate road-rail-airport network to get people and goods to and from a firm's offices or factory. Heavy traffic congestion can be the trigger that persuades a firm to move out of a region when commuting becomes so lengthy and onerous that employees start to suffer unacceptably high degrees of stress.

A citistate's downtown is important, too, DePrez notes. Even if a firm is going to locate in the suburbs, its image of the citistate is formed largely by the appearance of the downtown area. No corporation relishes moving to a city with a center considered ugly or dangerous. Firms believe their own image is enhanced by being associated with a city that has a positive image. (Such conditions are especially important for headquarters or professional offices but are less critical in manufacturing and back office site locations, DePrez observes.)

Physical safety and a tolerable crime rate are also important for corporations. Every citistate has reason to examine possibilities for community-based policing, the opportunity to *prevent* rather than simply *solve* crimes, as discussed in our Baltimore and Dallas reports.

High-quality air and water are critical for a citistate's future, as important to individuals to protect their personal health and enjoy a good quality of life as they are to employers looking for satisfactory work sites. Neither of those issues, nor the planning for landfills, incinerators, recycling, and management of the entire waste stream, can be handled by municipalities alone; regionwide approaches are already critically important and will become even more so over the next years.

The perfidious effects—environmental, fiscal, social—of metropolitan regions' unplanned, sprawling physical growth patterns were reviewed in the introduction to this book. American citistates will be at a disadvantage unless they move to curb unnecessary land consumption, establish minimum densities, locate work places and residential areas closer to each other, and make mass transportation an ever-larger factor in regional planning. There are excellent examples of this kind of planning in Europe and even a handful in America, especially the combination state land-use plan and urban growth boundary, originally passed in 1973, that has protected Portland, Oregon, from substantial wasteful development. Every citistate that cares a whit about its environment and social future should move to establish an urban growth boundary, beyond which neither jobs nor new housing developments are allowed to go. Where citistates lack the legal authority, they should go to state legislatures and get it.

The time is more ripe than ever for an alliance of interests, environmentalists opposing development at the urban periphery joining with inner-city minorities to keep more job-producing firms within reach in established urban areas and away from distant greenfield sites unserved by mass transit. In the late 1970s, we attended a conference in Detroit, cosponsored by the Sierra Club and the Urban League, trying to forge just such an alliance of "the greenies and the smoggies." Sadly, the alliance never came to be, though in Boston and other regions we keep hearing of renewed interest. Clearly, the citistate level is *the* most appropriate—probably the only feasible—arena for such coalition building.

A move toward compactness runs against the grain in America, but can produce far more desirable communities. Travel distances between home and work can be reduced, traffic congestion alleviated, dependence on fossil fuels reduced. Contrary to popular fears, Marcia D. Lowe of the

Worldwatch Institute notes, population density itself is not a cause of crime or blight. The Hong Kong citistate is the world's most densely populated, yet has the 12th-lowest murder rate among the globe's top 100 metropolises. Cities such as Vienna and Stockholm are compact, yet have high living standards and are a positive joy to walk around.[24]

By facing the growth issue forcefully, American citistates could also contribute importantly to the economic strength of the United States at large in the 1990s. There is no greater national priority than reduction of the overwhelming national deficit, which would reduce our dependence on fickle international capital and enable us to invest in productive infrastructure and enterprises to build our own future. Yet that is unlikely to occur if we again squander a massive share of our available capital on new rings of suburban and exurban development. Theodore Hershberg and Joseph Duckworth put the case convincingly:

> Capital for investment in infrastructure is growing increasingly scarce. The practices of the past decades—allowing our cities to decay while building anew the urban infrastructure in the suburbs and exurbs— cannot be sustained. Global competition for capital is accelerating with new demands from Eastern Europe and the Middle East. In America, capital is already scarce. The national debt is $4 trillion. The annual federal deficit is approaching $400 billion. Our declining rate of productivity means we are producing less wealth. It is strategically senseless to squander capital reproducing the urban infrastructure outside our cities and existing suburbs. Consider the opportunity costs of such a policy. Scarce dollars spent recreating what already exists—airports and rail hubs, art and cultural institutions, universities and hospitals, major office and sports complexes—means dollars unavailable for investment in vital assets such as health care, education and job training, research and development, and existing roads and bridges.[25]

Fight hard for fiscal equity.

Citistates could be the most efficient form of organization for the modern world economy. They generate the lion's share of the wealth of nations. But American citistates lack an important ingredient of power and sovereignty: an independent tax base. A huge portion of their tax yield is preempted by governments "above"—the state governments and the federal government. Or all the taxes are collected "below," by the individual cities and counties. Citistates in Europe and Japan are comparatively better off, with guaranteed shares of national taxes and much greater regional revenue control.

This does not, however, mean that American citistates need be "toothless tigers," mere debating societies. Their capacity for internal reform, and then for mobilizing political clout to influence state legislatures and the national Congress, should be immense.

What citistates especially need to recognize is that the poverty that afflicts their very low-income neighborhoods will, in time, exact a price on the entire region in terms of social service demands, crowded courts, overburdened prisons, and reduced public safety. The entire citistate ought to be pressing the state legislature for substantial, targeted aid for the fiscally distraught inner city—an argument we underscored most strongly in our Baltimore report.

The issue is hardly academic. The 1990s may represent the last chance to avert an almost complete suburban-inner city standoff in America, with good jobs flying to the metropolitan periphery while entire cities sink, on the model of Detroit, Newark, Camden, and East St. Louis, or Los Angeles's South Central, ever deeper into disinvestment, underclass life, crime, and despair.

Part of the solution must be internal, within the citistate. Every American citistate should consider adopting a system of regionwide tax-base sharing, much like the shining (but singular) example of Minnesota's Twin Cities. Since 1971, 40 percent of the tax base created by new commercial and industrial development in the region has gone into a pool that is then redistributed according to a formula combining population and the comparative wealth of communities. The program has been a godsend for the older cities, which predictably get a lot less new commercial-industrial growth. In our St. Paul chapter, we suggest the fiscal condition of that old city would be "calamitously worse" without the tax-base-sharing law. Sadly, no other American region has such a law.

The struggle for greater equity within citistates will require, in fact, multiple programs and partnerships. Examples might include regionwide preschool programs and open public school enrollment, sharing of the burdens of homeless populations, and setting regional benchmarks for the eradication of poverty.

Most of this agenda involves suburbanites championing the interests of center cities in a way they rarely if ever have. The center cities themselves, however, must also change; they must summon a new will to cooperate with the other communities in their regions. As we noted specifically in our Baltimore and St. Paul reports, center cities often remain stubbornly sovereign, acting as if sophisticated and capable suburban governments had not grown up all about them. The will to cooperate is a prisoner of entrenched union contracts, overlaid civil service rules, and a politicized style of management. Despite the cruel budget setbacks that the center cities have suffered in recent years and the start of management reform in many, the remaining agenda for internal reform is huge. The more rapidly center cities show willingness to reform their internal operations, the friendlier they're likely to find suburbs to broader cooperation and addressing the equity issue.

Equally important to achieving equity, however, is help from the outside. The policy leaders of a citistate should be on the side of expanded federal aid for poor people and neighborhoods across the nation.

Even dedicated regionalists underscore this point. The University of Pennsylvania's Theodore Hershberg, for example, has spent much time over the last years organizing regular meetings of regional business executives with state legislators from Philadelphia *and* the region's suburbs, pressing them to work together for city and regional interests. But Hershberg has no illusion that a measure of expanded state aid for Philadelphia would be sufficient. As he told a conference in June 1992:

> If ever one could say we're in a defining, watershed moment for America's cities, it is now. No matter how squeaky clean we make our good government machine, the game is over for America's cities unless there is substantial intervention by state and national governments. There is simply not the tax base for the cities to do it on their own. Population drop and migration out of the cities has drastically cut the base for supporting the essential services. The added social costs cities have had to take on since 1980—AIDS, homelessness, plagues of crack and crime—are staggering. In response to the loss of revenue, cities have raised their taxes. In the process, they have become extraordinarily uncompetitive. Our national government simply *must* accept a greater share of responsibility for our cities.

To a marked degree, that means a national government launching real efforts in income redistribution. It's fine to laud community empowerment and self-sufficiency, notes New Jersey Transportation Commissioner Thomas Downs. But "if a community or a center city has no real income base and growth potential," he adds, "power over decay is another way of managing a ghetto. If people suffer a real decline in income, nothing's left to invest in community businesses and community services."[26]

Create work for everyone—even if public money is required.

We are aware the very words of this subheading will sound frighteningly "socialistic" to many. But the profound change in the world economy, destroying so many low-skill jobs, leaving so many millions of people without gainful employment and mired in welfare and nonproductivity, is pure social dynamite. The resultant chaos in families and neighborhoods, the human misery it causes, threaten to tear America's social contract to shreds. Who honestly believes that our citistates would be visited by today's degree of drug addiction, child abuse, teenage pregnancy, burglary and assault and bulging prisons, if adequate work were available?

Some of the barriers to employment would seem relatively simple to resolve. A big part of the problem surely lies in work force preparedness. In region after region, it has become clear that the workers are simply unprepared for the work that *is* available. Citistate leaders are discovering that if the people they govern are not adequately prepared, nothing else matters. Adequate schools, apprenticeship programs, and community colleges are clearly critical to the solution. Job training programs can yield rich dividends—especially ones of sufficient quality so that the graduates are prepared to land jobs of real substance and potential (not just minimum-wage jobs that leave them mired in poverty anyway).

Jobless people also need a variety of special "assists" to get them into the world of real work and help them stay there. Some would love to be entrepreneurs and simply need a "microenterprise" loan or the like to get going. For others, the lack of day care stands as a seemingly insurmountable hurdle. For some, it is the fear of losing Medicaid benefits if they take a regular job. (Living literally "at the edge," they recognize that one sickness could shatter them or their small families.) The day-care and health problems were addressed—at least for people getting off Aid to Families with Dependent Children (AFDC) welfare—by way of short-term benefits included under the 1988 federal welfare reform bill. But the welfare safety net misses many people, and no citistate can depend on it totally.

Another barrier for many would-be workers is that they're too poor to own a car and find there's simply no public transportation to the suburban sites where jobs would be available. Urban expert Mark Hughes cites the example of the Seltzer organization, owner-manager of business parks in the Philadelphia suburbs, which noted in 1986 that many of the firms it

313

located were having major difficulty finding lower-wage workers. So Selt-zer approached the regional public transit operator, the Southeastern Pennsylvania Transportation Authority (SEPTA), to provide a "reverse-commute" service for workers from the inner city. SEPTA came up with a schedule of new morning and evening bus lines running directly from suburban commuter rail stops to the business park sites. The employers had to guarantee the difference between the actual fare box receipts and SEPTA's break-even cost of providing the service. The new bus lines proved quite successful, some even becoming self-supporting. Such reverse-commute arrangements illustrate the partnerships that can make a citistate more viable. They are no less vital than trying to help inner-city groups acquire capital for new job-producing enterprises close to their homes. We need, in fact, a *both-and,* not an *either-or,* approach.

The fact is that most hurdles to the employment of poor people are surmountable, given appropriate government or public-private partner-ships. Publicly supported day care, back-up health benefits, provision of special transportation to suburban work sites—it would be ideal if higher governments provided them routinely. But no citistate need stand hopeless in the absence of subsidies from afar. With enough ingenuity, an immense amount can be negotiated and implemented locally, benefiting the entire metropolitan region.

Additionally, there are ways governments can subsidize private em-ployers to open up or create jobs with long-term growth potential—jobs that will be likely, in time, to pay well beyond the poverty level that today's minimum wages entail. Robert Stumberg of the Washington-based Center for Policy Alternatives is enthusiastic about this set of possibilities. He notes such innovations as the Minnesota Employment and Economic Development Program, which for several years in the 1980s provided $4 an hour in wages plus $1 an hour in benefits for each new job that private employers were willing to create for a welfare recipient or a person with expired unemployment benefits. The private employers, in turn, had to promise to keep the new worker on the payroll beyond the length of the subsidy. The vast majority of participating firms turned out to be small businesses, and some 90 percent of them used their subsidies to invest in new equipment or to otherwise broaden their economic activity. Fashion such programs to target small enterprises and community development corporations, Stumberg suggests, and it's likely that significant benefits could be registered in any community.[27]

Even with such strategies in place, there will still be unemployed people. For such cases, the Europeans, whose urban social conditions are worsening but are still dramatically better than ours, are applying some constructive countermeasures. Germany has a work creation program for the jobless, something like our old WPA (Works Progress Administration), with people engaged in all manner of public works and other productive activity. In Rotterdam, a city with large immigrant populations and thousands of people out of work, the city tries to give long-term unemployed people jobs, such as "assistant caretaker," for which they are paid their normal social security benefits plus a slight extra stipend. The idea is to provide useful work that contributes to the public good, while also building up the low self-esteem often found among long-term jobless individuals.

We believe that for the hardest to employ in American citistates, a parallel type of program is needed—a payment a little above welfare, perhaps with some basic day care and health benefits, for persons willing to clean and rehabilitate parks, maintain city streets, tend to aged people, assist teachers or community police officers, or work directly with disturbed children and families. The system ought to see to it that people who are willing to work get constructive employment—and don't remain poor.

Not only would lives of pointlessness get diverted into constructive activity—we are often reminded of the old adage that "idle hands are the devil's workshop"—but there could be tangible, immediate public benefit as well. The citistate would have more tax payers, fewer tax eaters. And every cleaned and graffiti-free street, every renewed and well-maintained park, every quality day-care operation or strengthened school or policing operation, creates the reality, and the image, of a more attractive, safe, desirable city. While the jobless gain self-esteem, the citistate's competitive position could be materially enhanced.

If the idea of government-guaranteed employment seems just too radical for Americans, the system could be made into a market-driven device, linking newly created government jobs to higher productivity. Bounties could be offered to any unit of local or state government able to show how, in taking on previously unemployed people without discharging its existing workers, it is able to improve productivity and serve the public better. With a little luck, such a system might even be designed to avoid the knee-jerk, negative reaction of government employee unions fearful about losing job slots and membership. Indeed, it might be worthwhile involving the unions *in the planning* for such experiments.

The other question is whether great citistates may not *need* many more public workers than most American cities have ever felt necessary. An international comparison springs to mind: Paris. Of Paris's 38,000 public employees, 4,500 are reported to be sweepers. Most are of Arab or African descent. They sweep *each* street in Paris daily. Paris spends about $1,000 per resident per year just on cleanliness.[28] Walk the streets of Paris and you see the delightful results.

Of course, it's unlikely that either America's federal or state governments will ever lavish the attention on our citistates that the French do on Paris. The central French government provides 40 percent of Paris's $23-billion operating budget and covers a huge chunk of local costs for schools, day-care centers, hospitals, police, and firefighters. In the United States, by contrast, federal aid to cities was never high and has been plummeting like a rock. (In 1977 direct federal aid amounted to 34 percent of what the nation's 15 largest cities raised from their own sources—property, sales, and income taxes, and user fees. By the late 1980s, the ratio had fallen below 10 percent.[29])

Is there any chance American citistates might hope, realistically, for adequate national and state government support—plus full employment? The answer is probably no until the citistates' corporate and political leaders learn to speak up more forcefully. They need to telegraph a compelling case for more federal and state financing. Then, at the grassroots, operational level, they have to develop new systems to maximize the use of every national, state, and local dollar available. Higher governments can subsidize; but the systems to get people working, cities cleaned up, public agendas met, can only be designed and implemented locally.

Make governance work.

Governments operating at sixes and sevens, duplicating services, unable to reach the most fundamental cooperative agreements, fighting over economic scraps, pushing environmental or social problems off to their neighbors, create the image (and too often the reality) of a malfunctioning, divisive citistate.

And the stakes are becoming ever greater. Recent years have brought a groundswell of recognition, metropolitan specialist William R. Dodge notes, of the implications of economic interdependence, a realization that "regional economies determine our economic fate—locally, nationally and throughout the world."[30]

Yet without some form of regional planning and decision-making structure, how can a citistate make rational plans for its economic positioning, critically needed capital facilities, quality job training and continuing education? Without a legal requirement that municipalities and counties be part of a regional governance structure that at least has the power to resolve differences among them, how can one be certain that plans for economic development are brought on-line and in balance with conservation, quality land use, and the goal of compact, cost-effective growth? How else can one expect any kind of equitable distribution of social burdens and expenses, so that older cities and suburbs are not made paupers of the region, a constant economic drag and deep moral blemish on the citistate? And without a formalized and respected regional authority, who can bargain, cajole, lobby effectively before the federal and state governments for the interests of the *entire* citistate?

We raised precisely these issues in virtually all our city reports, from Phoenix to Seattle to Baltimore to Dallas. Yet in each case it was clear to us that the problem was only partially governmental—that it was critical that a region simultaneously develop ways to draw all manner of other players into regionwide problem solving. Major business groups, nonprofits, citizen organizations, universities, and foundations are indispensable participants. Cumulatively, working with government, they become *the* governance structure of the region. Is there any middle way to get the benefits of regional governance without some form of overarching structure? Some politicians suggest all the cohesion necessary can be achieved by voluntary intergovernmental agreements. These have been increasing rapidly as individual municipalities and counties recognize it's cheaper, or more efficient, to make agreements with their neighbors to share equipment, contract services to one another, or create mutual aid agreements for public safety emergencies. But the agreements are spotty, they're easily blocked by local politicos with a stake in the status quo, and they rarely reach the level of citistatewide accords.

Councils of governments (COGs) have been on the scene for decades and were once assigned rather important "sign-off" authority on federal grants within their regions. Some have done top-notch planning for their areas all along. Their role may again be enhanced as many are designated the metropolitan planning organizations (MPOs) to reach regional consensus and decisions on highway and transit funding under the 1991 federal transportation bill, "ISTEA," that we discussed in the first chapter. And the early 1990s have brought indications of some major metropolitan area COGs (in Atlanta, Raleigh, Denver, and other cities) moving into broader alliances with governments, universities, and citizen groups.

The ongoing legal drawback of COGs is that, in the final analysis, they are made up of representatives of local governments, not the populace directly, and that a dissident local government can effectively torpedo a major COG initiative. Hundreds of COGs subsequently suffer systemic anemia. A telling survey in 1990 revealed that 60 percent of COG executive directors surveyed nationwide reported that most key decisions in their regions are made *outside* of their councils.[31]

A familiar response to problems insoluble in a single constituency is to create special districts. In 1992 the United States had some 33,100 such districts, addressing every problem from air quality to mosquito control to economic development.

But do these approach the ideal of true citistate governance? Not really. State laws creating such agencies rarely if ever require tradeoffs among their various single-purpose objectives. As John Kirlin notes, the special purpose agencies are "rarely held politically accountable within the region in which they act, rarely effectively involve citizens or local elected officials in their deliberations, and commonly become captured by technicians or the interests most dependent upon their rule making."[32]

The Los Angeles region provides what may be America's prime example of special districts run amok. The South Coast Air Quality Management District exercises such immense powers over vehicle use, traffic congestion, land use, and job growth that many people call it a *de facto* regional government—albeit unelected and essentially unaccountable. The L.A. region also has multihundred-million or billion-dollar-a-year special districts in charge of transportation, water supply, waste disposal. Each agency's professionals do what seems logical from their own narrow point of view—building roads or transit lines, cleaning up L.A.'s putrid air, dealing with toxic wastes, for example. But *not one of them* is entrusted with the whole—seeing whether and how the pieces fit together. Cumulatively, for example, they spend $71 million a year on planning activities, virtually none of it coordinated.

Another half-way step to metropolitanism is to cede most regional authority to a single county government. Where there's one that embraces the entire metropolitan area (Maricopa County around Phoenix, for example), the county as *de facto* government may make a lot of sense. Due in part to their expansive geography, William Dodge notes, urban counties in the 1980s assumed responsibility for providing a widening constellation of services, among them transportation, solid waste, and public health. Counties have gained in professionalism, and many have been willing to confront state governments on issues of unfunded mandates and other burdensome state demands. "If counties had not existed at the beginning of the decade, something like them would probably have been invented by the end of it," Dodge observes.[33]

But rare are the cases in which counties actually embrace the full territory of a citistate. Many are denied full home-rule powers by their legislatures. And cooperation among counties is as hard to achieve as is voluntary accord, on tough issues, among cities and towns.

Clearly, none of these halfway steps toward regionalism gets citistates to the point of clear and shared governance, the ability to plan strategically and act cohesively, that they need to advance, compete, and prosper in today's world.

Again and again as we focused on the individual citistates in this volume, we were driven to the conclusion that a region simply *must* have some form of umbrella regional governance structure. At a minimum, such an organization needs the power to resolve disputes between individual governments of the region. At a maximum, it would assume direct control of, and coordinate, the major cross-regional functions (transit, air quality, and so on) now performed by independent special authorities.

The L.A. 2000 Partnership put its finger on the central need in its 1990 report, *Managing Growth in Southern California:*

> A democratic, responsive, accountable regional political structure is required to integrate now-fragmented policy making and to set policies within which local governments and single-purpose agencies can address local needs in concert with regional policies. That regional political structure must provide opportunities for regional political leaders and regional citizenship, both now impossible. Regional institutions and public policies must meet the challenges. They cannot generate paralysis or turf wars.[34]

Specifically, the L.A. 2000 Partnership called for a Southern California regional council, with some members elected by direct vote of the citizenry and others representing local governments. The council would be responsible for bringing all the strands of municipal and county and special authority planning into some kind of coherent whole.

Under the emerging outline of the L.A. 2000 Partnership and the Southern California Association of Governments, the planning of the big special service districts would have to be coordinated. City and county plans would be accepted as long as they didn't conflict with those of other jurisdictions or the regional plan. There'd be carefully orchestrated negotia-

319

tions to resolve differences. But eventually the regional council would have the right to resolve issues. There'd be no new single metropolitan *government,* but there *would* be a system of regional governance.

That approach is in line with the National Civic League's prescription. Life in urban and suburban America, the league warned in 1989, will decline seriously if the "big" governance issues, from education to social services to land use patterns to assuring a quality work force for the future, are *not* guided and ultimately directed on a regionwide basis. The league said a two-tier system was essential, with most existing subunits left in place, but with new metropolitan authorities formed to plan regionally and resolve conflicts between existing cities and counties.

These, we believe, must be the guiding principles for successful American citistate governance in the years to come. To those who argue that any new metropolitan authority represents just "another level of government"— the last thing Americans need or want—we reply that Americans are already finding they have more and more governments, special authorities, and agencies to deal with. The problem is the absence of governance that ties the problems together, sets priorities, and comes up with coherent solutions on the level that counts—the citistate.

Yet, the right kind of citistate governance must be developed in a consultative, "bottoms-up" process involving a wide range of civic players, neighborhood leaders up to the level of top corporate leadership. Mutual trust needs to be built among the parties. It would be an error for a state government to impose a regional government without broad consultation with the local community. By the same token, state legislatures must be willing to listen when local business-government-citizen partnerships tell them the time has come to authorize and legitimize regional governance. The future of citistates—and the economic and social health of states themselves—is at stake.

In the end, we need metropolitanwide accords in which everyone, from proud inner-city political organizations to thornily independent residents of a far-out suburb, give up a little. An example of such an approach has recently surfaced in Rotterdam, in which there's a call for political unity in order to modernize the port and transportation networks—a necessary step, it's argued, to maintain Rotterdam's role as a key shipping center for Europe. Rotterdam leaders are keenly aware that the suburbs are reluctant to cooperate with the city because it is so much bigger and might dominate any collaboration. So they have suggested that the city proper be reorganized into 10 to 12 new districts comparable in size to the suburbs. Once that's done, they suggest, the municipalities could feel comfortable in creating a new metropolitan authority, without today's center city dominating the whole.[35]

A companion requirement should be that whatever governments a citistate has, they function well. The 1990s, James Crupi notes, are a time when citizens expect government to be smaller, more efficient, more professional, able to deliver more services with scarcer resources. The successful citistate, he suggests, will have precisely those forms of public administration.[36]

We focused on this challenge in our St. Paul report, suggesting that even in Minnesota, with its fabled "good government" culture, there's immense need for demanding a reexamination of how government functions—the type of reform agenda spelled out by David Osborne and Ted Gaebler in their 1992 book, *Reinventing Government*.[37] One of the Osborne-Gaebler ideas, for example, is that governments have to learn to "steer rather than row." Instead of retaining massive public worker cadres to deliver services, governments have to be catalysts to get businesses, nonprofits, public-private partnerships into the game of governance as well. Another critical concept is that top government executives must be persuaded to "let go," to give managers increased scope, and then judge the results—just as restructured businesses are doing. (Many of these ideas relate as well to the newly popular concepts of TQM—"Total Quality Management"—that are increasingly being tried in government as they were initially in business.)

Stressing slim, efficient local government, we would underscore, is not the same as embracing the so-called public choice philosophy about local government that rose to prominence in the 1980s. Public choice advocates suggest that fragmented, even overlapping, governments are not so bad, that such entities spend less money in the aggregate, that they provide citizens with easily accessible local governments as a first recourse, and that they are more accountable.[38]

To a degree, they're right. There is much to criticize in large, bureaucratized, often heavily unionized city governments that carry high per capita costs. On the other hand, it's disputable whether small jurisdictions invariably deliver government at lower cost. If public choice boils down to fragmented enclaves that simply provide protection for "look-alikes"—people with similar economic standing, lifestyle interests, and public service needs—then public choice stands for *de facto* social and economic segregation and is clearly *not* a valid philosophy for democratic or equitable governance in a variegated metropolitan region.

Much therefore is required to achieve successful citistate governance. The process must join efficient government with a strong push for equity, public-private partnerships with clear accountability, participatory decision making, and new ways to reach clear, final, strong decisions for the entire region's benefit. It is an immense challenge. But the times demand no less.

Undergird governance with a strong citizen organization for the citistate.

Work consciously to build new and strengthened leadership cadres. In place after place we have been struck by the logic of creating some form of regionwide citizen organization, working for the shared and common good over pressure from special interests and the parochial positions of fragmented local governments. (Especially full expositions appear in the Baltimore and Dallas chapters.)

Such organizations—an appropriate 1990s term for them might be *metropolitan partnerships*—operate in numerous regions across the country. The oldest are in Seattle and Cleveland. The best known may be the Citizens League of the Minnesota Twin Cities area, which sparked the creation of the Metropolitan Council there in 1967 and helped inaugurate the country's first and best system of regional tax-base sharing. Typically the metropolitan partnerships organize interested citizens into policy task forces that work hard to research, think through, and then sell public policy makers on sound approaches to problems ranging from solid waste disposal to regional workforce preparedness, early childhood education to regional parks and recreation.

Our sense is that all the existing metropolitan partnerships need strengthening and that new ones are needed in citistates nationwide. The need is underscored by the serious—one might say appalling—lack of coherence and focus in advocating effectively for regionwide solutions in our society today. Regionalist William Dodge notes perceptively that unless a citistate has a well-developed problem-solving process to bring together the critical players from throughout the metropolitan area—government, business, nonprofit, civic—"opportunities are lost and threats become crises."[39] But all too often, there's simply no coherent voice to call for creation of such processes and then provide them with needed public support and backup as they develop.

Metropolitan partnerships need *significant* backing from businesses and individuals—up to $1 million to get launched and budgets of several hundreds of thousands of dollars afterward. They need such funds to attract and hold large memberships, not only from policy elites but from every class, income, racial, and geographic group across a metropolitan area, and to effectively use sophisticated tools of communication. Expertly prepared videotapes, for example, could describe policy problems and opportunities and be shown to various audiences—business, nonprofit, civic, neighborhood, church, school, and university.

It is true that the culture of any citistate will determine how a metropolitan partnership gets formed, what it selects as its early signature issues, how its board is constituted, and much more. Some cities' culture makes it much easier for them to launch such new and inventive partnerships than it is for others. But we think it fatal to throw up one's hands in despair and say, "Oh, a regional citizen organization or metropolitan partnership just won't work here. People in this region rarely agree on anything." Or a companion excuse: "The business community calls the tune here; if it's not 100 percent theirs, it won't happen." Or: "With all the Hispanics and Asians and other immigrants we have pouring in here, there's no common cultural base for us to work off anyway."

All those special circumstances simply mean that careful thought and planning have to go into a metropolitan partnership *before* it is launched. That's a role a group of leading citizens, from across the region, might undertake. (In our Baltimore and Dallas reports, we actually suggested names of regional luminaries who might be on an organizing committee.) Or the impetus might come from a community-oriented foundation, taking seriously its obligation to think strategically about the region's future. A school of public affairs, such as Theodore Hershberg's Center for Greater Philadelphia at the University of Pennsylvania, can provide the stimulus.

In some of our city reports we suggested that established leadership organizations for young professionals, such as Leadership Baltimore, Leadership Dallas, or Leadership Inc. in Philadelphia, could provide an initial cadre of active participants. Members of the leadership organizations (there are over 250 operating across the United States) typically have gone through a course introducing them to the major institutions and activities of their city and region. The monthly training sessions range from education to economic development, health and human services to the arts. Bankers learn about welfare, civil rights activists about job creation, journalists about the excruciating process of actually making things happen. But the groups' even more critical role is networking—linking emerging leaders from across the whole spectrum of American community life.

The common shortcoming of leadership groups is that they don't look forward—that they brief potential leaders on current conditions but too rarely get them to think or organize, to address future agendas. It's precisely at that juncture that we see opportunities for the leadership organizations to play an exciting and expanding role in America's citistates, preparing their graduates for important roles in new metropolitan partnerships.

Nor have enough American regions followed the example of Atlanta, which, through the leadership of the Atlanta Regional Commission and Metro Business Forum, has formed a Regional Leadership Institute designed to involve public and private sector leaders in strategizing to improve the region's governance, economy, and quality of life. Formation of a parallel Leadership Council, to serve the citistate encompassing Raleigh, Durham, and the Research Triangle Park in North Carolina, was sparked by the Triangle J Council of Governments late in 1992.

In some cities there's still a nostalgia for the brand of decisive leadership exerted by a few exalted power brokers. The most classic story may be the one that tells how banker Richard King Mellon and Democratic Mayor David Lawrence coalesced in the mid-1940s to save Pittsburgh from the pall of thick industrial smoke that darkened its noondays and coated every building and resident with grime. Together they spearheaded a Pittsburgh renaissance—clean air, fine buildings, highways and dams to prevent disastrous floods—that gave new life to a near-dead city.

Today the Mellon-Lawrence act can be seen as heavily elitist, a relic of a time when small power cliques controlled each American city and brooked little opposition. The old titans, the small bunch of senior white males that met in exclusive clubs to make decisions that swayed cities' whole futures, are a virtually extinct species. Power in American communities seems to have been atomized by the rise of fresh power groups: upstart industries and businesses, powerful developers, ethnic alliances, organized blacks and Hispanics and Asians, environmental and women's and social service groups, and many more.

Cities have also seen their traditional business leaders figuratively blow away in a hurricane of business buyouts, mergers, and closures. When such events occur, communities lose the leadership talent of executives who considered the cities their homes for life, who knew how to put together economic development deals, organize new civic projects, attract investment dollars. In their place come branch managers, imported from some other town and anxious to climb the corporate ladder in another. These are often the types, Norton Long is fond of saying, who exhibit as much concern for the town's long-term welfare as managers of United Fruit used to exhibit for the banana republics where they were doing business.

In virtually every city there is a cry for *leadership*—for *someone* to take a strong hand to organize the town for the future. Yet an individual who tries to take too prominent a role or steps on the toes of any interest group suddenly finds himself or herself under fire, oftentimes in the local press.

None of that means we need leaders any less. As our colleague Ralph Widner pointed out at a 1992 metropolitan planning conference in Toronto, the ability of each citistate to find the niche that will permit it to compete and survive "rests ultimately on the leadership base of the city—articulating a vision, mobilizing civic energy."

A central civic challenge for today's citistates is thus to nurture, encourage, and advance a replacement generation of civic entrepreneurs. Some will surely be from businesses large or small. But others need to be from universities, citizen groups, minority communities, and especially the expanding professions of the new service economy, from law to medicine to accounting.

There are inherent problems in civic undertakings, even with a wide cast of players. With corporate chieftains preoccupied with their national and international survival, they may leave local civic activity to more junior officials and fail to back them up with sufficient energy and resources. Timing, notes Tom Condon of the *Hartford Courant*, can be a big snag: if the process of attacking some issue is too short, it can seem superficial; if it's too long, people may lose interest.[40] The media may not be understanding or supportive. Racial groups may doubt the integrity of a process in which they don't think they're dealt a fair share. A community can suffer from *too many* plans never implemented—a phenomenon known in San Francisco as "S.P.O.T.S."—"Strategic Plan on the Shelf."

Nevertheless, the *absence* of effective leadership, a citistate totally adrift, is a *more* frightening prospect. The nurturing of new leaders and the creation of metropolitan partnerships that open a way for those leaders to play important regionwide roles are two of the most critical challenges for American citistates in the 1990s.

Notes

Chapter 1 — The New Citistate Age

1. Commentary by Joel Kotkin, author of *Tribes: How Race, Religion and Family Determine Success in the New Global Economy* (New York: Random House, 1993).

2. Benjamin R. Barber, "Jihad vs. McWorld," *The Atlantic Monthly,* March 1992, 53.

3. Interview with the author, August 4, 1992.

4. Peter Karl Kresl, "The Response of European Cities to EC 1992" (Paper prepared for the Eighth International Conference of Europeanists, Chicago, March 27–29, 1992).

5. For law and regulations in this area, see Brandon Roberts, *Investment Across the Atlantic: New Competition and Challenges for States* (Denver and Washington, D.C.: National Conference of State Legislatures, 1992).

6. Thomas Boswell, "Brighter Days May Be on Horizon," *The Washington Post,* September 28, 1992.

7. Local governments are not mentioned in the U.S. Constitution. Moreover, a longstanding principle of municipal law is "Dillon's rule." Named after Judge John F. Dillon for his decision in an 1868 case, this principle holds that local governments are "creatures of the state" and can exercise only those powers specifically granted them by state legislatures or those powers indispensable for carrying out the responsibilities that the legislatures have assigned them. Thus states have substantial constitutional power.

8. Luigi Mazza, "European Viewpoint: A New Status for Italian Metropolitan Areas," *Town Planning Review* 62, no. 2 (April 1991): 143.

9. Harry Elmers Barnes, *The History of Western Civilization,* vol. 2 (New York: Harcourt Brace & Co., 1935), 455.

10. C. D. Darlington, *The Evolution of Man and Society* (New York: Simon & Schuster, 1969), 539.

11. H. G. Wells, *The Outline of History* (New York: Doubleday & Co., 1971), 824.

12. Richard Eells and Clarence Walton, eds., *Man in the City of the Future: A Symposium of Urban Philosophers* (London: Arkville Press, 1968), 4.

13. H. A. Davies, *An Outline History of the World,* 5th ed. (London: Oxford University Press, 1968), 126–137.

14. William Reginald Halliday, *The Growth of the City State: Lectures on Greek and Roman History* (1923; reprint, Chicago: Argonaut Inc., 1967), 90.

15. Scott Greer, *Governing the Metropolis* (New York: John Wiley and Sons, 1962), 3.

16. Davies, *Outline History,* 338–340.

17. Richard G. Fox, *Urban Anthropology: Cities in Their Cultural Settings* (Englewood Cliffs, N.J.: Prentice-Hall, 1977), 97.

18. Ibid., 110.

19. Ibid., 113.

20. Examples drawn from the "Civitex" data base of the National Civic League, Denver, Colo.

21. John W. Gardner, *On Leadership* (New York: The Free Press, 1990), 97.

22. Quoted in Jane Jacobs, *The Economy of Cities* (New York: Random House, 1969), 175.

23. Interview with the author, April 19, 1992.

24. Donald Southerland, "The Rise of the Texas Tekkies," *The Washington Post,* Nov. 11, 1992.

25. Interview with the author, January 18, 1992.

26. Mark Hughes, from informal remarks in a lecture at Princeton University, Woodrow Wilson School of Public and International Affairs, April 24, 1992.

27. "Two Trials Reflect City's Two Worlds," *The New York Times,* March 24, 1992.

28. Tom Condon, series in *Hartford Courant,* March 17–24, 1991.

29. Richard Voith, "City and Suburban Growth: Substitutes or Complements," Federal Reserve Bank of Philadelphia *Business Review,* September/October 1992, 21–31.

30. H. V. Savitch et al., "Ties That Bind: Central Cities, Suburbs, and the New Metropolitan Region" (Paper prepared for the 1992 Annual Meeting of the American Political Science Association, Chicago, September 3–6, 1992).

31. Neal Peirce, "High Cost of Suburban Separatism," Baltimore *Sun,* March 23, 1992.

32. Paul Glastris, "A Tale of Two Suburbias," *U.S. News & World Report,* November 9, 1992, 32–33.

33. Edward Banfield, *The Unheavenly City* (Boston: Little, Brown, 1968); Richard Lawton, ed., *The Rise and Fall of Great Cities* (London: Bellhaven Press, 1989); Eugene J. Meehan, "Urban Development: An Alternative Strategy," in *Urban Revitalization,* ed. Donald B. Rosenthal (Beverly Hills: Sage Publications, 1980), 279–301; Paul E. Peterson, *City Limits* (Chicago: University of Chicago Press, 1981); and Douglas Yates, *The Ungovernable City* (Cambridge: MIT Press, 1978).

34. Yates, *The Ungovernable City,* 5.

35. Dennis R. Judd and Randy L. Ready, "Entrepreneurial Cities and the New Politics of Economic Development," in *Reagan and the Cities,* ed. George E. Peterson and Carol W. Lewis (Washington, D.C.: Urban Institute Press, 1986), 209–247; Terry Nichols Clark and Lorna Crowley Ferguson, *City Money: Political Processes, Fiscal Strain, and Retrenchment* (New York: Columbia University Press, 1983); and Deil S. Wright, *Understanding Intergovernment Relations,* 3rd ed. (Pacific Grove, Calif.: Brooks/Cole, 1988), 172–188.

36. Robert Warren, Mark S. Rosentraub, and Louis F. Weschler, "Building Urban Governance: An Agenda for the 1990s" (Paper prepared for the National Association of State Universities and Land Grant Colleges, Division of Urban Affairs, Urban Policy Project, 1992).

37. David Howard Davis, "The Zone of Transition as a Political Phenomenon" (Paper prepared for the Annual Meeting of the Midwest Political Science Association, Chicago, April 1991).

38. Richard P. Nathan, *A New Agenda for Cities* (Ohio Municipal League, 1992), 52–55.

39. Marcia D. Lowe, *Shaping Cities: The Environmental and Human Dimensions,* Worldwatch Paper 105 (Washington, D.C.: Worldwatch Institute, 1991), 11.

40. Christopher B. Leinberger, "Business Flees to the Urban Fringe," *The Nation,* July 6, 1992, 10.

41. U.S. Department of Transportation/Federal Highway Administration, *New Perspectives in Commuting* (Based on the 1990 Decennial Census and 1990 Nationwide Personal Transportation Study), (Washington, D.C.: U.S. Department of Transportation, July 1992), 2–7.

42. Leinberger, "Business Flees," 10.

43. Joel Garreau, *Edge City: Life on the New Urban Frontier* (New York: Doubleday, 1991), 222.

44. Letter to the author, December 31, 1992.

45. Letter to the author, June 13, 1989.

46.   Peter Karl Kresl, "The Response of European Cities to EC 1992" (Paper prepared for the Eighth International Conference of Europeanists, Chicago, March 27–29, 1992), 17.

47.   Peter Karl Kresl, "North American Cities and Free Trade," in *The Nation-State Versus Continental Integration* (Bochton, Germany: Universitaetsverlag Dr. N. Brockmeter, 1991), 255.

48.   John W. Walls, "Consolidated Government in Indianapolis and Marion County—Some Reasons and Results" (Indiana Chamber of Commerce, undated).

Chapter 8 — Guideposts for Citistates

1.   Royce Hanson, ed., *Rethinking Urban Policy: Urban Development in an Advanced Economy* (Washington, D.C.: National Academy Press, 1983).

2.   John R. Logan and Harvey L. Molotch, *Urban Fortunes: The Political Economy of Place* (Berkeley: University of California Press, 1987), 258–277.

3.   Panayotis Soldatos, *The Nice Project — The New "International Cities Era" Project* (Montreal: University of Montreal, 1989).

4.   Peter Hall, *World Cities*, 2nd ed. (New York: McGraw-Hill, 1977), 1–3.

5.   R. Scott Fosler, "Revitalizing State-Local Economies," in *A Decade of Devolution: Perspectives on State Local Relations,* ed. E. Blaine Liner (Washington, D.C.: Urban Institute Press, 1989), 98.

6.   Ibid., 92–93.

7.   Theodore Hershberg and Joseph Duckworth, "The City and Suburbs Must Change Course," *The Philadelphia Inquirer,* March 3, 1992.

8.   Michael Porter, *The Competitive Advantage of Nations* (New York: The Free Press, 1990).

9.   Letter to the author, October 25, 1992.

10.   Interview with the author, October 1992.

11.   *Divided Cities in a Global Economy: The 1992 European–North American State-of-the-Cities Report* (Washington, D.C.: German Marshall Fund of the United States, 1992), ii.

12.   Interview with the author, March 18, 1992.

13.   Peter L. Berger and Richard John Neuhaus, *To Empower People: The Role of Mediating Structures in Public Policy* (Washington, D.C.: American Enterprise Institute, 1977).

14.   *Divided Cities*, 10.

15.   Estimate by Leon Bouvier, demographer, Tulane University.

16. Mary K. Nenno, "Urban Policy Revisited—Issues Resurface with a New Urgency," *Journal of Planning Literature* 3, no. 3 (Summer 1988): 253.

17. Joel Kotkin, *Tribes: How Race, Religion and Family Determine Success in the New Global Economy* (New York: Random House, 1993), 257–258.

18. Interview with the author, April 19, 1992.

19. Neal Peirce, "L.A. Epicenter of Pacific Rim Growth—But Will It Choke on Its Own Growth?" December 6, 1988.

20. Norton E. Long, "The City as a Political Community," *Journal of Community Psychology* 14 (January 1986): 74.

21. Tony Hiss, *The Experience of Place* (New York: Alfred A. Knopf, 1990).

22. Interview with the author, August 4, 1992.

23. Peter Karl Kresl, "North American Cities and Free Trade," in *The Nation-State Versus Continental Integration* (Bochton, Germany: Universitaetsverlag Dr. N. Brockmeter, 1991), 252.

24. Marcia D. Lowe, *Shaping Cities: The Environmental and Human Dimensions,* Worldwatch Paper 105 (Washington, D.C.: Worldwatch Institute, 1991), 22.

25. Hershberg and Duckworth, "City and Suburbs."

26. Letter to the author, May 14, 1992.

27. Interview with the author, April 27, 1992.

28. Steven Greenhouse, "Why Paris Works," *The New York Times Magazine,* July 19, 1992, 29.

29. Roy W. Bahl, "States and the Financial Condition of Cities," *Proceedings of the Eighty-Second Annual Conference of National Tax Association-Tax Institute of America,* 1989.

30. William R. Dodge, *The Emergence of Intercommunity Partnerships in the 1980s* (Denver: National Civic League Press, 1990), 17.

31. Robert W. Gage, "Survey Examines COG Roles, Priorities," *Regional Reporter,* July 1990.

32. John J. Kirlin, in materials prepared for Intra-Regional Relations Task Force of Southern California Association of Governments, October 19, 1989.

33. Dodge, *Intercommunity Partnerships,* 15.

34. *Managing Growth in Southern California,* Report of the 2000 Partnership (Los Angeles, 1990), 8.

35. *Divided Cities,* 28.

36. Interview with the author, August 4, 1992.

37. David Osborne and Ted Gaebler, *Reinventing Government* (Reading, Mass.: Addison-Wesley, 1992).

38. See, for example, Ronald J. Oakerson and Roger B. Parks, "Citizen Voice and Public Entrepreneurship: The Organizational Dynamic of a Complex Metropolitan County," *Publius: The Journal of Federalism* 18, no. 4 (Fall 1988): 91–112.

39. Dodge, *Intercommunity Partnerships,* 12.

40. Tom Condon, series in *Hartford Courant,* March 17–24, 1991.

Bibliography

Author's note: This bibliography is selective, not exhaustive. Generally, items selected for inclusion met one or more of the following criteria:
Theoretical relevance—offers insights into concepts we were interested in, including regional governance, metropolitan change, city states, limits on local government, citizen involvement in changing local governance, impacts of changing global economics and national intergovernmental affairs on urban places and problems.

Comprehensiveness—examines a relatively wide range of data, cases, time, and literature. Many of these selections contain fairly complete literature reviews and lengthy bibliographies.

Objectivity—reflects reasonable scholarship and methods.

Problem-solving relevance—offers insight; suggests approaches to workable change, solutions to public problems. Accordingly, there is a bias toward recent studies, although several cited "classics" maintain practical as well as theoretical relevance.

Part I: Challenge and Change

Global Change, Global Economics

Barber, Benjamin R. 1992. "Jihad vs. McWorld." *The Atlantic Monthly,* March, 53–63.
    This brilliant essay argues that two conflicting forces of our age—tribalism and globalism—clash at every point except one: they may both be threatening to democracy. The best hope for survival of democratic processes is a "confederal option."

Fosler, R. Scott. 1989. "Revitalizing State-Local Economies." In *A Decade of Devolution: Perspectives on State Local Relations,* edited by E. Blaine Liner. Washington, D.C.: Urban Institute Press.
    Fosler provides an exceptionally coherent explanation of the relationship between modern regional and international economies. The essay underscores the critical interaction between public services, quality of life, ability of governments to meet citizen demands, and economic development.

Jacobs, Jane. 1969. *The Economy of Cities.* New York: Random House.

_____.1984. *Cities and the Wealth of Nations.* New York: Random House.
    Jacobs has written the seminal works showing the central role of cities and urban regions in economic invention and growth throughout world history.

Kasarda, John D. 1988. "America's Urban Dilemma." In *A World of Giant Cities*, edited by Mattei Dogan and John D. Kasarda, 56–84. Newbury Park, Calif.: Sage Publications.
> The author provides an excellent assessment of the effects of "economic transformation of America" on modern U.S. urban areas, including key demographic, economic, educational, and policy changes.

Knight, Richard V., and Gary Gappert. 1990. *Cities in a Global Society.* Newbury Park, Calif.: Sage Publications.
> The authors examine multiple challenges faced by cities in a "globalizing" world through the perspective of city planning and urban economics.

Porter, Michael E. 1990. *The Competitive Advantage of Nations.* New York: The Free Press.
> This is a definitive, contemporary assessment of economic competition in the new global economy. Using in-depth research on 10 nations and more than 100 industries, Porter articulates strategies for companies, governments, and nations. Importantly, the author concludes that nations can make a difference in economic competition, but national public policies can have unfortunate, unintended consequences. A key cross-cultural finding with major implications for our work is that "competitive advantage is created and sustained through a highly localized process" (p. 19).

Social Conflict and Urban Problems

Banfield, Edward C. 1968. *The Unheavenly City Revisited.* Boston: Little, Brown.
> In this updated version of Banfield's deterministic critique of U.S. cities and urban policies, the author draws social scientific conclusions about the state of urban affairs. The main conclusion is that rational management will not solve the problems and, in fact, will make the problems worse.

Cisneros, Henry. 1992. Untitled speech to the American Newspaper Publishers Association, New York City, May 6.
> In this dramatic speech delivered within days of the 1992 Los Angeles riots, the former mayor of San Antonio and future Secretary of Housing and Urban Development provided compelling evidence that "our cities are smoldering" because of economics, race, and rage. Newspaper publishers were challenged to provide and stimulate community leadership as a part of the solution.

Fainstein, Susan S., and Norman Fainstein, eds. 1972. *The View from Below: Urban Politics and Social Policy.* Boston: Little, Brown.
> In this volume, academics as well as advocates "present the view of cities from below" by describing cultural and structural conditions faced by the urban poor, their relations with the bureaucracy, the effects of government policy, and the political activities the poor and their advocates can take to overcome their problems.

Goldsmith, William W., and Edward J. Blakely. 1992. *Separate Societies: Poverty and Inequality in U.S. Cities.* Philadelphia: Temple University Press.

The authors demonstrate how segregation by race, social background, geography, and economics, combined with new international economic conditions, leave the urban poor locked in place and allow the wealthy and middle classes to rationalize poverty. They contend that only through local empowerment efforts involving grassroots organizations and neighborhood groups can the nation's political economics be changed.

Rubenstein, Richard. 1992. "The Los Angeles Riots: Causes and Cures." *ICAR Newsletter* 5 (Summer). Institute for Conflict Analysis and Resolution, George Mason University.

The author presents a thoughtful assessment of systemic and strategic issues of conflict resolution associated with the riots in Los Angeles and potentially in other urban areas.

The Urban Institute. 1992. *Confronting the Nation's Urban Crisis: From Watts (1965) to South Central Los Angeles (1992).* Washington, D.C.: Urban Institute Press.

This report summarizes the views of a group of senior urban scholars in the wake of the 1992 Los Angeles riots. The group, led by George Peterson of the Urban Institute, provides a concise review of what is known concerning the underlying causes of the riots and what has been learned about urban problems over the past 25 years. They conclude that a separate "urban" policy will not work and call for an integrated approach that addresses city problems within the following guidelines: (1) choose programs as social investments, (2) define a consistent social contract between society and those who receive government program benefits, (3) attack spatial segmentation, and (4) recognize that all levels of government and the community itself have critical roles to play.

Wideman, John Edgar. 1992. "Dead Black Men and Other Fallout from the American Dream." *Esquire,* September.

A brilliant report on the aftermath of the Los Angeles riots by an esteemed black American author. Wideman transports the reader to the place and the perspective of the black American, thereby explaining real problems in almost poetic terms.

Cities and Change

German Marshall Fund of the United States. 1992. *Divided Cities in a Global Economy: The 1992 European–North American State-of-the-Cities Report.* Washington, D.C.: German Marshall Fund of the United States.

Report of a joint North American–European team of urban observers that visited the Chicago, Atlanta, Toronto, Glasgow, Rotterdam, and Frankfurt citistates to gauge how they're dealing with their social problems.

Hall, Peter. 1979. *The World Cities.* New York: McGraw-Hill.

Hall analyzes the factors that contributed to the enormous growth of seven great world metropolitan centers and examines the administrative machines in host countries for dealing with the demands of those cities.

_____. 1989. "The Rise and Fall of Great Cities." In *The Rise and Fall of Great Cities,* edited by Richard Lawton. London: Bellhaven Press.

In discussing the problems of cities today—polarization, poverty, dependence, unemployment, and deterioration of the built environment—Hall finds the heart of cities at a great crossroads.

Hartman, Richard. 1991. "The Kennedy School Conference, the Evolution of Local Government, Regional Governance," *Regional Reporter* (September) Washington, D.C.: National Association of Regional Councils.

A group of the nation's leading regionalists met at the Kennedy School of Government at Harvard in July 1991 to consider future prospects in the field. Richard Hartman's excellent summary outlines the major conditions in contemporary American life making regionalism more relevant than ever—yet both enhancing and hampering its advance.

Herson, Lawrence, and John M. Bolland. 1990. *The Urban Web: Politics, Policy, and Theory.* Chicago: Nelson-Hall.

This comprehensive text portrays cities as the authors believe ancient Greeks saw them, as webs of interconnecting attributes; a city is seen as a government, an urban place, a sociological network, and an economic activity.

Jacobs, Jane. 1961. *The Death and Life of Great American Cities.* New York: Vintage Press.

This is a classic critique of postwar city building and associated economic and land-use issues.

Karp, David A., G. P. Stone, and W. C. Yoels. 1991. *Being Urban: A Sociology of City Life.* 2nd ed. Westport, Conn.: Praeger.

The authors examine important social-psychological issues associated with experiencing and living in modern American cities. These include the "rediscovery of community within the city"; processes underlying such paradoxes as urban involvement vs. indifference, intimacy vs. anonymity; and such phenomena as "public privacy" and "urban tolerance."

Lawton, Richard, ed. 1989. *The Rise and Fall of Great Cities.* London: Bellhaven Press.

This book is an anthology of chapters by various authors who write about the development of cities in western Europe and North America, their salad days, their eventual decline, and the reasons that led to each.

Morgan, David R. 1989. *Managing Urban America.* 3rd. ed. Pacific Grove, Calif.: Brooks/Cole.

Morgan describes how cities are managed, including the environment of urban management, the making and implementation of policy, and the internal workings of city government.

Nathan, Richard P. 1992. *A New Agenda for Cities.* Columbus: Ohio Municipal League Educational and Research Fund.

This short but insightful monograph sketches a strategy for meaningful, long-term urban problem solving that covers such points as urban hardship, management, mutual obligation needs, education for the public service, neighborhood-based reforms, the role of nonprofits, schools, and targeting.

The book contains reactions to the Nathan agenda by Charles Royer, former mayor of Seattle, president of the National League of Cities, and director of the Institute of Politics at the John F. Kennedy School of Government, Harvard University; Nicholas Lemann, author and national correspondent for *The Atlantic Monthly;* and Donald Weatherspoon, minority business advocate and former deputy director of the Michigan Department of Commerce.

Pike, Burton. 1981. *The Images of the City in Modern Literature.* Princeton, N.J.: Princeton University Press.

Pike sketches the story of the city in fiction, including the ambivalence toward it, its frenetic pace, and its penchant to alienate.

Rusk, David. 1993. *Cities Without Suburbs.* Washington, D.C. and Baltimore: Woodrow Wilson Center Press/Johns Hopkins University Press.

Rusk shows how American cities that have expansive borders, are not hemmed in by close-in suburbs, tend to be more prosperous and integrated.

Tuttleton, James W. 1990. "City Literature: States of Mind." *Modern Age* 33 (Fall).

"On the whole, the American novel of city life has been a vehicle of anti-urban passions and sentiments," writes Tuttleton, and such can be found throughout Western literature.

Waste, Robert J. 1989. *The Ecology of Policymaking.* New York: Oxford University Press.

Waste argues that there is a common life cycle of city policy making in America and identifies the interrelated factors in his model of urban policy-making ecology.

Quality of Life Issues

Landis, John D., and David S. Sawicki. 1988. "A Planner's Guide to the Places Rated Almanac." *Journal of the American Planning Association* 54 3 (Summer): 336.

This article presents the results of a survey which found that quality of life ratings have not had a great impact on urban policies. They are most important to citizens and community groups.

"Measuring the Quality of Life." 1986. *The Futurist* 20 (May/June): 58.

This review of Susan Cutter's *Rating Places* reveals that industry, real estate, marketing firms, and individuals are now using quality of life ratings as bases for locational decisions. It is contended that these ratings, which help winners and hurt losers, could be used by government to set an agenda for improving the quality of life nationwide.

Nathan, Richard P., and Charles Adams, Jr. "Four Perspectives on Urban Hardship." *Political Science Quarterly* 104 (Fall 1989): 483–509.

A classic treatment of the measurement of urban and city hardship, and the policy implications of such analysis.

Norris, Darrell. 1986. "Places Rated Berated." *American Demographics,* 8 3 (March 1986): 8.
    The author finds *Places Rated Almanac* to be newsworthy, but falling short on accuracy and usefulness. It misuses statistical techniques; it "measures, but does not measure up."

Fiscal Issues

Bahl, Roy W. *Financing State and Local Government in the 1980's.* New York: Oxford University Press, 1984.

Bahl, Roy, William Duncombe, and Wanda Schulman. 1990. "The New Anatomy of Urban Fiscal Problems." In *The Future of National Urban Policy,* edited by Marshall Kaplan and Franklin James, 32–57. Durham, N.C.: Duke University Press.
    This comprehensive article examines the fiscal health of the nation's cities, and state and local governments; discusses implications of the changing U.S. economy and changing federal policies for the economic strength of large urban areas; analyzes the fiscal responses of large urban governments to these economic and federal policy changes; and develops three hypotheses concerning urban fiscal problems and explores their implications for the future.

Clark, Terry Nichols, and Lorna Crowley Ferguson. 1983. *City Money.* New York: Columbia University Press.
    The authors provide an exhaustive analysis of the causes and effects of fiscal strain in American cities, based on data from 62 cities over two decades.

Dearborn, Phillip. 1986. "Fiscal Conditions in Large American Cities, 1971– 1984." Paper prepared for the National Academy of Sciences, Committee on National Urban Policy.
    This is a report on comparative, changing fiscal conditions of cities by one of the nation's foremost city budget experts.

Ladd, Helen F., and John Yinger. 1989. *America's Ailing Cities: Fiscal Health and Design of Urban Policy.* Baltimore: Johns Hopkins University Press.
    This book provides comprehensive, in-depth analysis of the problems with finance, intergovernmental relations, economics, municipal services, and urban policy faced by cities in this country today, whether of their own creation or from some outside force.

Levine, Charles H. 1978. "Organizational Decline and Cutback Management." *Public Administration Review* 38 (July/Aug.): 316–325.

_____. 1981. *The Politics of Retrenchment: How Local Governments Manage Fiscal Stress.* Beverly Hills, Calif.: Sage Publications.
    As the guru of "cutback management," Levine argues most effectively for changing budget and management processes to enhance the capacity of local government to cope with fiscal stress.

Pammer, William J., Jr. 1990. *Managing Fiscal Strain in Major American Cities: Understanding Retrenchment in the Public Sector.* New York: Greenwood Press.

Stein, Robert M. 1990. *Urban Alternatives: Public and Private Markets in the Provision of Local Services.* Pittsburgh: University of Pittsburgh Press.
 Stein examines the organization of cities and the effects of different types of organization and finance patterns on what cities do and how well they carry out their policies.

Limits of Local Government and Problems of Urban Polities

Baker, C. Douglas. 1992. "The Role of Governmental Fragmentation on Metropolitan County Expenditures." Paper prepared for the annual meeting of the American Political Science Association, Chicago, Sept. 2–6.
 This important analysis of recent spending data disputes earlier claims about local government limits and finds metropolitan counties engaged in substantial public economic redistribution.

Banfield, Edward C. 1966. *Big City Politics.* New York: Random House.
 Banfield describes the population, economy, organization of government, workings, elections, interest groups and influentials, and handling of issues in nine important American cities.

Banfield, Edward C., and James Q. Wilson. 1963. *City Politics.* New York: Vintage Books.
 The authors explain how politics operates in American cities, including those with city managers and nonpartisan elections.

Barnekov, Timothy, and Daniel Rich. 1989. "Privatism and the Limits of Local Economic Development Policy." *Urban Affairs Quarterly* 25 (December): 212–238.
 This article provides a set of propositions that define "common limitations" of local economic development policies based on privatism assumptions.

Fainstein, Susan S., Norman T. Fainstein, Richard C. Hill, Michael P. Smith, P. Jefferson Armistead, and Marlene Keller. 1986. *Restructuring the City: The Political Economy of Urban Redevelopment.* Rev. ed. New York: Longman.
 Through a comparison of case studies by several authors, this volume attempts to generalize the overarching questions about urban change, focusing on redevelopment issues.

Judd, Dennis. 1988. *The Politics of American Cities: Private Power and Public Policy.* Glenview, Ill.: Scott Foresman.
 This classic text examines the impact of changing national politics and policies on cities, tensions among urban public and privates interests, and influences of the private sector on the development of urban public policy.

Kantor, Paul. 1987. "The Dependent City: The Changing Political Economy of Urban Economic Development in the United States." *Urban Affairs Quarterly* 22 (June): 493–520.

Kantor contends that within the larger politico-economic order, city governments are captives of many slowly changing forces that shape and limit community choices.

_____. 1988. *The Dependent City: The Changing Political Economy of Urban America.* Glenview, Ill.: Scott Foresman.

Kantor writes of the need for a holistic approach to urban policymaking—understanding the past, uncovering present conditions, and proposing political alternatives that will shape the urban future. The result is an excellent, comprehensive view of urban political economy that critiques prevailing community power, public choice, and neo-Marxist theories. Although the author concludes that cities are dependent on multiple external economic and political forces, he provides some discussion of potential changes that could affect the future of the "dependent city."

Krumholz, Norman, and John Forester. 1990. *Making Equity Planning Work: Leadership in the Public Sector.* Philadelphia: Temple University Press.

Krumholz, former Cleveland city planning director, is one of America's leading thinkers on how to make urban planning work for the poor as well as the affluent.

Molotch, Harvey. 1988. "Strategies and Constraints of Growth Elites." In *Business Elites and Urban Development,* edited by Scott Cummings. New York: SUNY.

In this chapter, Molotch clarifies his belief that elites in communities use growth as the means to benefit themselves and their communities, in that order.

Orum, Anthony M. 1991. "Apprehending the City: The View from Above, Below, and Behind." *Urban Affairs Quarterly* 26 (June).

Orum presents a discussion of power, municipal government, and growth in American cities and towns. Growth shapes the city, Orum believes, but when growth impinges on citizens, dissent results.

Peterson, Paul E. 1981. *City Limits.* Chicago: University of Chicago Press.

This is a classic exposition on the limits of local government in the U.S. intergovernmental system. Peterson maintains that local governments' competition for economic resources and dependency on funds from national and state treasuries limit their autonomy and ability to redistribute resources. To remedy this, Peterson calls for greater centralization of economic decision making, taking the redistributive decision away from individuals at the local level and giving it to the national government.

Schneider, Mark. 1989. *The Competitive City: The Political Economy of Suburbia.* Pittsburgh: University of Pittsburgh Press.

Schneider tests the Peterson redistribution hypothesis in different types of local governments and finds it most applicable to affluent suburbs, which contributes to their exclusionary nature.

Yates, Douglas. 1978. *The Ungovernable City: The Politics of Urban Problems and Policy Making.* Cambridge, Mass.: MIT Press.

Well-known as one of the most pessimistic appraisals of local government capacity, this book contends that for many reasons, the American city is "fundamentally ungovernable."

Part II: Change and Response—City-State Solutions

City-States

Davies, H. A. 1968. *An Outline History of the World.* 5th ed. London: Oxford University Press.

Davies presents a well-written overview of world history, with substantial attention to the evolution of communities and city-states across cultures.

Eells, Richard, and Clarence Walton, eds. 1968. *Man in the City of the Future: A Symposium of Urban Philosophers.* London: Arkville Press, Macmillan.

This collection of essays by such notables as Margaret Mead, Peter Hall, and James Rouse was produced out of the Columbia University School of Business shortly after the urban crises of Watts and other cities in the late 1960s. It provides eloquent testimony to the fundamental importance of the city to civilization, demonstrating the relevance of earlier forms, such as the Greek city state, to modern America.

Fowler, W. Warde. 1904. *The City-State of the Greeks and Romans.* New York: Macmillan.

This is a detailed treatment of the early history of the city-state, with excellent detail and assessment of its contributions to political organization.

Fox, Richard G. 1977. *Urban Anthropology: Cities in Their Cultural Settings.* Englewood Cliffs, N.J.: Prentice-Hall.

Fox provides an in-depth examination of urban institutions and their cultural settings in many different societies and times. The book includes particularly good descriptions of city states in medieval European cities and Asian port cities and bazaar towns.

Halliday, William Reginald. 1967. *The Growth of the City State: Lectures on Greek and Roman History.* Reprint of 1923 ed. Chicago: Argonaut, Inc.

In this lively, well-written history of the ancient city state, the author provides particularly good insights concerning the social and political conditions of the times.

Hammond, Mason. 1951. *City-State and World State: In Greek and Roman Political Theory Until Augustus.* Cambridge, Mass.: Harvard University Press.

Hammond presents an interesting historical review and critique of ancient city-states, concluding that city-states failed when they stagnated, when they became orthodox and dominated the politics of the times as nation-states have dominated the political thought of the 20th century.

Ledebur, Larry C., and William R. Barnes. 1992. *Metropolitan Disparities and Economic Growth.* A research report of the National League of Cities.
The authors present an empirical analysis demonstrating that regions with the greatest income differentials between center cities and suburbs have suffered the most severe economic consequences—greater job loss, lower per capita income—during the current recession.

Maitland, Judith. 1992. "Dynasty and Family in the Athenian City State: A View from Attic Tragedy." *Classical Quarterly* 42:26–40.
Maitland provides interesting insights into the power struggles associated with the shift from rule by powerful families to the city-state, particularly as that shift affected "ordinary families" and women.

Mazza, Luigi. 1991. "European Viewpoint: A New Status for Italian Metropolitan Areas." *Town Planning Review* 62:143–146.

Putnam, Robert D., Robert Leonardi, and Raffaella Nanetti. 1992. "Governance and the Civic Community." Paper presented at the International Conference on Culture and Development in Africa, The World Bank, Washington, D.C., April 2–3.
These are accounts of the development since 1970 of 20 new regional governments in Italy.

Veyne, Paul. 1990. *Bread and Circuses: Historical Sociology and Political Pluralism.* English translation. London: Allen Lane, Penguin Press.
This is a classic treatment of the thousand years of history between the Greek city state of the fifth century B.C. through the assent, decline, and fall of the Roman Empire. The author provides a particularly good description and assessment of the development of civic consciousness and the public service commonweal motives of these societies.

Regional Reality: Governance, Economics, and Development

Bernard, Richard M., ed. 1990. *Snowbelt Cities: Metropolitan Politics in the Northeast and Midwest Since World War II.* Bloomington: Indiana University Press.
Through a series of essays, this book presents a pattern of urban political competition among the leaders of business, white ethnics, reform movements, blacks, neighborhoods, and suburbs. The essays describe ways in which 12 city states of the "Snowbelt" have attempted to rebuild and retool their economies to meet regional challenges.

Bollens, John C., and Henry J. Schmandt. 1982. *The Metropolis.* 4th ed. New York: Harper and Row.
Although dated, this remains the only comprehensive textbook on the topic of metropolitan governance.

Cervero, Robert. 1986. *Suburban Gridlock.* New Brunswick, N.J.: Center for Urban Policy and Research.
Cervero explores the mobility and congestion problems posed by rapid office and business growth on America's urban fringes, and discusses various design, land use, and management strategies.

Downs, Anthony. 1989. *The Need for a New Vision for the Development of Large U.S. Metropolitan Areas.* New York: Solomon Brothers.

Downs maintains Americans' popular vision of metropolitan life—detached single-family homes on spacious lots, private automobile ownership, low-rise office buildings and shopping centers, small and locally controlled governments—is self-destructing. The reasons: excessive travel, lack of housing for low-wage workers, lack of consensus on how to finance infrastructure fairly, and inability to accommodate LULUs (locally unacceptable land uses). The alternative vision Downs spells out includes encouraging people to live closer to where they work, some regional governmental coherence, and incentives to make individuals take a more realistic account of their behavioral choices.

_____. 1992. *Stuck in Traffic: Coping with Peak Hour Traffic Congestion.* Washington, D.C., and Cambridge, Mass.: Brookings Institution and Lincoln Institute of Land Policy.

Downs critically addresses several of the anticongestion remedies suggested in recent years, including raising gas taxes by more than a dollar a gallon, building more HOV lanes, better coordinating traffic lights on city arterials, and constructing new residential and commercial subdivisions with higher densities.

Fry, Earl H. 1989. *The New International Cities Era: The Global Activities of North American Municipal Governments.* Provo, Utah: David M. Kennedy Center for International Studies, Brigham Young University.

Garreau, Joel. 1991. *Edge City: Life on the New Frontier.* New York: Doubleday.

A popular, journalistic description of the dispersal and concentration of economic activity to outer suburbia that raises important questions concerning the causes and consequences of edge cities for regional governance and economics.

Greer, Scott. 1962. *Governing the Metropolis.* New York: John Wiley and Sons.

Greer's early and influential work called for a focus beyond big cities and on the "metropolitan" community, its problems and its governance.

Kresl, Peter Karl. 1992. *The Urban Economy and Regional Trade Liberalization.* Westport, Conn.: Praeger.

Kresl provides leading thought on how the breakdown of trade barriers places city states in direct global competition, together with a rich series of analyses and comparisons of challenges facing individual cities of Europe and North America, and how they can learn from each other.

Ledebur, Larry C. and William R. Barnes. 1992. *Metropolitan Disparities and Economic Growth.* A research report of the National League of Cities, in updated and corrected version.

This is an empirical analysis demonstrating that regions with the greatest income differentials between center cities and suburbs have suffered the most severe economic consequences—greater job loss, lower per capita income—during the current recession.

Lewis, Paul G. 1992. "Urban-Regional Political Economy and the Development of 'Edge City': Toward a Comparative Theory." Paper prepared for the annual meeting of the American Political Science Association, Chicago, Sept. 3–6.

Lewis presents an excellent empirical analysis, based on national census data, of the relationship between different regional governance arrangements, political fragmentation, and regional economic development. In the process, the author provides superb and balanced critiques of Garreau's "edge city" hypothesis (according to Lewis, local governments can and have taken authoritative action to shape regions that Garreau does not attempt to detect) and such staples of urban political economy theory as "the growth machine" (Logan and Molotch), city limits (Peterson), regime theory, and the HERE Tiebout hypothesis.

Logan, John R., and Harvey L. Molotch. 1987. *Urban Fortunes: The Political Economy of Place.* Berkeley: University of California Press.

In this book, the authors argue that local conflicts over growth are central to the organization of cities as opposed to being merely related to means of production or a response to conditions of demand and supply. Big cities and surrounding regions are often "growth machines" run by local elites. The book attempts to blend existing economic and sociological theory with urban economic reality.

Lowe, Marcia. 1991. *Shaping Cities: The Environmental and Human Dimensions.* Worldwatch Paper 105. Washington, D.C.: Worldwatch Institute.

The author argues for more compact metropolitan settlements, in the United States and throughout the world.

Lyons, W. E., and David Lowery. 1989. "Governmental Fragmentation Versus Consolidation: Five Public-Choice Myths About How to Create Informed, Involved, and Happy Citizens." *Public Administration Review* (Nov.–Dec.): 533–543.

National Civic League. 1990. *The Emergence of Intercommunity Partnerships in the 1980s.* Reprints from the *National Civic Review.* Denver: National Civic League Press.

William R. Dodge and Stephen C. Forman provide incisive discussions of how the metropolitan issue matured in the United States in the 1980s.

_____. 1989. "Metropolitan Governance Statement." *Civic Action* (November–December).

Osborne, David, and Ted A. Gaebler. 1992. *Reinventing Government: How the Entrepreneurial Spirit Is Transforming the Public Sector.* Boston: Addison-Wesley Publishing.

This book popularized the idea of consumer-driven, more responsive government at all levels in the United States.

Porter, Douglas R., ed. 1992. *State and Regional Initiatives for Managing Development: Policy Issues and Practical Concerns.* Washington, D.C.: Urban Land Institute.

This work presents essays by such knowledgeable observers as Florida's John DeGrove on the growth management issues that are so critical for rational citistate physical development.

344

Savitch, H. V., et al. 1992. "Ties That Bind: Central Cities, Suburbs and the New Metropolitan Region." Paper prepared for the annual meeting of the American Political Science Association, Chicago, Sept. 3–6.
    Based on a comprehensive analysis of 59 U.S. metropolitan areas from 1979 through 1987, this paper chronicles the close relationship between economic prosperity in central cities and surrounding suburbs. The authors use different measures over time to provide the most conclusive validation available that suburbs that surround healthy cities stand a far better chance of vitality than those that surround sick cities. Suburban "self-sufficiency" is not a sufficient defense against economic difficulties.

The [Los Angeles] 2000 Partnership. 1990. *Managing Growth in Southern California*.
    This is a state-of-the-art report on how a massive metropolitan region might reform its governance to cope with the environmental and social realities of the 1990s.

Community Building, Neighborhoods, and Nonprofits
(Re-creating Community at the Grassroots)

Anton, Thomas J., and Alison R. Flaum. 1992. "Theory into Practice: The Rise of New Anti-Poverty Strategies in American Cities." *Urban News* 5 (Winter).
    This article in the newsletter of the Urban Politics Section of the American Political Science Association chronicles a series of important collaborative antipoverty efforts in cities involving local governments, nonprofit organizations, and citizens. These new programs are seen as evidence challenging conventional notions about poverty as a national problem and limitations of community problem solving.

Bellah, Robert, Richard Hadsen, William Sullivan, Ann Swidler, and Steven Tipton. 1991. *The Good Society*. New York: Alfred A. Knopf.
    The authors acknowledge that Americans live in and through various institutions and that these institutions can and should be better understood and reformed.

Elazar, Daniel J. 1987. *Building Cities in America: Urbanization and Suburbanization in a Frontier Society*. Lanham, Md.: Hamilton Books.
    The distinctive character of American cities is the focus of this book. It examines the nature of politics and evolution of metropolitan regions, and argues for maintaining autonomy and growth in American cities. Elazar maintains that the restoration of community attachments is the first priority for the future of American self-government.

Elkin, Stephen L. 1987. *City and Regime in the American Republic*. Chicago: University of Chicago Press.
    Using empirical and normative arguments, Elkin proposes a "commercial republic" as a way to achieve equality and efficiency in urban democracies. He advocates institutional change to foster a broader and deeper citizen focus on the "commercial public interests of the city" and therefore the common good of the commercial republic.

Fitzgerald, Frances. 1986. *Cities on a Hill: A Journey Through Contemporary American Cultures*. New York: Simon and Schuster.
    An in-depth examination of four very different, new, U.S. communities, including the Castro gay male area of San Francisco; the Florida retirement community Sun City; and the religious communities of the Rajneeshee in central Oregon and Jerry Falwell's Moral Majority of Lynchburg, Virginia. This Pulitzer Prize–winning journalist concludes that despite vast differences in these communities, de Tocqueville's observations concerning Americans' capacity to "reinvent themselves" through building new communities remains valid after 150 years.

Kross, Jessica. 1983. *The Evolution of an American Town: Newtown, New York, 1642–1775*. Philadelphia: Temple University Press.
    Kross traces the changes in the political, social, and economic spheres of an American town for 133 years.

Long, Norton E. 1991. "The Paradox of a Community of Transients." *Urban Affairs Quarterly* 27 (September): 3–12. Also 1986. "The City as a Political Community." *Journal of Community Psychology* 14 (January): 72–80.
    In the title of the first article, Professor Long, acknowledged dean of the study of American communities, presents a governance paradox crucial to our times: How can transients make a community? Not easily, is the answer. Yet Long celebrates the role of the city in the Hellenistic and Roman empires as the "social cement that held them together" and contends that modern U.S. problems are largely grounded in local governance and must be solved by regional citizenship and committed regional leadership.

Morone, James A. 1990. *The Democratic Wish: Popular Participation and the Limits of American Government*. New York: Basic Books.
    This book provides historical perspective on the development of American democracy and the effects of that development on public policy. The author contends that Americans dread public power yet yearn for communal democracy, and he shows how that tension has at times resulted in weak, ineffective bureaucratic solutions to important public problems. Morone concludes that "more competent government" is required and should be built by "returning to the ideals that led Americans out of past perplexities," including the public good and communal democracy.

Salamon, Lester M. 1987. "Of Market Failure, Voluntary Failure, and Third-Party Government: Toward a Theory of Government-Nonprofit Relations in the Modern Welfare State," *Journal of Voluntary Action Research* 16 (January): 29–49.

_____. 1987. "Partners in Public Service: The Scope and Theory of Government-Nonprofit Relations." In *The Nonprofit Sector: A Research Handbook*, edited by Walter Powell. New Haven, Conn.: Yale University Press.
    Salamon's work describes and analyzes how social and human services are delivered in American communities through a long-standing but changing partnership between the nonprofit sector and government at all levels. His analysis concludes that government is now *the* major philanthropist in many traditional areas. By focusing on the partnership, rather than looking

in isolation at volunteerism or local government, Salamon provides theorists and practitioners with a powerful tool to consider for community building and change.

Warren, Robert, Mark S. Rosentraub, and Louis F. Weschler. 1992. "Building Urban Governance: An Agenda for the 1990s." Paper prepared for the National Association of State Universities and Land Grant Colleges, Division of Urban Affairs, Urban Policy Project.

The authors provide a comprehensive review of local government literature. They challenge the "limits on local autonomy" and "breakdown of local governance" literature and provide the best existing theoretical framework for optimism concerning the capacity for local self-governance.

Citizen Organization, Leadership Development

Ehrenhalt, Alan. 1991. *The United States of Ambition: Politicians, Power, and the Pursuit of Office.* New York: Times Books.

Concentrating on the question "Who sent us the leaders we have?" the author concludes that self-generated leadership, without benefit of party or establishment approval, has destroyed much of the cohesion in American society.

Gardner, John W. 1990. *On Leadership.* New York: The Free Press.

Gardner provides an extraordinarily insightful and comprehensive treatment of the complex topic of leadership in modern society. Particularly good on the need to promote diversity while building unity, this is a demanding but optimistic view of the future of leadership.

Svara, James H. 1990. *Official Leadership in the City: Patterns of Conflict and Cooperation.* New York: Oxford University Press.

Svara examines how local officials and forms of city government play a role in promoting patterns of conflict or cooperation within cities.

Welch, Susan, and Timothy Bledsoe. 1988. *Urban Reform and Its Consequences: A Study in Representation.* Chicago: University of Chicago Press.

This is a comprehensive and recent empirical examination of the central questions concerning the effects of different types of local election structures on representation, leadership, and community conflict. The work is based on a sample of nearly 1,000 council members and communities with populations between 50,000 and 1 million across 42 states.

Local Governments in the Intergovernmental Context

Frug, Gerald E. 1987. "Empowering Cities in a Federal System." *The Urban Lawyer* 19:553–568.

According to Frug, cities have substantial autonomy that should be asserted to enhance local democracy.

_____. 1988. *Local Government Law.* St. Paul, Minn: West Publishing Co.

This legal casebook's 1,000-plus pages are packed with case law and excerpts from a wide range of commentary on democracy; community; power; decentralization; local government; and legal-constitutional relationships between cities and states, between cities and the federal government, between cities and their citizens, and among neighboring cities.

Kaplan, Marshall, and Franklin James, eds. 1990. *The Future of National Urban Policy.* Durham, N.C.: Duke University Press.

An excellent collection of thoughtful essays on urban policy options in an era of "tough choices and elusive answers." Essays cover urban needs and finances; urban problems; the notion of "national urban policy"; institutional change; and future urban initiatives.

Kirschten, Dick. 1989. "More Problems, Less Clout." *National Journal,* 21 (August 12): 2026.

Big cities and their mayors have no end of problems; but as their cities lose population and economic strength, and as intergovernmental and political games change, mayors are losing their clout.

Orlebeke, Charles J. 1990. "Chasing Urban Policy: A Critical Retrospect." In *The Future of National Urban Policy,* edited by Marshall Kaplan and Franklin James. Durham, N.C.: Duke University Press.

National attempts at urban policy in the 1960s and 1970s gave way to "nonurban" policy of the Reagan-Bush years. The fundamental question for future national policy makers is whether to ". . . address again the challenge of place-oriented national policy" required to deal with the country's more vexing and permanent urban problems.

Peterson, George E., and Carol W. Lewis, eds. 1986. *Reagan and the Cities.* Washington, D.C.: The Urban Institute Press.

One of the earliest systematic analyses of the effects of national domestic budget cuts on cities, this work contains national data as well as case studies of a diverse sample of U.S. cities.

Wright, Deil S. 1988. *Understanding Intergovernmental Relations.* 3rd. ed. Pacific Grove, Calif.: Brooks/Cole.

This is a very comprehensive and objective treatment of U.S. intergovernmental affairs and actors. Wright's discussion of the "Rise and Fall of the Intergovernmental City" (chapter 5) is particularly insightful.

Index

worker preparedness linked to
social problems, 20–21, 299–300
Cities, European
low crime despite high density,
310
social problems in, 299
Citistates
and aid from federal government,
312–313
attracting industry, 164–165
barriers to employment in, 313–
316
barriers to prospering in United
States, 17 (see also United States,
governance gap in; United States,
socioeconomic state of; United
States, sprawling growth in)
citizen leadership through
metropolitan partnerships, 322–
325
compared with states and
provinces, 13
counties' relationship with, 32–33
creating "apartheid," 30
definition of, x
determining size of, 13
development, 27, 28–30
economics' role in, 10–13, 19
economy tied to quality of life,
308
environmental preservation, 309–
310
in era of "democratization of
power," 133
ethnicity's role in, 10
examples of problems in, 35–36
fostering identity among residents,
306–308
immigration's role in, 4
independent tax base needed for,
310–311
indivisibility of, 291–292
modern rebirth, 11–12
multicultural makeup, 303–306
poverty's effects on, 311
qualities needed to flourish, 12–
13, 46, 178–179
qualities to be international, 16–
17, 293–294
reasons for revival of, 1–2
regional governance in, 316–322
role in international economy,
194, 292–298
state governments' relationship
with, 5–6

telecommunications' role in, 2–3,
31
trade's role in, 3–4
typology of, 292–293
unleashing potential of, 36–37
world population in, 3–4
City-states
historic role of, 6, 7–11
Civic league
funding for, 218–219
qualities of, 217
Clark, Terry Nichols, 21
Clean Air Act Amendments, 6, 32
Cleveland, 27, 34
citizen leadership, 322
funding for social services, 64
Community development corpora-
tions (CDCs), 25
The Competitive Advantage of
Nations, 295
Concurrency, 94
Condon, Tom, 325
Conrad, Eleanor, 218
Coomes, Paul, 16
Crupi, James A., 2, 4, 5, 12, 218, 308

D

D'Alesandro, Tommy, 3rd, 130
Daily Life of Ancient Rome, 11
Daley, Richard, 270
Dallas, 195–241
assets, 209
business community, and
downtown's future, 223, revitalizing southern Dallas, 231–232, 241,
role in education, 212
citizen leadership, by proposed
Metropolitan Citizens League,
216–219
civic culture, 212
crime, 221, 233
cultural attractions, 221
"culture shock" as new replaces
old thinking, 209–212
current problems, 35
demographics, 195
economic development, role of
Frito-Lay in, 231, role of Texas

260, 264, 267–268, 270, 272–273
taxes, 275, 311
transportation, and freeway
improvement, 251, 254, linking
sights with trolleys, 252–253, 290
urban development, 251, by
creating a university center, 255–
256, 257, 290, along riverfront,
253–254
as walking capital, 251

Starr, Roger, 24

Stumberg, Robert, 314

SunCor Development, 57

Swain, Phil, 102

T

Tandy, Charles, 230

Telecommunications
role in citistates, 2–3, 31

Texas Instruments, 15, 231
3M, 15, 249

Thurow, Lester, 17

Tocqueville, Alexis de, 22

Total Quality Management, 12, 268

Trade
role in citistates, 3–4

Transportation. *See also individual cities*
auto, 308
commuting, 28
metropolitan planning organizations and, 6

U

Ueberroth, Peter, 23

United States. *See also* Cities,
American; *individual states and cities* barriers for citistates, 17
Constitution, 327
end of "effortless superiority," 17
foreign immigration into, 4,
303–304
governance gap in, 32–35
nationalism's beginning in, 7
socioeconomic state of, 17–27
sprawling growth in, 27–32
trade with Canada, 3

V

Vedesco, Steve, 15

Venetoulis, Theodore, 133

Virginia
Hampton Roads, 33

Voith, Richard, 19

W

Walls, John W., 34–35

Warren, Otis, 136

Warren, Robert, 21

Washington
freeholder governance, 99
land use, 96
new suburban topology, 117
unemployment, 95

Washington, D.C.
murder rate, 279

WaxWorks, 165, 173, 183

Weinstein, Bernard L., 209

Wells, H. G., 7

Weschler, Louis, 21

Westinghouse Communities, 57

Weyerhaeuser, 85, 109

Whitely, Peyton, 91

Wilder Foundation, 284

Woodward, Terry, 165, 173, 174

Wright, Deil, 21

Y

Yates, Douglas, 21

Yeager, J. Frank, 172, 180

Z

ZEOS, 249